THE EVERYTHING®

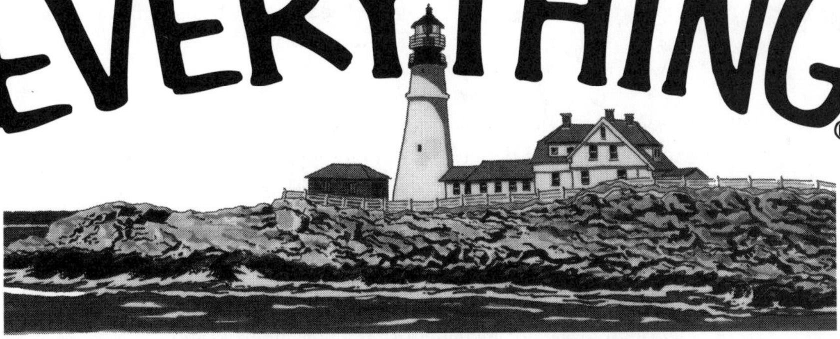

GUIDE TO NEW ENGLAND

Lodging, restaurants,
beaches, and
must-see attractions

Kim Knox Beckius

Adams Media Corporation
Avon, Massachusetts

Publishing Director: Gary M. Krebs
Managing Editor: Kate McBride
Copy Chief: Laura MacLaughlin
Acquisitions Editor: Allison Carpenter Yoder
Development Editor: Michael Paydos
Production Director: Susan Beale
Production Manager: Michelle Roy Kelly
Series Designer: Daria Perreault
Layout and Graphics: Arlene Apone, Paul Beatrice, Brooke Camfield, Colleen Cunningham, Daria Perreault, Frank Rivera

Published by Adams Media, an F+W Publications Company
57 Littlefield Street, Avon, MA 02322 U.S.A.
www.adamsmedia.com

ISBN: 1-58062-589-4
Printed in Canada.

J I H G F E D C

Library of Congress Cataloging-in-Publication Data
Knox, Kimberly.
The everything guide to New England book : a complete state-by-state guide to hotels, restaurants, beaches, and must-see attractions / by Kimberly Knox.
p. cm.
ISBN 1-58062-589-4
1. New England–Guidebooks. I. Title.
F2.3 .K59 2002
917.404'44–dc21 2001053591

This publication is designed to provide accurate and authoritative information with regard to the subject matter covered. It is sold with the understanding that the publisher is not engaged in rendering legal, accounting, or other professional advice. If legal advice or other expert assistance is required, the services of a competent professional person should be sought.

–From a *Declaration of Principles* jointly adopted by a Committee of the American Bar Association and a Committee of Publishers and Associations

Cover Illustrations by Barry Littmann.
Cartography by Ken Dumas.

Contents

Acknowledgments

I have my parents, George and Carol Snyder, to thank for instilling in me a love of books and writing. They also had a knack for turning even our short family vacations—often to New England destinations—into adventures that my brother Michael and I still remember vividly.

Special thanks to Barb Doyen for "finding" me and presenting me with the opportunity to write this guide.

I am indebted to all the visitors to my Web site since 1998 who have shared their travel experiences, provided insight into the questions New England travelers ask, and kept me on my toes. I am also grateful for the assistance of all the tourism and public relations professionals who are always ready to answer my questions and who keep me abreast of what's new and exciting in the region.

My deepest appreciation goes to colleagues, friends, and family members who reviewed this manuscript and made helpful suggestions: Bruce Beckius, Ramona Beckius, Barbara Raymond, George Snyder, and particularly Margot Weiss, whose thoughtful review and supportive comments helped me through the homestretch.

A big thank you to Debby Fowles, my Maine travel buddy, who lent her expertise in reviewing the Maine chapter.

For traveling with me, laughing with me, and being my greatest fan, I owe my husband, Bruce, my thanks and my love.

Introduction

HAVE YOU BEEN TO NEW ENGLAND? Even born and bred New Englanders may have difficulty answering that question with an authoritative affirmative. Though New England is a relatively compact region by size, its vacation possibilities are vast. You could literally spend a lifetime exploring New England's nooks and crannies, and then you'd need at least another lifetime to revisit them all again at a different time of year, when they are blanketed in fresh snow, bedazzled with spring blossoms, baked in summer sun, or brush-stroked by the magical hues of autumn.

The good news is, the sheer variety of things to do, places to see, and experiences to collect during all four unique seasons makes it possible to tailor a New England vacation to your own particular passions. Do you love art? history? literature? mansions? regional microbrews? lighthouses? hiking? horseback riding? seafood? storied inns? snow sports? Then there is a New England travel itinerary just waiting for you.

The bad news is, with all of these options, once you decide to visit New England, you may find yourself overwhelmed by the number of choices still to be made.

In more than three years of producing one of the largest New England travel sites on the World Wide Web (*http://gonewengland.about.com*), I've seen travelers struggling time and time again with where to begin.

Here are some questions I'm asked time and again:

- Should I stay in a B&B?
- When is the best time to see fall leaves?
- Where should I propose to my girlfriend?
- What can a family with three children do on Cape Cod?
- Where can I go to paint outside with my grandmother?
- Where should I take visitors from overseas who want to see a "classic" New England village?
- Could you recommend some sites that you wouldn't miss for the world?

Of the millions of travelers who visit New England each year from points both near and far, I'd wager a guess that many find themselves asking similar questions.

A few answers are obvious. New England's peak tourism season is definitely the fall, when nature puts on its annual color bonanza. Many prospective leaf peepers book their accommodations as much as a year in advance for predicted peak foliage weeks, and you'd be hard-pressed to find a last-minute opening anywhere in the region from late September through mid-October.

Massachusetts is the region's most visited state. Its central position within the New England region makes it a hub that many New England travelers arrive via or pass through, even if they are en route to other destinations. Its proximity to metropolitan New York also makes Massachusetts an ideal weekend getaway for a large population. In addition, the state of Massachusetts ranks sixth overall in the nation for tourism-promotion spending—the tourism budget for 2000–2001 weighed in at a hefty $24.5 million. With New England's largest city, Boston, and several of its most popular vacation hot spots including the Berkshires, Cape Cod, and the islands of Martha's Vineyard and Nantucket, within its boundaries, Massachusetts has drawing power that is unmatched in the region.

However, you'll find that some of the less obvious destination selections may actually offer you a unique getaway that's more memorable and less crowded and harried.

This *Everything® Guide* is designed to help you narrow the field of New England possibilities to the few that have the greatest appeal to you and your traveling companions. Designed to spark your thinking with descriptions of a little bit of everything that each New England state and region offers, it will lay out ideas and travel basics, then point you to appropriate resources for further planning and investigation. For each New England state, you'll find information on accommodations, attractions, dining, outdoor recreation, and shopping, organized by region.

If you are already familiar with New England, you'll also discover within these pages a wealth of tips on lesser known activities and attractions that you have yet to uncover on your own. Even locals may find a few new haunts to frequent.

Check the appendix for a look at helpful New England Web sites and a comprehensive guide to tourism organizations for each state. These regional promotion organizations are happy to provide you with additional information and free brochures to help you design and enjoy a New England vacation all your own.

PART I

New England—Land of Leaves, Lighthouses, and Lobsters

New England

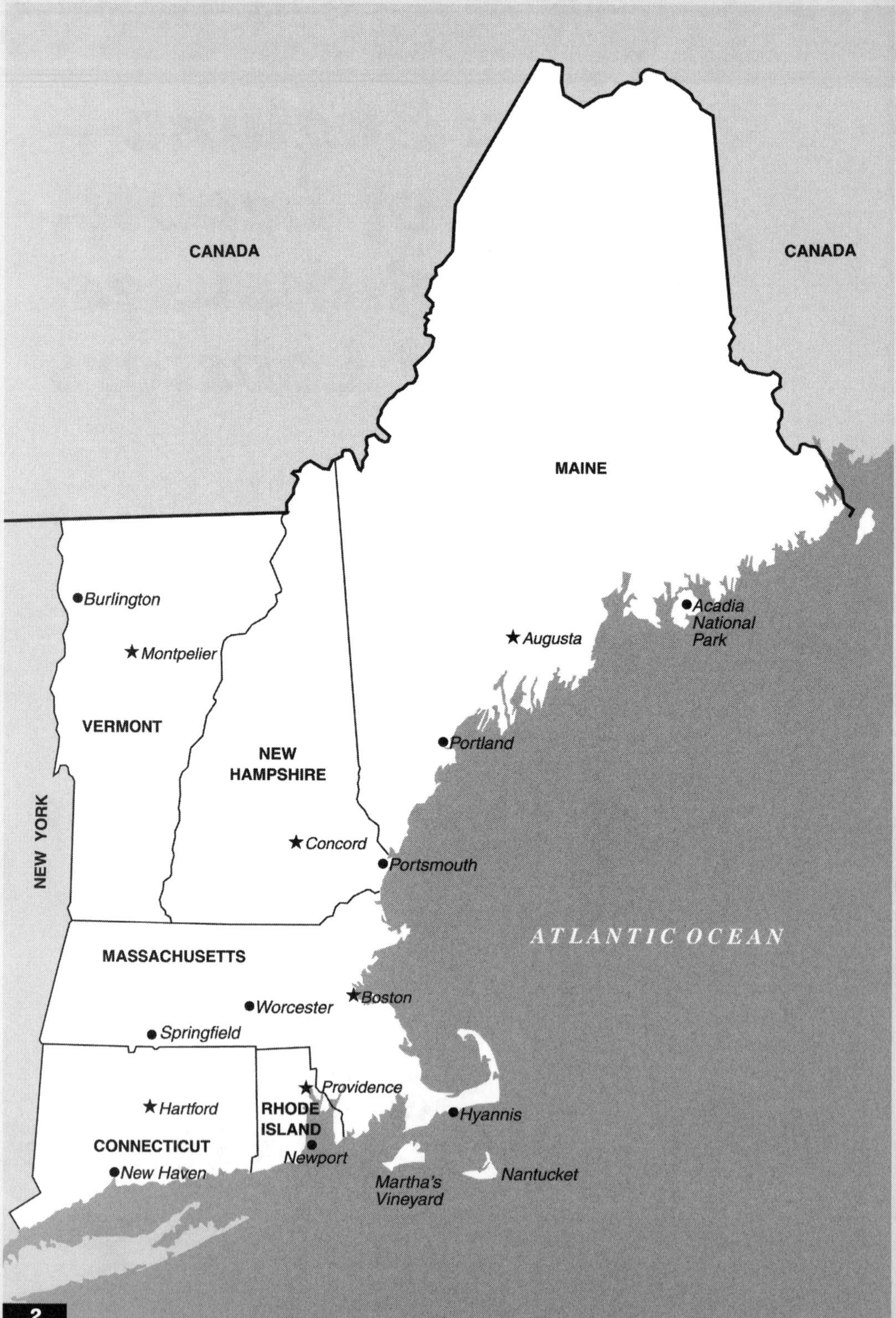
CANADA
CANADA
MAINE
Acadia National Park
Augusta
Portland
Burlington
Montpelier
VERMONT
NEW HAMPSHIRE
NEW YORK
Concord
Portsmouth
ATLANTIC OCEAN
MASSACHUSETTS
Boston
Worcester
Springfield
Providence
Hartford
RHODE ISLAND
Hyannis
CONNECTICUT
Newport
New Haven
Nantucket
Martha's Vineyard

Why Visit New England?

THERE'S SOMETHING ABOUT NEW ENGLAND that has earned it fans the world over, even among those who have visited it only through words and pictures. What is it that draws people to New England and makes the six-state region—Connecticut, Maine, Massachusetts, New Hampshire, Rhode Island, and Vermont—one that travelers return to again and again, throughout their lifetimes? While New England is a thoroughly modern region, there's a pervasive aura of timeless permanence present that hearkens back to simpler times. Idyllic images of New England—covered bridges and white-steeple churches, maple trees tapped for sap, horse-drawn sleigh rides, cider mills, and wooded acres blazing with autumn hues—are truly not at all removed from the reality visitors can experience when they cross into the land of leaves, lighthouses, and lobsters.

No United States region is home to more historic sites, none more steeped in the American patriotic tradition. From the Pilgrims' first feast of thanksgiving, recreated each year at Plimoth Plantation in Plymouth, Massachusetts; to the Revolutionary War battlefields at Lexington and Concord; to the seeds of political and intellectual influence embodied in the Adams and Kennedy families and writers such as Mark Twain, Harriet Beecher Stowe, Nathaniel Hawthorne, Herman Melville, Ralph Waldo Emerson, and Henry David Thoreau; many of the traditions and ideas that have shaped and continue to guide the destiny of America were born and nurtured in New England.

FAST FACT

Mark Twain said, "There is a sumptuous variety about the New England weather that compels the stranger's admiration—and regret." The record high temperature recorded in New England was 107° Fahrenheit on August 2, 1975, in both New Bedford and Chester, Massachusetts. The record low was –50°, recorded on December 30, 1933, in Bloomfield, Vermont.

Adding to the region's appeal are the four distinct seasons that continually paint New England with a changing palette of colors, even as time seemingly stands still. Each change in weather and temperature opens the door to new recreational possibilities—skiing, snowmobiling, garden strolling, fishing, biking, boating, and raking up and jumping into piles of crunchy leaves. And, the region's compactness makes it feasible for folks to plan a visit that incorporates an endless variety of activities. Travelers can spend a day walking the Freedom Trail in history-filled and bustling Boston and by evening find themselves either nestled inside a cozy cabin listening to the haunting cry of loons on a sleepy New Hampshire lake, breathing in salty ocean air and feasting on fresh seafood in a seaside Rhode Island town, or lazing on a blanket under the stars listening to the strains of a symphony at Tanglewood, the Boston Symphony Orchestra's summer home in Western Massachusetts's Berkshires.

While history, climate, and identity unify the region, each of the six states that comprise New England also has its own distinct appeal. Connecticut is New England's gateway, and it provides interesting juxtapositions of old and new that nevertheless blend together in perfect harmony. Historic whaling towns are a stone's throw away from the flashing lights and twenty-four-hour action of the world's largest casino. Maine visitors are equally entranced by outlet shopping bargains and frequent moose sightings. Massachusetts can't be beat for historic attractions, miles of sandy beaches, delectable chowder, performing arts centers, quaint island escapes, scenic highways, and world-class museums. New Hampshire satisfies vacationers' hunger for mountain vistas and lakeside retreats, while also surprising them with the offbeat—from llama treks to sky rides to attractions such as America's Stonehenge and Clark's Trading Post with its dancing bears. Rhode Island may be America's most diminutive state, but it can brag of 400 miles of coastline and one of the nation's densest concentrations of historic landmarks. Vermont's rural stretches and sparse population make it the cure for everyday hassles and a coveted destination for hikers and skiers.

Whether you are planning your first or fiftieth trip to New England, this guide will orient you to the region, provide destination inspiration, steer you toward helpful travel resources, and help you to maximize your precious time in this corner of the world. Hopefully, you will turn to it again and again as you join the loyal legion of fans who have fallen in love with New England.

FAST FACT

You'll see scrod on seafood menus throughout New England, particularly in Boston—but there is actually no such fish. The term is usually applied to the best white fish of the day, frequently cod or haddock. The term scrod probably evolved from the Dutch "schrod," meaning "to fillet."

A Brief History of the Region

NEW ENGLAND HAS LONG BEEN THE INCUBATOR for American ideas. Much of the region's mystique lies in its intricate and compelling history and its vital role in weaving the political, cultural, and intellectual fabric of American life. Visiting New England is truly akin to leaping inside the pages of a history textbook and meeting larger than life characters face-to-face on their own turf.

The "New" England

John Smith is credited with giving the region its Eurocentric nomenclature in 1614, but the land he called "New England" was home to native peoples long before European explorers and settlers arrived on the scene. Little is known, though, of New England's earliest inhabitants. Fossil evidence of human habitation found in Shawville, Vermont, places a date of 9000 B.C. on New England's earliest civilization, but no clear connection has been established between these early peoples and the thriving Algonkian civilization that arose during the fourteenth or fifteenth centuries, and was firmly established by the time Europeans began to explore the area in earnest. Mystery also continues to swirl around the question of whether Viking explorers from Scandinavia ever touched ground as far south as New England.

Though "related," the Algonkians were splintered into many small tribes—the Narragansetts in Rhode Island, the Abenaki in Maine, the Massachusetts in, of course, Massachusetts, and many others. They were frequently engaged in wars amongst themselves, and their lack of unity would eventually contribute to the Europeans' domination of those who had at first befriended them.

English interest in the land that would later be known as New England picked up in the early 1600s, but it would be several decades before a permanent settlement would be established here. Profit seekers found little in the way of gold or diamonds to entice them to stick around, but a group of Puritans, whom we know today as the Pilgrims, did find something of immeasurable value on New England's shores—religious freedom.

In mid-December 1620, after more than two months aboard the *Mayflower*, the Pilgrims landed at Plymouth Rock after first touching ground on what is now Provincetown on the outmost tip of Cape Cod. More than half of them died during the first miserable winter, but with spring came the help of Squanto and the Wampanoag tribe, and by fall, the Native Americans and Pilgrims joined in a feast in celebration of their first harvest—our country's First Thanksgiving.

In 1628, another group of Puritans formed the Massachusetts Bay Colony, settling in the Boston area, and from there, religious leaders dispersed with followers to establish settlements in neighboring New England states. Oddly enough in light of their own desire for freedom from religious persecution, the Puritans were an intolerant bunch, and in 1636, upstart preacher Roger Williams, who asserted, "forced worship stinks in God's nostrils," established the colony of Rhode Island after being banished from Massachusetts Bay Colony.

FAST FACT

Included on the menu for the Pilgrims' first Thanksgiving was lobster and beer! President Abraham Lincoln proclaimed Thanksgiving a national holiday in 1863, three months after the Battle of Gettysburg in the American Civil War. Lincoln designated the last Thursday of November as Thanksgiving Day. President Franklin Delano Roosevelt changed it to the fourth Thursday in 1939.

Colonial Revolt

Mother England pretty much left her colonies to toddle along on their own until the 1760s, when King George III, Prime Minister Lord North, and Parliament began imposing new taxes on colonial subjects. Needless to say, the Americans were not amused, primarily because they lacked representation in Parliament and had little recourse as new taxes and laws—the Sugar Act of 1764, the Stamp Act of 1765, the Townshend Acts of 1767—were handed down. Tensions mounted, resistance reverberated, and in 1770, British troops opened fire on an angry crowd, killing five in the Boston Massacre. To pacify the colonists, Parliament repealed some repressive laws, but the tea tax remained as a sign of England's heavy hand. Defiant patriots responded in 1773 by demanding that a ship loaded with tea leave Boston Harbor and return to England. When it did not, the rebels, including Sam Adams and John Hancock, disguised themselves as Native Americans, stormed the ship, and tossed its cargo of more than 300 crates of tea into the ocean.

You know what happens next—war. The American Revolution broke out in New England with Paul Revere warning of the coming of British troops on his famous midnight ride from Boston to Lexington, and minutemen standing in defense of freedom as the "shot heard round the world" was fired at Lexington. Massachusetts also saw the war's first major engagement, the Battle of Bunker Hill, where the Brits were victorious but suffered heavy losses. On July 4, 1776, fourteen New Englanders were among the signers of the Declaration of Independence.

FAST FACT

The Old Farmer's Almanac is North America's oldest continuously published periodical and one of the best sources for New England lore. It's been around since 1792, during George Washington's second term! The secret formula for long-range weather forecasting devised by its first editor Robert B. Thomas is kept in a black tin box at the *Almanac* offices in Dublin, New Hampshire.

Post-Revolution New England

When the war was finally won in 1781, New Englanders returned to the business of building the economy of the Northeast, while some of the most prominent among them, including John Adams and his son, John Quincy Adams, turned their attention to shaping the fledgling democracy. Much of New England's early prosperity was tied to its success in using its key natural resource—the ocean. The fishing, whaling, and shipbuilding industries and overseas trade bolstered the development of harbor towns.

The nineteenth century brought with it impediments to a maritime economy—wars, trade embargoes—but resilient New Englanders used their ingenuity to develop a new economic model—manufacturing. From the launch of Samuel Slater's cotton mill in Rhode Island in 1789 to the rise of mill towns in the Merrimack Valley of Massachusetts in the first half of the century, New England was at the forefront of the Industrial Revolution in America.

New England also took the lead in social reform during this era. Abolitionists spoke out against slavery and sheltered escaped slaves, helping them achieve freedom through the Underground Railroad. In 1800, Rhode Island was the site of the nation's first labor strike.

Dorothea Dix crusaded on behalf of the mentally ill in Massachusetts. Artistic, literary, and intellectual accomplishments had their epicenter here, too. The 1800s saw the creation of the nation's oldest continuously operating art museum, Hartford, Connecticut's Wadsworth Atheneum (1842); the opening of the first free municipal public library, the Boston Public Library (1854); and the debut of the Boston Symphony (1881) and the Boston Pops (1885). Writers who shaped not only the thinking of the nation but the world called New England home—Henry David Thoreau, Emily Dickinson, Ralph Waldo Emerson, Henry Wadsworth Longfellow, Nathaniel Hawthorne, Herman Melville, Mark Twain, and Harriet Beecher Stowe.

The nineteenth century also saw an influx of "new" New Englanders. During the Great Potato Famine of 1845–1850, Irish immigrants arrived in Boston at a rate of more than 1,000 per month. Others arrived from Italy, Portugal, Eastern Europe, and Canada. Digestion of the new mass of opportunity seekers led to a few hiccups and bellyaches as these groups forged their own political and cultural identity in New England's cities and towns.

By the twentieth century's dawn, New England was losing its grasp on economic leadership as new methods of manufacturing made it possible for factories to move to locations where labor was less expensive. The stock market crash of 1929, World War II, and the postwar recession contributed to wild fluctuations in the region's fortunes. But the latter half of the century marked a resurgence of prominence for the region. The election of an extraordinarily popular president from New England in 1960, John F. Kennedy of Massachusetts, showed beyond the shadow of a doubt that the region and indeed the country had overcome its anti-immigrant sentiments. Kennedy was the first Irish Catholic and (at that time) the youngest person ever elected to the nation's top office. The growth, too, of an information economy in the late 1900s and early part of the twenty-first century boded well for the current and future economic strength of the region—home to distinguished universities and leading technology companies.

FAST FACT

The job of preparing the first Thanksgiving feast, a three-day celebration for fifty colonists and ninety Native Americans, fell to the four married women who survived the Pilgrims' first winter in Plymouth. Martha Stewart was not the first amazing New England hostess!

What the Future May Hold

New Englanders are proud of the region's rich history and traditions, but they are not ones to opt for stagnancy and complacency. The next "revolution" in American history may well be nurtured inside the fertile minds of imaginative, ingenious New Englanders.

Getting There and Back

ONE OF THE PERKS OF NEW ENGLAND is its accessibility. By air, sea, road, or rail, there is never a shortage of travel options for this first step in planning your Northeastern getaway.

By Car

Most of New England is well connected by interstate highways, and traveling to and around the region by car allows the highest degree of itinerary-planning flexibility. New England's compact geography makes it possible to explore multiple states within the course of even a weekend getaway. Even if you are flying to New England or arriving by rail or bus, you may want to seriously consider renting a car for the duration of your stay. Boston is really the only New England destination where you won't need a car—in fact, you're better off without one.

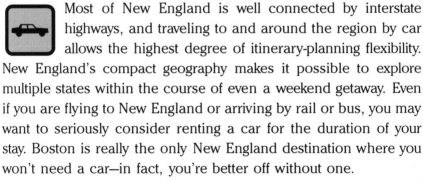

Major interstate highways include: I-95, which runs north and east from New York City through Connecticut, Rhode Island, Massachusetts, New Hampshire, and Maine; I-84, which enters Connecticut at Danbury and traverses the state, connecting to I-90, also known as the Massachusetts Turnpike, at Sturbridge; I-91 runs due north from New Haven, Connecticut, through Hartford and Springfield, Massachusetts, bisecting the Massachusetts Turnpike, then along the Vermont/New Hampshire border before taking a turn into northern Vermont; I-93 branches off from I-95 near Boston and runs through New Hampshire, meeting up with I-91 at St. Johnsbury, Vermont.

The speed limit on most interstate highways is 65 miles per hour, but is often lower around many major cities. So be alert for posted speed limits as you approach cities and towns. Also be sure to obey speed limits posted on local roadways. Keep in mind that highway routes may be your fastest option, but there may be more scenic alternatives if travel time is not a major issue for you.

Traffic can be a hassle, particularly if you are traveling a popular "escape route" on a Friday afternoon. Traffic through Boston, into Maine, and especially entering Cape Cod can be nightmarish during peak travel weekends. If you can plan your drive for "off-peak" times, you may have a smoother journey.

By Plane

Boston's Logan International Airport is by far the region's busiest airport. Major carriers also serve Bradley International Airport in Windsor Locks, Connecticut; T. F. Green International Airport in Warwick (near Providence), Rhode Island; and smaller airports in Manchester, New Hampshire; Portland and Bangor, Maine; Burlington, Vermont; and Hyannis and Worcester, Massachusetts. New England is also an accessible destination to those arriving at airports in Albany and New York City, New York, and Montreal, Canada.

Bradley International Airport

Bradley International Airport (BDL), (860) 292-2000 or (888) 624-1533, located just fifteen minutes north of Hartford in Windsor Locks, is an easily accessible transportation hub that serves the Greater Hartford/Springfield area as well as western New England. It is the New England region's second largest airport, serving more than 7 million passengers annually.

Bradley International Airport is located at exit 40 off I-91. Airport Connection, (860) 627-3400, offers transportation services between the airport and Hartford hotels. Connecticut Transit, (860) 525-9181, also operates buses that provide transportation connecting the airport and the Old State House in downtown Hartford.

The airlines serving Bradley International Airport are:

American
(800) 433-7300 *www.aa.com*

America West
(800) 235-9292 *www.americawest.com*

Continental
(800) 525-0280 *www.continental.com*

Comair
(800) 221-1212 *www.fly-comair.com*

Delta
(800) 221-1212 *www.delta.com*

Delta Express
(800) 325-5205 *www.delta.com/prog_serv/delta_express*

MetroJet
(800) 428-4322 *www.usairways.com/metrojet*

Midway
(800) 446-4392 *www.midwayair.com*

Midwest Express
(800) 452-2022 *www.midwestexpress.com*

Northwest
(800) 225-2525 *www.nwa.com*

Southwest
(800) 435-9792 *www.southwest.com*

TWA
(800) 221-2000 *www.twa.com*

T.F. Green International Airport

T.F. Green International Airport (PVD), (401) 737-8222 or (888) 268-7222, located just twelve minutes south of Providence in Warwick, is an easily accessible, hassle-free transportation gateway that serves the state of Rhode Island as well as southern New England. It is even a reasonable alternative to busy Logan Airport in Boston. More than 5 million passengers utilize T.F. Green Airport each year.

T.F. Green International Airport is located at exit 13 off I-95. Aero-Airport Limousine Service, (401) 737-2868, offers transportation services from the airport to Providence hotels, the train station, Civic Center, the Convention Center, and Brown University. Cozy Cab, Inc., (401) 846-1500 or (800) 846-1502, operates a shuttle between the airport and Newport.

The airlines serving T.F. Green International Airport are:

Air Ontario
(888) 247-2262 *www.airontario.com*

American/American Eagle
(800) 433-7300 *www.aa.com*

Cape Air
(800) 352-0714 *www.flycapeair.com*

Continental/Continental Express
(800) 525-0280 *www.flycontinental.com*

Delta
(800) 221-1212 *www.delta.com*

Delta Express
(800) 325-5205 *www.delta.com/prog_serv/delta_express*

MetroJet
(888) 638-7653 *www.flymetrojet.com*

Northwest
(800) 225-2525 *www.nwa.com*

Southwest
(800) 435-9792 *www.southwest.com*

United/United Express
(800) 241-6522 *www.ual.com*

US Airways/US Airways Express
(800) 428-4322 *www.usair.com*

Logan International Airport

Logan International Airport (BOS), (617) 561-1600 or (800) 23-LOGAN, is located in East Boston. The nation's seventeenth busiest airport, it serves more than 26 million passengers each year. This 2,400-acre transportation center is New England's largest.

Logan International Airport is located off the I-93 Expressway at the Callahan Tunnel/Logan Airport exit. Stay to the right at the end of the tunnel, and the second exit will put you onto the Logan Airport access roadway. The airport is also accessible via the Ted Williams Tunnel. However, access to the Ted Williams Tunnel may be limited due to construction. The Logan Shuttle offers complimentary transportation around the terminals, to the airport's subway station on the MBTA Blue Line, and to the Water Transportation Terminal. Boat service to downtown Boston is provided by the Airport Water Shuttle, (617) 439-3131; Harbor Express, (617) 376-8417; and seasonally, on-call by City Water Taxi, (617) 422-0392. Harbor Express also provides boat service to the South Shore at the former Quincy shipyard.

The Logan DART shuttle bus, (800) 23-LOGAN, provides service between downtown Boston's Financial District via South Station and Logan Airport's five terminals. The Logan DART departs from South Station every fifteen minutes Sunday through Friday from 6 A.M. until 8 P.M. There is also a pickup from the MBTA bus stop at the Stone and Webster Building on Summer Street.

Shared van transportation between Logan Airport and points downtown including hotels is provided by a number of companies including U.S. Shuttle, (617) 889-3366 or (877) SHUTTLE; Back Bay Coach, (617) 746-9909 or (888) 222-5229; Boston Beats Limo, (617) 267-5856; Logan/Boston Hotel Shuttle, (617) 561-

9500 or (877) 315-4700; and City Transportation, (617) 561-9000. Call ahead for pricing and schedule information. Some services require twenty-four-hour advance reservations. Taxi service is also readily available twenty-four hours a day to transport you from Logan to your destination. All drop-off points within a 12-mile radius of downtown Boston are charged at a metered rate. Beyond the 12-mile radius, a flat fee is assessed. Passengers are responsible for tunnel tolls. For sample fares, see Massport's Logan Airport Web site, *www.massport.com.*

Eight rental car companies operate at or near Logan International Airport: Alamo, (800) 327-9633; Avis, (800) 831-2847; Budget, (800) 527-7000; Dollar, (800) 800-4000; Enterprise, (800) 325-8007; Hertz, (800) 654-3131; National, (800) 227-7368; and Thrifty, (800) 367-2277.

TRAVEL TIP

Massport offers shuttle service to Logan Airport from Braintree to the south, Framingham to the west, and Woburn to the north, with secure parking available in all three locations. Buses stop at all airport terminals. For schedule, rates, and directions, call (800) 23-LOGAN.

Worcester Regional Airport

For New England travelers whose destination is in central or western Massachusetts, Worcester Regional Airport (ORH), Airport Drive, (508) 799-1741 or (888) FLY-WORC, is a viable, growing alternative to the much more congested Logan International Airport in Boston. Four major carriers offer flights in and out of Worcester: American Eagle, (800) 433-7300; Delta, (800) 221-1212; Pan Am, (800) 359-7262; and US Airways (800) 428-4322.

Worcester Regional Airport is located north of the Mass Pike (I-90) off I-290. Worcester Airport Limousine Service, (800) 660-0992, provides door-to-door transportation between the airport and surrounding areas.

Portland International Jetport

Portland International Jetport (PWM), ☏(207) 772-0690, serves northern New England from its convenient location off the Maine Turnpike. Passenger traffic through Portland's airport has grown substantially during the past twenty years to more than 1 million travelers annually.

Portland International Jetport is located at exit 7A off I-95. Airlines serving Portland include Air Nova, ☏(800) 272-9662; American Airlines, ☏(800) 433-7300; Continental Airlines, ☏(800) 525-0280; Delta, ☏(800) 221-1212; Northwest, ☏(800) 225-2525; TWA, ☏(800) 221-2000; United Airlines, ☏(800) 241-6522; and US Airways, ☏(800) 428-4322.

Companies offering scheduled airport shuttle service include: Concord Trailways, ☏(800) 639-3317; Greyhound/Vermont Transit, ☏(207) 772-6587; Mermaid Transportation, ☏(800) 696-2463; and Shuttlebus/Zoom, ☏(877) THE-ZOOM. Many Portland-area hotels also provide courtesy vans for their guests. Taxis and bus service are also readily available.

Bangor International Airport

Bangor International Airport (BGR), ☏(207) 947-0384, serves northern Maine and Canada from its convenient location off I-95. There are more than sixty domestic flights to and from Bangor daily.

To reach the airport, take exit 47 for Union Street off I-95 and follow signs. Airlines serving Bangor include American Eagle, ☏(800) 433-7300; Continental Airlines, ☏(800) 525-0280; Delta Connection, ☏(800) 221-1212; Finnair, ☏(800) 950-5000; Pan Am, ☏(800) 359-7262; and US Airways Express, ☏(800) 428-4322.

Companies offering scheduled airport shuttle service include: Concord Trailways, ☏(207) 945-4000 or ☏(800) 639-3317; The Bus, ☏(207) 947-0536; and West's Coastal Connection, ☏(207) 546-2832 or ☏(800) 596-2823. Several local hotels offer free airport shuttle service. Taxis and limousine service are also readily available.

Manchester Airport

Manchester Airport (MHT), (603) 624-6539, is conveniently located off I-93 and is a growing transportation hub that serves northern New England. It is also an alternative for some travelers to Boston's busy Logan International Airport. Passenger traffic tripled at Manchester Airport between 1997 and 2000.

To reach Manchester Airport, follow signs from I-93 to 293/Route 101 to exit 2 for Brown Avenue. Follow Brown Avenue for one mile, then take a left on Airport Road. Airport shuttles are operated by Flight Line, (603) 893-8254 or (800) 245-2525; Hampton Shuttle, (603) 659-9893 or (800) 225-6426; and Mermaid Transportation Company, (207) 772-2509 or (800) MY-MAINE. Taxis and limousines are also readily available.

The airlines serving Manchester Airport:

Air Canada
(888) 247-2262 *www.aircanada.ca*

American Eagle
(800) 433-7300 *www.aa.com*

Continental/Continental Express
(800) 525-0280 *www.continental.com*

Delta Airlines
(800) 221-1212 *www.delta-air.com*

Delta Connection/Comair
(800) 354-9822 *www.fly-comair.com*

MetroJet
(888) 638-7653 *www.usairways.com/metrojet*

Northwest Airlines
(800) 225-2525 *www.nwa.com*

Southwest Airlines
(800) 435-9792 *www.southwest.com*

United Airlines
(800) 241-6522 *www.ual.com*

US Airways/US Airways Express
(800) 428-4322 *www.usairways.com*

Burlington International Airport

Burlington International Airport (BTV), (802) 863-2874, is New England's third busiest airport, serving about 900,000 passengers annually. Airlines serving Vermont include American Airlines, (800) 433-7300; Continental Express, (800) 523-3273; Delta Connection, (800) 221-1212; JetBlue Airways, (800) 538-2583; Northwest, (800) 225-2525; United Airlines/United Express, (800) 241-6522; and US Airways/US Airways Express, (800) 428-4322. Burlington International Airport is located four miles east of Burlington off Route 2.

Smaller Airports

There are several other small airports for certain niches throughout New England. Some of the most popular include those that serve Cape Cod, Martha's Vineyard, and Nantucket in Massachusetts; Block Island in Rhode Island; Nashua and Lebanon in New Hampshire; and New London and New Haven in Connecticut. When applicable, these airports are discussed in the book.

By Train

Amtrak, (800) 872-7245, *www.amtrak.com*, is the region's major rail carrier. The NortheastDirect route connects Newport News, Virginia, with Boston, with stops along the way in Washington, D.C., Baltimore, Philadelphia, New York's Penn Station, and New Haven, Connecticut. At New Haven, the line splits, and travelers may choose stops along the Hartford route including Springfield and Worcester, Massachusetts, or along the shoreline route, including Mystic, Connecticut, and Providence, Rhode Island. The Vermonter route is popular with skiers and fall foliage seekers. With daily service from Washington, D.C., and New York, this train makes stops in Vermont at Brattleboro, Bellows Falls, Windsor-Mt. Ascutney, Waterbury-Stowe, Burlington, and St. Albans. There are also stops at New Haven, Hartford, and Windsor,

Connecticut, and you can continue on to Montreal by bus from St. Albans. The Ethan Allen Express route connects New York City to Rutland, Vermont, with several New York stops along the way.

Metro North, ✆(212) 340-3000 or ✆(800) 638-7646, operates from New York's Grand Central Station and offers more affordable service to points in Connecticut. The New Haven line carries passengers between Grand Central and points along Connecticut's shoreline as far east as New Haven. There is connecting service from Stamford to New Canaan, from South Norwalk to Danbury, and from Bridgeport to Waterbury. Metro North offers a wide variety of special excursion packages including round-trip rail transportation from New York City to Connecticut destinations such as Mystic Seaport and Foxwoods Casino.

FAST FACT

The Acela is Amtrak's high-speed rail service that makes travel along the Washington, D.C.–New York–Boston corridor speedy and convenient. The train's top speed of 150 miles per hour is the fastest of any Amtrak service in the nation. The Acela schedule is designed specifically for business travelers going between New York and Boston, but it's also a good transportation choice for vacationers. For schedule information and reservations, call Amtrak at ✆(800) USA-RAIL.

By Bus

Interstate bus companies that provide service to many points in New England include Greyhound Bus Line, ✆(617) 526-1800 or ✆(800) 231-2222; Bonanza Bus Line, ✆(617) 720-4110 or ✆(800) 556-3815; Peter Pan Trailways, ✆(617) 426-7838 or ✆(800) 343-9999; and Concord Trailways, ✆(617) 426-8080 or ✆(800) 639-3317.

Cruising New England

Though New England may not be the first destination that comes to mind when you're planning a cruise vacation, there are several cruise lines that stop at ports of call along New England's coast such as Boston, Portland, and the islands of Nantucket and Martha's Vineyard. The majority of departures coincide with fall foliage season.

American Canadian Caribbean Line
(800) 556-7450 *www.accl-smallships.com*

American Cruise Lines
(800) 814-6880 *www.americancruiselines.com*

Clipper Cruise Line
(314) 727-2929 or (800) 325-0010 *www.clippercruise.com*

Cunard Line
(800) 7-CUNARD *www.cunard.com*

Holland America
(206) 281-3535 or (877) SAIL HAL *www.hollandamerica.com*

Norwegian Cruise Line
(800) 343-0098 *www.ncl.com*

Princess Cruises & Tours
(800) 774-6237 *www.princesscruises.com*

Regal Cruises
(800) 270-7245 *www.regalcruises.com*

Silversea Cruises
(800) 722-9955 *www.silversea.com*

Planning Your Trip

"PEAK" AND "OFF-PEAK" TRAVEL TIMES are closely linked to the changing seasons. Overall, fall is New England's busiest tourism season as "leaf peepers" descend upon the region from near and far. Hotel reservations can be extraordinarily hard to come by if you have not made plans well in advance. You'll struggle with crowds, too, if you visit the area's seaside destinations during summer weekends and particularly the Fourth of July holiday week. Finding a ski chalet in Vermont can be tricky during school vacation weeks in December and February. Your best bet is to plan as far ahead as possible, to make sure you understand individual lodging properties' cancellation policies, and to be prepared for lines at attractions and restaurants if your trip coincides with peak season. Keep in mind that you can uncover special "off-peak" deals by visiting ski resort areas in the spring and summer, Cape Cod and other oceanside spots in the fall through early spring, or just about any destination during the first few weeks of September before the annual foliage-viewing rush.

Time Zone

All six New England states are on U.S. Eastern Time (GMT minus five hours). Daylight Savings Time is observed. Clocks are set forward one hour at 2:00 A.M. on the first Sunday morning in April, and

Eastern Standard Time resumes at 2:00 A.M. on the last Sunday morning in October.

Public Holidays

These public holidays are observed in New England: New Year's Day (January 1), Martin Luther King, Jr.'s Birthday (third Monday in January), Presidents' Day/Washington's Birthday (third Monday in February), Patriots' Day (Monday closest to April 19—Massachusetts and Maine only), Memorial Day (last Monday in May), Independence Day (July 4), Labor Day (first Monday in September), Columbus Day (second Monday in October), Veterans Day (November 11), Thanksgiving (fourth Thursday in November), Christmas Day (December 25).

Business Hours

Typical public and private office hours are Monday through Friday, 8 or 9 A.M. to 5 P.M. Banking hours are typically Monday through Friday, 9 A.M. to 3 P.M., but many banks, particularly those with branch offices inside retail establishments such as grocery stores, offer extended hours on selected evenings and on Saturday mornings. Many gas stations and grocery/convenience stores are open twenty-four hours. Post offices are usually open from 8 or 8:30 A.M. until 5 P.M. Monday through Friday and until noon or later on Saturday. Most stores are open Monday through Saturday from 9:30 or 10 A.M. until 6 P.M. or later and on Sunday from 11 A.M. or noon until 5 or 6 P.M.

Finding Accommodations

Accommodations are abundant nearly everywhere you go in New England, except perhaps in the far northern wilderness reaches of Maine and New Hampshire. Your most difficult decision will be choosing a type of lodging from the diverse array available—luxury hotels, rustic cabins, spacious resorts, rental cottages, lakeside campsites, family-run motor inns, antique-filled bed and breakfasts, historic mansions . . . heck, there's even a nude campground in Foster, Rhode Island–Dyer Woods Nudist Campground, ✆(401) 397-3007. This guide will point you to some of the region's unique places to stay and to resources for researching lodging options. Contact regional and state tourism organizations for more leads on accommodations to suit your needs, and be sure to ask friends who have visited New England for their recommendations.

Advance reservations are always a good idea, and during fall foliage season, they are absolutely critical. After all, you don't want to spend valuable vacation minutes searching aimlessly for a place to catch some shuteye.

What to Pack

Two factors will influence the contents of your suitcase when you're packing for your trip to New England–the time of year and your planned activities.

In general, you'll want to take along lightweight clothing for visits between late June and early September, but be sure to pack a jacket or sweater, especially if you're visiting areas along the coast, where breezes can have a decidedly cooling effect. Bathing suits, towels, and sunscreen are critical for ocean-side or lakefront getaways. An insect repellent containing DEET is essential for protecting yourself from Lyme disease (which is carried by ticks), especially if you're planning to spend time outdoors in wooded, brushy, or overgrown grassy areas.

In the spring and fall, temperatures can be quite cold at night even when daytime temperatures are comfortably moderate. You'll want to bring along a warmer jacket or raincoat. Pack items that can be worn in layers.

If you visit between November and March, you'll want to be prepared with a heavy winter coat, scarf, waterproof boots, and gloves or mittens. If you are planning a ski vacation, you can take your own gear along or rent equipment at the slopes.

An umbrella is always a good idea no matter what the season. Be sure to pack any prescription medications you may need, maps and brochures with information on the sights you plan to visit, airline and other tickets, passports, credit cards and/or travelers checks. Many hotels provide hair dryers and toiletry items such as shampoo, soap, and body lotion, but it is always wise to inquire ahead. B&Bs are less likely to offer these amenities. You may need to furnish your own linens at rental accommodations, so be sure to ask ahead.

Don't forget your camera so that you'll have lasting images of your New England discoveries, and be sure to pack plenty of film. Film will cost you a premium if you wait to buy it at one of New England's historic attractions.

Safety Tips

As a general rule, New England is a safe place to travel. That said, visitors to the region should stay alert and use common sense to protect themselves and their belongings. Here are a few things to keep in mind:

- Don't carry large amounts of cash. Travelers checks and credit cards are much safer choices, or withdraw small amounts of cash at Automated Teller Machines (ATMs), which are commonplace throughout the region.
- Carry valuables—passports, visas, money, jewelry—close to you at all times. Do not leave valuables unattended in your hotel room. Instead, check with your hotel for the availability of a safe.
- Lock your hotel room door and use the deadbolt where available. Lock your car doors, too, whether you're parked or driving.
- Do not leave luggage or purchases visible in your car.
- Whenever possible, stay in well-traveled, populated areas, particularly after dark.
- In most of New England, you can dial 911 from any telephone to access the emergency response system. If 911 service is not available, dial 0, and an operator can connect you to the appropriate emergency services.

- Fill your car with gas before heading to remote areas, and don't underestimate the usefulness of a good map of the area where you are traveling.
- Deer and moose, and slick, wet fall leaves can all create driving hazards. In the autumn, watch out, too, for drivers who are looking at leaves instead of watching the road.

Health Care

Most sizable cities in New England have their own hospitals with emergency rooms. Highway signs with the hospital symbol–a white "H" on a blue background–can direct you to the nearest facility. Many cities and towns also have walk-in clinics for minor emergencies and ailments. Over-the-counter drugs are available at pharmacies and grocery and convenience stores, and even many discount and department stores. If you require prescription medications, it is a good idea to bring along an adequate supply. Prescription drugs are available at licensed pharmacies only with a prescription from a doctor licensed in the state you are visiting.

Safety Belt and Child Restraint Laws

In New England, laws requiring the use of safety belts and car seats for children vary by state. Here is a quick summary:

Connecticut–Safety belts are required for all front seat passengers ages four and up. Children three years old and younger and less than forty pounds must be secured in rear seat child restraints.
Maine–Passengers ages four and up in all seats must wear seatbelts. Children ages three and younger must ride in the rear of the vehicle in a car seat.
Massachusetts–Safety belts are required for passengers ages five and up in all seats. Children four years old and younger or who weigh less than forty pounds must ride in a rear seat child restraint.
New Hampshire–Children three years old and younger must be

secured in a rear seat child restraint. Children ages four through seventeen must wear a seatbelt. There is no safety belt law applying to adults in New Hampshire.

Rhode Island—Passengers ages seven and up must wear safety belts in all seats. Children six years and younger and less than 54 inches and less than eighty pounds must ride in a car seat. Children six years and younger and greater than 54 inches and eighty pounds must be seated in the rear of the vehicle if space is available.

Vermont—Everyone five and up must wear a safety belt in any seat of a vehicle. Child restraints are required for children ages four and younger.

For more information about highway safety laws and potential fines, call the Insurance Institute for Highway Safety at (703) 247-1500 or visit the nonprofit organization's Web site at *www.hwysafety.org*.

Helmet Laws

Laws pertaining to helmets for motorcycle drivers and passengers also vary by state. In Connecticut and New Hampshire, helmets are required for riders seventeen and younger only. In Maine, they are required for riders fourteen and younger. In Rhode Island, riders twenty years old and younger are required to wear helmets. In Massachusetts and Vermont, all riders must wear helmets.

Connecticut, Maine, Massachusetts, and Rhode Island also have laws requiring the use of helmets by young bicyclists. In Connecticut, Rhode Island, and Maine, riders younger than sixteen must wear a helmet. In Massachusetts, bicycle riders older than one and younger than thirteen must wear helmets.

Liquor Laws

The legal drinking age in New England is twenty-one. A photo ID is often required for admission to nightclubs or bars. State-imposed "blue laws" restrict the days and hours during which alcoholic beverages can be sold.

New England's Top Events

JANUARY
Sleigh Rally, Lyndonville, VT, ✆(800) 627-8310
Boston Cooks!, Boston, MA, ✆(800) 733-2678

FEBRUARY
Winterfest, East Millinocket, ME, ✆(207) 723-4443

MARCH
New England Spring Flower Show, Boston, MA, ✆(617) 536-9280
St. Patrick's Day Parade, Boston, MA, ✆(617) 268-8525
Maine Maple Sunday, statewide, ✆(207) 287-3871

APRIL
Boston Marathon, Boston, MA, ✆(617) 236-1652
Daffodil Festival, Meriden, CT, ✆(203) 630-4259

MAY
Edible Art, Boston, MA, ✆(617) 349-8586
Brimfield Outdoor Antiques and Collectibles Show, Brimfield, MA, ✆(413) 283-6149

Nantucket Wine Festival, Nantucket, MA, ✆(508) 228-1128
Dogwood Festival, Fairfield, CT, ✆(203) 259-5596

JUNE
Old Port Festival, Portland, ME, ✆(207) 772-6828
Schweppes Great Chowder Cook-off, Newport, RI, ✆(401) 846-1600
Festival of Historic Houses, Providence, RI, ✆(401) 831-7740
Discover Jazz Festival, Burlington, VT, ✆(802) 863-7992
Rose and Garden Weekend, Hartford, CT, ✆(860) 242-0017
Ben & Jerry's One World One Heart Festival, Fayston, VT, ✆(802) 846-1500 or ✆(800) BJ FESTS
Windjammer Days, Boothbay Harbor, ME, ✆(207) 633-2353

JULY
Brownsville Baked Bean Suppers, West Windsor, VT, ✆(802) 484-7285
Boston Harborfest/Fourth of July, Boston, MA, ✆(617) 227-1528
Native American Festival, Bar Harbor, ME, ✆(207) 487-5387
The Newport Flower Show, Newport, RI, ✆(401) 847-1000 ext. 140
International Festival of Arts & Ideas, New Haven, CT, ✆(203) 498-1212
Maine Potato Blossom Festival, Fort Fairfield, ME, ✆(207) 472-3802
Vermont Quilt Festival, Northfield, VT, ✆(802) 485-7092
Yarmouth Clam Festival, Yarmouth, ME, ✆(207) 846-3984
Lowell Folk Festival, Lowell, MA, ✆(978) 970-5000

AUGUST
Newport Folk Festival, Newport, RI, ✆(401) 847-3700
League of New Hampshire Crafts, Sunapee, NH, ✆(603) 224-3375
Maine Lobster Festival, Rockland, ME, ✆(207) 596-0376 or ✆(800) 562-2529
JVC Jazz Festival, Newport, RI, ✆(401) 847-3700
Vermont State Zucchini Festival, Ludlow, VT, ✆(802) 228-5830
North Country Moose Festival, Pittsburg, Colebrook, and Errol, NH, ✆(603) 237-8939

SEPTEMBER
Mark Twain Days, Hartford, CT, ✆(860) 525-1000
Norwalk Seaport Association Oyster Festival, East Norwalk, CT, ✆(203) 838-9444
Seafood Festival and Sidewalk Sale Days, Hampton Beach, NH, ✆(603) 926-8718 or ✆(800) 438-2826
Bourne Scallop Festival, Buzzards Bay, MA, ✆(508) 759-6000
The Big E (Eastern States Exposition), West Springfield, MA, ✆(413) 737-2443
New Hampshire Highland Games, Lincoln, NH, ✆(603) 229-1975 or ✆(800) 358-7268
Stowe Oktoberfest, Stowe, VT, ✆(802) 253-8506

OCTOBER
Head of the Charles Regatta, Cambridge, MA, ✆(617) 868-6200
Hildene Farm, Food, & Folk Art Fair, Manchester, VT, ✆(802) 362-1788
Haunted Happenings, Salem, MA, ✆(978) 744-0013
Haunted Newport, Newport, RI, ✆(800) 976-5122
Mystic Seaport Chowderfest, Mystic, CT, ✆(860) 572-5315 or ✆(888) 9-SEAPORT
Cranberry Harvest Festival, South Carver, MA, ✆(508) 295-5799
Keene Pumpkin Festival, Keene, NH, ✆(603) 358-5344

NOVEMBER
Thanksgiving at Plimoth Plantation, Plymouth, MA, ✆(508) 746-1622 ext. 8366

DECEMBER
Bright Nights at Forest Park, Springfield, MA, ✆(413) 733-3800
Berkshire Museum Festival of Trees, Pittsfield, MA, ✆(413) 443-7171
Christmas in Newport, Newport, RI, ✆(401) 849-6454
Mystic Seaport Lantern Light Tours, Mystic, CT, ✆(860) 572-5315 or ✆(888) 9-SEAPORT
First Night Boston, Boston, MA, ✆(617) 542-1399

PART II

Connecticut

Connecticut

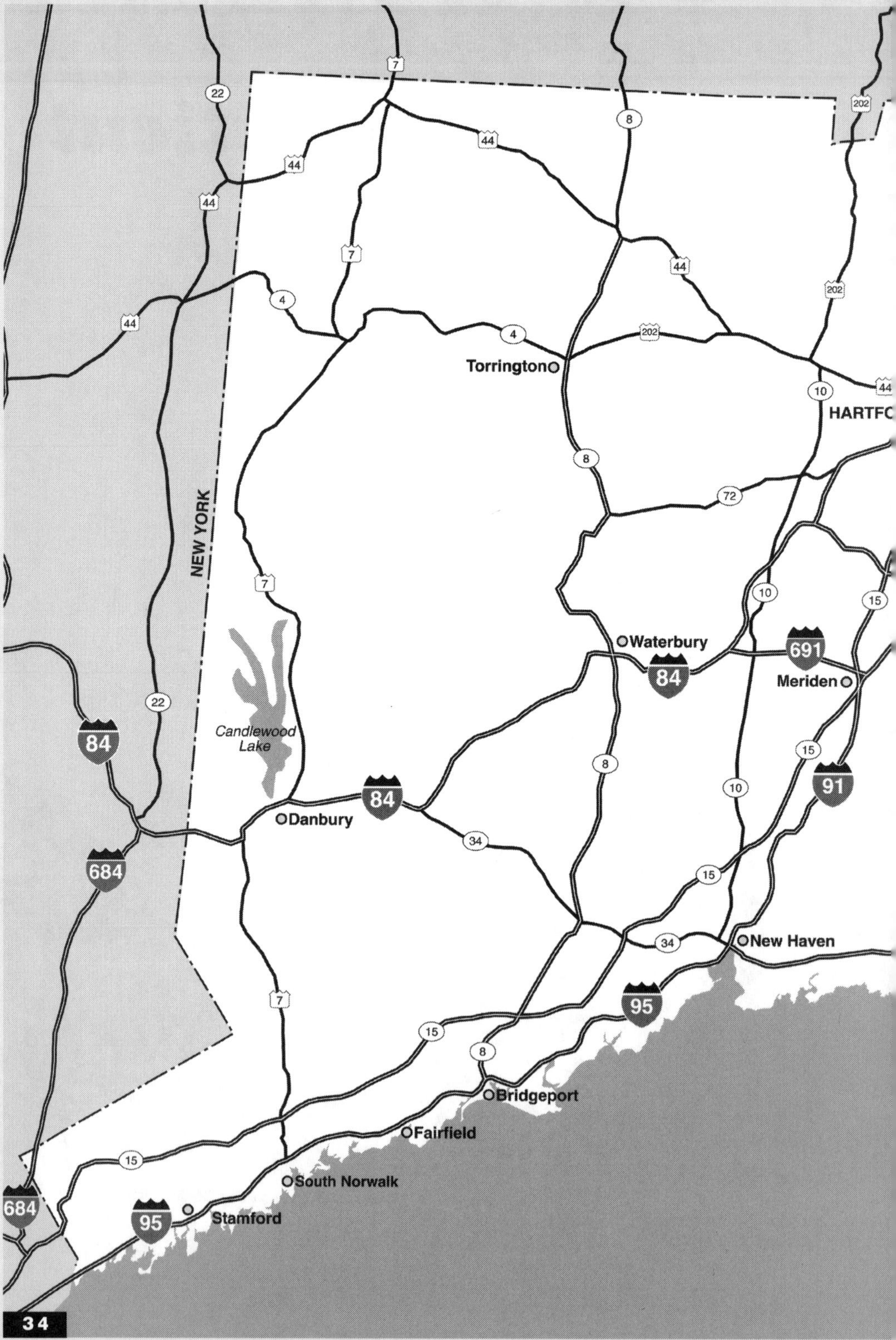

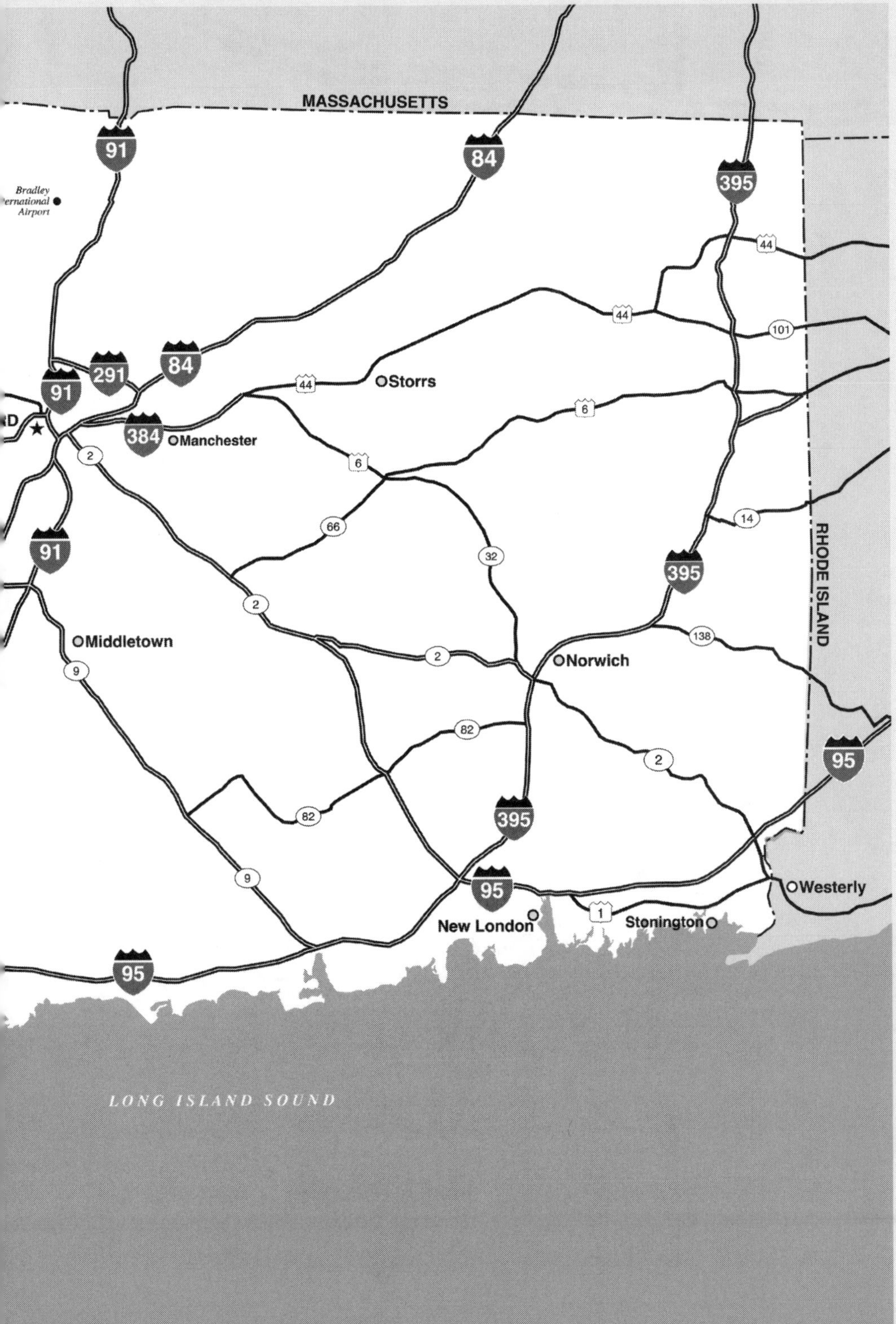

MASSACHUSETTS
91
84
395
Bradley
ernational
Airport
44
44
101
291
84
91
44
Storrs
6
RD
384
Manchester
2
6
66
32
14
RHODE ISLAND
91
395
2
138
Middletown
2
Norwich
9
82
2
95
82
395
9
95
Westerly
1
New London
Stonington
95
LONG ISLAND SOUND

Hartford, Connecticut

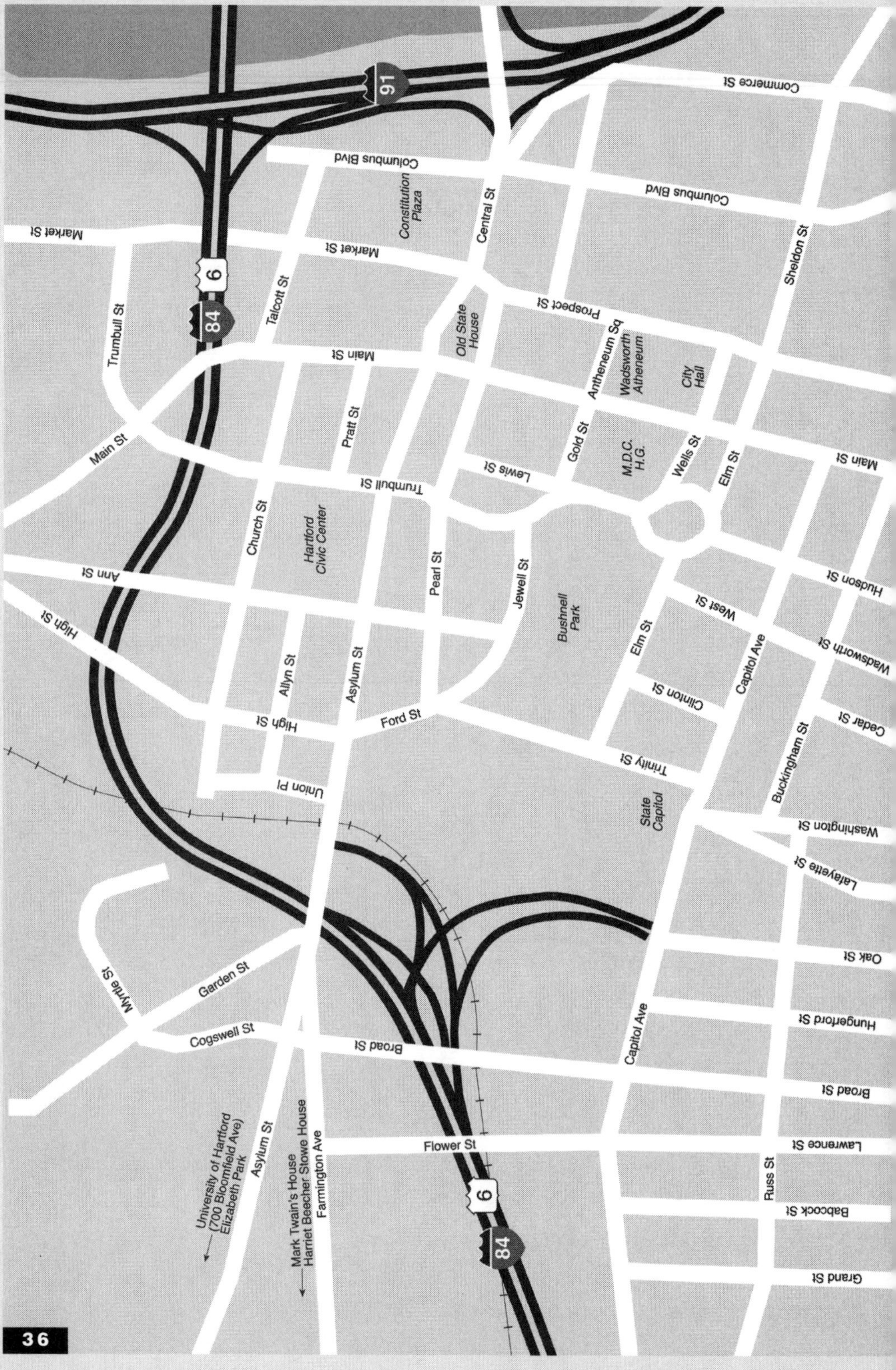

New Haven, Connecticut

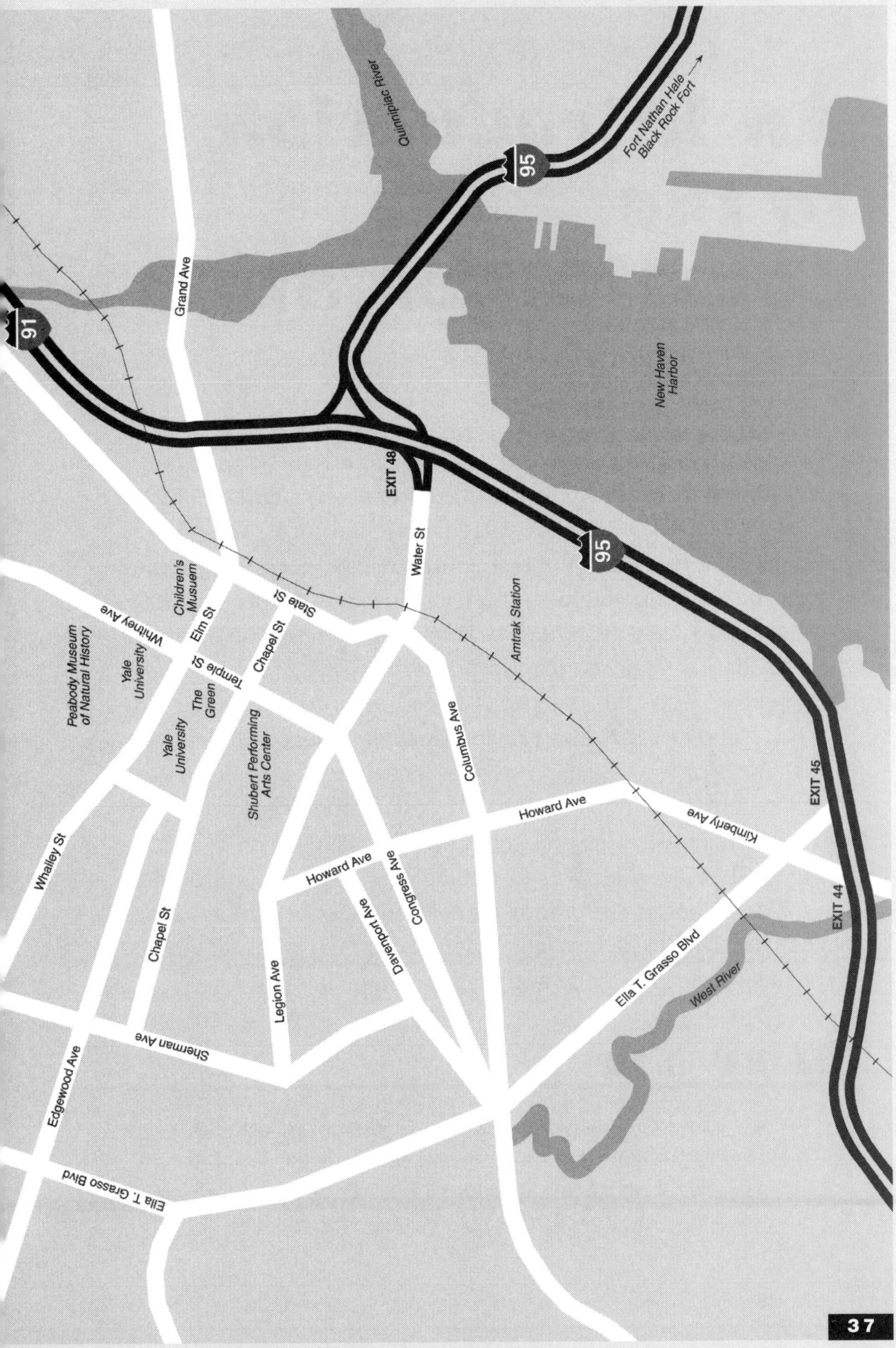

An Introduction to the Constitution State

AMERICA'S FIRST TURNPIKE, its first town library, and its first newspaper can all be credited to Connecticut. Connecticut inventors gave the world the first sewing machine, cotton gin, helicopter, nuclear submarine, and artificial heart. And we even have Connecticut to thank for the first Frisbee—bored Yale students got their hands on some empty pie plates from Mrs. Frisbie Pies in Bridgeport in 1920, and the rest is flying toy history.

This "land of firsts" also provides many travelers with their very first glimpse of New England as they enter the region from New York City and other points south and west. Unfortunately, many see little more than the trees and green highway signs lining Interstates 84, 91, and 95 on their way to further-flung New England destinations. Connecticut may be the third smallest state in the United States, but it's no lightweight when it comes to historic sites, museums, attractions, and vacation destinations all its own.

TRAVEL TIP

Request your free Connecticut Vacation Guide packed with information on attractions, accommodations, and recreational activities statewide by calling toll free, (800) CT-BOUND, or by completing the online form at *www.ctbound.org/vgorderform.htm*.

Connecticut as a Vacation Destination

Coastal Fairfield County offers art museums, a zoo, and historic mansions and lighthouses to explore. New Haven is home to historic Yale University. The Mystic area, a whaling and shipbuilding center in the seventeenth through nineteenth centuries, is now a popular family destination featuring historic and marine life attractions. Elsewhere along the state's Long Island Sound shoreline and inland along the Connecticut River, visitors will find spectacular scenery, steam train rides, beaches, and even a castle.

The central part of the state surrounding Connecticut's capital city, Hartford, is home to historic houses, apple orchards, and one of the country's oldest amusement parks still in operation. Connecticut's "Quiet Corner" in the northeast pocket of the state offers unique possibilities from antiquing to roaming with buffalo. And the Litchfield Hills in the western part of the state are home to vineyards, fabulous outdoor recreational opportunities, and some of the state's most romantic and charming inns.

Connecticut can't be beat for a quick getaway—there's so much to experience in a close, accessible area. Couple compact geography with the state's amazing contrasts, and you'll be able to engage in a wide variety of vacation activities, even if your travel plans allow for little more than a weekend in the Constitution State.

Connecticut harmoniously blends old and new, large and small. Historic whaling towns are a stone's throw from the glamour and glitz of the world's largest casino, Foxwoods. Urban Fairfield County, an extension of the New York metropolitan region, is bisected by one of the nation's most scenic highways, the Merritt Parkway. Though only three states are more densely populated, nearly three-quarters of Connecticut is rural.

So don't simply speed through Connecticut. Make savoring the sights in captivating Connecticut your first New England travel priority.

FAST FACT

Connecticut's Official:

Song—"Yankee Doodle"
Bird—American Robin
Tree—White Oak
Flower—Mountain Laurel
Animal—Sperm Whale
Insect—Praying Mantis
Mineral—Garnet
Shellfish—Eastern Oyster

Top Connecticut Highlights

The following are some of the "must-see" attractions in the state. One of the beauties of touring this compact state is that if any two or three of these locales are appealing, you can most likely fit them all into one day's adventure.

The Barnum Museum

820 Main Street, Bridgeport
(203) 331-1104
www.barnum-museum.org

P. T. Barnum, America's crown prince of oddities and mastermind behind "The Greatest Show on Earth," was born in Connecticut, and he and his cast of characters—General Tom Thumb, Chang and Eng the Siamese twins, Jumbo the Elephant, and others—come to life at the only museum dedicated to the life of the famous showman.

Beardsley Zoo

1875 Noble Avenue, Bridgeport
(203) 394-6565
www.beardsleyzoo.org

Connecticut's only zoo is home to more than 120 species of wildlife including endangered Siberian tigers and red wolves that are being raised as part of the Species Survival Plan. While you're there, be sure to stroll through the indoor re-creation of a South

American rain forest in the New World Tropics building. Children will be delighted by the zoo's carousel museum, working carousel, and New England farmyard.

Foxwoods Resort Casino

Route 2, Mashantucket
(800) PLAY-BIG
www.foxwoods.com

The world's largest casino isn't in Las Vegas, Monte Carlo, or Atlantic City. It's in Connecticut! The Mashantucket Pequot tribe's Foxwoods Resort Casino offers twenty-four-hour gaming action and boasts more than 5,500 slot machines and a Bingo Hall that goes on forever. You'll also find three on-site hotels, thirty dining options, headline entertainment in the 1,450-seat Fox Theatre, and the Mashantucket Pequot Museum, America's largest Native American museum, which is a five-minute shuttle ride away. A smaller and cozier competing casino, **Mohegan Sun** (1 Mohegan Sun Boulevard, Uncasville, (888) 226-7711), is about a fifteen-minute drive away.

FAST FACT

Connecticut has New England's most temperate climate. Temperatures rarely top ninety degrees or fall below zero. Autumn is peak season, with dazzling foliage displays in the Litchfield Hills, the Connecticut River Valley, and along the Merritt Parkway. Winter offers lantern light tours at Mystic Seaport, Christmas festivities in Bethlehem, and skiing. Spring brings opportunities to hike, bike, and explore the outdoors; summer offers swimming and boating along the shore and festivals celebrating seafood favorites from lobster to clams to oysters. Keep in mind that some attractions are closed in the winter, and beaches and amusement parks are often not open until the last weekend in May.

Hartford

www.ci.hartford.ct.us

Connecticut's capital city offers visitors sightseeing opportunities galore. In downtown Hartford, you can: tour the gold-domed State Capitol Building; ride an antique 1914 carousel in the nation's first municipal park built with public funds—Bushnell Park; see America's oldest Civil War monument; and explore the country's oldest continually operated art museum, the Wadsworth Atheneum, with a collection of 40,000 works. Nearby, visit Mark Twain's Hartford home for a unique look into the life and humor of this American author. Also visit Twain's literary neighbor—the Harriet Beecher Stowe House is part of the same complex. And don't miss Elizabeth Park, the country's first municipal rose garden, known for its 900 varieties of roses.

Lake Compounce

822 Lake Avenue, Bristol

(860) 583-3300

www.lakecompounce.com

Connecticut is home to America's oldest amusement park—Lake Compounce. Today, this historic family attraction that dates to 1846 seamlessly blends the old and the new on 325 acres in Bristol. You'll find a 1911 carousel, a vintage trolley, and a classic wooden roller coaster alongside modern bumper cars, thrill rides, and the Splash Harbor Water Park. Choose the Ride All Day admission pass, or purchase the much more affordable general admission pass available for those who would rather not jostle their internal organs.

HOT SPOT

Connecticut is home to the **Carousel Museum of New England,** 95 Riverside Avenue, Bristol, (860) 585-5411, where handcrafted carousel horses from bygone days are preserved and displayed. Nearby in downtown Hartford's Bushnell Park, you can clamber aboard a vintage 1914 carousel, which operates from May through mid-October.

The Maritime Aquarium

10 North Water Street, Norwalk

(203) 852-0700

www.maritimeaquarium.org

More than 1,000 marine animals native to Long Island Sound and its watershed, including oysters, lobsters, seahorses, fish, sharks, rays, and river otters, call the Maritime Aquarium home, and you may just have a tricky time getting the kids to leave for home when they discover the shark touch tank, seal pool, Jellyfish Encounter exhibit, and larger-than-life IMAX movies. If you're looking for adventure, the aquarium offers a chance to go see the animals in their natural habitat on their summertime study cruises on Long Island Sound.

HOT SPOT

Deep River Navigation Company, (860) 526-4954, offers Connecticut River and Long Island Sound cruises including Sunday Brunch Cruises and Lighthouse Cruises. Departure points are Hartford, Old Saybrook, and Middletown. Check their schedule online: *www.deeprivernavigation.com*.

Mystic Aquarium and Seaport

www.mysticaquarium.org

www.mysticseaport.org

A shipbuilding and whaling center from the seventeenth to nineteenth centuries, Mystic is now home to several popular Connecticut attractions including Mystic Seaport, a 17-acre living history museum that recreates maritime life in the 1800s; Mystic Marinelife Aquarium featuring more than 6,000 water-loving creatures from around the world including the only captive whales in New England and a penguin pavilion; Olde Mistick Village with its sixty shops and restaurants; and, of course, Mystic Pizza, the setting for the movie of the same name that launched Julia Roberts's career.

New England Air Museum

Route 75, Windsor Locks

(860) 623-3305

www.neam.org

Located near Bradley International Airport, this museum has one of the world's largest collections of antique aircraft and aviation artifacts including planes dating from 1909 to the present, helicopters and gliders, and exhibits on such fascinating themes as Early French Aviation and the History of Air Mail. For a real blast, take the controls of the jet fighter cockpit simulator.

HOT SPOT

Take your kids to a trashy place . . . the **Garbage Museum** in Stratford, (203) 381-9571. Home to the Trash-o-saurus, the museum teaches kids the importance of recycling. Admission is free. Hours are limited.

USS *Nautilus*

One Crystal Lake Road, Groton

(860) 694-3174

(800) 343-0079

www.ussnautilus.org

The Submarine Force Museum in Groton is the permanent home of the world's first nuclear-powered submarine, the USS *Nautilus*. The historic ship was christened in 1954 by First Lady Mamie Eisenhower. It shattered all submerged speed and distance records and made an historic first journey under the North Pole. You'll be able to climb aboard for a self-guided audio tour of this historic craft, then learn more about submarines by exploring the museum's exhibits of memorabilia, working periscopes, and even a submarine control room.

Yale University

Visitor Information Center, 149 Elm Street, New Haven
(203) 432-2300
www.yale.edu

Yale University is an often-overlooked treasure that should be on Connecticut visitors' lists. Take a free guided tour of the historic campus, founded in 1701 and located permanently in New Haven in 1718. You can see a rare Gutenberg Bible and original Audubon bird prints at the Beinecke Rare Book and Manuscript Library; art from Europe, America, Africa, and the Near and Far East at the Yale Art Gallery; more than 9 million specimens, including dinosaurs and meteorites, at the Peabody Museum of Natural History; and the most extensive assemblage of British art outside of Britain at the Yale Center for British Art.

HOT SPOT

Marvel at the size of the extinct beasts as you amble through the Great Hall of Dinosaurs at the **Peabody Museum of Natural History at Yale University,** 170 Whitney Avenue, New Haven, (203) 432-5050. Then, make tracks to Hartford County's Dinosaur State Park, 400 West Street, Rocky Hill, (860) 529-8423, where one of North America's largest collections of fossilized dino tracks, imprinted in the Earth 200 million years ago, is housed under a dome.

Southwestern Connecticut/ Fairfield County

SOUTHWESTERN CONNECTICUT'S FAIRFIELD COUNTY might remind you of the Buddhist parable of the blind men and the elephant. Just as each blind man experienced a very different creature depending upon whether he touched the elephant's head or ears or tusk or trunk or tail, you'll find a variety of experiences await you as you feel your way around Fairfield County. Touch Greenwich, and you'll leave impressed with the affluence and sophistication of the region. Touch Stamford, and you'll swear you're in the heart of a major commercial center. Touch Westport, and you'll take home memories of seaside elegance and creative, cultured living. Touch Norwalk, and the sensation is different again—a former thriving seaport searching for a new life as a trendy shopping and sightseeing destination. Touch Bridgeport, and you'll get the notion that this is a blue-collar, post-industrial area struggling to find a new identity. New England sneaks up on you subtly as you enter and travel through this gateway region. Fairfield County is above all a region of transition.

Lodging Options

As a pseudosuburb of New York City, Fairfield County's lodging options are dominated by business-class and chain hotels.

The Greenwich and Stamford Area

The **Budget Hospitality Inn,** 19 Clarks Hill Avenue, Stamford, (203) 327-4300 or (800) 362-7666, beats neighboring hotels' rates, as does the Super 8, 32 Grenhart Road, Stamford, (203) 324-8887.

The **Hyatt Regency Greenwich,** 1800 East Putnam Avenue, Old Greenwich, (203) 637-1234, designed in English Manor style, is convenient to I-95.

The **Howard Johnson,** 1114 Boston Post Road, Riverside, (203) 637-3691, allows pets with a deposit.

The **Holiday Inn Select,** 700 Main Street, Stamford, (203) 358-8400.

Sheraton Stamford Hotel, 2701 Summer Street, Stamford, (203) 359-1300.

Stamford Marriott Hotel, 2 Stamford Forum, Stamford, (203) 357-9555.

Westin Stamford, 1 First Stamford Place, Stamford (203) 967-2222.

The **Stanton House Inn,** 76 Maple Avenue, Greenwich, (203) 869-2110, is an historic mansion, designed by Stanford White.

Harbor House, 165 Shore Road, Old Greenwich, (203) 637-0145, is a short stroll to the beach.

TRAVEL TIP

For assistance locating the perfect bed and breakfast, try one of Connecticut's B&B reservation services: **Bed and Breakfast, Ltd.,** (203) 469-3260, which has 125 properties or **Nutmeg Bed & Breakfast Agency,** (860) 236-6698 or (800) 727-7592, with more than 100 statewide B&B listings for tourists and business travelers.

In Darien and Norwalk

The **Howard Johnson Inn,** 150 Ledge Road, Darien, (203) 655-3933, with its distinctive orange roof, is two blocks from the train station.

The **Doubletree Club Hotel,** 789 Connecticut Avenue, Norwalk, (203) 853-3477.

Courtyard by Marriott, 474 Main Avenue, Norwalk, (203) 849-9111

Four Points Hotel by Sheraton, 426 Main Avenue, Norwalk, (203) 849-9828

Hilton Garden Inn Norwalk, 560 Main Avenue, Norwalk, (203) 523-4000

Silvermine Tavern, 194 Perry Avenue, Norwalk, (203) 847-4558, is a traditional New England country inn featuring romantic, antique-furnished guest rooms.

In Stratford, Bridgeport, and Fairfield

The showcase hotel is the **Holiday Inn Hotel & Conference Center,** 1070 Main Street, Bridgeport, (203) 334-1234.

Ramada Inn Stratford, 225 Lordship Boulevard, Stratford, (203) 375-8866.

The **Fairfield Inn,** 417 Post Road, Fairfield, (203) 255-0491 or (800) 347-0414, offers 80 rooms and a free continental breakfast. The four-room **Nathan Booth House,** Main Street, Stratford, (203) 378-6489, is a circa 1843 Federal-Greek Revival farmhouse listed on the National Register of Historic Places.

HOT SPOT

National Helicopter Museum Eastbound RR Station, off Main Street, Stratford, (203) 375-5766. Discover the history of helicopters and see a fully restored Sikorsky S-76 cockpit. Open Wednesday through Sunday.

Fairfield County for Art Aficionados

The **Bruce Museum of Arts and Science,** 1 Museum Drive, Greenwich, (203) 869-0376, showcases a collection of fine and decorative art from around the world with a particular emphasis on American art. The **Silvermine Guild Arts Center,** 1037 Silvermine Road, New Canaan, (203) 966-5617, dates to 1922 and is one of America's oldest arts communities; set on five acres, the center is home to five galleries with works on view and for sale. The **Whitney Museum of Art at Champion,** One Champion Plaza, Stamford, (203) 358-7630, is

Connecticut's arm of the prestigious New York City museum; changing exhibits focus particularly on twentieth-century American art. Norwalk is home to one of the nation's most significant Depression-era art collections, the largest collection of murals resulting from the Federal Art Project of the Works Progress Administration (WPA); murals are on view at Norwalk City Hall, Norwalk Community College, the Maritime Aquarium, and the Norwalk Public Library. Just north of Fairfield County in Ridgefield, see surrealism and more at the **Aldrich Museum of Contemporary Art,** 258 Main Street, (203) 438-4519, which is also home to a fascinating Sculpture Garden.

TRAVEL TIP

Want to see some art while on a limited budget? Check out the following:

The **Artists' Market,** 163 Main Street, Norwalk, (203) 846-2550. This gallery has exhibited and sold the works of Dutch artist M. C. Escher, known for his imaginative works of illusion, for more than twenty years. Open daily.

Housatonic Museum of Art, 900 Lafayette Boulevard, Bridgeport, (203) 332-5000. Holds more than 4,000 works by European, American, Asian, African, and Hispanic artists. Open daily.

Historic Sites to See

Take a guided tour of the Second Empire-style mansion built by investment banker and railroad tycoon LeGrand Lockwood; the **Lockwood-Mathews Mansion,** 295 West Avenue, (203) 838-1434, is open mid-March through December, closed Mondays. **Ogden House and Gardens,** 1520 Bronson Road, Fairfield, (203) 259-1598, offers a wildflower walk, herb garden, and circa 1750 farmhouse on the National Register of Historic Places to explore May through mid-October.

You'll find a collection of fine American furniture and American impressionist art at the **Bush-Holley Historic Site,** 39 Strickland Road, Greenwich; the site was once a boarding house for Connecticut's first art colony. See a restored blacksmith's home in Stamford; the **Hoyt-Barnum House,** 713 Bedford Street, (203) 329-1183, is open Sundays May through September. See carriages, farm equipment, and an historic 32-acre homestead at **Boothe Memorial Park,** 134 Main Street, Stratford, (203) 381-2068; free admission year round. Also take in Connecticut's only National Historic Site, **Weir Farm,** 735 Nod Hill, Wilton, (203) 834-1896, the summer home and studio of American impressionist painter J. Alden Weir for forty years.

HOT SPOT

The **Stamford Museum and Nature Center,** 39 Scofieldtown Road, Stamford, (203) 322-1646, boasts a working farm, planetarium, observatory, and nature exhibits. Youngsters will find interactive exhibits featuring science, arts, culture, history, safety, and health to delve into at the **Children's Museum of Southeastern Connecticut,** 409 Main Street, Niantic, (860) 691-1111.

Amusements and Attractions

Captain's Cove Seaport at Black Rock Harbor in Bridgeport, (203) 335-1433, is home to the Revolutionary War-era frigate HMS *Rose* and *Lightship #112 Nantucket,* plus a fish market and specialty shops. The **Beardsley Zoo,** 1875 Noble Avenue, Bridgeport, (203) 394-6565, provides a habitat for more than 120 species of animals. The **Barnum Museum** at 820 Main Street, Bridgeport, (203) 331-1104, pays homage to master promoter and Connecticut native P.T. Barnum. Meet more than 1,000 different marine animals at the **Maritime Aquarium,** 10 North Water Street, Norwalk, (203) 852-0700. Cheer on the **Bridgeport**

Bluefish, Fairfield County's only professional sports team. The minor league baseball team plays at the Harbor Yard Baseball Complex in Bridgeport. Call (203) 334-TIXX for tickets. Bet on the dogs at **Shoreline Star Greyhound Park,** 255 Kossuth Street, Bridgeport, (203) 576-1976 or (888) GO-DOG-GO.

Dining Highlights

Fairfield County restaurants dish up cuisine to please any palate. Here's a smattering of some of the region's notable places to nosh.

Bloodroot, 85 Ferris Street, Bridgeport, (203) 576-9168, is a feminist, vegetarian restaurant with views of Long Island Sound. Other great waterfront dining spots include **Rowayton Seafood Restaurant**, 89 Rowayton Avenue, Norwalk, (203) 866-4488, where you'll also find a seafood market, and the **Crab Shell,** 46 Southfield Avenue, Stamford, (203) 967-7229, where you can snuggle up to a bowl of hot chowder by the fireplace in the winter or sit outside and watch the world sail by in the summer.

Beer connoisseurs can sample the region's microbrews at **Bank Street Brewing Co.,** 65 Bank Street, Stamford, (203) 325-2739, which is housed in an eighty-five-year-old bank building; **New England Brewing,** 13 Marshall Street, South Norwalk, (203) 866-1339; and at **Lost City Brewing Co.,** 955 Connecticut Avenue, Bridgeport, (203) 333-2337.

For something decidedly elegant, consider **Jean-Louis,** 61 Lewis Street, Greenwich, (203) 622-8450, for cosmopolitan French cuisine; **Thomas Henkelmann,** 420 Field Point Road, Greenwich, (203) 869-7500, for French food in an atmosphere of Victorian high society; or **Da Pietro's,** 36 Riverside Avenue, (203) 454-1213, Westport, which offers Italian-Southern French cooking in an atmosphere you'll find either cramped or cozy depending on whether your glass is half empty or half full.

FAST FACT

Connecticut's oyster farmers harvest and sell more than 188 million oysters per year, second only to Louisiana. Oyster cultivation has been an important Connecticut industry for more than a century. There are more than 52,000 acres of oyster farms along Connecticut's Long Island Sound coast. Each September, this delectable mollusk's role in the economy of the Constitution State is celebrated at the Norwalk Seaport Association's annual **Oyster Festival.** Call (203) 838-9444 for dates and information.

Shopping Discoveries

Fairfield County boasts a number of shopping destinations. **Greenwich Avenue** in Greenwich is lined with upscale shops and trendy boutiques. While you're in Greenwich, you may want to at least do some drive-by shopping at **Miller Motorcars,** 342 West Putnam Avenue, (203) 629-3890, a Ferrari and Aston Martin dealer that always has some head-spinning vehicles parked out front. Upscale retail also dominates both the **Stamford Town Center,** 100 Greyrock Place, (203) 356-9700, America's first high-rise, downtown shopping mall, and Main Street in Westport.

If it's antiques you're after, you'll definitely want to stop at **Stamford's United House Wrecking,** 535 Hope Street, (203) 348-5371; with 30,000 square feet of treasures to dig through, it's been Connecticut's largest antiques center for more than a decade. Representing 200 dealers, the **Stratford Antiques Center,** 400 Honeyspot Road, (203) 378-7754, is another biggie.

Specialty shops abound in South Norwalk, which is also home to the **Cigar Factory Outlet,** 27 Hanford Place, (203) 854-9594. For something completely different, move on over to the Disneyland of Dairy, **Stew Leonard's,** 100 Westport Avenue,

Norwalk, ☏(203) 847-7213, designated the “World’s Largest Dairy Store” by Ripley’s Believe It or Not. This remarkable grocery store features animatronic animals dancing in the aisles, a petting zoo, and other surprises; a great place to pick up picnic foods, too.

HOT SPOT

Boothe Memorial Park Main Street, Stratford, ☏(203) 381-2046. This homestead with a carriage house, gardens, and more is a National Historic Landmark. Park is open daily year-round. Buildings are open summer through fall.

New Haven and Connecticut's Southern Shore

THE CITY OF NEW HAVEN serves as an invisible line of demarcation between the Connecticut that could be construed to be part of the New York City metropolitan area and the Connecticut that is purely and truly New England. In fact, travelers who choose the southeastern coastal region of Connecticut as their destination will be treated to a bit of everything that New England is and has been.

After all, where else can you go to the largest museum dedicated to Native American culture, to Captain Kidd's hideout, to one of the country's oldest universities, to the scene of the bloodiest battle of the American Revolution, to a recreated nineteenth-century seaport, to the birthplace of the world's first nuclear-powered submarine, and to the world's largest casino, all within an hour's driving distance?

Lodging Options

You can find just about every type of accommodation imaginable in southeastern Connecticut. Among the array, you'll find colonial homes filled with antiques such as the **Bee and Thistle Inn,** 100 Lyme Street, Old Lyme, (860) 434-1667 or (800) 622-4946, built in 1756, or **Deacon Timothy Pratt House,** 325 Main Street, Old Saybrook, (860) 395-1229, which dates to 1746 and has three period-style rooms. The **Old Mystic Inn,**

52 Main Street, Mystic, (860) 572-9422, was built in 1784, and each guest room is named for a New England author. Victorian homes turned B&Bs are abundant, too. The **Three Chimneys Inn,** 1201 Chapel Street, New Haven, (203) 789-1201, dates to the 1870s and is just a block from Yale. There's even a farmhouse B&B in Old Mystic called **Hell's Blazes,** Long Country Drive (860) 535-2335 or (888) MY DEVIL—just think of the fun you'll have telling your friends where you're staying!

FAST FACT

Lyme disease, a tick-borne illness, is named for Old Lyme, Connecticut, where it was first diagnosed. Connecticut remains one of the states with the highest number of cases of the disease each year. Lyme-carrying ticks are especially prevalent during spring and summer. Protect yourself while outdoors by wearing long pants and long-sleeved shirts, tucking pants into socks, using insect repellent, and checking yourself and your children for ticks daily. If you do discover a tick, remove it carefully with tweezers. Keep an eye on the bite area, and if any swelling or discoloration occurs, contact a physician.

You'll find three hotel choices right on site at **Foxwoods Resort Casino**: the **Grand Pequot Tower,** the **Great Cedar Hotel,** and **Two Trees Inn.** Call (800) FOXWOODS for reservations at any of the three hotels. The Mohegan Sun will debut hotel accommodations at its casino property early in 2002.

Other notable choices are the **Lighthouse Inn,** 6 Guthrie Place, New London, (860) 443-8411, a Mediterranean-style mansion built by steel magnate Charles S. Guthrie in 1902 and a former retreat for film stars such as Bette Davis and Joan Crawford; the **Norwich Inn & Spa,** 607 West Thames Street, (860) 886-2401 or (800) ASK-4SPA, a great place for a healthy country escape; and **Water's Edge Resort,** 1525 Boston Post Road, Westbrook, (860) 399-5901 or (800) 222-5901, which offers great getaway packages.

HOT SPOT

At **Sports Haven,** 600 Long Wharf Drive, New Haven, (203) 946-3201, *www.ctotb.com/sportshaven.asp,* adults can watch and wager on horse and greyhound racing and jai alai in a 38,000-square-foot complex with four movie-size, high-resolution screens. But the wildest thing is the **Shark Bar's** 2,800-gallon tank teeming with exotic sharks.

Seeing the Sights of New Haven

It's much easier to get into Yale if you're *not* applying to be a student. If you do only one thing while you're in New Haven, take a free, student-led tour of the historic **Yale University** campus, the alma mater for many U.S. presidents. Tours are available at 10:30 A.M. and 2 P.M. on weekdays and at 1:30 P.M. on weekends. They depart from the Visitor Information Center, 149 Elm Street, (203) 432-2300. If you can spend additional time at Yale, take in the **Yale Center for British Art,** 1080 Chapel Street, (203) 432-2800, home to the largest collection of British art outside the United Kingdom; the **Yale University Art Gallery,** 1111 Chapel Street, (203) 432-0600, with a collection of 80,000 objects including works by van Gogh, Monet, and Picasso; the **Beinecke Rare Book and Manuscript Library,** 121 Wall Street, (203) 432-2977, which houses among its 600,000 volumes one of the few preserved Gutenberg Bibles; or the **Peabody Museum of Natural History,** 170 Whitney Avenue, (203) 432-5050, with fascinating exhibits related to plant, animal, and human evolution and the Great Hall of Dinosaurs.

Off campus, **Fort Nathan Hale** and **Black Rock Fort,** 36 Woodward Avenue, (203) 787-8790, a restored Revolutionary War fort and a restored Civil War fort, respectively, are open free to the public seasonally. Catch a show or make an appointment to take a backstage tour of the **Shubert Performing Arts Center,** the centerpiece of New Haven's expansive cultural scene. Dating to 1914, this theatrical gem was the stage for the world premieres of such long-loved shows as *Carousel, South Pacific, The King and I, The Sound of Music, A Streetcar Named Desire,* and *My Fair Lady.*

Just outside the city, visit the **Eli Whitney Museum,** 915 Whitney Avenue, Hamden, (203) 777-1833, dedicated to the legacy of the Connecticut-born cotton gin inventor. In Ansonia, tour the **General David Humphreys House,** 37 Elm Street, (203) 735-1908, for a peek at the lifestyle of a Revolutionary War hero and America's first ambassador.

HOT SPOT

Visit a castle . . . the East Haddam "castle" built by Connecticut actor William Gillette, known for his stage portrayals of Sherlock Holmes, is now a state park. Inside **Gillette Castle,** (860) 526-2336, you'll find intricate hidden mirrors and creative decor including a replica of the sitting room at Sherlock Holmes's 221B Baker Street. Park admission is free; there is a charge to tour the castle. The park is scheduled to reopen Memorial Day 2002 following extensive renovations.

River and Shore

Stony Creek is the departure point for boat tours of the Thimble Islands, steeped in lore for serving as Captain Kidd's hideout, among other things. For a real adventure, paddle through the Thimbles. **Stony Creek Kayak,** 327 Leetes Island Road, (203) 481-6401, offers guided tours of the islands.

As I-95 continues to follow Connecticut's shoreline east, the temptation to turn away from the shore and head inland intensifies. That, of course, is due to the Connecticut River, the major artery first navigated by a European, Dutchman Adriaen Block, in 1614. The Connecticut River Valley was home to some of Connecticut's earliest settlers, and today the towns that dot the riverfront retain a sense of timelessness.

The **Essex Steam Train & Riverboat Ride,** One Railroad Avenue, Essex, (860) 767-0103 or (800) 377-3987, is a great way to soak up the area's ambience in an economical time period. First climb aboard a 1920s-era coach pulled by a steam-powered locomotive, then board a riverboat for a relaxing inland excursion. From the water, you'll see the nineteenth-century **Goodspeed Opera House,** home to Goodspeed Musicals, Route 82, East Haddam, (860) 873-8668, a wonderful place to see a performance if you're staying in the region.

Mystic and More

The Mystic area is Connecticut's top travel destination, and while much of the tourist traffic can be attributed to the mesmerizing lure of the state's two Native American casinos, this seaport region's other attractions make it a richly diverse vacation choice.

At **Mystic Seaport,** 75 Greenmanville Avenue, Mystic (860) 572-5315 or (888) 9-SEAPORT, immerse yourself in the nineteenth-century world of shipbuilding, fishing, sailing, and whaling. This 37-acre, sixty-building living history complex is home to the largest collections of antique vessels and maritime photography in the world. Once your appetite for maritime history has been whetted, be sure to visit the **Submarine Force Museum** in nearby Groton, One Crystal Lake Road, (860) 694-3174 or (800) 343-0079, where you can climb down into the belly of the world's first nuclear-powered submarine, the USS *Nautilus*.

Mystic Aquarium, 55 Coogan Boulevard, Mystic, (860) 572-5955, offers families a one-stop oceanic trip around the world. The million-gallon "Alaskan Coast" habitat is home to seals and beluga whales. The 300-gallon "Coral Reef" houses 500 exotic species of fishes from around the globe. And the interactive "Challenge of the Deep" exhibit will take you on an underwater odyssey. After a day of sightseeing, sip sweet cider and munch on just-baked mini doughnuts at **B.F. Clyde's Cider Mill,** 129 North Stonington Road, Old Mystic, (860) 536-3354. Clyde's is the only remaining steam-powered cider mill in the United States and the country's longest continuous producer of hard cider.

FAST FACT

The Battle of Groton Heights lasted only forty minutes, but when it was over, eighty-eight of the 165 defenders stationed at Fort Griswold and fifty-one British attackers were dead. Today, visitors to the site of this battle of the American Revolution, **Fort Griswold Battlefield State Park,** 57 Fort Street, Groton, (860) 445-1729, can relive that September day in 1781 when Connecticut native Benedict Arnold, who had deserted the American cause a year earlier, led British troops into an area that he knew quite well.

Free admission to tour the historic fort, a Revolutionary War museum, and the **Ebenezer Avery House,** which sheltered the wounded.

Connecticut's Casinos

It may come as a surprise that Connecticut is one of America's premier gambling destinations. Since opening in February 1992, the Mashantucket Pequot tribe's 46,000-square-foot **Foxwoods High Stakes Bingo & Casino,** Foxwoods, Route 2, Mashantucket, (800) PLAY BIG, has grown exponentially to emerge as the world's largest resort casino.

Foxwoods never closes, and more than 40,000 people enter this unreal world daily. It truly is possible to lose all sense of space and time once you've entered the Foxwoods zone. The omnipresent din of cha-chinging slot machines and craps dealers shouting, "Coming out," the flashing lights and amazing sights (the length of the buffet line alone is enough to blow you away), and the sheer enormity of it all make Foxwoods a place to include on your Connecticut itinerary, even if you don't plan to gamble a cent.

From the casino, a free shuttle will take you to the **Mashantucket Pequot Museum and Research Center,** 110 Pequot Trail, Mashantucket, (860) 396-6839 or (800) 411-9671, the nation's largest museum dedicated to Native American culture. The 308,000-square-foot multimedia museum tells the Pequot tribe's story from prehistoric to present times. Allow three to five hours to explore its life-size displays and changing exhibits.

The Mohegan tribe boosted Connecticut's draw as a gaming outpost in 1996 when it opened **Mohegan Sun,** One Mohegan Sun Boulevard, Uncasville, (888) 226-7711. With 179,000-square-feet of gaming space, it's just over half the size of Foxwoods. The Mohegan Sun's décor reflects the four seasons; as you wander the circular layout of the casino, the carpet pattern changes from bright spring flowers to summer hues to orange and gold fall leaves to a winter walkway, and the leaves overhead change with the seasons, too. If you can't get to New England during fall foliage season, it's fall year round at the Mohegan Sun's Autumn Casino. At the casino's core, you'll find the Wolf Den, which offers an astonishingly fine line-up of free shows.

An $800 million expansion scheduled for completion in April 2002 will add a 1,200-room, thirty-four-story hotel; more than 100,000 square feet of meeting space including the largest ballroom in the Northeast; the Sky Casino, with 115,000 square feet of additional gaming space; a 16,000 square foot spa, salon, and fitness center; an additional 175,000 square feet of premium retail and entertainment space; and a new 10,000-seat arena to the Mohegan Sun empire, making it even more competitive with its neighbor to the south.

Dining Highlights

Louis' Lunch, 261–263 Crown Street, New Haven, (203) 562-5507, cooked the country's first hamburger sandwich in 1900, and you can still order one cooked on the original grill. New Haven also claims America's first pizza pie, and the same brick ovens at **Frank Pepe's Pizzeria Napoletana,** 157 Wooster Street, (203) 865-5762, where they still crank out what many call the state's most delectable pizza.

You don't have to be a guest of **Water's Edge Resort,** 1525 Boston Post Road, Westbrook, (860) 399-5901 or (800) 222-5901, to enjoy the spectacular views and tasty dishes served in the resort's dining room. Another favorite waterfront dining spot, albeit a bit touristy, is **Abbott's Lobster in the Rough,** 117 Pearl Street, Noank, (860) 536-7719, where you can feast on lobster, steamers, and other seafood delights indoors or outdoors at picnic tables right at the ocean's edge. Diners are allowed to bring their own alcoholic beverages.

For something truly unusual, make reservations at **Randall's Ordinary,** Route 2, North Stonington, (860) 599-4540, where colonial recipes are prepared entirely in an open-hearth fireplace. And for something straight out of a movie scene, grab a bite at **Mystic Pizza,** 56 West Main Street, Mystic, (860) 536-3700, the setting for the movie of the same name that launched Julia Roberts's career.

You'll find around-the-clock dining at southeastern Connecticut's two casinos. Both offer expansive buffets and dozens of other enticing options from casual cafés to elegant steakhouses and New England seafood restaurants. **Mohegan Sun's Brew Pub** crafts its very own Sachem's Ale and Matahga Lager, named for Mohegan chiefs.

Shopping Discoveries

Deal seekers will love this region's outlet shopping malls including the more than sixty-five designer and name brand outlets at **Westbrook Factory Stores,** 314 Flat Rock Place, Westbrook, (860) 399-8739 or (888) SHOP-333; more than seventy upscale outlet stores at **Clinton Crossing Premium Outlets,** 20-A Killingsworth Turnpike, Clinton, (860) 664-0700; and twenty-four national brand outlets at **Mystic Factory Outlets,** Coogan Boulevard, Mystic, (860) 443-4788.

New Haven is home to Connecticut's oldest flea market, the **Boulevard Flea Market,** 510 Ella T. Grasso Boulevard (Route 10), (203) 772-1447, operating on Saturdays and Sundays.

Don't miss the more than sixty cute shops and restaurants at **Olde Mistick Village,** Route 27 and Coogan Boulevard, Mystic, (860) 536-4941. And for a truly unique New England shopping experience, lose yourself inside the 10,000-square-foot craft mecca **Raspberry Junction,** 417 Route 2, North Stonington, (860) 535-8410, which markets the works of more than 300 New England crafters.

Hartford and the Connecticut River Heritage Valley

HARTFORD IS CONNECTICUT'S CAPITAL CITY and America's insurance capital, too. The American insurance industry was born in Hartford in 1810—largely to protect important Connecticut River shipping interests. Today, the Greater Hartford area is home to about forty major insurance companies.

As cities go, Hartford suffers a bit of an identity crisis, situated as it is about halfway between the larger, more urbane cities of New York and Boston. Its petite skyline is punctuated by the glittering, gold-domed State Capitol Building and the "blue onion" dome atop the Colt Building. By day, downtown Hartford is a bustling commercial center. At night and on weekends, when the business crowd flees to suburbia, Hartford can seem terribly ghostly unless a concert or sporting event at the Civic Center has drawn folks downtown.

Nevertheless, the 350-year-old city, and particularly the thriving communities that surround it, retain the cultural and intellectual flair and the air of prosperity and abundance that spurred American literary icon Mark Twain to make Hartford his home in 1871. You may just find, as Twain wrote in 1868 following his first visit to the city, "Of all the beautiful towns it has been my fortune to see this is the chief. . . . You do not know what beauty is if you have not been here."

Lodging Options

The **Sheraton Hotel** at Bradley International Airport, (860) 627-5311, is connected to both airport terminals and provides convenient accommodations for those flying to and from Bradley. Other hotels close to Bradley that offer free airport shuttle service include **Hartford-Days Inn Windsor Locks/Bradley International Airport,** 185 Turnpike Road, (860) 623-9417; **Doubletree Windsor Locks/Bradley Airport,** 16 Ella T. Grasso Turnpike, (860) 627-5171; **Homewood Suites Hartford Windsor Locks,** 65 Ella Grasso Turnpike, (860) 627-8463; and **Ramada Inn at the Airport,** 5 Ella T. Grasso Turnpike, (860) 623-9494.

In downtown Hartford, centrally located hotels include the **Hilton Hartford,** 315 Trumbull Street, (860) 728-5151, which is attached to the Hartford Civic Center; the **Marriott Residence Inn Hartford/Downtown,** 942 Main Street, (860) 524-5550, which offers fully equipped suites ideal for those who plan extended stays; and the **Goodwin Hotel,** One Haynes Street, (860) 246-7500 or (888) 212-8380, which combines classic styling with modern amenities.

Outside the city, you might choose to stay at the **Charles R. Hart House,** 1046 Windsor Avenue, Windsor, (860) 688-5555, a restored Victorian bed and breakfast; the **Simsbury Inn,** 397 Hopmeadow Street, Simsbury, (860) 651-5700 or (800) 634-2719, a 100-room classic New England inn with full-service amenities, an indoor pool, tennis, and an art gallery; or the **Avon Old Farms Hotel,** 279 Avon Mountain Road (Route 44), Avon, (860) 677-1651 or (800) 836-4000, a charming, 160-room hotel complex in the heart of the Farmington Valley.

FAST FACT

Central Connecticut is home to the **National Iwo Jima Memorial Monument,** located just off Route 9 on the New Britain–Newington line. The eternal flame burns as a tribute to the Americans who died on the island of Iwo Jima during World War II. The monument resembles the famous photograph by Joe Rosenthal of the raising of the American flag on Mount Suribachi on February 23, 1945. Sculpted by Joseph Petrovics, the Iwo Jima Memorial was dedicated on the fiftieth anniversary of the flag raising.

Insurance-City Sights

Whether your interests run to history, art, landscaping, or literature, there's a Hartford attraction to capture your imagination. Explore the **Wadsworth Athenaeum,** 600 Main Street, (860) 278-2670, one of the country's oldest art museums and home to more than 45,000 works of art. Take a free, one-hour tour of the gold-domed, Victorian Gothic **State Capitol Building,** 210 Capitol Avenue, (860) 240-0222. Visit the changing exhibits at the **Old State House,** 800 Main Street, (860) 522-6766, the oldest state house in the United States and site of the signing of the country's first written constitution.

Spend time in **Bushnell Park,** between Elm and Jewell Streets, (860) 522-6400. America's oldest public park is home to the Soldiers and Sailors Memorial Arch, a Civil War memorial; an antique carousel; and the Pumphouse Gallery. Visit Hartford's **Ancient Burying Ground** at Gold and Main Streets, the final resting place of early settlers and Revolutionary War soldiers.

Just outside the downtown area, tour **Mark Twain's House,** 351 Farmington Avenue, (860) 493-6411, and sample the humor and achievements of this American literary giant. Next door, tour the **Harriet Beecher Stowe House,** Farmington Avenue and Forest Street, (860) 525-9317, home to the *Uncle Tom's Cabin* author from 1871–1896. Breathe in the sweet scents at **Elizabeth Park** on Prospect Avenue, (860) 543-8876, America's oldest municipal rose garden, which is at its blossoming peak in June. The **Pond House Café,** (860) 231-8823, in Elizabeth Park is a great choice for tranquil dining overlooking a duck pond. Take a peek at presidential political campaigns from the past at the **Museum of American Political Life at the University of Hartford,** 200 Bloomfield Avenue, West Hartford, (860) 768-4090.

HOT SPOT

Amy's Udder Joy Exotic Animal Farm, 27 North Road, Cromwell, (860) 635-3924, provides a home for injured, orphaned, abused, and unwanted rare and exotic animals. The facility is open to the public seasonally for self-guided tours. There's also a petting zoo and animal feeding area.

Exploring the Outskirts

While the areas surrounding Connecticut's capital city are primarily residential, there are some sightseeing "nooks" to discover.

Bristol is home to the Hartford region's top family attraction, **Lake Compounce,** 822 Lake Avenue, (860) 583-3300. It's America's oldest continuously operating amusement park, and its combination of antique and updated rides, games, and entertainment make it a full-day outing. Lake Compounce is open daily mid-June through Labor Day and operates on an abbreviated schedule in the spring and fall. Also in Bristol, see more than 3,000 clocks at the **American Clock and Watch Museum,** 100 Maple Street, (860) 583-6070.

Take a leisurely drive through **Old Wethersfield,** (860) 529-9013, where more than 150 homes predate 1850; the quaint shops and cozy restaurants create an aura of bygone days.

Near Bradley Airport, don't miss the more than 80 historic aircraft on view at the **New England Air Museum,** Route 75, Windsor Locks, (860) 623-3305. And in East Granby, marvel at the underground dungeon where prisoners were held at the **Old New-Gate Prison and Copper Mine,** Newgate Road, (860) 566-3005.

TRAVEL TIP

Each summer, the 152-acre **Hill-Stead Museum in Farmington,** (860) 677-9064, hosts the largest free poetry reading event in the United States. The Sunken Garden Poetry Festival features distinguished poets reading from their works in the museum's garden on selected Wednesday evenings. Each evening of readings also features a special musical performance. Tours of the museum, a 1901 Colonial Revival mansion with an impressive collection of Impressionist paintings, are available at half price on festival evenings.

Dining Highlights

In Hartford, **Max Downtown,** 15 Lewis Street, (860) 522-2530, offers upscale Italian dining in a classy atmosphere. It's a favorite among the preconcert/pretheater crowd, and reservations are a must on show nights. Another downtown Italian dining option, **Hot Tomato's,** 1 Union Place, (860) 249-5100, is a bit more hip and boisterous. Homemade breads, desserts, and fresh mozzarella are the perfect accompaniments to a wide selection of entrees. **Carbone's Ristorante,** 588 Franklin Avenue, (860) 296-9646, has been located in the city's Italian end for more than sixty years and features recipes passed down through the chefs' families.

Black-eyed Sally's BBQ & Blues, 350 Asylum Street, (860) 278-RIBS, serves up great Cajun food and live blues Wednesday through Saturday evenings. There's a **Morton's** at 30 State House Square (860) 724-0044, if you're a steak lover. For casual dining and more than thirty TV screens, head to **Coach's Sports Bar,** 187 Allyn Street, (860) 52-COACH. And for Hartford's only original brews, hop on over to **City Steam,** 942 Main Street, (860) 525-1600, for a beer and a bite to eat.

For a relaxed luncheon, head for **Pumpkin's,** 54 Pratt Street, (860) 278-1600, where you'll find gourmet sandwiches, soups, and salads. Head straight for the restaurant's back room, which is furnished with overstuffed couches and chairs, clever lamps, coffee tables, library shelves lined with books and board games, and provocative paintings. After your meal, play Trivial Pursuit, Yahtzee, Scrabble, or one of the other available board games while you sip one of Pumpkin's specialty coffee drinks. **Xando,** 103 Pratt Street, (860) 244-8233, is another good choice for light dining and an especially good choice for dessert—perch yourself on an antique couch in the upstairs loft and make your own s'mores over a fondue pot flame. There's a **Xando in West Hartford,** too, at 970 Farmington Avenue, (860) 521-2178.

HOT SPOT

The Ultimate Albert Einstein Carrot Cake, the Ultimate Chocolate-Covered Banana Cheesecake, the Ultimate Cecilia Bartoli Luscious Chocolate-Covered Italian Almond Cake . . . they're the products of renowned dessert maker David Glass. Visit **Desserts by David Glass,** (860) 525-0345, in Hartford's Colt Building, where you can buy seconds and irregulars that are every bit as tasty at substantial savings.

Outside the city, the **Avon Old Farms Inn,** Routes 44 and 10, Avon, (860) 677-2818, a former stagecoach stop, is one of the twenty oldest restaurants in the United States, and its Sunday brunch has consistently been voted one of the best in the state. Dare to devour a two-foot hot dog at **Doogie's,** Berlin Turnpike, Newington, (860) 666-1944. Or, right next door, you can feast on sumptuous steaks at **Ruth's Chris Steak House,** 2513 Berlin Turnpike, (860) 666-2202. The **Mill on the River,** 989 Ellington

Road, South Windsor, (860) 289-7929 or (888) 344-4414, offers romantic river views and a multicultural menu.

Shopping Discoveries

Westfarms Mall on the Farmington/West Hartford town line, (860) 561-3024, is one of the state's most elegant shopping centers, offering more than 130 upscale stores. You'll find a nineteenth-century dairy farm turned shopping center in Avon at **Riverdale Farms Shopping,** Route 10 North, (860) 677-6437, which features shops selling antiques, gifts, jewelry, clothing, and more.

Shopaholics will love West Hartford Center. The area around Farmington Avenue and LaSalle Street features galleries, designer boutiques, jewelers, restaurants, and coffee bars. Souvenir seekers can't beat the gift shop at the **Mark Twain House,** 351 Farmington Avenue, (860) 493-6411, where you can pick up everything from huckleberry candy to gifts featuring Twain-isms.

Connecticut's Quiet Corner

IF GETTING AWAY FROM EVERYDAY FRENZY is your primary travel objective, Northeast Connecticut, nicknamed the state's "Quiet Corner," may provide the escape you're craving. Nowhere is the state's rural character more evident, and yet, you need not fear boredom—a vacation outpost here puts you within a half hour's drive of Connecticut's casinos, Hartford, Mystic, and Providence, Rhode Island.

And while this corner may speak to visitors in hushed tones, it's certainly not silent. You can poke around in antique shops, see vestiges of the region's early heritage, stroll through gardens, and even roam with buffalo without ever leaving this well-preserved pocket of rustic New England.

Lodging Options

Small inns and B&Bs dominate the list of available accommodations in the twenty-one-town area known as the "Quiet Corner." A sampling includes B&B at **Taylor's Corner,** 880 Route 171, Woodstock, (860) 974-0490 or (888) 503-9057, an eighteenth-century colonial with eight fireplaces; **Lord Thompson Manor,** Route 200, Thompson, (860) 923-3886, a country manor estate set on 42 acres; **Chickadee**

Cottage B&B, 70 Averill Road, Pomfret, (860) -963-0587, a tiny hideaway adjacent to a bird sanctuary; and the **Fitch House,** 563 Storrs Road, Mansfield, (860) 456-0922, a Greek Revival mansion listed on the National Register of Historic Places.

For something out of the ordinary, **Little Red Schoolhouse,** 25 Lisbon Road, Canterbury, (860) 546-6238, is a circa 1849 one-room schoolhouse that sleeps four and is available for weekly rentals. Or pamper yourself at the **Spa at Grand Lake,** 1667 Exeter Road, Lebanon, (860) 642-4306, where package plans include daily massages.

Quiet Things to Do

Nathan Hale is Connecticut's "state hero," and the life of this legendary figure is told in Coventry at the **Nathan Hale Homestead,** 2299 South Street, (860) 742-6917. The state also has an official "heroine," Prudence Crandall, and her story comes alive at the **Prudence Crandall House Museum,** Routes 14 and 169, Canterbury, (860) 546-9916. Crandall founded the state's first school for black women, which is now a National Historic Landmark. History buffs will also want to visit **Roseland Cottage,** Route 169, Woodstock, (860) 928-4074, the 1846 Gothic Revival home of abolitionist publisher Henry C. Bowen, which has one of the country's oldest indoor bowling alleys and where Presidents Grant, Hayes, Harrison, and McKinley all attended Fourth of July parties.

Roam with the buffalo at **Creamery Brook Bison,** 19 Purvis Road, Brooklyn, (860) 779-0837, where wagons will take you rumbling through a dairy farm and out to the fields where the fascinating beasts will come out to greet you. Or spend a tamer afternoon amid the more than thirty herb gardens at **Caprilands Herb Farm,** 534 Silver Street, Coventry, (860) 742-7244. Make reservations for the high tea featuring zesty, herb-flavored dishes served on Sundays at 2 P.M.

Dining Highlights

Scenic dining opportunities abound in the Quiet Corner. At the **Golden Lamb Buttery,** 499 Wolf Den Road, Brooklyn, (860) 774-4423, dinner is preceded by a hayride through the 1,000-acre farm and cocktails in the barn—reservations are a must. For fine dining in front of a cozy, crackling fireplace, head for the **1734 Altnaveigh Inn,** Route 195, Storrs, (860) 429-4490. The **Harvest,** 37 Putnam Road, Pomfret, (860) 928-0008, features four individually decorated dining areas and the Black Cat Lounge with its 20-foot cherry wood bar.

For lighter fare and a touch of the unusual, you'll feel caught in a time warp at **Zip's Diner,** Routes 12 and 101, Dayville, (860) 774-6335, which dates to 1954. At the **Traveler Restaurant,** Route 171 (I-84 exit 74), (860) 684-4920, every meal comes with a free book. **Willimantic Brewing Co. & Main St. Café,** 967 Main Street, Willimantic, (860) 423-6777, is housed in a granite and limestone 1909 post office building. Try their house beers made on the premises or sample selections from other New England microbreweries.

Shopping Discoveries

Putnam is truly a town for antique lovers, featuring more than 450 dealers in seventeen shops within the town's **Route 44 Antique District,** (800) 514-3448.

Collectors and browsers alike will find **Lou's Olde Tyme Sheet Music Shoppe,** 229 Cook Hill Road, South Killingly, (860) 779-2183, a unique spot. **Queen Anne Station,** 8 Tolland Turnpike/Route 74, Willington, (860) 429-8143, features the works of seventy-five artisans in an eight-room Queen Anne-style house.

If you're a gardener, don't miss **Martha's Herbary,** 589 Pomfret Street, Pomfret, (860) 928-0009, where the gift shop is overflowing with herbal gifts and indoor and outdoor gardening tools and accessories.

It's Christmas year round at **G&L Christmas Barn,** Route 14, Windham, (860) 456-1154, and the **Christmas Barn,** 835 Route 169, Woodstock, (860) 928-7652.

The Rolling Hills of Litchfield

IF THERE IS SUCH A THING AS SOPHISTICATED rusticity, then Connecticut's picturesque Litchfield Hills can claim that label. Located in the state's northwest corner, this Berkshire Mountains foothills region lies within a two-hour drive of either New York City or Boston. And indeed it is "city folk" who seem to choose this land of lakes, antiques, and outdoor expanses as a convenient weekend destination. It's close enough for a quick getaway and yet worlds apart from the hubbub of urban living.

Litchfield's tourist businesses cater to the uniqueness of their clientele, coupling country charm with cosmopolitan hospitality. There's no other Connecticut region where you can pack whitewater rafting in the morning, a wine tasting in the afternoon, dinner at a five-star inn, and an evening of chamber music into one vacation day.

HOT SPOT

Take your clubs! **Richter Park,** 100 Aunt Hack Road, Danbury, (203) 792-2550, an eighteen-hole municipal championship golf course, is consistently ranked one of the state's and even the country's best public golf facilities by national golf publications. For automated tee time reservations, call (203) 748-5743.

Lodging Options

The Litchfield Hills are home to some of the state's best-loved inns including Connecticut's only five-star property, the **Mayflower Inn,** Route 47, Washington, (860) 868-9466, a former school that was transformed into an inn in 1920 and hosted Eleanor Roosevelt in 1933. The **Boulders,** East Shore Road, New Preston, (860) 868-0541 or (800) 55-BOULDERS, with its views of Lake Waramaug and its classic decorative touches, is another favorite. The **Old Riverton Inn,** 436 East River Road, Riverton, (860) 379-8678 or (800) EST-1796, is a former stagecoach stop now listed on the National Register of Historic Places. **Manor House,** 69 Maple Avenue, Norfolk, (860) 542-5690, an 1898 Tudor mansion, sparkles with twenty stained-glass windows designed by Louis Tiffany.

For young singles, **Club Getaway** in Kent, (860) 927-3664 or (800) 6 GETAWAY, can't be beat for recreation and entertainment. **Interlaken Inn,** 74 Interlaken Road, Lakeville, (860) 435-9878 or (800) 222-2909, is a country resort that offers 30 acres of recreational amenities and a variety of rooms and suites including some that accommodate pets.

For business-class hotels, look to the cities of Danbury and Waterbury. The **Hilton Danbury & Towers,** 18 Old Ridgebury Road, (203) 794-0600, is convenient to I-84, as is the **Sheraton Waterbury Hotel,** 3580 East Main Street, (203) 573-1000.

TRAVEL TIP

There is one toll-free number to call for camping reservations in all Connecticut state park and forest campgrounds: (877) 668-CAMP.

For a directory of privately owned and operated campgrounds, contact the **Connecticut Campground Owners Association,** (860) 521-4704, or visit their online directory, *www.campconn.com*.

Out and about in Lovely Litchfield

Litchfield's attractions make the outdoors irresistible. Schedule a meditative walk at Connecticut's first outdoor labyrinth at **Wisdom House Retreat Center,** 229 East Litchfield Road, Litchfield, (860) 567-3163, or spend a leisurely morning bird watching at the **Sharon Audubon Center,** 325 Route 4, Sharon, (860) 364-0520. The 4,000-acre **White Memorial Foundation,** Route 202, Litchfield, (860) 567-0857, is Connecticut's largest nature center. The grounds are open free daily and boast 35 miles of trails for hiking, cross-country skiing, bird watching, picnicking, and boating.

For family adventure, head for **Quassy Amusement Park,** Route 64, Middlebury, (203) 758-2913 or (800) FOR-PARK, where you'll find 20 acres of amusements on the shores of Lake Quassapaug including the Big Flush, a water coaster with a 400-foot vertical drop. Or get your motor running and take in the NASCAR and other auto racing action at **Lime Rock Park,** Route 112, Lakeville, (860) 435-5000 or (800) RACE-LRP. Lime Rock Park is also the site for **Skip Barber Racing School** courses, (860) 435-1300 or (800) 221-1131. Call for a schedule if you've always wanted to be in the driver's seat.

For a historic snapshot, visit the **Glebe House Museum** and **Gertrude Jekyll Garden,** Hollow Road, Woodbury, (203) 263-2855. While the 1750s farmhouse where the first Episcopalian bishop in America was elected is significant, even more magical is the garden designed in 1926 by famed English horticulturist Gertrude Jekyll to accompany the home's transformation to a museum. Delve even deeper into history with a stop at the **Institute for American Indian Studies,** 38 Curtis Road, Washington, (860) 868-0518, where a seventeenth-century Algonkian village comes to life.

Dining Highlights

Have a Yankee feast for an all-inclusive price at Connecticut's oldest inn, **Curtis House,** 506 Main Street South, Woodbury, (203) 263-2101. The **Fife 'n Drum Restaurant and Inn,** Route 7, Kent, (860) 927-3509, is a place for warm food and furnishings, gentle piano music, and, most of all, wine. The restaurant's cellar has more than 1,000 wine selections from across the globe. **Pub and Restaurant,** Route 44, Norfolk, (860) 542-5716, provides a touch of old England and boasts the state's largest selection of beers. The **Yellow Victorian Restaurant,** 6 Riverton Road, Riverton, (860) 379-7020, is known not only for its romantic and historic ambience, but also for its Sunday brunches.

Even if you're not staying overnight at the five-star **Mayflower Inn,** Route 47, Washington, (860) 868-9466, the inn's elegant dining room is open to the public by reservation.

For a family spot, try the **Cookhouse,** 31 Danbury Road, New Milford, (860) 355-4111, where barbecue reigns supreme, and the ribs are slow-roasted for ten hours over hardwoods before they ever touch the grill.

TRAVEL TIP

Connecticut's Top Foliage Viewing Spots

- **Stone Tower** at Haystack Mountain State Park, West Norfolk, offers a 360-degree view of the countryside.
- The **Cobble Mountain Trail** at Macedonia Brook State Park, Warren.
- **Lookout Tower** in Mohawk State Forest, Cornwall.
- **Stone Tower** in Sleeping Giant State Park, Hamden.
- **Heublein Tower** in Talcott Mountain State Park, Simsbury. The tower observation level provides views of the Farmington River Valley.

Shopping Discoveries

The Litchfield area is a shopper's paradise. While finding the magical merchants tucked away around each bend on your own is half the fun, here's a quick list of shopping spots you'll actually want to schedule into your travels.

Do you consider yourself a connoisseur of tea? No matter how many tea varieties you've sipped in your lifetime, you're bound to discover a new blend you adore when you stop into the tasting room at **Harney & Sons Fine Teas,** 11 Brook Street, Lakeville, (860) 435-5050 or (800) TEA-TIME. Open daily for free tastings, you're welcome to sample tea until you're steeped.

Skitch Henderson, founder and director of the New York Pops, and his wife, Ruth, own the **Silo at Hunt Hill Farm,** 44 Upland Road/Route 202, New Milford, (860) 355-0300 or (800) 353-SILO, where you'll discover wondrous kitchen gadgetry and everything you need to create a New England dining environment in your own home. The Silo is more than just a store, though. It's also an art gallery and a cooking school, where you can learn from guest "chefs in residence" during weekend courses.

HOT SPOT

Connecticut souvenir hunters will hit the jackpot at The **Connecticut Store,** 120140 Bank Street, Waterbury, (203) 753-4121 or (800) 474-6728. The warehouse-like shop is a showcase for items made in Connecticut, from Wiffle balls and Pez candy dispensers to fine-crafted clocks, crafts, candies, clothing, and more.

Bargain seekers will find hand crafted furnishings at the **Hitchcock Chair Company Factory Store,** Route 20, Riverton, (860) 379-4826, and hundreds of pewter gift items at the **Woodbury Pewter Factory Store & Outlet,** 860 Main Street South, Woodbury, (203) 263-2668 or (800) 648-2014, where you'll also get to see live pewter-making demonstrations weekdays.

Gardeners throughout the United States know **White Flower Farm** for its selection of annuals, perennials, bulbs, and ornamental plants. When you're in northwestern Connecticut, you can visit them at Route 63, Litchfield, (860) 567-8789, for a chance to wander among the flowers and shop in the on-site store.

HOT SPOT

Antiquers would be hard-pressed to find a more ideal destination than Woodbury, Connecticut. The Litchfield region town is home to more than forty-five independent dealers. A directory of shops is available online at *www.antiqueswoodbury.com*.

To reach Woodbury, take exit 15 from I-84 and follow Route 6 East for a few minutes. On Saturdays, from March through December, the Woodbury Antiques & Flea Market, offers browsers an extraordinary, ever-changing selection of antiques. There's no charge for admission or parking.

PERSONAL ITINERARY NOTES

A DAY OF LIGHT

Early A.M. Start your "day of light" at the **Old Lighthouse Museum** in Stonington, 7 Water Street, (860) 535-1440. Here, you'll see the Stonington Harbor Lighthouse, which dates to 1823. It was moved to its current location on higher ground in 1840. The lighthouse, now a museum, has seasonal hours, so be sure to call ahead.

Late A.M. From Stonington, follow Route 1 West to Route 27 to **Mystic Seaport,** 75 Greenmanville Avenue, (860) 572-5315 or (888) 9-SEAPORT. Here, among its many maritime attractions, you'll find a replica of the second oldest lighthouse in New England, the 1746 Brant Point Lighthouse on Nantucket. You may want to grab a light lunch of New England clam chowder and a sandwich at the **Galley,** Mystic Seaport's casual, food court-style restaurant.

Early P.M. You may want to spend the afternoon exploring Mystic Seaport more thoroughly—after all, this living history museum can occupy visitors for a full day or more. If you'd rather spy another lighthouse, take I-95 South to the Colman Street exit, head south to Montauk Avenue, which ends at Pequot Avenue, four blocks from the New London Harbor Lighthouse. This historic 1760 structure, which marks the entrance to the Thames River, is Connecticut's oldest lighthouse and New England's fourth oldest. It remains active and is viewable only from the exterior, as it is a private residence.

Late P.M. Leave plenty of time for the hour and a half drive along I-95 to South Norwalk, and cruise to **Sheffield Island Lighthouse,** completed in 1868. Sound Navigation, (888) LI SOUND, *www.soundnavigation.com,* operates a regular schedule of outings to the island and tours of the lighthouse, from Hope Dock in South Norwalk. Sound Navigation's schedule includes Thursday Night Clambakes on Sheffield Island, Friday Night Sunset Cruises to the lighthouse, and other late-day options in season. Call for a complete schedule and reservations.

A LONG FALL WEEKEND

Day One The Litchfield Hills are a favorite among leaf peepers in Connecticut. At the **Danbury Railway Museum,** 120 White Street, Danbury, (203) 778-8337, you can ride aboard one of the vintage trains for a look at the leaves. If you are looking for a different angle, **Mooney Time** at 72 Railtree Hill Road, Woodbury, (203) 263-0167, offers champagne hot-air balloon flights over the sprawling Litchfield Hills. Or you can plan a picnic at **Squantz Pond State Park,** Route 39, New Fairfield, along the shores of Candlewood Lake, the state's largest lake.

Day Two There are more than 35 miles of hiking trails at **White Memorial Foundation and Conservation Center,** Route 202, Litchfield, (860) 567-0857. Just north, in Norfolk, you can tour the town in a horse-drawn carriage by making reservations with **Loon Meadow Farm,** 41 Loon Meadow Drive, (860) 542-6085. Loon Meadow Farm also hosts hayrides and bonfires, so call ahead for a schedule.

Day Three On the final day of your extended weekend, motor around the Litchfield Hills making possible stops at the **Silo Gallery,** 44 Upland Road/Route 202, New Milford, (860) 355-0300 or (800) 353-SILO, a gallery in a hay barn featuring artists from all over the world; the **Institute for American Indian Studies,** 38 Curtis Road, Washington, (860) 868-0518; **Hopkins Vineyard,** 25 Hopkins Road, New Preston, (860) 868-7954, for views of Lake Waramaug and wine tasting; and **Haight Vineyard and Winery,** 29 Chestnut Hill Road, Litchfield, (860) 567-4045, where you can learn about the winemaking process and sample the finished product.

Remember, accommodations can be hard to come by in the busy fall months, so make a reservation before you leave home.

FIVE DAY TRIPS FROM HARTFORD IN SPRING OR SUMMER

Day One Spend your first day leisurely exploring the downtown area including the **State Capitol Building,** 210 Capitol Avenue, (860) 240-0222; the **Old State House,** 800 Main Street, (860) 522-6766; **Bushnell Park**, Trinity Street at Elm Street, (860) 232-6710; and the **Wadsworth Athenaeum** art museum, 600 Main Street, (860) 278-2670.

Day Two On the western outskirts of the city is the **Mark Twain House,** 351 Farmington Avenue, (860) 247-0998, and the **Harriet Beecher Stowe House at Nook Farm,** Farmington Avenue at Forest Street, (860) 525-9317. If time allows, travel farther west on Farmington Avenue and explore the shops in West Hartford Center. Plan an early evening picnic in the fragrant, historic rose gardens of **Elizabeth Park,** Prospect Avenue, (860) 242-0017, or at the **Park's Pond House Café,** (860) 231-8823.

Day Three Take a day trip to Bristol, where you can explore the **Carousel Museum of New England,** 95 Riverside Avenue, (860) 585-5411, and spend the rest of the day playing at **Lake Compounce,** 822 Lake Avenue, (860) 583-3300, America's oldest amusement park.

Day Four In the state's northeast "Quiet Corner," you'll find antique shops to explore in Putnam. In Coventry, tour the **Nathan Hale Homestead,** 2299 South Street, (860) 247-8996, and taste the fruit of the vine at **Nutmeg Vineyards Farm Winery,** (800) Bunker Hill Road, (860) 742-8402. If you've got kids in tow, there's an authentic mine in Oneco at **River Bend Mining and Gemstone Panning,** 41 Pond Street/Route 14A, (860) 564-3440, where you can pan for your own gems.

Day Five Plan a day trip by bus or by car from Hartford to **Foxwoods Resort Casino** or **Mohegan Sun Casino**. Leaving the lure of the casinos for last ensures that you'll have sufficient funds for your entire stay!

A WEEK ALONG THE CONNECTICUT COAST

Day One Start out at the **Maritime Aquarium** at Norwalk, 10 North Water Street, (203) 852-0700, to explore the marine life of Long Island Sound and take in a colossal IMAX movie. In the afternoon, take I-95 North to exit 27 and visit the **Barnum Museum** in Bridgeport, 820 Main Street, (203) 331-9881, a monument to the Greatest Showman on Earth.

Day Two Set out the next day continuing north on I-95 to exit 47 for New Haven, home of historic **Yale University.** Tour the campus in the morning and spend the afternoon exploring one or two of the university's splendid museums of art, rare books, or natural history.

Day Three Continue north on I-95 to exit 63, stopping in Clinton at the **Clinton Crossing Premium Outlets,** 20A Killingsworth Turnpike, (860) 664-0700, or to exit 65 for the **Westbrook Factory Stores,** 314 Flat Rock Place, (860) 399-8739 or (888) SHOP-333, for bargain shopping. If the temperatures are sweltering, you may want to spend some time relaxing on the beach at nearby **Hammonasset Beach State Park** at exit 62 in Madison. Have dinner overlooking Long Island Sound at **Water's Edge Resort,** 1525 Boston Post Road, Westbrook off exit 65, (860) 399-5901 or (800) 222-5901.

Day Four Take Route 9 from I-95 to explore the Connecticut River towns of Old Saybrook, Essex, and East Haddam. The quirky **Gillette Castle** in East Haddam, (860) 526-2336, is a must-see attraction. Essex is home to the **Connecticut River Museum,** 67 Main Street, (860) 767-8269, with changing exhibits focusing on the region's history. You'll find quaint shops, art galleries, and seafood restaurants tucked away in these river towns. Plan to dine aboard the 1920s-era dinner train operated by **Valley Railroad** in Essex, One Railroad Avenue, (860) 767-0103 or (800) 377-3987.

Day Five I-95 should feel like an old friend by now. Heading north once again, stop at exit 90 for the town of Mystic, one of Connecticut's most popular destinations. Explore the town's whaling history at **Mystic Seaport,** 75 Greenmanville Avenue, (860) 572-5315 or (888) 9-SEAPORT. Grab lunch at **Mystic Pizza,** 56 West Main Street, (860) 536-3700, made famous by the movie of the same name. Then spend the afternoon with whales, dolphins, and penguins at the **Mystic Aquarium,** 55 Coogan Boulevard, (860) 572-5955. If it's a perfect summer evening, dine in nearby Noank at **Abbott's Lobster in the Rough,** 117 Pearl Street, (860) 536-7719, where you can feast on the freshest seafood at a picnic table overlooking the Sound as the sun sets.

Day Six Grab your bingo marker, bolster your bluffing abilities, limber up to do battle with one-arm bandits, and continue on to exit 92 off I-95, your route to the world's largest casino, **Foxwoods,** Route 2, Mashantucket, (800) PLAY BIG. Even if you're not a gambler, you'll find wonderful shops and shows, a plethora of dining options, and the Mashantucket Pequot Museum, dedicated to preserving the 11,000-year legacy of the region's Native Americans.

Day Seven Can you believe it's already time to bid adieu to the Connecticut coast? If you're returning home on I-95 south, stop along your way at exit 86 and submerge yourself in the nautical marvels of the **Submarine Force Museum at Groton,** One Crystal Lake Road, (860) 694-3174 or (800) 343-0079, where you can tour the USS *Nautilus*, the world's first nuclear-powered submarine.

PART III

Rhode Island

Rhode Island

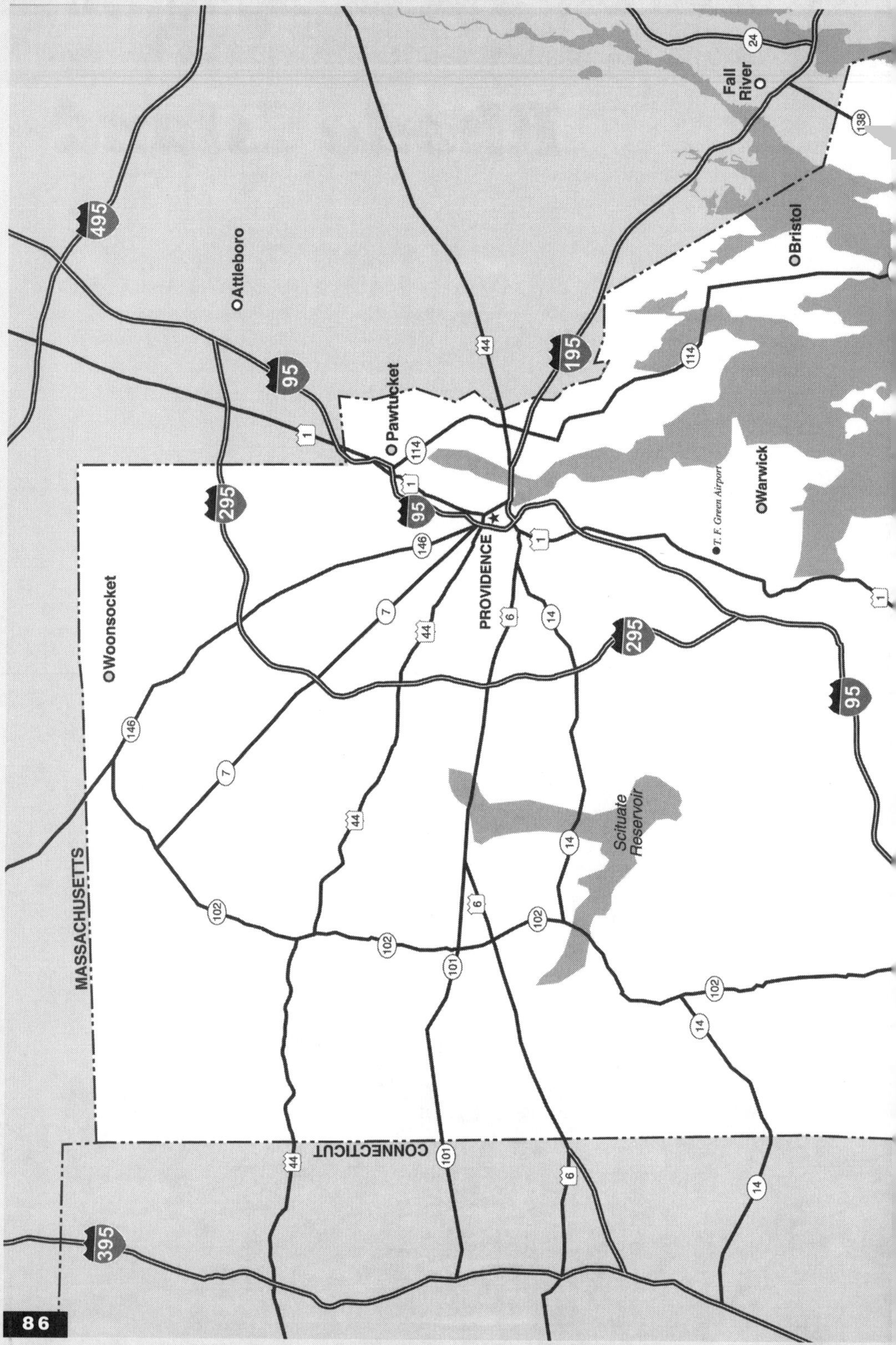

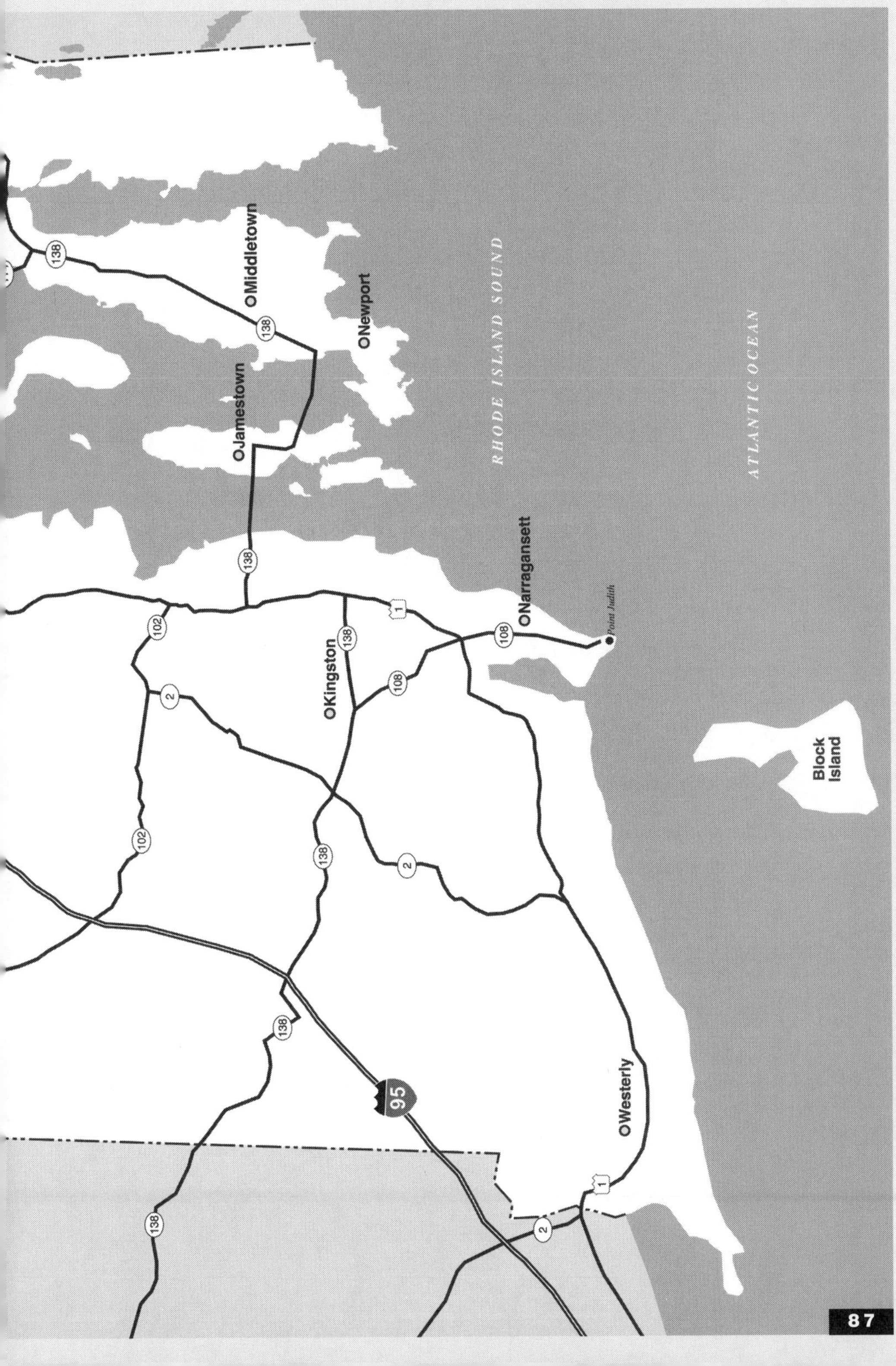

Middletown
138
Newport
RHODE ISLAND SOUND
ATLANTIC OCEAN
Jamestown
138
138
Narragansett
Point Judith
1
108
Kingston
138
102
2
108
Block
Island
102
138
2
138
95
Westerly
1
2
138

Newport, Rhode Island

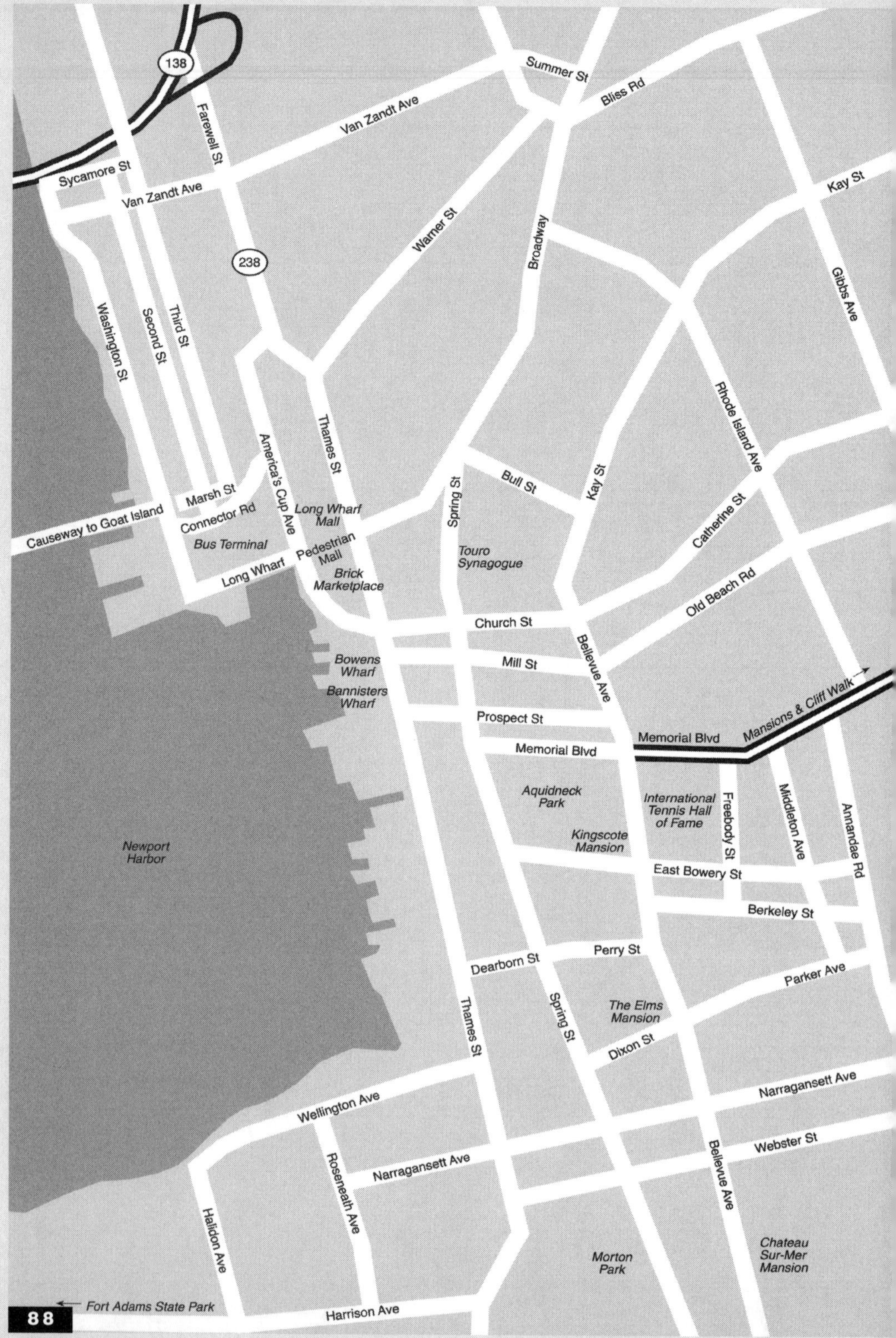

Providence, Rhode Island

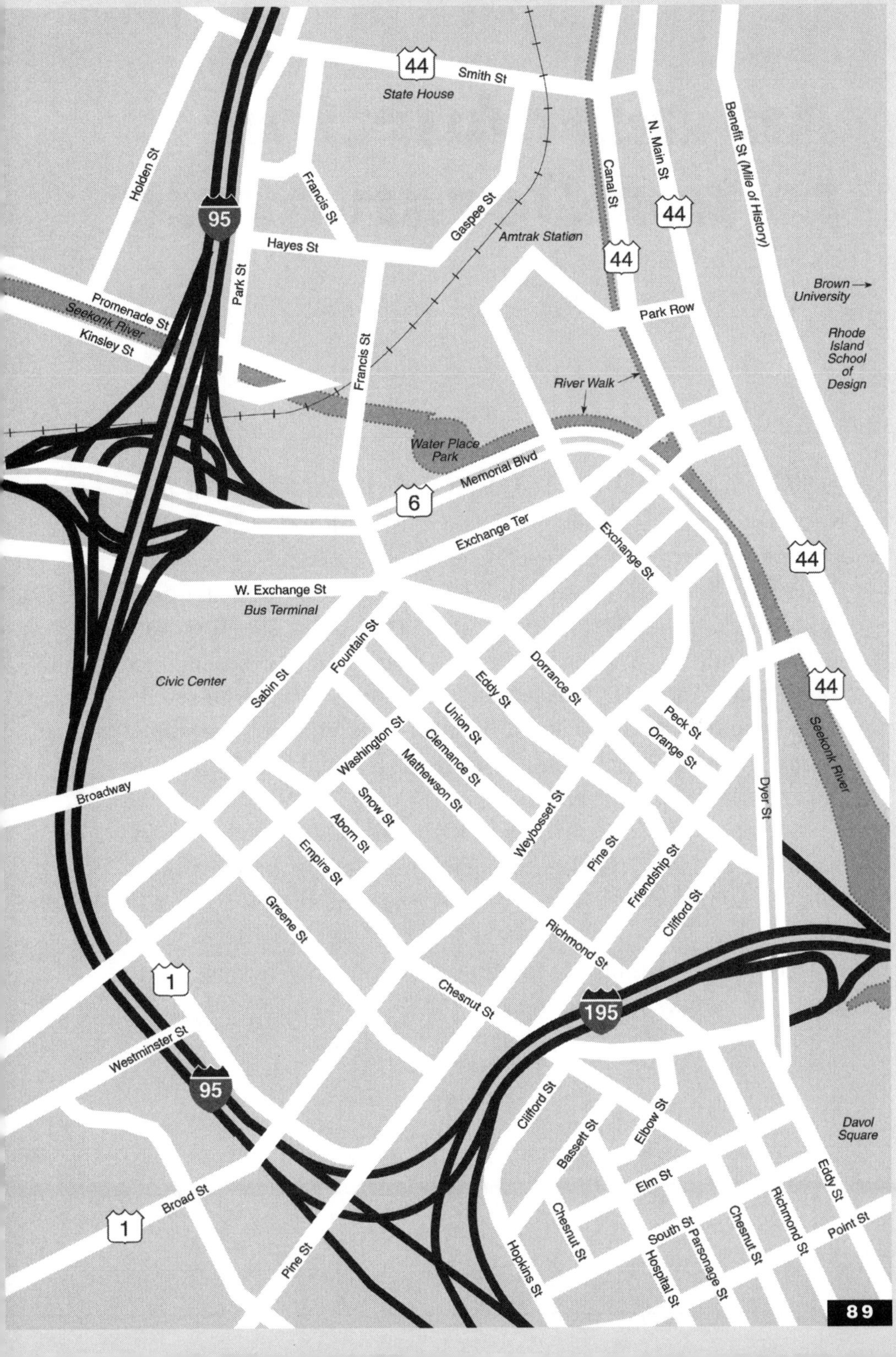

An Introduction to the Ocean State

ONCE YOU'VE VISITED RHODE ISLAND, you'll think twice about calling it "little." Facts are facts–Rhode Island is the smallest state not only in New England but also in the entire United States. But this petite place is feisty–did you know that Rhode Island declared its own independence from Great Britain on May 4, 1776, a full two months before the Declaration of Independence was signed? And it is practically bursting at the seams with scenic, historic, and cultural wonders. In spite of its compact geography, Rhode Island is home to an incredible 20 percent of the country's National Historic Landmarks.

Rhode Island is blessed with 400 miles of coastline including 100 miles of sandy beaches. Combine that with its premium location–just 60 miles from Boston and 180 miles from New York City–and it is easy to see why some of the biggest names in America flocked to Rhode Island at the turn of the century, turning it into their own summer playground.

FAST FACT

If you've seen any of these movies, you've already "visited" Rhode Island. All were filmed totally or partially in the Ocean State.

Amistad
Dumb and Dumber
Me, Myself, and Irene
Meet Joe Black
Outside Providence
Reversal of Fortune
There's Something about Mary
True Lies

Rhode Island as a Vacation Destination

Today, Rhode Island offers an astounding variety of vacation possibilities. Newport's marvelous mansions are a must-see for visitors, as is the natural beauty of Block Island, called "one of the twelve last great places in the Western Hemisphere" by the Nature Conservancy. Capital city Providence has undergone extensive urban renewal, and the River Walk and WaterPlace Park are permanent monuments to the city's rejuvenation. Travelers and locals alike flock to see the spectacular "WaterFire" displays on the Providence riverfront—a musical score accompanies the crackling bonfires that float along the river, casting a warm, shimmering glow on the vibrant city center.

The Blackstone Valley in the northern part of the state was the birthplace of America's Industrial Revolution—Samuel Slater opened his famous cotton mill there in 1793. And of course, you can't leave for home until you've played on the beaches of South County. Ocean lovers have been lured to these shores for more than a century.

The good news is, these days, your name doesn't have to be Vanderbilt or Astor for you to immerse yourself in all of the pleasures of this seaside paradise. From mansions to boating excursions to beaches to outdoor concerts to seafood dinners, Rhode Island offers a little something for everyone.

TRAVEL TIP

While summer is a spectacular time to enjoy beaches, boating, and famous outdoor music festivals, there are alternatives to fighting peak season crowds. Narragansett Bay breezes keep Rhode Island winters less frigid than elsewhere in New England. Off-season rates kick in after the summer tourist population swell subsides. Newport's mansions are especially spectacular when decked out in Christmas finery. Keep in mind some attractions close in the off-season, and beaches usually open the last weekend in May.

Ten Rhode Island Highlights

Rhode Island may be small, but it is no small task to list all the best places to visit there! The following are a few of the highlights you should seriously consider checking out on your visit.

Birds and Butterflies

Middletown, Rhode Island, is home to the **Norman Bird Sanctuary**, 583 Third Beach Road, (401) 846-2577, a 450-acre preserve with 7 miles of walking trails and a natural history museum, and the **Butterfly Zoo at the Newport Butterfly Farm,** 594 Aquidneck Avenue, (401) 849-9519, a screened greenhouse where you can mingle with flitting specimens from all over the world.

Block Island

Block Island has been designated "one of the twelve last great places in the Western Hemisphere" by the Nature Conservancy and is home to more than forty species of rare and endangered plants and animals. Highlights include beaches, boating, bicycling, fishing, lighthouses, and sweeping views of the sea from the 185-foot clay cliffs at Mohegan Bluffs.

TRAVEL TIP

The Rhode Island Public Transit Authority (RIPTA) operates the downtown Providence LINK, vintage-style trackless trolleys. Two routes take visitors to stops at twenty city parking lots and at major city attractions. Cost: fifty cents a ride or $1.50 for one day of unlimited rides. Tokens and passes are available at Kennedy Plaza and the Interim Sales and Information Outlet located at 129 Washington Street. Visit the RIPTA Web site, *www.ripta.com*, for more information on stops and schedules, or call (401) 781-9400.

The Enchanted Forest

Route 3, Hopkinton, (401) 539-7711

This storybook-themed amusement park has a carousel, roller coaster, and other rides, plus a petting zoo, miniature golf, go-carts, and batting cages. The park is open from May through September and offers special holiday programming during weekends in December.

Green Animals Topiary Garden

Cory's Lane, Portsmouth, (401) 683-1267

This splendid Victorian estate boasts America's oldest topiary gardens, first planted in 1880. California privet, golden boxwood, and American boxwood trees are artfully "carved" into geometric and ornamental designs and even animal shapes such as an elephant, a camel, and a teddy bear. Also visit the rose garden, the antique toy collection in the main house, and the plant shop.

Historic Carousels

Rhode Island is home to three historic carousels. In East Providence, you'll find the 1895 Crescent Park Carousel, designated a National Historic Site and a National Historic Landmark. You'll have trouble choosing your mount from the sixty-six hand-carved figures designed by Charles I.D. Looff. Slater Memorial Park in Pawtucket is home to Looff's earliest carousel, this one built in 1894 and installed in the park in 1910. It features forty-two intricate horses, plus three dogs, a lion, a camel, and a giraffe. The oldest carousel in America, Westerly's Flying Horse Carousel, was constructed in 1883 and has twenty horses that were each hand carved from a single piece of wood.

International Tennis Hall of Fame

194 Bellevue Avenue, Newport, (401) 849-3990

The International Tennis Hall of Fame and the world's largest tennis museum are housed at the Newport Casino, where the first American tennis National Championships were held in 1881. The complex also features thirteen grass tennis courts—the only competition grass courts in the country that are open to the public.

FAST FACT

When it opens in 2003, the **Heritage Harbor Museum** will depict Rhode Island's legacy and traditions like no other attraction. Narragansett Electric donated the decommissioned South Street Power Station in Providence to house this new breed of museum that will encompass theater, art, interactive exhibits, children's play areas, and unique restaurants, shops, and galleries.

To check on its progress, call (401) 751-7979 or visit the museum's Web site, *www.heritageharbor.org.*

Newport Mansions

A visit to Rhode Island isn't complete without a visit to at least one or two of Newport's magnificent seaside mansions. The Preservation Society of Newport, (401) 847-1000, operates eleven historic properties including Cornelius Vanderbilt II's seventy-room "cottage," the **Breakers,** and William K. Vanderbilt's **Marble House,** which features 500,000 cubic feet of marble. Don't miss the privately owned Astors' **Beechwood Mansion,** 580 Bellevue Avenue, (401) 846-3772, where costumed guides portray family members, servants, and guests. Several other privately operated mansions are also open for tours. Make sure you leave time to stroll the three and one-half mile Cliff Walk along the Atlantic, which will take you past many of these famous, historic homes.

HOT SPOT

Newport may have the mansion market cornered, but a lovely 33-acre turn-of-the-century mansion and estate in Bristol is worth visiting. **Blithewold Mansion and Gardens,** 101 Ferry Road/Route 114, (401) 253-2707, the former summer home of Pennsylvania coal magnate Augustus Van Winkle, has forty-five rooms. The landscaped grounds overlooking Narragansett Bay include an arboretum with the largest giant redwood east of the Rocky Mountains, a Japanese water garden, and formal gardens that feature 50,000 flowering spring bulbs.

Rhode Island Beaches

Rhode Island has 400 miles of coastline, so if the ocean calls to you, you'll be pleased with your options—a total of forty-eight public beaches. South County boasts the state's most popular spots including South Kingstown Town Beach, Roger Wheeler State Beach, Blue Shutters Town Beach, and Misquamicut State Beach, which also offers family amusements. You'll also find public beaches in Bristol, Jamestown, Middletown, Narragansett, Newport, Portsmouth, Tiverton, Warwick, and on Block Island.

Roger Williams Park Zoo

1000 Elmwood Avenue, Providence, (401) 785-3510

Providence is home to the country's third oldest zoo, which has been a popular family attraction since 1872. The widely acclaimed zoo is home to more than 900 animals representing 150 different species.

WaterPlace Park and River Walk

WaterPlace is the 4-acre urban park along the Woonasquatucket

River that is the centerpiece of revitalization in Rhode Island's capital city—Providence. The charming cobbled walkways, footbridges, and amphitheater will remind you of Venice, and you'll do a double take when you spot a gondola gliding along with a gondolier at the stern and a smiling, picnicking couple aboard. Believe it or not, a company called **La Gondola, Inc.,** ✆(401) 421-8877, offers gondola outings from a landing at WaterPlace; call ahead to make reservations.

TRAVEL TIP

Rhode Island has five B&B reservation services: **Anna's Victorian Connection,** ✆(401) 849-2489 or ✆(800) 884-4288, has 200 B&B listings, mostly in private homes within fifteen minutes of Newport; **Bed & Breakfast Referrals of South County Rhode Island,** ✆(800) 853-7479, offers twenty-one B&Bs along the state's southern coastline; **Bannister Bed & Breakfast Reservation Service,** ✆(401) 846-0059; **Bed & Breakfast Newport,** ✆(401) 846-5408 or ✆(800) 800-8765; and **Bed & Breakfast of Rhode Island,** ✆(401) 849-1298 or ✆(800) 828-0000.

Divine Providence

AFTER BOSTON, IF YOU CAN CHOOSE ONLY ONE other New England city to visit, make it Providence. Even before the NBC television series that bears the city's name raised the profile of this urban enclave, Providence had emerged as one of the most dynamic centers of learning, culture, and architecture in the Northeast. Since the early 1980s, Rhode Island's capital has undergone a multimillion-dollar urban renewal project focused on the city's waterfront, and yet, care has been taken to preserve the historical character of one of the oldest cities in America. Religious leader Roger Williams founded Providence in 1636, and today it is the only major U.S. city that has its entire downtown listed on the National Register of Historic Places.

Providence has a youthful exuberance that you'll sense as you meander its streets and the central River Walk because it is home to five major colleges and universities, including the Ivy League's Brown University, New England's third oldest college; Rhode Island School of Design, a forward-thinking college of the arts established in 1877; and Johnson & Wales University, which graduates some of the region's top chefs from its culinary school. Providence is quite compact and easily explored on foot. As you discover the Venice-inspired riverfront walkways and bridges of WaterPlace Park, the bustling pubs and trendy shops of Thayer Street, and the cultural richness provided by the city's museums and performing arts centers, you'll understand why *Money* magazine named Providence "The Best Place to Live in the East" in 2000. Not only is Providence a nice place to visit, but you may just find yourself wanting to live there, too.

TRAVEL TIP

Set sail on a day or overnight trip aboard the ***Continental Sloop Providence,*** a replica of the tall ship commanded by John Paul Jones that was America's first commissioned warship. Call (401) 274-7447 for a schedule of departures from Providence's India Point Park, or visit the sloop on the Internet, *www.sloopprovidence.org*.

Lodging Options

For accommodations right at T.F. Green Airport, try the **Comfort Inn Airport,** 1940 Post Road, Warwick, (401) 732-0470; the **Radisson Airport Hotel,** 2081 Post Road, Warwick, (401) 739-3000; or **Sheraton Inn Providence Airport,** 1850 Post Road, Warwick, (401) 738-4000. In the heart of downtown Providence, you'll find a grand old hotel that is an attraction in and of itself. Built in 1922, the **Providence Biltmore, Kennedy Plaza,** (401) 421-0700 or (800) 294-7709, offers more than 200 rooms and suites and a rooftop grand ballroom with skyline and waterfront views. The **Westin Providence,** One West Exchange Street, (401) 598-8000, is the city's largest hotel, and you'll also find convenient, central accommodations at the **Holiday Inn Downtown,** 21 Atwells Avenue, (401) 831-1717.

For unique lodgings, head just outside the city to Cranston, where you'll find **Edgewood Manor Bed & Breakfast,** 232 Norwood Avenue, (401) 781-0099 or (800) 882-3285, an eighteen-room Greek Revival mansion constructed in 1905. About 10 miles from Providence in Seekonk, Massachusetts, **Historic**

Jacob Hill Farm Bed and Breakfast Inn, 120 Jacob Street, (508) 336-9165, dates to between 1722 and 1723 and offers cozy suites and a pool that is lit for night swimming. Closer to downtown, you'll find canopied beds, fireplaces, and other charming touches at the **State House Inn,** 43 Jewett Street, Providence, (401) 351-6111, which was built in 1889.

TRAVEL TIP

Providence has a very nice central location in the Northeast and makes a nice base-camp for extended stays. If you are driving, the city is:

30 miles from New Bedford, MA
32 miles from Newport, RI
43 miles from Worcester, MA
48 miles from Mystic, CT
52 miles from Boston, MA
56 miles from Cape Cod, MA
70 miles from Hartford, CT
175 miles from New York, NY

Perusing Providence

The four-acre WaterPlace Park and River Walk in the heart of downtown Providence is the most visible manifestation of the city's recent renaissance. Creating the series of Venetian-like canals, bridges, and riverside walkways was no easy task. Railroad tracks were removed, and two rivers were rerouted through the city to create this scenic centerpiece where you can stroll, picnic, watch outdoor theater presentations, and even embark on a gondola ride. Call **La Gondola, Inc.,** (401) 421-8877, May through October to reserve your forty-minute ride for a party of up to six people. Bring your own bottle of wine–cheese and salami are provided.

For a romantic option on land, see the River Walk and city

sights from a horse-drawn carriage. **Slide Hill Farm Carriage Rides** depart from Kennedy Plaza on weekends Memorial Day through Columbus Day. Call (401) 377-2426 for information.

History and architecture buffs won't want to miss the College Hill neighborhood of Providence, home to Benefit Street, Providence's "Mile of History." Wealthy colonial businessmen began building houses along Back Street, now Benefit Street, in 1758, and the street today can boast of the largest concentration of Colonial homes in America. Early Federal period and interesting nineteenth- and twentieth-century architectural styles can be seen, too. The Providence Preservation Society, (401) 831-7440, offers information on self-guided walking tours of Benefit Street. While you're there, you can visit the **Old State House,** 150 Benefit Street, (401) 222-2678, where the Rhode Island General Assembly renounced allegiance to King George III of England a full two months before the rest of the American colonies officially did so with the signing of the Declaration of Independence.

Nearby at 52 Power Street at Benefit Street, visit the **John Brown House,** (401) 331-8575. John Brown was a prosperous Providence merchant, and this 1786 Georgian mansion is filled with examples of Rhode Island craftsmanship.

The **Rhode Island School of Design (RISD) Museum,** 224 Benefit Street, (401) 454-6500, is open to the public Tuesday through Sunday. It exhibits an impressive collection of more than 85,000 works ranging from ancient Greek and Roman sculpture to French impressionist paintings to contemporary art.

One of the most distinctive architectural gems of Providence's skyline is the **State House,** Smith Street, (401) 222-2357, designed by McKim, Mead, and White and completed in 1901. It sports one of the largest self-supported domes in the world. Free guided tours are available weekdays.

The National Park Service–operated **Roger Williams National Memorial,** 282 North Main Street, (401) 785-9450, includes a landscaped park and a visitor's center, where the story of Rhode Island's founder is told.

TRAVEL TIP

The Rhode Island Public Transportation Authority's (RIPTA) summer Rack N' Ride program makes it easy for cyclists to take advantage of the state's miles of biking paths. RIPTA buses are equipped with easy-to-use bike racks on the front that hold two bikes, which can be loaded and unloaded independently. There is no extra charge for transporting your bike on the bus. For a free guide to cycling, call (401) 222-4203, ext. 4042.

On the Outskirts

Just outside of downtown Providence, you can spy elephants, snow leopards, polar bears, and more in natural settings at the nation's third oldest zoo, **Roger Williams Park Zoo,** 1000 Elmwood Avenue, (401) 785-3510. The widely acclaimed zoo is home to more than 900 creatures. Don't miss the **Marco Polo Trail,** which traces explorer Marco Polo's three-year journey through Asia.

In Cranston, show the tykes how milk gets from the cow to the carton at **Nature's Best Dairy World,** 2032 Plainfield Pike/Route 14, (888) 315-TOUR. There's an antique carousel at Dairy World, and in East Providence, don't miss the **1895 Crescent Park Carousel,** designated a National Historic Site and a National Historic Landmark.

Take a free guided tour of the historic **Brown University** campus, College and Prospect Streets, (401) 863-1000. Tours led by undergraduate students are offered most weekdays at 10, 11, 1, 3, and 4. From mid-September through mid-November, tours are also available on Saturdays at 10, 11, and noon.

TRAVEL TIP

If you can possibly time your visit to Providence to coincide with WaterFire, do! **WaterFire** is a fusion of fire, water, music, and art. Sculptor Barnaby Evans created the first WaterFire in 1994 and a second for the International Sculpture Conference in 1996. Soon thereafter, supporters raised funds to keep it going. Today, WaterFire has ninety-seven flaming braziers that cast their gaze-monopolizing glow along the Woonasquatucket and Moshassuck Rivers. Schedule of WaterFire events at *www.waterfire.com*, or call (401) 272-3111.

Dining Highlights

Federal Hill, the neighborhood west of downtown Providence, is home to the city's "Little Italy." Dine on classic Italian dishes at the second-oldest family-run restaurant in the United States, **Camille's Roman Garden,** 71 Bradford Street, (401) 751-4812. Then pop into **Roma Gourmet Foods,** 310 Atwells Avenue, (401) 331-8620, for homemade pastries.

Thayer Street, which runs through the Brown University campus, is dotted with ethnic eateries and outdoor cafes, many of which cater to the college crowd by offering generous portions at affordable prices and staying open late. **Café Paragon,** 234 Thayer Street, (401) 331-6200, is a casual, trendy, Mediterranean eatery by day, but show up after midnight, and it's even got a different name–Viva–as it is transformed into a techno dance club. **Channels Internet,** 272 Thayer Street, (401) 841-0100, has multiple incarnations, too. It's a sandwich and coffee shop, an Internet café, and a jazz club all in one.

Beer enthusiasts should chug on over to the **Union Station Brewery,** 36 Exchange Terrace, (401) 274-BREW, for a pint and some pub fare inside a historic brick building that was formerly the Providence train station. Or try the **Trinity Brewhouse,** 186

Fountain Street, (401) 453-2337, Rhode Island's largest brewery.

For a decidedly upscale meal, head to **Capital Grille,** 1 Union Station, (401) 521-5600, for dry-aged steaks. **Federal Reserve Restaurant,** 170 Westminster Street, (401) 621-5700, is in a restored bank building with its own turn-of-the-century vault, towering ceilings and windows, and a marvelous, 60-foot marble bar.

CAV Restaurant, Antiques and Gifts, 14 Imperial Place, (401) 751-9164, serves fresh, creative dishes with a Mediterranean and vegetarian slant in an antique-filled loft where you might just find an unusual gift while you dine.

After dinner, sip coffee on a couch while watching foreign and independent films at **Cable Car Cinema & Café,** 204 South Main Street, (401) 272-3970.

FAST FACT

Rhode Islanders have stamped their state's name on their own variety of clam chowder. Unlike traditional, creamy, milk-based New England clam chowder or tomato-based Manhattan clam chowder, Rhode Island clam chowder features quahogs, celery, onions, and potatoes in a clear broth.

Shopping Discoveries

Even shopping can be a blast from the past in Providence. The **Arcade,** 65 Weybosset Street, (401) 521-2665, is America's oldest indoor shopping mall, and it's on the National Register of Historic Places. The 1828 mall now houses three floors of shops, boutiques, and eateries. The Arcade is closed on Sundays.

Providence also boasts a modern shopping center, the **Providence Place Mall,** Francis Street and Memorial Boulevard, (401) 270-1017, which opened in 1999 and features popular restaurants, an IMAX theater, and 150 specialty shops.

Gallery Flux, 260 Weybosset Street, (401) 274-9120, showcases functional art created by Rhode Islanders. You'll also find the works of Rhode Island natives among the gifts and decorative items at the **Opulent Owl,** 195 Wayland Avenue, (401) 521-6698.

Funky shops and boutiques along Thayer Street beckon to college students and tourists alike. **OOP!,** 297 Thayer Street, (401) 455-0844, features whimsical works by more than 100 artisans. If you need an inflatable moose head, this is your shop.

The Blackstone Valley

THE BLACKSTONE VALLEY, the region that stretches north and west of Providence to Rhode Island's borders with Massachusetts and Connecticut, is named for the Reverend William Blackstone, an English preacher who established the first settlement in what is now Boston before moving south to what is now Cumberland, Rhode Island. But while the Valley and the River that shaped its history bear Blackstone's name, the character of this region was indelibly imprinted by another man—Samuel Slater.

Slater was born in England, but his ingenuity and defiant spirit made him a natural-born Yankee and an American hero of sorts. Of course, his countrymen might've labeled him a thief and a traitor. At the age of fourteen, Slater was apprenticed to Jedediah Strutt, a partner of the English inventor of cotton-spinning machinery, Sir Richard Arkwright. In order to protect its textile monopoly, English law forbade textile workers from leaving the country, but Slater, after carefully memorizing machine specifications, secretly emigrated to America in 1789. Slater's unique knowledge of textile mill construction and operation gave an unprecedented boost to America's fledgling textile industry, and the water-powered mill he built in Pawtucket became the model that changed the course of the country's industrial development.

When you visit this region that cradled the American Industrial

Revolution, you'll glimpse a way of life that accompanied the country's emergence as an economic force. You'll also see how the ravages of industrialization are being combated. The Blackstone River played a vital role in the industrial development of the area, and the river's environmental cleanup is key to its new post-industrial, recreational role. The contrasts between the valley's former "mill towns" and its appealing rural expanses, while still obvious, are beginning to blur as efforts to preserve the historical legacy of the entire region gain momentum. The 1986 creation by Congress of the Blackstone River Valley National Heritage Corridor, which incorporates forty-six miles of river and twenty-four Rhode Island and Massachusetts towns and is overseen by the National Park Service, ensures the future preservation and linkage of parks, historic sites, attractions, and recreation areas that tell the valley's fascinating story.

FAST FACT

McCoy Stadium has been the home of the Pawtucket Red Sox, the International League's AAA affiliate of the Boston Red Sox, since 1973. The historic stadium was a 1942 Works Progress Administration (WPA) project. General admission tickets are very affordable (just $5 at the time of this book's printing) and can be ordered by calling (401) 724-7300.

Lodging Options

For traditional, chain hotel accommodations, try the **Comfort Inn in Pawtucket,** 2 George Street, (401) 723-6700, which has an outdoor pool and an on-site Ground Round restaurant or the **Holiday Inn in Woonsocket,** 194 Fortin Drive, (401) 769-5000 or (800) 465-4329, which offers an indoor pool and fitness center and caters to both corporate and leisure travelers.

If you're seeking something cozy and unique, consider the **Pillsbury House Bed and Breakfast,** 341 Prospect Street,

Woonsocket, (401) 766-7983 or (800) 205-4112, an 1875 inn with a kitchenette available to guests; or stay in a 1736 farmstead that is on the National Register of Historic Places, the **Whipple-Cullen Farmstead B&B,** 99 Old River Road, Lincoln, (401) 333-1899.

Evolutionary Sights

Before Samuel Slater arrived on the scene, the Blackstone River Valley was dotted with farming communities. When you visit **Dame Farm,** 29 Brown Avenue, Johnston, (401) 222-2632, you'll get a glimpse of what it was like to earn a living from the land. Now a 500-acre state park, the property features buildings dating from the 1760s through 1925 that are listed on the National Register of Historic Places and restored to the period in which they were built. The state leased 170 acres to the Dame family, the owners of the farm from 1890 to 1969, and they continue to operate a working farm on the site.

The mill that precipitated cataclysmic change in not only the region but also the nation is a must-see. **Slater Mill Historic Site,** 67 Roosevelt Avenue, Pawtucket, (401) 725-8638, is a museum complex that includes the original yellow clapboard textile mill built by Slater in 1793, the 1810 Wilkinson Mill and machine shop, and the 1758 Sylvanus Brown House, home of a master craftsman who contributed to Slater's success by making machine patterns and wooden machine parts for the textile mill. Tours are available daily, though the schedule is very limited December through May.

While you're in Pawtucket, see the historic 1894 carousel in **Slater Memorial Park,** entrances from Routes 1A and 15, (401) 728-0500, ext. 252. You can take a spin on one of the carousel's horses or choose one of the dogs, a lion, a camel, or a giraffe, for just a quarter per ride from late May through early September.

If you've not yet had your fill of mills, you can also delve into the lives of the French Canadians who left their Quebec farms behind for work in the mills at the interactive **Museum of Work and Culture,** 42 South Main Street, Woonsocket, (401) 769-WORK.

Finally, for an up-close look at the state of the mighty Blackstone River today, venture aboard the *Blackstone Valley Explorer*, a forty-nine-passenger riverboat that departs from various locations for cruise tours. For schedule information, contact the **Blackstone Valley Tourism Council,** (401) 724-2200.

HOT SPOT

The Patriots, New England's NFL football team, call Massachusetts home, but each summer the team's training camp is held in Rhode Island on the grounds of Bryant College, 1150 Douglas Pike, Smithfield. Not only can you watch your favorite team members in action during two scheduled practices on most days while camp is in session, but also you can participate in the Patriots Experience—an interactive football theme park that allows you to "get in the game." Parking and admission are free. For a schedule, directions, and more information, call Bryant College at (401) 232-6480.

Dining Highlights

Egg rolls and jazz? If they don't seem to go together at first glance, you may be convinced otherwise by **Chan's Fine Oriental Dining,** 267 Main Street, Woonsocket (401) 765-1900, where live jazz is on the menu Friday and Saturday nights. All music performances require advance ticket purchases.

The Blackstone Valley region is famous for its family-style, all-you-can-eat chicken dinners. They're served up at more than a dozen of the region's restaurants. The largest is **Wright's Farm Restaurant,** 84 Inman Road, Burrillville, (401) 769-2856, which serves about 300 tons of chicken annually.

For a flashback, stop into the first diner to appear on the National Register of Historic Places, a 1941 stainless steel diner, paradoxically named the **Modern Diner,** 364 East Avenue, Pawtucket, (401) 726-8390.

Shopping Discoveries

The town of Glocester is home to **Chepachet Village,** known for antiques and collectibles shopping and for seasonal farm stands. It's also where you'll find **Brown and Hopkins Country Store,** 1179 Putnam Pike/Route 44, (401) 568-4830, one of the country's oldest continuously operating general stores, dating to 1809.

The **Greenhouse at Daggett Farm,** located within Slater Memorial Park, Pawtucket, is a project of the Blackstone Valley Chapter RI ARC, which provides services and support to persons with mental retardation and their families. Your purchase of plants and gifts at the greenhouse supports the organization's "horticultural therapy" program.

TRAVEL TIP

The **Rhode Island Wine Trail,** (401) 222-2781, not only takes you to four vineyards for a sample of the local fruit of the vine turned into wine but also provides a route through some of the state's most picturesque countryside.

Greenvale Vineyards, Portsmouth, (401) 847-3777, is situated alongside the scenic Sakonnet River and is listed on the National Register of Historic Places.

Newport Vineyards, Middletown, (401) 848-5161, is a family-run winery just outside of Newport that is open daily for tours and tastings.

Diamond Hill Vineyards, Cumberland, (401) 333-2751 or (800) 752-2505, has beautiful gardens and grounds to explore before or after you taste award-winning wines inside the owners' 200-year-old home.

Sakonnet Vineyards, Little Compton, (401) 635-8486, is open daily for tours and tastings of its regionally distinctive wines.

South County Seaside Escapes

SOUTHERN RHODE ISLAND IS DEFINITELY one of New England's top beach vacation destinations. It boasts 100 miles of dazzling coastline, more than a dozen public beaches, expansive ocean views, and some of New England's best surfing. Yes—diehard surfers ride Rhode Island's waves year-round. Some of the best swells accompany storms in the spring and fall, when water temperatures are, oh, a bit on the chilly side.

But if you're traveling to one of the eleven South County towns—Charlestown, Coventry, East Greenwich, Exeter, Hopkinton, Narragansett, North Kingstown, Richmond, South Kingstown, West Greenwich, or Westerly—you'll be glad to know that a bevy of other nonbeach attractions and enticements exist here. After all, your wet suit may be at the cleaners. It may rain. Or you might get sunburned on your first day!

Officially, there is no Rhode Island county named "South County," but this informal designation for the coastal area is pervasive. When you've tired of basking on the beach, you'll find plenty of other activities to occupy your days, from strolling classic New England Main Street shopping districts to exploring art, military, and Native American history, to squealing along with the kids as you plummet in a roller coaster car at a fairyland amusement park.

Though this seaside playland lies just ninety minutes from Boston and three and one-half hours from New York, you're bound to feel a world away if this is the place you choose to stay.

FAST FACT

Surprised that you can ski in Rhode Island? It *is* nicknamed the Ocean State, not the Mountain State, after all. But **Yawgoo Valley Ski Area** off Route 2 in Exeter does offer day and night skiing and snow tubing on twelve trails. Call (401) 294-3802 for ski conditions.

Lodging Options

You can hide away inside your own tiny "beach cottage" at **Hathaway's Guest Cottages Bed & Breakfast,** 4470 Old Post Road, Charlestown, (401) 364-6665.

Willows Resort Motel, Route 1, Charlestown, (401) 364-7727 is a 15-acre resort on a saltwater pond.

Blueberry Cove Inn, 75 Kingstown Road, Narragansett, (401) 792-9865 or (800) 478-1426, has seven great rooms and a whirlpool suite.

Have the run of the inn at the **Old Clerk House,** 49 Narragansett Avenue, Narragansett, (401) 783-8008, a Victorian home with just one guest suite.

Enjoy dramatic ocean views from another Victorian landmark, **Ocean Rose Inn,** 113 Ocean Road, Narragansett, (401) 783-4704.

Turn back the clock to the days when steamships sailed into Wickford Harbor at the **1906 Haddie Pierce House B&B,** 146 Boston Neck Road, North Kingstown, (401) 294-7674, a clapboard home with a widow's walk.

Stay close to the beach and have access to an outdoor pool at the **Holiday Inn,** 3009 Tower Hill Road, South Kingstown, (401) 789-1051

Be surrounded by stately old trees at the **Larchwood Inn,** 521 Main Street, South Kingstown, (401) 783-5454 or (800) 275-5450, which has its own restaurant and tavern.

Tuck yourself in beside a gurgling brook at **Brookside Manor,** 380-B Post Road, South Kingstown, (401) 788-3527, a circa-1690 manor house on 8 acres.

Choose a room, efficiency, or cottage at **Sand Dollar Inn,** 171 Post Road, Westerly, (401) 322-2000.

Have a golf course at your doorstep at **Winnapaug Inn,** 169 Shore Road, Misquamicut/Westerly, (401) 348-8350 or (800) 288-9906.

For privacy and flowering gardens call the **Villa,** 190 Shore Road, Westerly, (401) 596-1054 or (800) 722-9240.

For golf and tennis packages and water-view rooms go to the **Watch Hill Inn,** 38 Bay Street, Watch Hill, 401-348-6300 or (800) 356-9314.

Have business amenities and an indoor pool available to you at the **Best Western West Greenwich Inn,** 101 Nooseneck Hill Road, West Greenwich, (401) 397-5494.

Swim in a heated greenhouse pool at the **1790 Millstone Farm Bed & Breakfast,** 410 Plain Meeting House Road, West Greenwich, (401) 397-7737 or (401) 397-6517.

The Beaches of South County

You certainly won't be disappointed with the vast selection of beaches that line Rhode Island's coast. You may, however, be a bit chagrined that individual usage and parking fees at each make it costly to "beach hop," at least within the course of a day. Call ahead for prices and parking information. The South County Tourism Council is also a good central resource for help in selecting the best beach to suit your interests. Contact them at (401) 789-4422 or (800) 548-4662.

Charlestown

Blue Shutters Town Beach, East Beach Road off Route 1, (401) 364-1227 (summer), (401) 364-1222 (winter), very popular family beach

Charlestown Town Beach, off Route 1, (401) 364-1227 (summer),

(401) 364-1222 (winter), clean beach area with modest surf

Charlestown Breachway State Beach, Burlingame State Park, (401) 364-7000 (summer), (401) 322-8910 (winter), popular with campers

East Beach/Ninigret State Beach, off East Beach Road, (401) 322-0450 (summer), (401) 322-8910 (winter), unspoiled 3-mile area, no concessions/facilities

Quonochontaug Beach, off Route 1, (401) 364-1227 (summer), (401) 364-1222 (winter), area of exclusive homes, good fishing

Narragansett

Narragansett Town Beach, Ocean Road/Route 1A, (401) 789-1044, three beach areas with differing appeals—areas for surfers, families, and those seeking quiet relaxation

Roger W. Wheeler State Beach, 100 Sand Hill Cove Road, (401) 789-3563 (summer), (401) 789-8374 (winter), sheltered area with no undertow that is a good choice for families with small children

Salty Brine State Beach, 254 Great Road, (401) 789-3563 (summer), (401) 789-8374 (winter), tiny family beach

Scarborough State Beach (Scarborough North & South Beach Complex), 870 Ocean Road (Scarborough North), (401) 789-2324, 970 Ocean Road (Scarborough South), (401) 782-1319, (401) 789-8374 (winter), family spot, excellent for bodysurfing

North Kingstown

North Kingstown Town Beach, (401) 294-3331, narrow, rocky beach, good for strolling

South Kingstown

Carpenter's Beach Meadow, 855 Matunuck Beach Road, (401) 789-9301, snack bars and shops within walking distance

East Matunuck State Beach, 950 Succotash Road, (401) 789-8585 (summer), (401) 789-8374 (winter), popular for fishing and surfing and with teens and young adults

Roy Carpenter's Beach, Matunuck Beach Road exit off Route 1, (401) 789-9301, family beach surrounded by summer cottages

South Kingstown Town Beach at Matunuck, Matunuck Beach Road, Wakefield, (401) 789-9301, quaint family beach with moderate to heavy surf

HOT SPOT

Picture this . . . professional musical theater, historical surroundings, fragrant gardens, the Rhode Island shore, all rolled together in one enchanted evening. That's what you'll find at **Theatre-By-The-Sea,** 364 Cards Pond Road, Matunuck, South Kingstown, where professionally produced musicals and plays are performed in a 1933 theater that's on the National Register of Historic Places. Just steps away from the theater, you'll find casual dining at the **Seahorse Grill,** housed inside an original 1929 inn and tavern. For a schedule of summer shows and ticket information, call (401) 782-8587.

Westerly

Atlantic Beach Park, 321-328 Atlantic Avenue, (401) 322-0504, carousel, bumper cars, and other family amusements
Dunes Park Beach, north end of Atlantic Avenue, (401) 596-1543, small, family-oriented beach
Misquamicut State Beach, 257 Atlantic Avenue, (401) 596-9097 (summer), (401) 322-8910 (winter), Rhode Island's most popular beach area
Napatree Point, Bay Street, Watch Hill, (401) 596-1543, primarily a walker's beach, limited parking
Watch Hill Beach, Bay Street, Watch Hill, (401) 596-1543, crowded family beach near the historic Flying Horse Carousel
Westerly Town Beach, Atlantic Avenue, (401) 596-1543, picnicking facilities available

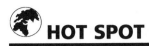

HOT SPOT

The **Flying Horse Carousel** off Route 1A in the village of Watch Hill in Westerly is both a National Historic Landmark and a lot of fun. This is the only surviving example of a flying horse carousel in America, where the horses are not attached to the floor but instead are suspended from a center frame and swing out as if flying. Only children are permitted to ride.

Beyond Beaches

Ready to put the boogie board aside and get to know the "other" South County? Start by introducing yourself to the first Rhode Islanders, the Native American tribes that populated the area for hundreds of years before Europeans arrived in the 1630s. The **Tomaquag Indian Memorial Museum,** 390 Summit Road, Exeter, is open Monday through Thursday afternoons and features local Native American artifacts and a gift shop where you can purchase items handmade by native peoples. In Charlestown, you'll find the **Narragansett Indian Reservation,** (401) 364-1100, where you can visit the **Royal Indian Burial Ground,** the resting place for the Narragansett tribe's chiefs and their families, and the Narragansett Indian Longhouse, the tribe's historic meeting place.

Fast forward to the Colonial era, 1678 to be exact, by visiting **Smith's Castle,** 55 Richard Smith Drive, North Kingstown, (401) 294-3521, one of the nation's oldest plantation houses. Hours vary seasonally, so call ahead. While you're in North Kingstown and your mindset is still on the Colonial period, you might also stop at **Casey Farm,** 2325 Boston Neck Road, (401) 295-1030, another plantation farm that dates to about 1750. Tours of the working farm are available Tuesdays, Thursdays, and Saturdays in season. And don't miss the **birthplace of Gilbert Stuart,** 815 Gilbert Stuart Road, (401) 294-3001. Our images of George

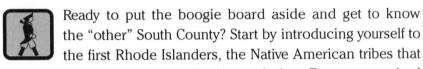

Washington are shaped largely by the work of this famous Rhode Island-born portrait painter. The home is open Thursday through Monday from April until October.

FAST FACT

There are several tales of Rhode Island vampires, but none more enduring than that of Mercy Brown. You can visit her gravesite in Exeter's Historical Cemetery No. 22 behind Chestnut Hill Baptist Church. According to stories, Brown died in 1892 at the age of nineteen, shortly following the deaths of her mother and sister. Her brother, Edwin, was also ill, and in an effort to save him from what appeared to be a curse on the family, the women's bodies were exhumed. Mercy's body had shifted inside the coffin, it appeared, and fresh blood was present in her heart, which was burned upon a nearby rock before Mercy was reburied. Feeding poor Edwin the heart ashes, alas, did not save him—he died two months later. But Mercy's legend lives on.

The **South County Museum at Canonchet Farm,** Boston Neck Road, Narragansett, (401) 783-5400, exhibits more than 20,000 artifacts of life in Rhode Island from the eighteenth to the early twentieth centuries in themed settings—a general store, country kitchen, Victorian bedroom, schoolroom, and working print shop, carpentry shop, blacksmith shop, and farm.

For a look at the turn-of-the-century social scene, visit the **Towers,** Ocean Road, Narragansett, (401) 782-0657. This landmark is the last remaining section of the glorious Narragansett Pier Casino that was at the center of the summer social season from the time it was built in 1883 until its untimely destruction by fire in 1900. Designed by famed architect Stanford White, the former playground of South County's swanky summer set is currently undergoing restoration. A visitor's center, gallery, and exhibit area are open on the first floor, and tours are available in the summer by appointment only.

Still not ready to go back to the beach? Jet over to the **Quonset Aviation Museum,** 488 Eccleston Avenue, North Kingstown, (401) 294-9540, a volunteer-run habitat for retired, historic aircraft that is open Friday through Sunday. Or hit the water without getting wet by taking a sightseeing cruise aboard the 149-passenger Southland Riverboat, which departs from State Pier #3, Port of Galilee, Narragansett, (401) 783-2954.

HOT SPOT

A single admission price allows you to ride all day at the **Enchanted Forest,** Route 3, Hopkinton, (401) 539-7711, an amusement park geared toward younger children that is open daily mid-May through September.

Dining Highlights

The only thing better than eating lobster on a vacation at the Rhode Island shore is eating an excessive amount of lobster! You can do just that at **Nordic Lodge,** 178 East Pasquiset Trail, Charlestown, (401) 783-4515, home of the Giant Viking Buffet featuring all-you-can-eat lobster and much more for about the price you'd pay for just two whole lobsters elsewhere. While you're there, be sure to sign the restaurant's guest book, as annual mailings include a free live-lobster-to-go offer. Nordic Lodge is open seasonally, as are many of the restaurants in this region.

For casual outdoor dining accompanied by the sounds of crashing surf, try **Paddy's Restaurant,** 155 Atlantic Avenue, Westerly, (401) 596–2610, or do as Rhode Island diners have done for more than eighty years—enjoy a traditional Rhode Island Shore dinner at **Aunt Carrie's Seafood Restaurant,** 1240 Ocean Road, Narragansett, (401) 783-7930. At **Champlin's Restaurant,** Great Island Road, Galilee, Narragansett, (401) 783-3152, you can watch fishermen unloading the day's catch—which might just become your supper.

For a touch of romance, mosey over to the **Grille at the Watch Hill Inn,** 38 Bay Street, Watch Hill, (401) 348-6300 or (800) 356-9314, where you can watch the sunset from one of three outdoor dining decks while sipping tropical beverages and feasting on lobster in the rough, or reserve a quiet table at the intimate **Spain Restaurant & Lounge,** 1144 Ocean Road, Narragansett, (401) 783-9770, a perennial favorite serving seafood and traditional Spanish dishes.

The **Coast Guard House,** 40 Ocean Road, Narragansett, (401) 789-0700, is known for its seaside Sunday brunches. Housed in an historic former Coast Guard lifesaving station that dates to 1888, the restaurant also serves lunch and dinner and hosts live entertainment on Friday and Saturday nights.

TRAVEL TIP

The first Wednesday of each month is **"Opening Night Westerly."** From 5 to 8 P.M., downtown nonprofit and commercial galleries and studios host opening receptions where you can meet artists, view their works, and enjoy refreshments and entertainment. For more information, call (401) 348-0733 or (401) 596-2877.

Shopping Discoveries

Are you dreaming of the quintessential "Main Street New England" shopping experience—tree-lined streets, white picket fences, gardens, old homes, church spires, and a snug harbor forming the backdrop for antique shops brimming with unique treasures, boutiques with clever wares, art galleries, gourmet food shops, and outdoor cafés? Then close your eyes, and don't open them until you get to **Wickford Village.** Okay, that might not be feasible, but the good news is that the picture-perfect image in your head is not at all far from the reality that you'll find at this historic North Kingstown village that is home to more than forty shops, galleries, and restaurants. For more information, call the Wickford Village Association at (877) 295-7200 or visit their Web site at *www.wickfordvillage.org*.

Another one-of-a-kind shopping experience awaits at the **Fantastic Umbrella Factory,** 4920 Old Post Road, Charlestown, (401) 364-6616, a nineteenth-century farmyard that is now home to a Main Store featuring eclectic gifts, Dave's Den featuring incense and tapestries and other mystical miscellany, an art gallery, a crafts cooperative, a natural foods restaurant, and a perennial garden.

In Exeter, you'll find New England's largest year-round **Christmas House,** 1557 Ten Rod Road, (401) 397-4255, surrounded by 23 acres of scenic woodland.

FAST FACT

Rhode Island's Narragansett Native American tribe originally named the quahog "poquahock," from which "quahog" evolved. Quahogs are found just below the surface of the sand between high and low tide and can be harvested by hand or rake. A quahog that is 1 to 2½ inches long is called a littleneck; a 2½- to 3-inch quahog is a cherrystone; and a 3-inch or larger quahog is a chowder. They're delicious raw, steamed in their shells, and in chowder and clam cakes.

Newport

NEWPORT'S POPULATION QUADRUPLES EACH YEAR between May and September. That alone speaks to the enormous popularity of this New England destination that has been called America's first resort.

Newport was founded in 1639 at the southern tip of Aquidneck Island, and by the 1700s, it was already one of the American colonies' most important ports. Unfortunately, the British realized this and, in 1776, they blockaded the port and occupied the town. By the time Newport was "freed" in 1780 by a fleet of French ships enlisted to support the colonies' cause in the American Revolution, the port city was in ruins. It would never recover its status as a thriving seaport.

No need to cry the blues for Newport, though. Surrounded by water on three sides and blessed with gentle, cooling breezes in the summer, it was discovered a century later by the nation's "aristocracy"—the Astors and Vanderbilts and other wealthy capitalists who transformed Newport into their own summer playground. Newport's Gilded Age was one in which its socially elite temporary residents continually strove to outdo each other by building larger, more ornate "cottages" and by hosting more and more lavish parties.

Today, Newport still knows how to celebrate summer, and the incomparable mansions that once were the setting for the grandest of events open their doors to tourists for a gander at the lifestyle of a bygone era. The summer season in Newport is packed with music festivals, yachting events, nightlife, and opportunities to see and be seen at the town's delightful shops and eateries and to stroll along the Cliff Walk, the only obstacle between the mansions and the churning sea. But Newport's tourism industry has made a conscious effort, too, to expand its "peak" season beyond that May to September timeframe. December is another particularly busy month, as Santa arrives by Coast Guard cutter and the Newport mansions dress up in fabulous holiday fashion. A month-long schedule of "Haunted Newport" events also has made October an appealing month for a trip to the "City by the Sea"–if you dare.

HOT SPOT

Have you ever dreamed of being a lighthouse keeper? Newport's **Rose Island Lighthouse,** built in 1870 and refurbished in 1993, is now a museum open to the public by day and a fantasy getaway for lighthouse lovers at night. The two keepers' bedrooms are available for overnight stays year-round. Or, you and three friends could be "Keeper for a Week." Your "rent" would include daily work projects. For reservations, call ✆(401) 847-4242.

Lodging Options

Though you're not likely to find accommodations to rival those the Vanderbilts and Astors had when they visited Rhode Island, there are many elegant lodging options in Newport. The 237-room **Hotel Viking,** One Bellevue Avenue, ✆(401) 847-3300 or ✆(800) 556-7126, is listed on the National Register of Historic Places. It was built by 100 of Newport's wealthiest residents in the 1920s to accommodate their numerous guests and can now be your home base when you visit Newport's mansions. **Castle Hill Inn & Resort,** Ocean Drive, ✆(401) 849-3800 or ☏(888) 466-1355, is the former mansion home of Harvard marine biologist Alexander Agassiz. Built in 1874, the mansion-turned-inn has ten guest rooms and a roaring fireplace and counts among its famous former guests author Thornton Wilder, Grace Kelly, and Montgomery Clift. Additional rooms are available at neighboring **Harbor House,** and there are beach cottages with kitchens available, too. The **Francis Malbone House,** 392 Thames Street, ☏(401) 846-0392 or ☏(800) 846-0392, was built for shipping merchant Francis Malbone in 1760 by architect Peter Harrison—noted for his design of Newport's Touro Synagogue. The **George Champlin Mason House,** 31 Old Beach Road, ☏(401) 847-7081 or ☏(888) 834-708, an 1873 Victorian designed by the architect responsible for one of Newport's famous mansions, Chepstow, oozes romance with its working room fireplaces and antique canopied beds. **Cliffside Inn,** 2 Seaview Avenue, ☏(401) 847-1811 or ☏(800) 845-1811, is the former home of artist Beatrice Turner who painted more than 1,000 self-portraits, many of which can be seen throughout the inn—that is, if you can manage to pry your gaze away from the sumptuous spread set out each afternoon at tea time.

TRAVEL TIP

If you would just as soon avoid the crowds of summer, there's another "most wonderful time of the year" to visit Newport. Newport's famous, ostentatious mansions are even more lovely when adorned with lush greenery, baubles, and bows. The Preservation Society of Newport County, which operates many of these historic mansions, selects a few of its prized properties to decorate and open for holiday season tours each year, and other privately owned mansions get into the spirit, as well.

For something a bit less "fancy," the **Marriott** at 25 America's Cup Avenue, ☏(401) 849-1000, provides a convenient location from which to explore Newport's sights. A cozy **Courtyard**

by Marriott, 9 Commerce Drive, Middletown, (401) 849-8000, lies just outside town and offers particularly good off-season rates. The **1855 Marshall T. Slocum House Bed & Breakfast,** 29 Kay Street, (401) 841-5120 or (800) 372-5120, offers warm hospitality, a chill-beating fireplace in the parlor, and hearty breakfasts. No time for a dog of your own? Combine your love of canines with a getaway at the **Labrador House,** 15 Ayrault Street, (401) 849-8660, an 1880s Victorian that has four guest rooms and two resident yellow Labrador retrievers.

The sheer abundance of hotels, inns, and B&Bs in Newport can make selecting the perfect accommodations to suit your tastes a daunting task. Newport boasts more than 2,000 rooms and the largest number of individual inns and B&Bs in the United States. The good news is, help is available. **NIBBs**, a consortium of Newport Inns and Bed and Breakfasts, offers an online directory at *www.newportinns.com* to help you select one of the many cozy inns or hospitable bed and breakfasts for your stay. **Newport Reservations,** (800) 842-0102, is a free reservation service that can assist you in locating available rooms.

Keep in mind that, especially during peak season, it will likely be impossible to book a stay in Newport for just one weekend night. You need not necessarily allow that to thwart your quick getaway plans, though. Remember that Rhode Island is tiny—just 37 miles east to west and 48 miles north to south—so staying in another part of the state or even in neighboring Connecticut or Massachusetts may help you to get around this restriction imposed by many lodging establishments.

A Guide to the Newport Mansions

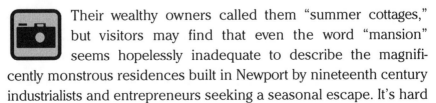

Their wealthy owners called them "summer cottages," but visitors may find that even the word "mansion" seems hopelessly inadequate to describe the magnificently monstrous residences built in Newport by nineteenth century industrialists and entrepreneurs seeking a seasonal escape. It's hard to imagine living in these splendid palaces, much less living in them for just a few short months each year.

There are so many mansions to see that plotting a plan of action can be a bit daunting. Here's a quick description of each mansion that is open to the public, listed in a suggested order from those that you simply must see to those that you might tour on another visit to Newport. Those marked with an asterisk (*) are under the umbrella of the **Newport Preservation Society,** (401) 847-1000, which offers discounted, multiproperty admission passes that are available at each mansion it operates.

The Astors' Beechwood Mansion

580 Bellevue Avenue, (401) 846-3772

www.astors-beechwood.com

Built in 1851 and bought in 1881 by William Backhouse Astor and his wife, Caroline, the undisputed queen of American society, this Victorian mansion was the setting for the 1911 wedding of their son, John Jacob Astor IV, who later embarked on an ill-fated honeymoon aboard the *Titanic.* Today, visitors to Beechwood return to the year 1891 and are welcomed as guests of *the* Mrs. Astor by actors and actresses in period character and costume.

The Breakers*

Ochre Point Avenue, (401) 847-1000

This seventy-room villa was completed in 1895 for Cornelius Vanderbilt II, heir to the family shipping and railroad fortune. It was designed by Richard Morris Hunt to resemble a sixteenth-century Italian palace. This is the grandest of all of the Newport mansions.

Rough Point

Bellevue Avenue, (401) 849-7300

The "newest" old mansion in Newport. Opened to the public in 2000, the dramatic, Gothic-style home was originally built in 1889 for Frederick W. Vanderbilt and was the home of tobacco heiress Doris Duke until her death in 1993. Rough Point houses one of the area's most significant private art collections. This mansion is not accessible by car. Shuttles depart from the Newport Gateway Information Center, 23 America's Cup Avenue.

Marble House*

Bellevue Avenue

This "summer cottage" was built between 1888 and 1892 for William K. Vanderbilt and his wife, who envisioned this as her "temple to the arts" in America. Of the $11 million spent on construction, $7 million went toward the purchase of the 500,000 cubic feet of marble that inspire the mansion's name.

Green Animals*

Cory's Lane, Portsmouth, (401) 683-1267

Located just outside of Newport, Green Animals is worth the trip to see its amazing topiary gardens. There are eighty topiary figures including geometric shapes, ornamental designs, and over twenty birds and animals including an elephant, a unicorn, and a giraffe. The Victorian country house that was home to the Brayton family features a collection of antique toys and dollhouses.

Belcourt Castle

657 Bellevue Avenue, (401) 846-0669

www.belcourtcastle.com

This sixty-room mansion was built for Oliver Hazard Perry Belmont, who inherited his fortune from his father, and served as the Rothschild banking representative in America. It was designed by Richard Morris Hunt to resemble a Louis XII-style castle. While Belcourt Castle remains privately owned, it is open daily for guided tours.

Chateau-Sur-Mer*

Bellevue Avenue, (401) 847-1000

This Victorian mansion was built in 1852 and enlarged in 1872 for retired banker William S. Wetmore. Until the Vanderbilts arrived on the social scene in the 1890s, this Victorian villa was Newport's most palatial residence.

Rosecliff*

Bellevue Avenue (401) 847-1000

This structure was completed in 1902 for Theresa Fair Oelrichs, daughter of one of the discoverers of the Comstock Silver Lode. Designed by Stanford White of the famed architectural firm McKim, Mead, and White to resemble the neoclassical Grand Trianon at Versailles, it houses Newport's largest ballroom.

The Elms*

Bellevue Avenue

Built in 1901 as a summer vacation home for Pennsylvania coal magnate Edward J. Berwind, it is a nearly perfect replica of a circa-1750 Parisian chateau.

Chepstow*

Narragansett Avenue

Chepstow was designed by local Newport architect George Champlin Mason and built in 1860. It houses the possessions of the Morris family, which acquired the property in 1911. Tours are by appointment only from May through October.

Kingscote*

Bellevue Avenue

This Gothic Revival-style mansion was the first Newport "cottage" built exclusively for summer use. Completed in 1841 for George Noble Jones, a Georgia planter, it was sold in the 1860s to Newport China trade merchant William Henry King and christened Kingscote. His collection of Oriental furnishings remains on view inside the house.

HOT SPOT

Don't let the name fool you. Sure, **Newport Grand Jai Alai,** 150 Admiral Kalbfus Road/Route 138, (401) 849-5000 or (800) 451-2500, features live jai alai action and wagering. In fact, the record for throwing a pelota—188 miles per hour—was set here in 1979. But this gaming and entertainment facility also offers a state-of-the-art simulcast theater with eleven giant screens and eighty individual televisions where you can watch and bet on thoroughbred, harness, and greyhound racing and jai alai year round. You'll also find hundreds of video poker, blackjack, and slot machines inside gaming rooms designed to reflect the opulent décor of the Newport mansions. Admission is free; you must be at least eighteen to get in.

More Than Mansions

Though the mansions, of course, are a must-see, there's so much more to do in historic Newport. At the **International Tennis Hall of Fame,** 194 Bellevue Avenue, (401) 849-3990, the legends of tennis are immortalized. This is the world's largest tennis museum, and it's also the spot where the first American tennis National Championships were held in 1881. The complex also features thirteen grass tennis courts, and they're open to the public for play in season. Reservations can be made at the **Pro Shop,** (401) 846-0642.

On all but the bitterest of cold days, you'll want to meander along the **Cliff Walk,** the three and one-half-mile National Recreation Trail that provides breathtaking views of Newport's shoreline and of the historic Bellevue Avenue mansions. Development of the Cliff Walk began in the 1880s, and while at times there have been disputes waged by homeowners along the trail, its public access has been preserved. The walk starts at the western end of Easton's Beach at Memorial Boulevard and continues south with major entrance points at Narragansett Avenue, Webster Street, Sheppard Avenue, Ruggles Avenue, Marine Avenue, Ledge Road, and Bellevue Avenue at the east end of Bailey's Beach. While the trail makes for a quite leisurely walk, you'll still want to be sure to wear comfortable shoes and to watch where you're going. The **Newport Historical Society**, (401) 841-8770, conducts walking tours of the Cliff Walk Saturday mornings at 10 A.M. May through September.

Fort Adams State Park, Harrison Avenue, (401) 847-2400, was the second largest bastioned fort in the U.S. from 1799 to 1845. Volunteers and staff of the Fort Adams Trust, (401) 841-0707, conduct guided tours of the 21-acre stone fort daily from 10 A.M. until 4 P.M. on the hour from mid-May through mid-October. The park is open free and is where you'll find famous events such as the Newport Jazz and Folk Festivals, plus a beach, picnic areas, fishing, a boat ramp, a Museum of Yachting, and ferry departures to Block Island. Tickets for festival events are generally available through **Ticketmaster,** (401) 331-2211.

Newport is also home to America's oldest synagogue. **Touro Synagogue,** 60 Touro Street, (401) 847-4794, established by Spanish and Portuguese Jews fleeing religious persecution, was dedicated in 1763 and is now a National Historic Site. Designed by Peter Harrison, it is renowned for its architecture. Free tours are available most days except for Saturdays and Jewish holidays. Services are open to the public as well.

In nearby Middletown, flock to the **Norman Bird Sanctuary,** 583 Third Beach Road, (401) 846-2577, a 450-acre preserve that offers 7 miles of walking trails and a small natural history museum. Then flit on over to the Butterfly Zoo at the **Newport Butterfly Farm,** 1038 Aquidneck Avenue, (401) 849-9519, a screened greenhouse where you can mingle with gorgeous specimens from all over the world. Another popular Middletown spot is **Purgatory Chasm,** Purgatory Road, (401) 846-2119, a narrow cleft in the rock ledges at Easton Point, which is a scenic Narragansett Bay overlook—don't forget your camera.

TRAVEL TIP

What better place to learn to sail than the "Sailing Capital of the World"—**Newport. Newport Sailing School and Tours, Ltd.,** Goat Island Marina, Dock A5, (401) 848-2266, offers a thirteen-hour, one weekend basic course for beginners. Instruction includes sailing terminology, boating rules, seamanship, proper tacking procedure, jibbing, proper landing procedure, water safety, knot tying, rigging, tides, man-overboard drills, mooring, and sailing a prescribed course. Intermediate and advanced courseware available. Visit the Newport Sailing School online at *www.newportsailing.com*.

Dining Highlights

Just when lunch or dinner time rolls around and you think you'll get a brief respite from the rigors of having to decide what to do next in Newport, you'll find that the local restaurant selection once again leaves you with decisions, decisions, decisions.

Let's start with your historic options. The **White Horse Tavern,** 26 Marlborough Street, (401) 849-3600, is America's oldest continuously operating tavern—it's been hosting guests since 1687. But don't let the tavern moniker and the restaurant's rustic New England appearance fool you. This is one of Newport's most sophisticated dining enclaves featuring cuisine that highlights fresh local ingredients. Jackets are required at dinner, and reservations are a must. **Canfield House,** 5 Memorial Boulevard, (401) 847-0416, is a fine restaurant, a pub, and a cigar-friendly piano bar, all under the roof of a former Victorian gambling casino that is on the National Register of Historic Places. **La Petite Auberge,** 19 Charles Street, (401) 849-6669, serves classic French cuisine inside a historic 1714 house. **Vanderbilt Hall,** 41 Mary Street, (401) 846-6200, was built by Alfred Vanderbilt in 1909 and given to the town of Newport for use as a YMCA. Now it's an inn, but you don't have to be staying in one of the fifty guest rooms to enjoy a memorable dining experience in this historic edifice.

For a completely out of the ordinary dining experience, book passage aboard the **Newport Dinner Train,** 19 America's Cup Avenue, (401) 841-8700. You'll enjoy a lovely meal served in a luxury dining car while you travel the rails for twenty-two miles along the scenic shore of Narragansett Bay.

If you eat chowder in only one place, make it the **Black Pearl,** Bannister's Wharf, (401) 846-5264. This crowded, noisy, casual tavern is an excellent choice for lunch or a late-night munch. For a traditional New England lobster dinner, the **Sea Fare's American Café,** Brick Market Place, (401) 849-9188, is always a solid choice. **Scales & Shells Restaurant,** 527 Thames Street, (401) 846-3474, is another favorite with seafood lovers.

For upscale cuisine in a fun, furry environment, try **Cheeky Monkey**, 14 Perry Mill Wharf, (401) 845-9494. There's spicy food on the menu and live blues on stage at the **Newport Blues Café,** 286 Thames Street, (401) 841-5510. Or, if you prefer jazz, check out the funky atmosphere of the **Red Parrot,** 348 Thames Street, (401) 847-3800.

For local microbrews, you'll have to head to nearby Middletown, where you'll find the **Coddington Brewing Company**, 210 Coddington Highway, (401) 847-6690, which has pub fare and beers brewed on the premises. And while there's no restaurant there, beer fans will also want to visit and tour **Coastal Extreme Brewing Company,** 307 Oliphant Lane, (401) 849-5232, if they're in Middletown on a Friday evening. Their Newport Storm beer is served at many Newport restaurants.

If your taste buds are still torn, plan your trip to coincide with the annual Taste of Rhode Island waterfront festival held in Newport each September, when you can sample it all!

Shopping Discoveries

Whether you're in search of a souvenir for yourself, something to wear to dinner, an antique treasure, or a perfect gift made in Rhode Island, Newport's three centrally located waterfront shopping areas, **Bannister's Wharf** and **Bowen's Wharf,** both located off America's Cup Avenue, and the **Brick Marketplace** between Thames Street and America's Cup Avenue, won't disappoint.

Bowen's Wharf has a special charm with its cobblestone and brick walkways, boat docks, raw bars, and blend of eighteenth-, nineteenth-, and twentieth-century architecture. You'll find Newport's oldest fine arts gallery here—the **Roger King Gallery of Fine Art,** 21 Bowen's Wharf, (401) 847-4359, which exhibits an ever-changing selection of New England regional and marine art. Scrimshaw artist Brian Kiracofe's store, **Newport Scrimshanders,** 14 Bowen's Wharf, (401) 849-5680 or (800) 635-5234, features works by thirty American artisans. At **Thames Glass Inc.,** 688 Thames Street, (401) 846-0576, you can watch skilled glassblowers create exquisite, one-of-a-kind pieces and bring home a Newport original.

Antiques addicts will want to explore the shops along Spring Street, and if you're a lover of old houses, don't miss **Aardvark Antiques,** 449 & 475 Thames Street, (401) 849-7233, purveyors of architectural and decorative elements salvaged from old houses.

You'll find gift shops at many of the Newport mansions as well. While selections are a bit pricey, you may just find a souvenir of one of your favorite Newport mansion memories.

If the perfect gift still eludes you, pop into **Lobstair,** 78 Clinton Street, (401) 846-0583 or (888) 456-9983, and overnight a live lobster to someone you love.

Block Island

YOU DON'T HAVE TO FLY AWAY TO AN ISLAND in the South Pacific to get away from it all. The same kind of hurry- and hassle-free escape awaits New England travelers if they choose Block Island as their destination. The tiny, pork chop-shaped island is just 10 square miles in size, but its natural beauty and unique variety of flora, fauna, and feathered creatures are unparalleled.

The Narragansetts lived here when Dutch navigator Adrian Block, for whom the island is named, stumbled across it in 1614. They called their home "Manisses," the "Island of the Little God." Permanent settlers began arriving in 1661. Today, the island's permanent population numbers about 800. Its 120 kindergarten through grade 12 students share a single school. But the population is augmented astronomically by tourists—about 15,000 visit each day during the high season.

The Nature Conservancy has called Block Island "one of the twelve last great places in the Western Hemisphere." Environmental preservation efforts began in earnest with the formation in 1971 of the Block Island Conservancy. Today, approximately a quarter of the island is protected as open space. Because it is home to more than forty species of rare and endangered plants and animals, visitors must be mindful to protect this fragile environment as they enjoy Block Island's beaches, boating, bicycling, fishing, lighthouses, and sweeping views of the sea from the clay cliffs at Mohegan Bluffs.

Getting to Block Island

Block Island is located twelve miles off the coast of Rhode Island. It is not connected to the mainland and is accessible only by air or by boat.

The **Block Island Ferry** is operated by the Interstate Navigation Company, ☏(401) 783-4613. Year-round service is available between Point Judith, Rhode Island, and Block Island. In the summer, ferries also depart for Block Island from New London, Connecticut. The trip takes about an hour from Point Judith, two hours from New London. Call for scheduled departure times, which vary seasonally, and pricing information. You should plan to arrive about an hour before your scheduled departure to allow ample time to park and board. Passenger tickets may be purchased on board the ferry.

It is extraordinarily difficult to take a car to Block Island. All vehicle reservations need to be booked and paid for in advance by telephone. Vehicle reservations for summer weekends and holidays should be booked four to five months in advance. Your reservation will be forfeited if you do not check your car in at the ferry ticket window at least one hour prior to departure. Reservations are not necessary for passengers, bicycles, and motorcycles.

Without a vehicle reservation, you can inquire about traveling standby on your date of departure. However, even if you manage to secure a standby slot, you will not be guaranteed a return reservation.

Island Hi-Speed Ferry, ☏(877) 733-9425, will get you from Galilee to Block Island in just thirty minutes. The ferry operates from early June through mid-October and provides passenger service only. Call ahead for a schedule and rates. Reservations are recommended, and tickets are nonrefundable.

New England Airlines, ☏(401) 466-5881 or ☏(800) 243-2460, provides air service between Westerly State Airport and Block

Island. The round-trip flight takes about twelve minutes, and adult airfare is about $70.

Action Airlines at Groton/New London Airport in Groton, Connecticut, (800) 243-8623, offers single- and twin-engine charter service to Block Island.

TRAVEL TIP

If you want to search for lighthouses on your own, get a copy of the Rhode Island Official State Map, which is available free at tourism centers statewide or by calling (401) 222-2601 or (888) U-UNWIND. The map pinpoints the locations of all the state's lighthouse treasures. Keep in mind that some of these structures are privately owned and may not be easily accessible. You'll also find helpful information on Rhode Island lighthouses online at the New England Lighthouses Web site, *http://lighthouse.cc/ri.html*.

Lodging Options

Block Island may be small, but it's not lacking for lodgings. After all, the majority of folks on the island on any given day need a place to stay. About half of the inns and hotels on the island close during the off-season, but you'll find deals on rates at those that remain open November through March.

Grand Victorian hotels proliferate. The twenty-one-room **Atlantic Inn,** High Street, (401) 466-5883 or (800) 224-7422, is an 1879 Victorian inn situated on a six-acre hilltop retreat with fabulous ocean views. **Hotel Manisses,** Spring Street, (401) 466-2421 or (800) MANISSE, is a nineteenth-century Victorian hotel with seventeen rooms decked out in period furniture; four have whirlpool tubs. The **National Hotel,** Water Street, (401) 466-2901 or (800) 225-2449, is a circa 1888, forty-five-room Victorian inn listed on the National Register of Historic Places and famous for its porch, where you can spend a lazy afternoon watching boats on the harbor. The island's oldest and largest resort, **Spring House Hotel,** Spring Street, (401) 466-5844 or (800) 234-9263, dates to 1852 and has hosted famous guests including President Ulysses S. Grant, author Mark Twain, and singer Billy Joel, as well as a Kennedy family wedding. The historic hotel has forty-nine rooms, a wraparound porch, and panoramic views.

If you prefer to stay in a smaller B&B or inn, options are abundant as well. The **Barrington Inn,** Beach & Ocean Avenues, (401) 466-5510, is an 1886 farmhouse turned nonsmoking B&B featuring corner rooms with decks and views of New Harbor and the Great Salt Pond. **Beach House,** Corne Neck Road, (401) 466-2924, is the only B&B located right on Crescent Beach, and its four guest rooms all have ocean views. The **Rose Farm Inn,** Roslyn Road, (401) 466-2034, was once a farmhouse and is now a cheery bed and breakfast with rooms that feature canopied beds, whirlpool baths for two, and ocean views.

If you're looking for a very private retreat, you might want to consider renting a Block Island cottage or home for a week or longer. Ferreting out a suitable vacation rental can be a bit of a project, as most are rented independently by their owners. The Internet is a wonderful resource for researching available rental properties. Several useful Web sites are:

- **10K Vacation Rentals** *www.10kvacationrentals.com*
- **CyberRentals.com** *www.cyberrentals.com*
- **U.S. Resort & Cottage Registry** *www.cottages.org*

You might also want to try the **Bellevue House,** High Street, (401) 466-2912, which counts among its accommodations options not only B&B rooms but six rental cottages and apartments.

For Block Island hotel, inn, B&B, and cottage reservations assistance, contact **Block Island Holidays, Inc.,** (401) 466-3137 or (800) 905-0590, or Block Island Reservations, (401) 466-2605 or (800) 825-6254.

Island Enticements

While many New England destinations tempt travelers seeking pure relaxation with a myriad of sights to see and things to do, Block Island is truly a spot where you'll be content in doing something close to nothing. From lazing on the sandy beach that runs along the eastern coast of the island to rocking away an afternoon on the porch of your inn while you watch the ferry boats come and go, this island hideaway truly provides relief from modern living's frenzied pace.

That said, if you're ready for some recreation, you'll soon discover why Block Island is a favorite with walkers, cyclists, bird watchers, and other outdoor sports lovers. You'll find miles of walking trails at **Rodman's Hollow,** Cooneymus Road, (401) 466-2129, an Ice Age-carved glacial depression with rolling hills and scenic ocean vistas. Rodman's Hollow is situated along the 25-mile Greenway network of interconnecting trails that starts at the heart of the island near Beacon Hill and traverses public and private lands.

For the island's most picturesque views, you'll want to climb **Mohegan Bluffs,** Mohegan Trail, (401) 466-5009. These clay cliffs soar to more than 200 feet above the shimmering sea. A staircase is available to facilitate your climb and descent. While you're there, visit Southeast Light, one of two lighthouses on the island. Built in 1875, erosion jeopardized its position on the edge of the bluffs until 1993, when the Victorian brick structure was moved inland. Block Island's other lighthouse, **North Light,** Corn Neck Road, (401) 466-2129, houses a maritime environmental center and museum and is open daily. Be prepared, as it's quite a hike to reach this light.

Intrigued by the island's unique history? The **Block Island Historical Society,** Old Town Road, (401) 466-2481, is open daily from June through September and exhibits historical artifacts that tell the island's tale. If you're traveling with little ones, plan a visit to the **Manisses Animal Farm** on the grounds of the **1661 Inn** and the **Hotel Manisses,** One Spring Street, (401) 466-2421, where you can pay a call on exotic animals including emus, llamas, and fainting goats, and visit a petting zoo, too.

HOT SPOT

If the salty air and ocean breezes have whetted your appetite to learn more about Rhode Island's yachting heritage, visit **Herreshoff Marine Museum and America's Cup Hall of Fame,** One Burnside Street, Bristol, (401) 253-5000, about 15 miles from Newport. The Herreshoff Manufacturing Company in Bristol built eight consecutive America's Cup-winning yachts between 1893 and 1934 and the first torpedo boats for the U.S. Navy. Visit this museum between May and October for a glimpse of forty classic sailing and power yachts built between 1859 and 1947, plus photographs and memorabilia that commemorate the America's Cup and the "golden age of yachting."

Dining Highlights

Savor the flavors of Block Island during a four-course dinner served in the dining room at the **Atlantic Inn,** High Street, (401) 466-5883, where dishes feature fresh herbs and vegetables from the inn's garden. President Bill Clinton and his family chose the Atlantic Inn for dinner on a 1997 visit to the island. Or, for something lighter, tapas and cocktail service are available on the wraparound verandah.

The **Hotel Manisses,** Spring Street, (401) 466-2836, offers a variety of dining experiences, from the sophisticated cuisine and romantic atmosphere of the main dining room to the casual ambience and diverse menu selections of the Gatsby Room to the flaming coffees, cognacs, and other after-dinner drinks served in the Upstairs Parlor, where you can delight in simple conversation or even play checkers or chess.

Can't stand to spend a moment indoors while you're on this

enchanted island? You'll find outdoor dining overlooking the harbor at **Finn's,** Water Street, (401) 466-2473, which is also a fish market, so you're sure to find the freshest of seafood on the menu. You can even eat breakfast outdoors on the harbor-view deck at **Ernie's Old Harbour Restaurant,** Water Street, (401) 466-2473. There's also an outdoor dining terrace at **Harborside Inn,** Water Street, (401) 466-5504 or (800) 892-2022, where you can feast on an expansive breakfast buffet in the morning, savor the island's finest chowder—it's won the coveted First Place Award in the annual Block Island Chowder Cook-off for three consecutive years—at lunchtime, and select from local seafood, homemade pastas, beef, veal, and poultry as the dinner hour rolls around.

The wait may be long, but you may just find that the portion size makes it all worthwhile when you join the throngs at **Eli's,** 456 Chapel Street, (401) 466-5230, for pasta, grinders, and a few menu surprises. This unassuming restaurant is popular with natives and tourists alike.

Shopping Discoveries

You probably came to Block Island to unwind, not to engage in retail pursuits. Still, you may be glad to know, especially on a rainy day, that there are some pleasant shops to explore on this tiny island.

Block Island's main shopping areas are **Dodge** and **Water Streets**. You'll find an eclectic selection of dolls, Victoriana, and locally made products at **Scarlet Begonia,** Dodge Street, (401) 466-5024. If you fall in love with the Maine- and Rhode Island–made furniture at **Red Herring,** 232 Water Street, (401) 466-2540, no worries. They'll arrange shipping for you.

The **Book Nook Bookstore,** Water Street, (401) 466-2993, has been an institution on Block Island for more than 25 years. It's a great place to pop in and pick up a beach read. And, if it's simply impossible for you to get away from it all on vacation, if you call ahead, they'll have the newspapers you need to stay "tuned in" in stock and on reserve for you for the duration of your stay.

Want to support the work of Block Island artists and craftspeople? The **Spring Street Gallery,** Spring Street, (401) 466-5374, represents products made by creative and entrepreneurial islanders.

Once you return home, if you find yourself longing for the scents and warm sensations of Block Island, order natural bath and body products crafted by island herbalist Johanna Ross from natural island ingredients online at *www.thymeandagainherbs.com* or by calling (401) 466-5563.

Itineraries

PERSONAL ITINERARY NOTES

A SHORT AND SWEET SUMMER HOLIDAY

Day One Head straight to the state's summertime playground, Newport, and tour one or two of the town's historic mansions on your first morning. In the afternoon, view several other stately homes from the outside as you meander along the Cliff Walk. In the evening, picnic at **Fort Adams State Park,** or feast on Rhode Island clam chowder and other seafood delights at one of the restaurants along the waterfront.

Day Two Set the alarm for an early call the next morning and allow at least forty-five minutes for the drive to Galilee, where you can catch the **Island Hi-Speed Ferry,** ☏(877) 733-9425, which will whisk you over to Block Island in just thirty minutes. Rent a bicycle or moped and spend the day visiting the island's two historic lighthouses and enjoying its sandy beaches. Return to Newport in the evening and, if you're not thoroughly exhausted, kick back and listen to the cool sounds at the **Newport Blues Café,** 286 Thames Street, ☏(401) 841-5510.

Day Three On your last day in Rhode Island, visit the **International Tennis Hall of Fame,** 194 Bellevue Avenue, Newport, ☏(401) 849-3990, perhaps even playing a match yourself on the only championship grass courts open to the public in America–you'll need a reservation. If time permits, take a short drive in the afternoon to Middletown, where you can frolic with butterflies at the **Newport Butterfly Farm,** 594 Aquidneck Avenue, ☏(401) 849-9519, or hike the trails at the **Norman Bird Sanctuary,** 583 Third Beach Road, ☏(401) 846-2577, before heading for home.

RHODE ISLAND FOR LIGHTHOUSE LOVERS

Early A.M. Start your lighthouse tour at one of Rhode Island's most distinctive beacons, the octagonal Point Judith Light, located on Route 108 in Point Judith. Originally constructed of wood in 1810, the structure you'll see when you visit the grounds of this lighthouse today is the brownstone lighthouse that replaced the original light in 1857.

Late A.M. Just around the corner, you'll be able to board the **Block Island Ferry,** ✆(401) 783-4613, for a one-hour trip to Block Island, home to two historic lighthouses. Don't catch the ferry back until you've seen the lovely, red-brick **Southeast Light,** ✆(401) 466-5009, built high on the Mohegan Bluffs in 1875 and moved further inland for protection in 1993.

Early P.M. Ready for a brisk autumn walk? Block Island's other lighthouse, **North Light,** ✉ Corn Neck Road, ✆(401) 466-2129, is a bit of an uphill hike, but you won't want to miss the environmental center and museum at this still-active light built in 1867 at the island's northern tip.

Late P.M. Return to Point Judith and head north on Route 1A to Route 138 East. Cross the Jamestown Bridge, and when you reach Conanicut Island, head to the island's southern tip to see the **Beavertail Light,** ✆(401) 423-3270, located in Beavertail State Park at the end of Beavertail Road, where the grounds and a museum in the assistant keeper's house are open to the public. The original lighthouse was built on this site in 1749 and was only the third Atlantic coast lighthouse ever constructed. Today, you'll see sweeping views of Narragansett Bay when you visit the 1856 lighthouse, the third structure to stand on this site.

A FIVE-DAY FAMILY SUMMER SAMPLER

Day One Begin your Rhode Island visit with a relaxing day at **Misquamicut Beach,** 257 Atlantic Avenue, (401) 596-9097, in South Kingstown. The family will enjoy the surf and the games and amusements. If a quieter beach is more your speed, South County's seaside towns provide plenty of other options.

Day Two Head for Galilee in the morning and take the half-hour trip to Block Island aboard **Island Hi-Speed Ferry,** (877) 733-9425. One of the best ways to see this island's spectacular scenery is to rent bicycles—the whole island is ideal for cycling. Return to the mainland at the end of the day.

Day Three Spend the morning in Newport viewing the magnificent mansions from the three and one-half-mile **Cliff Walk**. Choose one or two that intrigue you and venture inside for a tour in the afternoon. Children might particularly like the Astors' **Beechwood,** 580 Bellevue Avenue, (401) 846-3772, where costumed guides play period roles.

Day Four Drive from Newport to Providence, stopping along the way to see the historic yachts at the **Herreshoff Marine Museum,** One Burnside Street, Bristol, (401) 253-5000, and perhaps **Bristol's Blithewold Mansion and Gardens,** 101 Ferry Road/Route 114, (401) 253-2707, as well. Take an evening gondola ride on the Woonasquatucket River in Providence from the urban park, **WaterPlace,** which is at the hub of the capital city. Call **La Gondola, Inc.,** (401) 421-8877, for reservations.

Day Five Spend the last day of your family road trip at the country's third oldest zoo, Providence's **Roger Williams Park Zoo,** 1000 Elmwood Avenue, (401) 785-3510, before bidding adieu to Rhode Island.

A ROMANTIC RHODE ISLAND WEEK FOR TWO

Day One Rhode Island is the perfect place to rekindle your relationship. Start your week of romance by taking a walking tour of Rhode Island's capital city, Providence. Enjoy a picnic lunch aboard a gondola departing from WaterPlace Park. Call **La Gondola, Inc.,** (401) 421-8877, for reservations. In the afternoon, visit **Roger Williams Park Zoo,** 1000 Elmwood Avenue, (401) 785-3510, or, during baseball season, cheer on the minor league Pawtucket Red Sox at their nearby home field, **McCoy Stadium,** (401) 724-7300. In the evening, dine at one of Providence's brewpubs or, for something more upscale, try the **Capital Grille,** (401) 521-5600, at the former Providence train station. Then, cuddle up on a comfy couch and enjoy an offbeat or foreign film at the **Cable Car Cinema,** 204 South Main Street, (401) 272-3970, where the popcorn is all you can eat!

Day Two Embark on a leisurely drive south from Providence along Narragansett Bay. Stop first in North Kingstown and visit historic **Smith's Castle,** 55 Richard Smith Drive, (401) 294-3521, where Rhode Island founder Roger Williams is known to have preached. Peruse the shops and old houses in **Wickford Village,** (877) 295-7200, in the afternoon, stopping for iced tea at an open-air café.

Day Three Ready for some relaxation? Select from South County's numerous beaches and spend the early part of the day bodysurfing or relaxing on the beach. Find time in the afternoon to visit the **Towers,** Ocean Road, Narragansett, (401) 782-0657, the last remnant of a turn-of-the century casino that was a popular spot with wealthy South County vacationers prior to its destruction by fire in 1900. Be sure to call ahead for an appointment.

Day Four Take the **Block Island Ferry,** (401) 783-4613, from Point Judith. Your car can go along if you've made a reservation well in advance, but you might prefer to explore the island by bicycle–maybe even a bicycle built for two! Return by ferry to Point Judith in the evening.

Day Five Drive to Newport on your fifth day. In the afternoon, walk along the three and a half mile Cliff Walk, scoping out the magnificent mansions and choosing the most intriguing to tour the next day. In the evening, picnic at Fort Adams State Park or plan an intimate dinner at America's oldest operating tavern, **White Horse Tavern,** 26 Marlborough Street, (401) 849-3600.

Day Six Tour one or two of Newport's historic mansions in the morning. In the afternoon, visit the **International Tennis Hall of Fame,** 194 Bellevue Avenue, Newport, (401) 849-3990. When dinnertime arrives, feed each other lobster drenched in butter at one of Newport's terrific seafood restaurants, then head to the **Red Parrot,** 348 Thames Street, (401) 847-3800, for a nightcap and jazz.

Day Seven Spend the morning of your last day at **Green Animals Topiary Garden,** Cory's Lane, Portsmouth, (401) 847-1000, marveling at the ornamental trees and breathing in the rich floral fragrance of the gardens. In the afternoon, walk through the **Norman Bird Sanctuary,** 583 Third Beach Road, Middletown, (401) 846-2577. Before you blow a kiss good-bye to the Ocean State, take in the view of Narragansett Bay one last time from **Purgatory Chasm,** Purgatory Road, Middletown, (401) 846-2119

PART IV

Massachusetts

Massachusetts

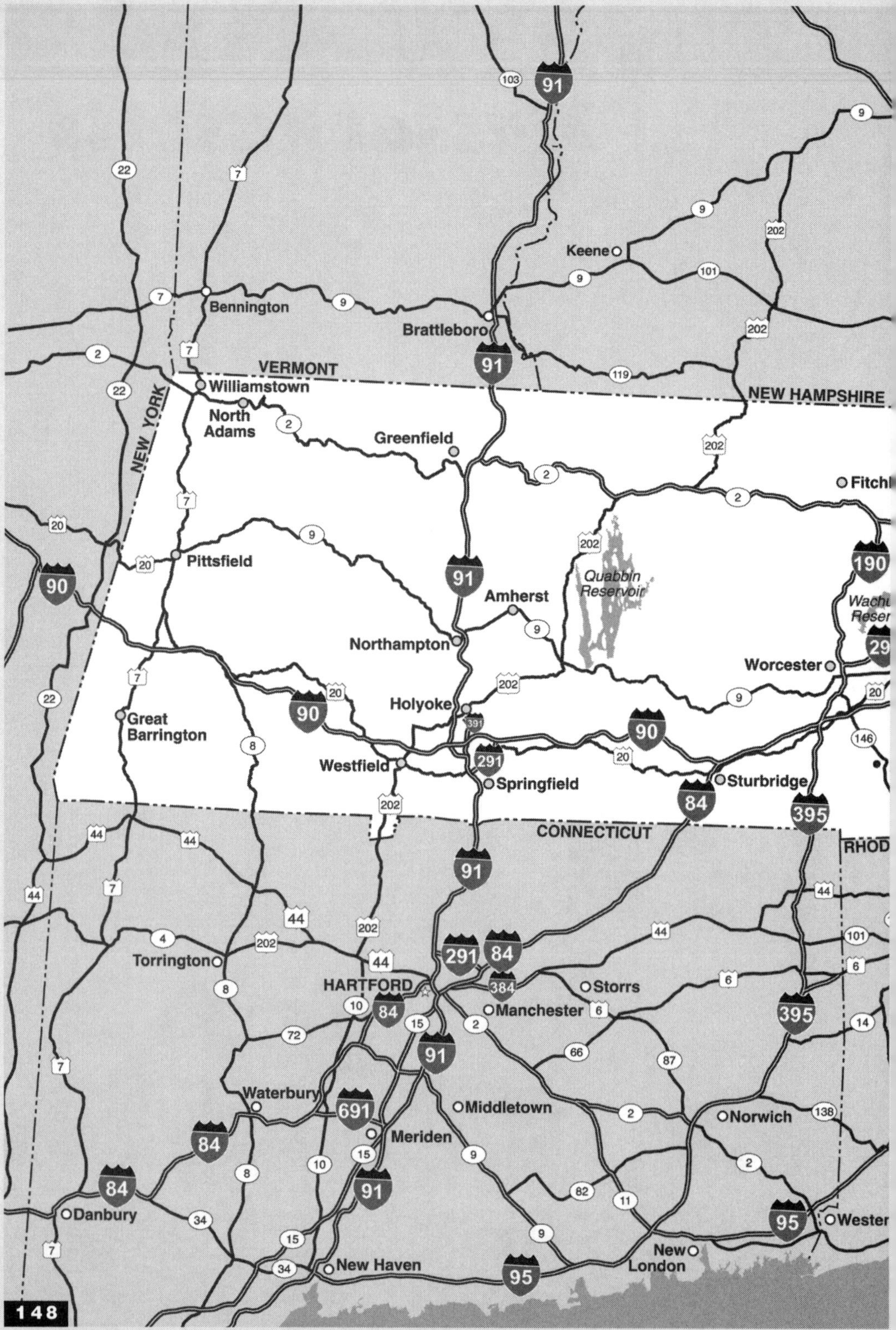

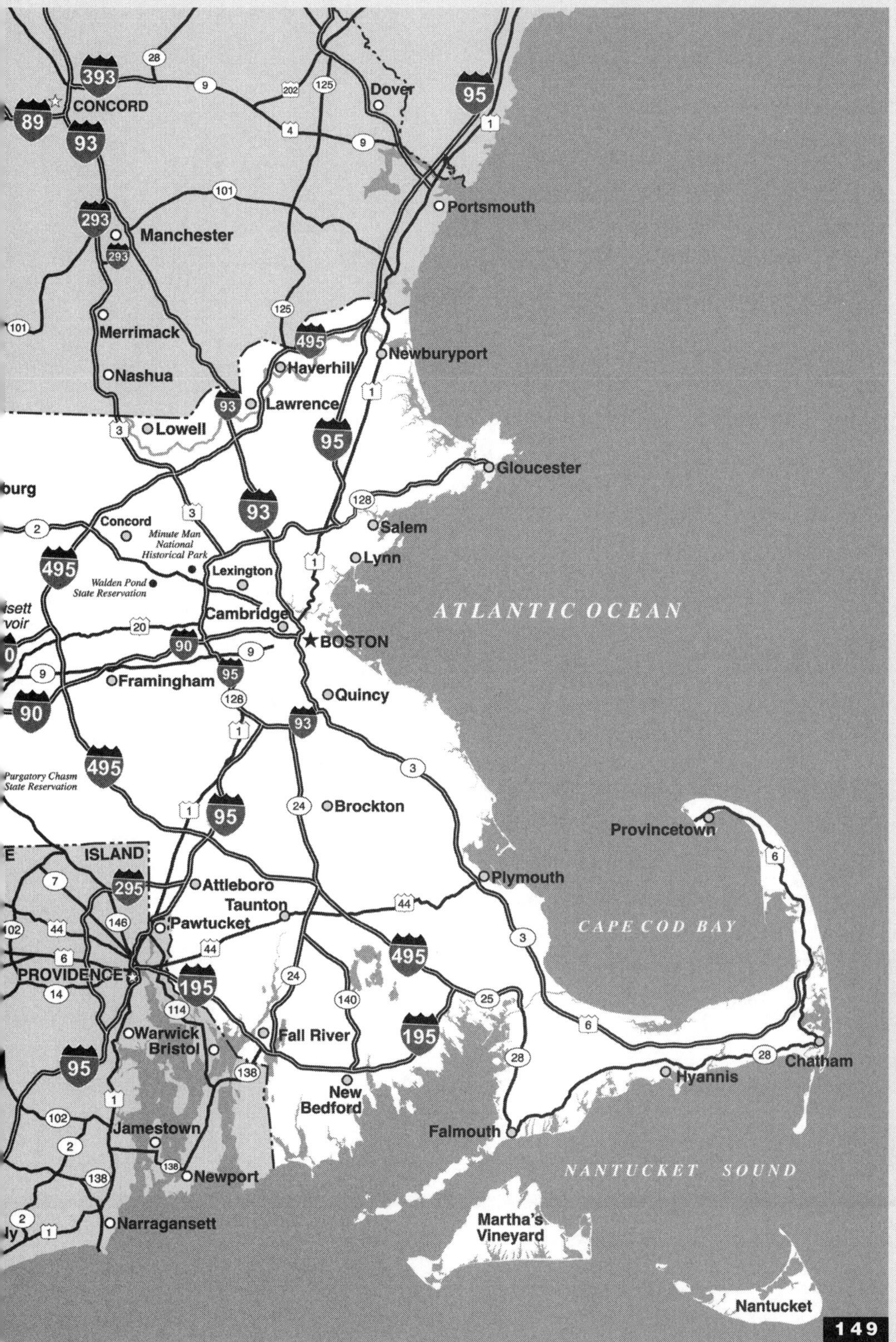
CONCORD
Dover
Portsmouth
Manchester
Merrimack
Nashua
Haverhill
Newburyport
Lawrence
Lowell
Gloucester
Concord
Minute Man National Historical Park
Salem
Lynn
Lexington
Walden Pond State Reservation
Cambridge
ATLANTIC OCEAN
BOSTON
Framingham
Quincy
Purgatory Chasm State Reservation
Brockton
Provincetown
ISLAND
Attleboro
Plymouth
Taunton
Pawtucket
CAPE COD BAY
PROVIDENCE
Warwick
Bristol
Fall River
Chatham
Hyannis
New Bedford
Falmouth
Jamestown
Newport
NANTUCKET SOUND
Narragansett
Martha's Vineyard
Nantucket

Boston and Cambridge, Massachusetts

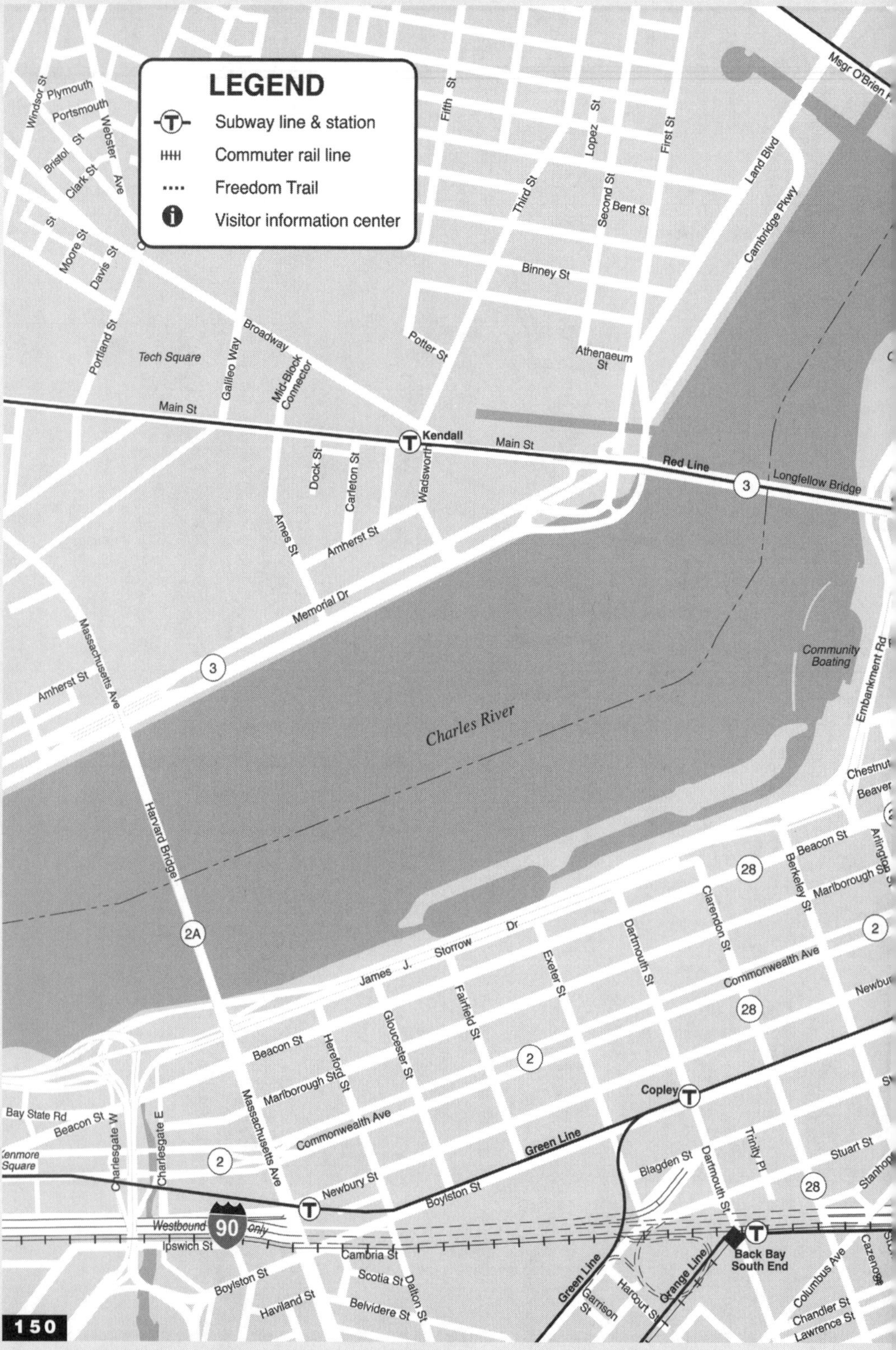

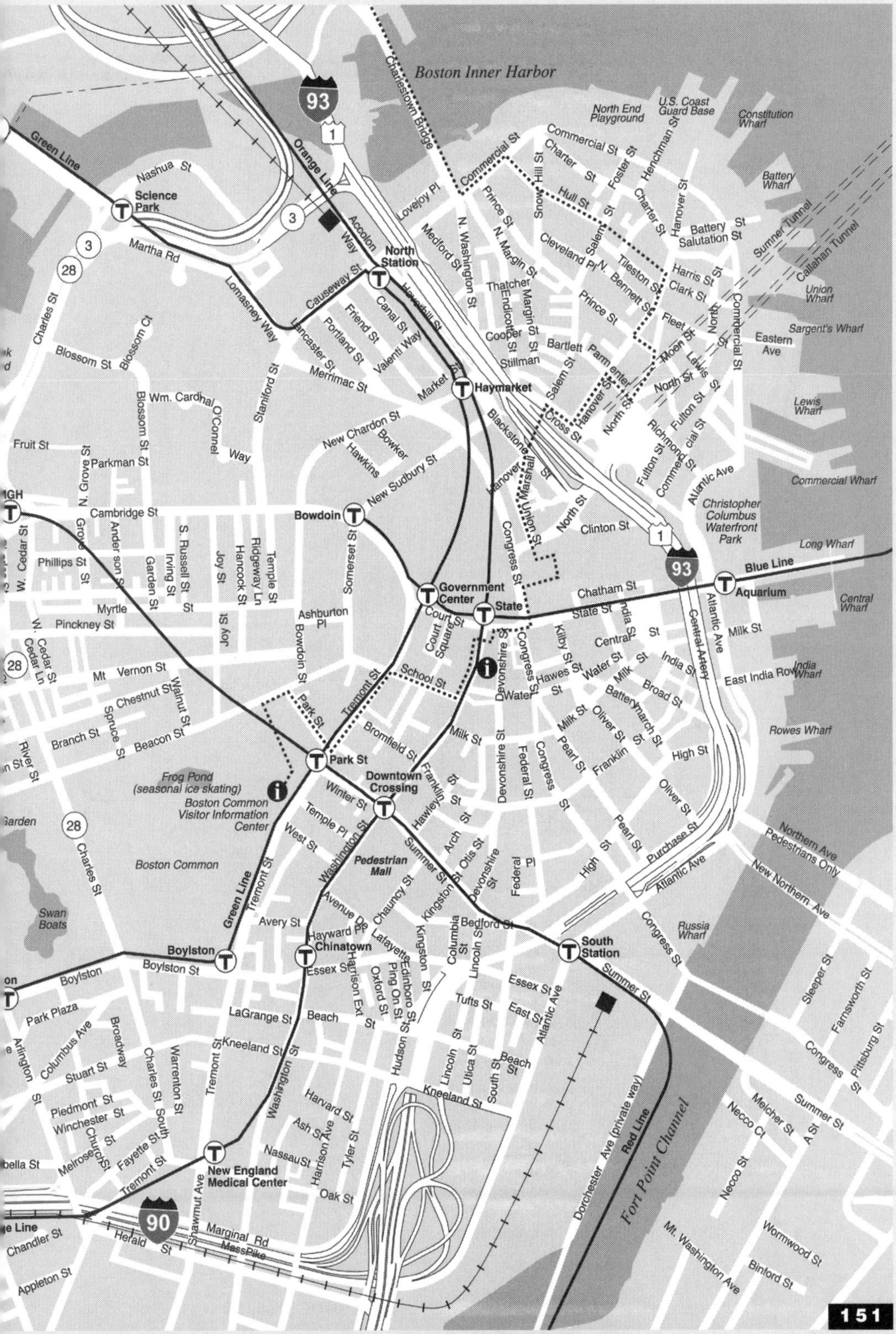
Boston Inner Harbor
Charlestown Bridge
93
1
3
28
Orange Line
Green Line
Blue Line
Red Line
Science Park
North Station
Haymarket
Bowdoin
Government Center
State
Aquarium
Park St
Downtown Crossing
Boylston
Chinatown
South Station
New England Medical Center
North End Playground
U.S. Coast Guard Base
Constitution Wharf
Battery Wharf
Union Wharf
Sargent's Wharf
Lewis Wharf
Commercial Wharf
Christopher Columbus Waterfront Park
Long Wharf
Central Wharf
India Wharf
Rowes Wharf
Russia Wharf
Sumner Tunnel
Callahan Tunnel
Eastern Ave
Commercial St
Charter St
Hull St
Foster St
Henchman St
Hanover St
Battery St
Salutation St
Harris St
Clark St
Fleet St
Moon St
North St
Lewis St
Fulton St
Richmond St
Atlantic Ave
Lovejoy Pl
Medford St
N. Washington St
Prince St
N. Margin St
Snow Hill St
Cleveland Pl
Salem St
Tileston St
N. Bennett St
Thatcher
Endicott St
Margin St
Cooper St
Bartlett
Parmenter
Stillman
Cross St
Blackstone St
Marshall
Union St
Clinton St
Congress St
Nashua St
Martha Rd
Lomasney Way
Accolon Way
Causeway St
Canal St
Haverhill St
Friend St
Portland St
Valenti Way
Lancaster St
Merrimac St
Market St
Staniford St
New Chardon St
Bowker
Hawkins
New Sudbury St
Charles St
Blossom St
Blossom Ct
Wm. Cardinal O'Connel Way
Fruit St
Parkman St
N. Grove St
Cambridge St
Grove St
Anderson St
W. Cedar St
Phillips St
Garden St
Irving St
S. Russell St
Joy St
Hancock St
Ridgeway Ln
Temple St
Somerset St
Myrtle St
Pinckney St
Cedar Ln
Mt Vernon St
Chestnut St
Walnut St
Spruce St
Branch St
Beacon St
River St
Ashburton Pl
Bowdoin St
Court St
Court Square
School St
Tremont St
Bromfield St
Milk St
Devonshire St
Chatham St
State St
India St
Kilby St
Central St
Hawes St
Water St
Broad St
Batterymarch St
Oliver St
Pearl St
Franklin St
High St
Federal St
Congress St
Central Artery
East India Row
Purchase St
Northern Ave
Pedestrians Only
New Northern Ave
Frog Pond (seasonal ice skating)
Boston Common Visitor Information Center
Boston Common
Swan Boats
Winter St
Temple Pl
West St
Washington St
Summer St
Hawley St
Arch St
Otis St
Pedestrian Mall
Chauncy St
Kingston St
Avenue De Lafayette
Hayward Pl
Avery St
Bedford St
Columbia St
Lincoln St
Federal Pl
Essex St
Harrison Ave
Edinboro St
Ping On St
Oxford St
Tufts St
East St
Boylston St
Park Plaza
Columbus Ave
Broadway
LaGrange St
Beach St
Kneeland St
Hudson St
Utica St
South St
Arlington St
Stuart St
Charles St South
Warrenton St
Piedmont St
Winchester St
Church St
Melrose St
Fayette St
Harvard St
Ash St
Tyler St
Nassau St
Oak St
Isabella St
Chandler St
Herald St
Shawmut Ave
Marginal Rd
MassPike
Appleton St
Dorchester Ave (private way)
Fort Point Channel
Steeper St
Farnsworth St
Pittsburg St
Melcher St
Necco Ct
Necco St
A St
Mt. Washington Ave
Wormwood St
Binford St

Springfield, Massachusetts

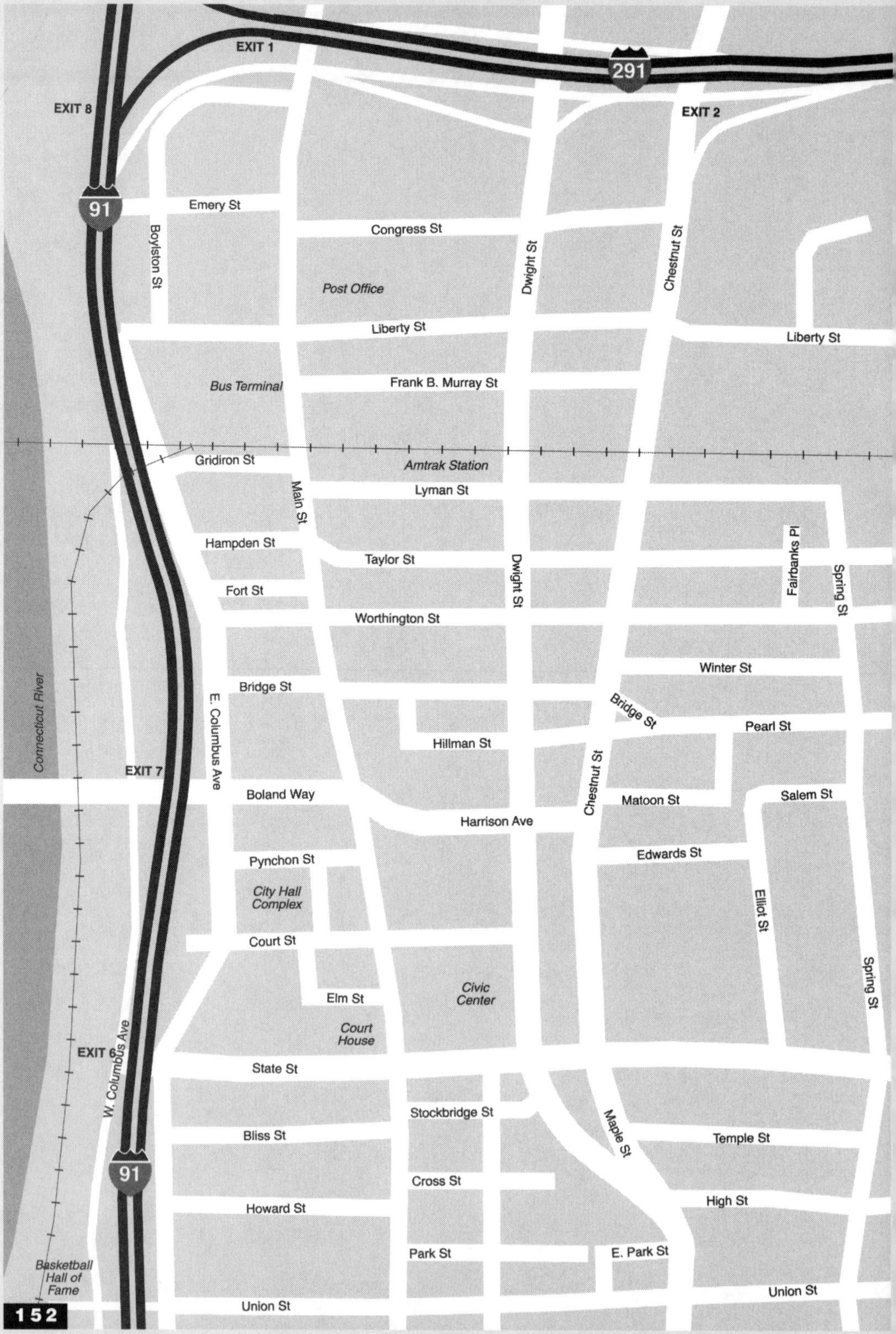

Worcester, Massachusetts

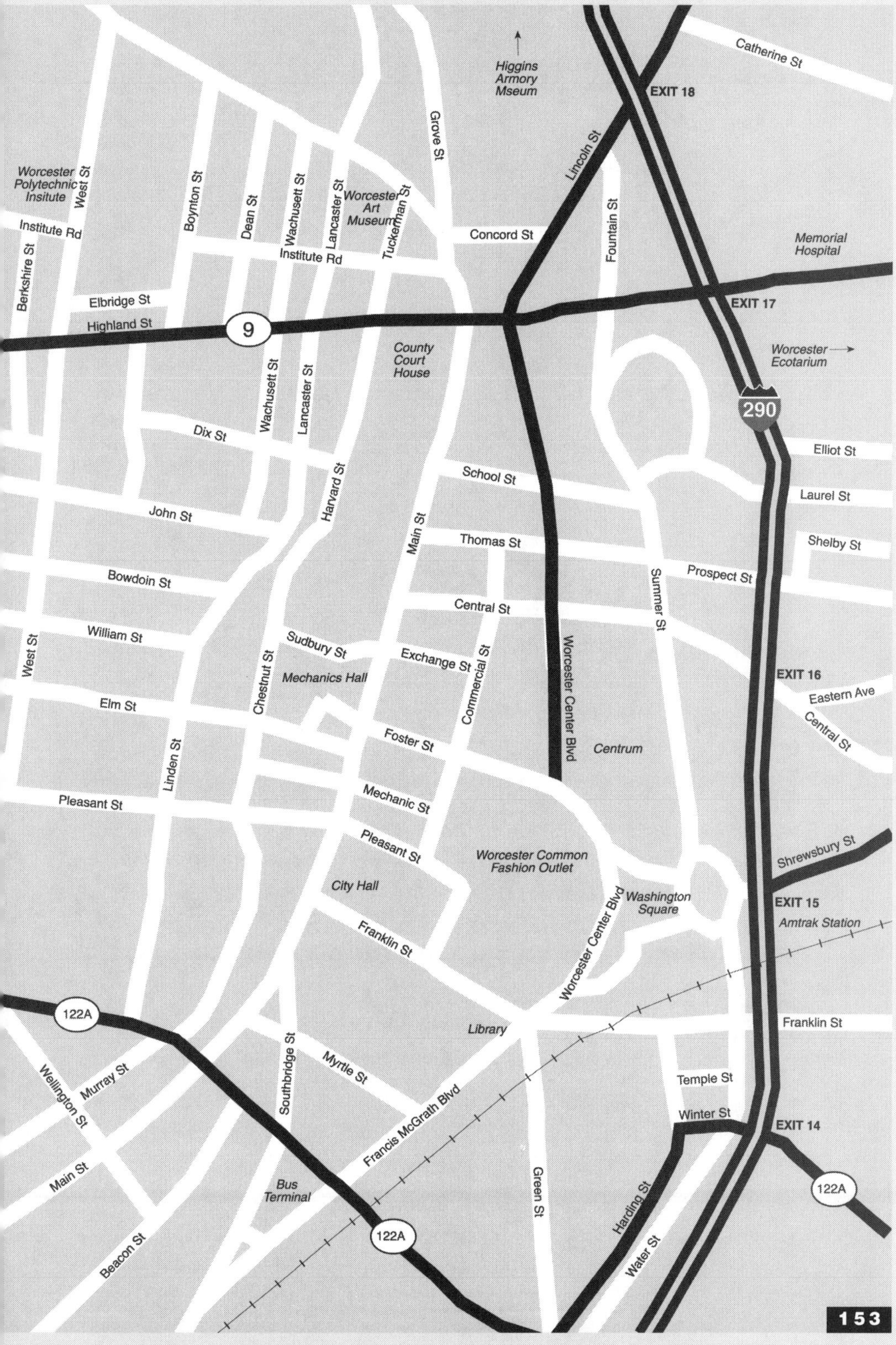

Cape Cod and the Islands

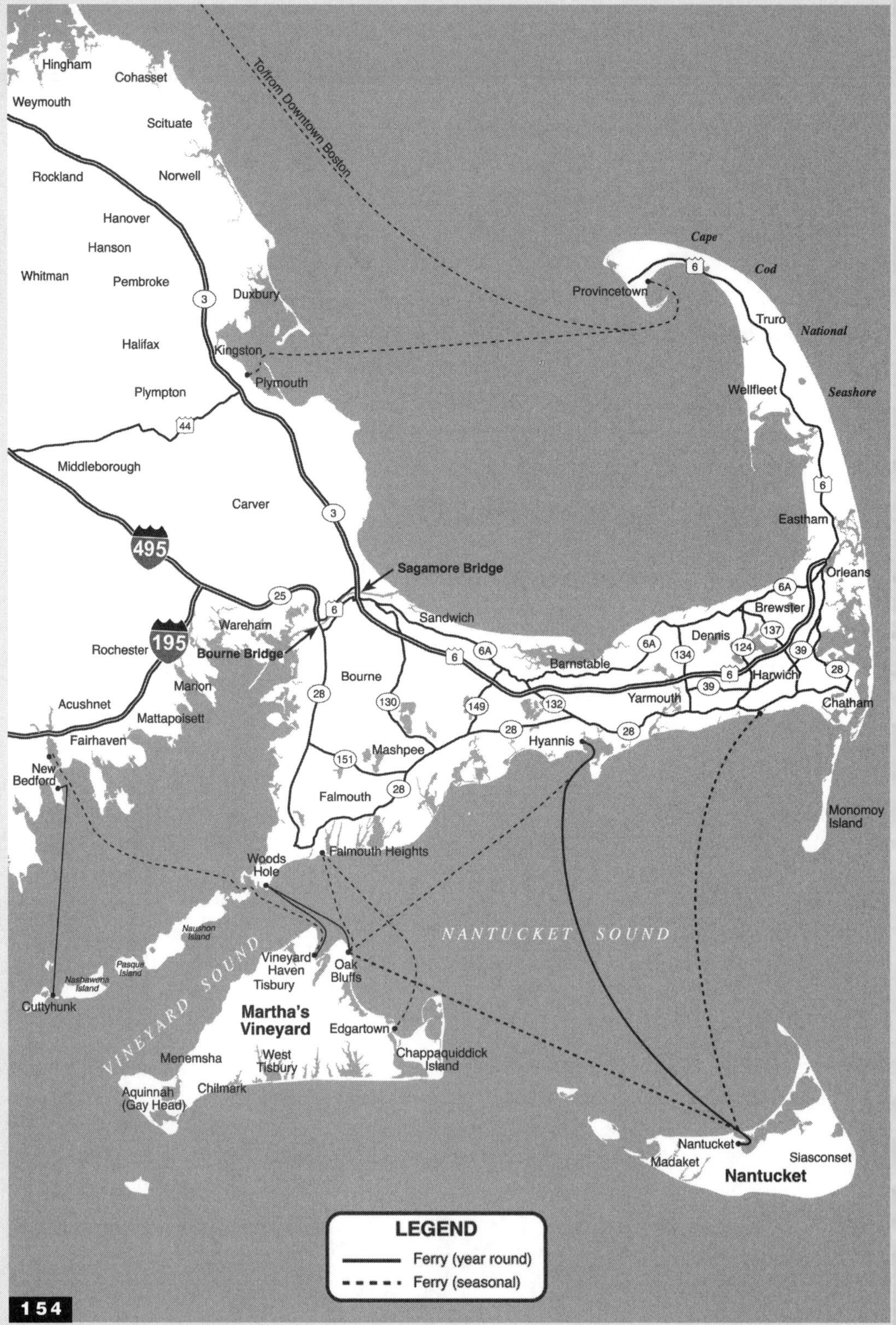
To/from Downtown Boston
Hingham
Cohasset
Weymouth
Scituate
Rockland
Norwell
Hanover
Hanson
Whitman
Pembroke
Duxbury
Halifax
Kingston
Plymouth
Plympton
44
3
Middleborough
Carver
495
Sagamore Bridge
25
6
Sandwich
Wareham
Rochester
195
Bourne Bridge
6A
Barnstable
Bourne
28
130
149
132
Marion
Acushnet
Mattapoisett
Fairhaven
New Bedford
151
Mashpee
Falmouth
Hyannis
Yarmouth
Falmouth Heights
Woods Hole
Cape
Cod
National
Seashore
Provincetown
Truro
Wellfleet
Eastham
Orleans
Brewster
Dennis
137
124
134
39
Harwich
Chatham
Monomoy Island
NANTUCKET SOUND
Naushon Island
Pasque Island
Nashawena Island
Cuttyhunk
VINEYARD SOUND
Vineyard Haven
Tisbury
Oak Bluffs
Martha's Vineyard
Edgartown
Chappaquiddick Island
Menemsha
West Tisbury
Aquinnah (Gay Head)
Chilmark
Nantucket
Madaket
Siasconset
Nantucket
LEGEND
Ferry (year round)
Ferry (seasonal)

An Introduction to the Bay State

MASSACHUSETTS IS TRULY THE HEART of New England. It borders every other New England state except for Maine, and even the Maine state line is just a handful of miles away.

But geography alone is insufficient to explain the state's vital position. Historically, politically, intellectually, and culturally, Massachusetts has long been at the center of developments not only in the region, but the nation. It was Massachusetts, after all, that took the lead in forging a separate national identity for the American colonies. From the fiery speeches of the Sons of Liberty at Boston's Faneuil Hall to the Boston Massacre to the Boston Tea Party to the midnight ride of Paul Revere to the Battle of Lexington and Concord that marked the start of war between the colonies and the motherland, Massachusetts ignited the rebellion and bore more than its share of the burden in America's fight for independence.

Some of the nation's greatest thinkers have called Massachusetts home—authors such as Ralph Waldo Emerson and Henry David Thoreau, social reformers including Dorothea Dix who crusaded on behalf of the mentally ill and Horace Mann who lobbied for universal education, beat generation spokesman Jack Kerouac, and popular illustrator Norman Rockwell, who captured enduring images of American life, not to mention several members of the Adams and Kennedy families who rose to positions of political prominence.

Travelers will find their own heartbeats quickening as they discover the multitude of historic attractions, museums, performing arts centers, scenic byways, beaches, and theme parks that line Massachusetts' arteries. Boston is not only the state's capital but also New England's major metropolitan area. It boasts some of the country's finest cultural institutions, museums, and professional sports arenas and more than 100 colleges and universities that keep Massachusetts at the forefront of intellectual debate and scientific discovery. North of Boston, Cape Ann's beaches and eclectic towns and the witchcraft lore of Salem are popular with visitors. The Merrimack Valley is home to the battlefields of Lexington and Concord and the former residences of Massachusetts literary legends. South of Boston, you can explore the state's whaling past and the lives of its first European settlers, the Pilgrims. Cape Cod, Nantucket and Martha's Vineyard have a flavor all their own—they're the perfect oceanside antidote to Boston's urban bustle. In the western part of the state, you'll find Springfield, the birthplace of basketball and Dr. Seuss, and college towns such as Amherst and Northampton. The Berkshire Hills of western Massachusetts are a summer haven for arts lovers, a photo-perfect paradise in autumn, and a winter wonderland for skiers.

Massachusetts practically pulsates with possibilities as it provides a matchless mix of past and present. Choose this land of patriots, Pilgrims, painters, and presidents as your launching pad for a grand tour of all of New England or as your primary destination.

Ten Massachusetts Highlights

The following are some of the "must-see" attractions in the state. Although Massachusetts may be a small state, it is perhaps a bit too stretched out to have access to all corners from a single locale. If you plan on visiting several regions in the state, it is most advisable to arrange for a few different, strategically placed accommodations.

TRAVEL TIP

Massachusetts has dozens of Lodging Reservation Services, including: **Bed & Breakfast Agency of Boston, Inc.,** (617) 720-3540 or (800) 248-9262, with 130 properties; **Bed & Breakfast Associates Bay Colony Ltd.,** (781) 449-5302 or (800) 347-5088, with 150 member properties; **Bed & Breakfast Cape Cod,** (508) 775-2772 or (800) 686-5252, with 175 B&Bs; **Berkshire Bed and Breakfast Reservation Service,** (413) 268-7244, with 130 listings; **DestINNations New England,** (508) 790-0566 or (800) 333-INNS, with forty properties; **Greater Boston Hospitality,** (617) 277-5430, representing eighty properties; **Martha's Vineyard and Nantucket Reservations,** (508) 693-7200 or (800) 649-5671, with 150 lodging options; and **Provincetown Reservations System,** (508) 487-2400, with 300 accommodations choices.

Naismith Memorial Basketball Hall of Fame

1150 West Columbus Avenue, Springfield

(413) 781-6500

www.hoophall.com

Did you know that Springfield, Massachusetts, is the birthplace of basketball? It's also home to the Naismith Memorial Basketball Hall of Fame, where you can pay tribute to the game's great players, teams, and coaches and even get into the game yourself with interactive exhibits.

Cape Cod and the Islands

Cape Cod juts out from Massachusetts, extending 70 miles into the Atlantic Ocean. The Cape and islands of Nantucket and Martha's Vineyard offer miles of glorious ocean beaches; quaint villages; art galleries; outdoor recreation including biking, hiking, and golf; and attractions that are a mix of past and present.

The Freedom Trail

Information booth on Boston Common at Tremont Street

(617) 227-8800

One of the best ways to see Boston's major historic landmarks is to follow the two and one-half mile Freedom Trail. It's easy to follow the red line that has been painted or bricked to permanently mark the route, and you'll find each of the sixteen stops along the trail marked with a sign. Boston Common, your best starting point, is the oldest public park in the United States.

Boston's Museums

The Boston metropolitan area is home to more than fifty museums for people of all ages. The museums cover an extensive range of topics and interests, including art history, children's, industry, and natural history. Boston is teeming with learning experiences waiting to be discovered.

Minute Man National Historical Park

174 Liberty Street, Concord

(978) 369-6993

www.nps.gov/mima

Relive the "shot heard 'round the world" that marked the beginning of the American Revolution when fighting broke out between the British and the American colonists at the Battle of Lexington and Concord. This 900-acre national historic site encompasses significant structures and landscapes associated with the Revolution's opening battles, plus original segments of the Battle Road traveled by the minutemen on April 19, 1775. Also within the park, you'll find the Hartwell Tavern, a restored eighteenth-century home and tavern offering tours led by costumed guides, and the Wayside, home at different times to three noted American authors—Louisa May Alcott, Nathaniel Hawthorne, and Margaret Sidney.

FAST FACT

April 19 is the anniversary of the outbreak of the American Revolution at Lexington and Concord, and the Monday closest to that date is a holiday in only two U.S. states—Maine and Massachusetts. Patriots' Day is also the day of the annual Boston Marathon.

The Mohawk Trail

www.mohawktrail.com

There are more than 100 attractions along this 63-mile stretch of highway that begins at the Massachusetts-New York border. A particularly scenic drive in autumn, Route 2, better known as the Mohawk Trail, is also lined with country inns, public and private camping areas, and quaint shops. This is also a spectacular region for winter skiing and summer white-water rafting adventures.

New Bedford Whaling Museum and Battleship Cove

Climb aboard a half-scale replica of a whaling ship and view the largest collection of artifacts and art devoted to America's whaling history at the **New Bedford Whaling Museum,** 18 Johnny Cake Hill, New Bedford, (508) 997-0046. In nearby Fall River, board a very different kind of ship—the battleship *Massachusetts* at **Battleship Cove,** (508) 678-1100, which is also home to the destroyer *Joseph P. Kennedy, Jr.* and the submarine *Lionfish.*

Old Sturbridge Village

Route 20, Sturbridge

(508) 347-3362

www.osv.org

One of central Massachusetts' leading attractions, this village recreates life in New England in the early 1800s. There are more than forty period buildings to explore at this 200-acre site, and costumed interpreters demonstrate spinning, weaving, blacksmithing, period cooking, and more as they interact with visitors and tell of their lives. There is also a working historical farm. Old Sturbridge Village hosts special events throughout the year—attend a gardening workshop, a re-creation of a town meeting, or special Christmas holiday celebrations.

Plymouth and Plimoth Plantation

137 Warren Avenue
(508) 746-1622
www.plimoth.org

A visit to the land of Pilgrims and Promise should include a stop at Plimoth Plantation, the living history museum that re-creates the lives of New England's first English settlers and their Native American friends and neighbors. You'll also want to tour the *Mayflower II*, a replica of the famous ship that carried the Pilgrims to New England's shores, and see Plymouth Rock—unimpressive in size but nostalgia-inspiring nonetheless. Both are located on the waterfront in Plymouth.

HOT SPOT

Nearly one million people visit **Plymouth Rock** each year. Since the earliest efforts to preserve the symbolic rock began in 1774, it has been dropped a few times and vandalized by tourists. The rock you'll see today has been sheltered since 1921 within a canopy designed by famed architects McKim, Mead, and White. To get to Plymouth Rock, follow Route 3 South to Route 44 East to the waterfront.

Salem

Forever branded by the hysteria in 1692 that led to the infamous witchcraft trials, Salem takes advantage of its wicked past, offering up its own trail of attractions that not only tell the story for which the town is best known but also celebrate the city's seafaring heritage and its most notable former resident, author Nathaniel Hawthorne. Must-see stops include the **Salem Witch Museum,** Washington Square, (978) 744-1692, where you'll hear and see a compelling retelling of the accusations, hysteria, trials, and executions of 1692 through life-size dioramas; the **Witch Dungeon Museum,** 16 Lynde Street, (508) 741-3570, where actors re-create the trials based on transcripts; the **Salem Wax Museum of Witches and Seafarers,** 288 Derby Street, (978) 740-2WAX or (800) 298-2WAX, where characters from Salem's past are re-created in wax; and the **House of the Seven Gables,** 54 Turner Street, (978) 744-0991, the inspiration for Hawthorne's novel of the same name.

New England's Hub: Boston and Cambridge

MARCH 5, 1770—THE BOSTON MASSACRE leaves five residents dead at the hands of British troops. December 16, 1773—Colonists disguised as members of the Mohawk tribe clamber aboard British ships and dump 342 chests of tea into Boston Harbor. June 16, 1775—Colonel Prescott gives American militiamen the command, "Don't fire until you see the whites of their eyes," before the Battle of Bunker Hill.

Legendary Boston lives in the pages of history books, but the string of dates and events familiar to practically every American is transformed from tedious text to exhilaratingly vivid reality when you actually set foot in what is arguably the nation's most historic and fascinating city. You can practically hear Paul Revere's horse galloping and his pulse pounding as you gaze up at the tower of the Old North Church, where the silversmith's eyes searched to see . . . one if by land, and two if by sea. And the high drama of the Boston Tea Party will be forever etched in your mind when you participate in the annual December re-enactment of the event—getting all fired up about the tax on tea at the Old South Meeting House before stealing away to the harbor to wreak havoc aboard a replica of a British ship.

Boston brilliantly blends all the benefits of a modern, urban center—fine restaurants, theater, luxury hotels, public transportation, chic shops, major league sports teams, cutting edge museums—with a pervasive sense of the past. The city is architecturally intriguing, culturally rich, and historically unequaled. It's also, quite simply, a lot of fun. Boston and nearby Cambridge, which is home to America's first institution of higher learning–Harvard University, combine to welcome hundreds of thousands of students to the compact area's more than 100 colleges and universities each year, giving the city and its surrounding neighborhoods a youthful energy. While not as frenetic as New York, Boston has a lively tempo that will propel you as you walk the Freedom Trail, slurp chowder from a bread bowl, root for the Red Sox, shop for antiques on Beacon Hill, ice skate in the winter, or laze aboard a swan boat in the summer in Boston Public Garden. The list of possibilities is endless, so be prepared to make tough choices once you've made the first easy choice–visit Boston.

TRAVEL TIP

Although Chicago is the "Windy City," Boston is actually America's windiest city. Summer is the high season on the Cape and along the North Shore—you'll find accommodations harder to come by and pricier. The Berkshires are at their best during summer's arts season or in winter for skiing. Because Boston is primarily a walking city, late spring and fall are the most comfortable times to visit. Autumn can be breathtaking statewide.

The T—The Mass Transit System of Eastern Massachusetts

Driving in Boston is notoriously tricky, and the difficulties of navigating the city's one-way streets and crowded highways have been compounded since 1991 by the Central Artery/Tunnel Project, more commonly known as the "Big Dig." This massive infrastructure project is not due for completion until the end of 2004. If you must drive in Boston, it's always a good idea to verify directions with someone at your destination shortly before your departure, as traffic patterns will be rerouted frequently for the duration of the Big Dig. Traffic advisories are also posted online at the Big Dig Web site, *www.bigdig.com.* Parking is expensive in Boston, too—upwards of $25 to $30 a day.

The good news is that even before Boston gave birth to the notion that the American colonies should be a free and independent nation, it had already originated another modern concept we take very much for granted today—mass transit. In 1631, Thomas Williams began operation of ferry service from Chelsea to Charlestown and on to Boston. In 1897, the nation's first subway line connected Boston's Park and Boylston Streets. Today, more than 819,000 one-way passenger trips are taken each day on the subway, bus, water ferry, and commuter rail systems operated by the Massachusetts Bay Transportation Authority (MBTA). MBTA service connects seventy-eight communities in the Greater Boston area, and commuter rail and interdistrict bus routes branch out to an additional sixty-four communities. The system encompasses a total of 181 routes and 252 stations. Stations and stops are marked with a black "T" in a circle, thus, the transportation system's nickname—the T.

Boston's mass transit system is known for being efficient, safe, and clean, and it provides visitors with an easy means of getting around the city without a car. Your best deal is likely the Boston Visitor Pass, which is valid for unlimited travel on the subway, local buses, and the inner harbor ferry. A one-day pass is $6, a three-day pass is $11, and a seven-day pass is $22. You can even buy your Visitor Pass before you leave home either online at *www.commerce.mbta.com* or by calling (877) 927-7277. Passes are also on sale at more than twenty MBTA stations in Greater Boston, including the Logan Airport subway station.

MBTA maps are posted at all stations and may be viewed online at *www.mbta.com.* Route and schedule information is also available by calling the MBTA Traveler's Information Center, (617) 222-3200 or (800) 392-6100 outside Massachusetts, or by visiting the MBTA Information Booth located at Park Street on the Green Line outbound platform. There's also a handy guide to museums and attractions along MBTA routes and best stops for accessing the sights you'd like to see online at: *www.mbta.com/newsinfo/geninfo/museums*.

Keep in mind that there is no subway service in the "wee" hours between about 1 A.M. and 5 A.M. Ferries stop running even earlier. If you plan to stay out late, you need to have an alternate means of transportation in mind.

Lodging Options

Boston gives Manhattan chase when it comes to room rates, which is an unfortunate reality for families and other leisure travelers. The good news is that prices are frequently lower on weekends when the business travel crowd ebbs. Keep in mind that in addition to the rate quoted for your overnight stay, you may be charged to park your vehicle, even if you are a guest of the hotel parking in the hotel's own garage. You may also be assessed a fee each time you move your car in or out of the garage throughout the duration of your stay. Boston is a walking city, so there is a definite benefit to staying right in the heart of downtown. However, you will find some less expensive accommodations options on the outskirts of the city. Looking for an outlying hotel that is close to public transportation may be one way to keep your Boston vacation affordable.

While an entire chapter could be devoted to the horde of hotels, inns, and B&Bs located in and around Boston and Cambridge, here's a selection of some of the most popular and intriguing options to help you start your planning.

The **Boston Harbor Hotel,** 70 Rowes Wharf, (617) 439-7000 or (800) 752-7077, is a 230-room luxury hotel overlooking the historic waterfront. It's convenient to the Financial District and a short walk from Faneuil Hall and Quincy Market.

The **Boston Park Plaza Hotel,** 64 Arlington Street, (617) 426-2000 or (800) 225-2008, was built in 1927 in Boston's historic

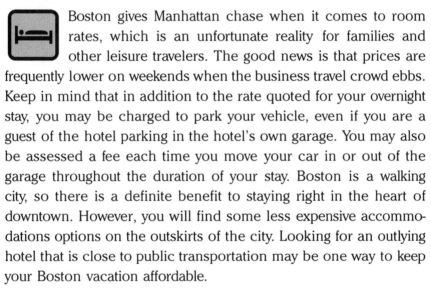

Back Bay. It has 960 rooms and suites and is the city's only member of Historic Hotels of America.

Boston Marriott Long Wharf, 296 State Street, (617) 227-0800, is just a block from Faneuil Hall and Quincy Market and appeals particularly to business travelers.

The **Colonnade,** 120 Huntington Avenue, (617) 424-7000 or (800) 962-3030, is a Back Bay landmark that has hosted three U.S. presidents and has a rooftop pool.

The **Fairmont Copley Plaza,** 138 St. James Avenue, (617) 267-5300, has provided elegant, centrally located accommodations since its gala 1912 opening.

XV Beacon, 15 Beacon Street, (617) 670-1500 or (877) XVBEACON, is one of the city's newest and boldest hideaways featuring individually styled, luxurious rooms and suites with unique features such as canopy beds and fireplaces. Complimentary Mercedes transportation to wherever you're going in Boston is provided.

The **Four Seasons Hotel,** 200 Boylston Street, (617) 338-4400, overlooks the Public Garden and puts you within walking distance of the city's premier attractions.

The **Gryphon House,** 9 Bay State Road, (617) 375-9003 or (877) 375-9003, is a B&B in the heart of Boston that has eight suites and free on-site parking.

Hilton Boston Logan Airport, 85 Terminal Road, (617) 568-6700, is right at the heart of the airport, and complimentary shuttle service is provided between the hotel and terminals.

Holiday Inn Boston Logan Airport, 225 McClellan Highway, (617) 569-5250, provides free parking and shuttle service to and from the airport.

Le Meridien, 250 Franklin Street, (617) 451-1900 or (800) 791-7781, is located in the 1922 Renaissance Revival building that once housed the Federal Reserve.

The **Omni Parker House,** 60 School Street, (617) 227-8600 or (800) 843-6664, is the oldest continually operating hotel in America, famous for inventing Parker House rolls and Boston cream pie.

Regal Bostonian Hotel, Faneuil Hall Marketplace, (617) 523-

3600, has 201 guest rooms including some with working fireplaces or French doors opening to balconies overlooking Boston.

The **Ritz-Carlton, Boston,** 15 Arlington Street, (617) 536-5700, has overlooked the Public Garden since 1927 and features 233 rooms and forty-two suites.

The **Ritz-Carlton Boston Common,** 10 Avery Street, (617) 574-7100, opened in September 2001, and overlooks the Boston Common. It has 193 luxury accommodations, 33 suites, and 46 Ritz-Carlton Club–level rooms and suites.

The **Seaport Hotel,** One Seaport Lane, (617) 385-4000 or (877) SEAPORT, is a high-tech, service-inclusive (no tipping)hotel located across from Boston's World Trade Center.

Taylor House Bed & Breakfast, 50 Burroughs Street, (617) 983-9334 or (888) 228-2956, is a restored Victorian in the Jamaica Plain neighborhood that has three guest rooms.

Union Park Guest House, 12 Union Park, (617) 421-1821, is a Victorian Brownstone in Boston's South End that offers guests individually decorated rooms with fireplaces.

The **Wyndham Boston,** 89 Broad Street, (617) 556-0006, puts you within easy walking distance of the Financial District, Quincy Market, and the New England Aquarium.

Reasonably priced accommodations aren't impossible to come by in Boston. The **Buckminster,** 645 Beacon Street, (617) 267-7370 or (800) 727-2825, is an older-style hotel located near Fenway Park that offers clean, comfortable rooms starting at $129 for a single or double, $159 for a suite. It just might be one of the city's best-kept "secrets."

Over in Cambridge, the **Charles Hotel in Harvard Square,** One Bennett Street, (617) 864-1200 or (800) 882-1818, features Shaker-style furnishings in its 249 rooms and forty-four suites. The distinctive, pyramid-shaped **Hyatt Regency Cambridge,** 575 Memorial Drive, (617) 492-1234, offers a complimentary shuttle to Boston. The **Inn at Harvard,** 1201 Massachusetts Avenue, (617) 491-2222 or (800) 458-5886, is an elegant option adjacent to Harvard Yard. The

Mary Prentiss Inn, 6 Prentiss Street, (617) 661-2929, is an 1843 Greek Revival B&B with high ceilings, four-poster beds, antique armoires, fireplaces, and Jacuzzis. The **Residence Inn Boston Cambridge Center,** 6 Cambridge Center, (617) 349-0700, is a good choice for long-term stays in the Boston area.

Farther away from downtown, you can find some more affordable accommodations options. **Amsterdammertje Euro-American Bed & Breakfast,** located south of Boston in Quincy, (617) 471-8454 or (800) 484-6401, is sparsely furnished but offers a place for the very value-conscious that is convenient to public transportation. Note that children under ten are not allowed. In Braintree, the **Days Inn,** 190 Wood Road, (781) 848-1260, has free parking and a free Continental breakfast. West of Boston in Watertown, the **Super 8,** 100 North Beacon Street, (617) 926-2200, offers free parking and easy access to the Massachusetts Turnpike.

The Massachusetts Office of Travel and Tourism serves as a clearinghouse for properties in the Boston area and all of Massachusetts that have online reservation and instant confirmation capabilities. Start your search at *www.massvacation.worldres.com/script/node.asp.*

Things to Do and See in Boston and Cambridge

There are so many things to do and see in Boston and Cambridge that it is hard to even skim the surface. This section highlights several of the most popular sites and touches on a few other gems.

The Freedom Trail

Each year, about 3 million people follow the red line that links the sixteen most significant sites related to Boston's role in the American Revolution, and if this is your first visit to Boston, walking the Freedom Trail is likely one of the first things you'll want to do.

The trail can be blitzed through in about an hour if you're in a real hurry and you don't plan to actually stop and look at anything. Your best bet, though, is to allow three hours or more to walk the trail at a leisurely pace and see all of its Revolutionary War landmarks.

While technically you can pick up the trail at any point, the best starting spot is the information booth at Boston Common, ☏(617) 536-4100. Here, you can pick up a map and brochure describing the trail sites. The two and one-half-mile trail is not a loop—it begins at Boston Common and ends in Charlestown at the Bunker Hill Monument. Admission to the sites along the trail is free with three exceptions: Paul Revere House, Old South Meeting House, and the Old State House. National Park Service rangers conduct guided tours of the Freedom Trail mid-April through early September. Call ☏(617) 242-5642 for a schedule.

TRAVEL TIP

Boston has its own half-price, day-of-show ticket outlets located in Copley Square and Faneuil Hall Marketplace. Half-price theater and show tickets go on sale at 11 A.M. each day. Visit BosTix online at *www.boston.com/artsboston* for directions and to see what's on sale today.

The Black Heritage Trail

For a look at the history and life of Boston's nineteenth-century African-American community, walk the one and six-tenths-mile Black Heritage Trail, which features fourteen sites primarily in the Beacon Hill area. You can venture inside two of the sites, the African Meeting House and the Abiel Smith School. For a self-guided walking tour—map and guide and information on guided tours, contact the **Museum of Afro American History,** ☏(617) 725-0022.

The Pru

From 1965 until 1976, Boston's tallest building was the **Prudential Building,** or the "Pru." Still one of the most recognizable landmarks in the Boston skyline, the building offers extensive shopping and dining options on its bottom floors and an observation deck on the fiftieth floor. **Top of the Hub,** found on the fifty-second floor, is considered by many the most romantic restaurant in the city.

TRAVEL TIP

Save money and see six of Boston's most popular attractions. **Boston CityPass** is available for purchase at any of the six participating locations: Harvard Museum of Natural History, John F. Kennedy Library and Museum, John Hancock Observatory, Museum of Fine Arts, Museum of Science, and the New England Aquarium. The CityPass price comes to about 50 percent of what the combined admissions prices would be. For more information, call (888) 330-5008 or visit CityPass online at *www.citypass.com*.

The New England Aquarium

Central Wharf

(617) 973-5200

www.neaq.org

A very popular family attraction. Watch three species of penguins at play in the 143,000-gallon Penguin Pool, see a whale skeleton, touch water critters in the hands-on touch pool, visit a coral reef without donning scuba gear, and more. If you don't want to pay the aquarium's admission price, you can still see the free, outdoor harbor seal exhibit.

Harvard University

Free daily campus tours of history-laden Harvard University leave from the Harvard Information Center in Holyoke Center, 1350 Massachusetts Avenue, Cambridge (617) 495-1573. From

September through May, tours depart at 10 A.M. and 2 P.M. Monday through Friday and at 2 P.M. on Saturday. From June through August, tours are available at 10 A.M., 11:15 A.M., 2 P.M. and 3:25 P.M. Monday through Saturday and 1:30 and 3 P.M. on Sunday.

Quincy Market

When you reach Faneuil Hall on your Freedom Trail tour, you may want to stop for a while to visit neighboring Quincy Market, off State Street, (617) 338-2323. Quincy Market, along with North Market and South Market all together are known as the Faneuil Hall Marketplace. This always lively indoor/outdoor market is home to more than fifty shops, souvenir and flower carts, fourteen full-service restaurants, forty food stalls offering the flavors of Boston and the world, street performers, loud bars, and even a comedy club, Comedy Connection, (617) 248-9700, which was named "Best Comedy Club in the Country" by *USA Today*.

TRAVEL TIP

If you want to see Boston's sights but aren't sure you have the time or the stamina to do a lot of walking, waddle over to the Prudential Center and book yourself passage on a **Duck Tour** to tour Boston's roads and waters in a World War II-era amphibious vehicle—a "duck." Your duck's captain will point out famous landmarks as you motor through the streets of Boston and, once you've plunged into the Charles River, he might even let you take the wheel. Tickets sell out fast, so be sure to get to the Prudential Center early in the day. For more information, call (617) 723-3825 or (800) 226-7442 or visit *www.bostonducktours.com*.

The Public Garden

The Public Garden, along Charles Street adjacent to Boston Common, is America's oldest botanical garden. Images of the pedal-powered swan boats, (617) 522-1966, that have occupied the garden's pond since 1877 are some of the city's most enduring. The good news is—you don't even have to do the pedaling, so sitting back and enjoying a summer day from your swan perch is a fabulously relaxing thing to do after all of the walking and sightseeing that Boston demands. In the winter, the pond is open to ice skaters.

Fenway Park

4 Yawkey Way

(617) 236-6666

Completed in 1912, Fenway Park is the oldest active baseball park in Major League Baseball. Plans are underway to replace historic Fenway Park, home of the Boston Red Sox, with a new, modern facility. Until then, guided tours of Fenway Park are available Monday through Friday, May through September.

TRAVEL TIP

You can use a credit card to purchase up to eight tickets for any home game by calling the **Red Sox** 24-Hour Touchtone Ticket System, (617) 482-4SOX. Tickets can also be purchased in person at the Red Sox Ticket Office, 4 Yawkey Way, (617) 267-1700, Monday through Friday from 9 A.M. to 5 P.M. Many games are sellouts; purchase tickets well in advance.

The Samuel Adams Brewery

30 Germania Street

(617) 522-9080

See how beer is made and sample some of Boston's signature brews at the Samuel Adams Brewery. Tours are offered Thursdays at 2 P.M., Fridays at 2 P.M. and 5:30 P.M., and Saturdays at noon, 1 P.M., and 2 P.M. In May through August, there are also tours at 2

P.M. on Wednesdays. The tour is open to all ages, though you must be twenty-one with proper ID to sample beer.

The Harbor Islands

www.nps.gov/boha

Hadn't thought of Boston as an island getaway? Think again! The Boston Harbor Islands, (617) 223-8666, thirty islands off the coast of the capital city, were designated a National Park in 1996. Several of the islands are open to the public during the summer months and accessible by ferry from Long Wharf in downtown Boston. Limited ferry service is also available from North and South Shore departure points. Private boats can also land on the islands. George's Island, the park system's central point of arrival, is home to Fort Warren, a Civil War landmark. Other islands feature beaches that call to sunbathers, walking trails, birding opportunities, and historic lighthouses. Call **Boston Harbor Cruises,** (617) 227-4321, for up-to-date ferry schedules, or visit the Boston Harbor Islands Information Booth at Long Wharf.

Marvelous Museums

M Boston is home to museums that rival those found anywhere else in the world. Whatever your interests, you're likely to find a museum you'll want to visit during your stay in Boston.

- The **Museum of Science, Science Park,** (617) 723-2500, is the city's most visited–it has more than 400 interactive exhibits, an IMAX theater, and a planetarium.
- The **Museum of Fine Arts, Boston,** 465 Huntington Avenue, (617) 267-9300, is the largest art repository in all of New England. Its holdings include the largest collection of works by French impressionist Claude Monet outside of France.
- The **Children's Museum,** 300 Congress Street, (617) 426-8855, will inspire the imaginations of young visitors.

- The **Boston Tea Party Ship and Museum,** Congress Street Bridge, (617) 338-1773, commemorates this historic 1773 event.
- The **Isabella Stewart Gardner Museum,** 280 the Fenway, (617) 566-1401, displays art masterpieces in an equally enchanting setting modeled after a fifteenth-century, Venetian-style palazzo.
- The **John F. Kennedy Library and Museum,** Columbia Point, (617) 929-4500 or (877) 616-4599, captures the legacy and leadership of one of America's most celebrated twentieth-century presidents.
- The **MIT Museum,** 265 Massachusetts Avenue, Cambridge (617) 253-5927, at the Massachusetts Institute of Technology is home to the world's largest collection of holograms and other fascinating exhibits of science, technology, and the potential of the human mind.

The Museums of Harvard University

Harvard University in Cambridge is home to a bevy of museums that could keep you busy for days. Start with the historic university's three art museums, (617) 495-9400. The **Arthur M. Sackler Museum** houses the university's collections of ancient, Asian, Islamic, and later Indian art. Treasures include Chinese jades, bronzes, sculptures, and cave paintings; Korean ceramics; Japanese woodblock prints; Greek and Roman sculpture and vases; and ancient coins. The **Busch-Reisinger Museum** is the nation's only museum devoted to the arts of Central and Northern Europe, particularly the German-speaking countries. The **Fogg Art Museum** is Harvard's oldest art museum, and its focus is on Western art from the Middle Ages to the present. Among the highlights here are impressionist and post-impressionist works and the Boston area's most important collection of works by Picasso.

Harvard also has a **Museum of Natural History**, 26 Oxford Street, (617) 495-3045, comprised of a Botanical Museum, the Museum of Comparative Zoology, and the Mineralogical and Geological Museum.

Museums for the Rest of Us

If stodgy, serious museums simply aren't your thing, there are museums in Boston for you, too. The **Museum of Bad Art,** (617) 325-8224, dedicated to "art too bad to be ignored," has a permanent gallery south of Boston in Dedham at the **Dedham Community Theater,** 580 High Street, which is open free to the public Monday through Friday from 6:30 to 10:30 P.M. and weekends from 1:30 to 10:30 P.M. And there's always the **Boston Beer Museum** at the Sam Adams Brewery, 30 Germania Street, (617) 522-9080, in the Jamaica Plain neighborhood of the city.

Touring Boston by Land and by Sea

Organized tours of Boston highlights can be an efficient way to see the city, especially if your time is limited or if you're exhausted just reading about all of the walking that visiting the city can entail. Local guides can provide you with an insider's view that you might not get from tourism brochures and maps. Boston is also known for its thematic tours—from ghosts to whales to literary greats to chocolate to the Boston Strangler, there are theme-tours to match every taste.

By Land

- **Bike! Boston,** 46 Beach Street, Suite 503, (617) 451-2153 or (877) 695-2153, offers guided, casually paced, ninety-minute cycle excursions.
- **Boston Adventures,** (617) 430-1900, offers nine different Boston sightseeing tours including the twice daily Boston Strangler Mystique Tour. Groups of ten or more can book a Pub Crawl tour or the Seafood Deluxe Tour.
- **Boston By Foot,** 77 North Washington Street, (617) 367-2345, is the city's oldest walking tour company. A variety of tours is offered May through October including Boston By Little Feet, designed to accommodate young walkers, and Boston Underground, a look at Boston's subways and underground waterways.

- **Boston Tours,** 56 Williams Street, Waltham, (781) 899-1454 or (800) 237-TOUR from within Massachusetts, caters to visitors staying in hotels in outlying Boston suburbs. They'll pick you up and show you the sights.
- **Brush Hill Tours,** 435 High Street, Randolph, (781) 986-6100 or (800) 343-1328, is a Gray Line affiliate offering fall foliage, Plymouth, Salem, and Cape Cod bus tours from Boston. They also operate the Beantown Trolley, which offers unlimited hop-on, hop-off service at twenty stops in the city. Trolley tickets include a harbor cruise in season.
- **Literary Trail Tours,** (617) 574-5950, depart each Saturday at 9 A.M. from the Omni Parker House at the corner of Tremont and School Streets. The half-day minicoach outing includes interior tours of the Omni Parker House, the Boston Public Library, the Concord Museum, and the Orchard House, home of the Alcott family.
- **Minuteman Trolley Tours,** 380 Dorchester Avenue, South Boston, (617) 269-3626, offers seventy-five-minute tours of Boston and Cambridge with unlimited reboarding at five stops. Departure points are the New England Aquarium, Harvard Square, USS *Constitution,* Hyatt Regency Cambridge, and the Holiday Inn Select Boston.
- **New England Ghost Tours,** (781) 235-7149, offers the Boston Spirits Walking Tour on selected evenings.
- **North End Tours Market Tours,** 6 Charter Street, (617) 523-6032, will take you to the butcher, the baker, the cheese maker, and other Italian specialty ingredient purveyors on regularly scheduled tours of Boston's Italian North End.
- **Old Town Trolley Tours,** (617) 269-7150 or (800) 868-7482, offers hop-on, hop-off service that allows you to see major Freedom Trail sites, the Bull & Finch Pub, Chinatown, and other attractions at your own pace. You can board at any stop and at major hotels, as well. Old Town Trolley Tours is also famous for its three-hour Boston Chocolate Tours in February and March.

By Sea (and River)

- **A.C. Cruise Line,** 290 Northern Avenue, (617) 261-6633 or (800) 422-8419, offers whale-watching excursions in the summer and fall and cruises to Gloucester, too.
- **Beantown Whale Watch,** 60 Rowes Wharf, (617) 542-8000, is operated by Massachusetts Bay Lines, Inc., and they guarantee you'll see whales.
- **Boston By Sea,** 175 Berkeley Street, (617) 574-5950, offers guided walking tours and boat tours of the Long Wharf area that explore Boston's maritime heritage.
- **Boston Harbor Cruises,** One Long Wharf, (617) 227-4321 or (877) SEE-WHALE, offers not only whale-watch excursions but also Boston Harbor Islands tours and a number of sightseeing cruises.
- **Charles Riverboat Company,** 100 Cambridgeside Place, Suite 320, Cambridge, (617) 621-3001, is Boston's only riverboat company offering daily, narrated Charles River sightseeing tours.
- **Odyssey,** Rowes Wharf on Atlantic Avenue, (888) 741-0282, combines harbor touring with fine dining for lunch, dinner, Sunday brunch, and moonlight cruises.
- The **Schooner *Liberty*,** 67 Long Wharf, (617) 742-0333, departs daily in season for midday, afternoon, and sunset views of Boston from aboard a tall ship.

Dining Highlights

Boston is without a doubt New England's dining capital, so pack an appetite. After all, this is the city that has even given its name to such widely loved dishes as Boston baked beans, Boston brown bread, and Boston cream pie. Boston restaurants can be busy, so make reservations ahead of time when possible.

Seafood is the main event when you're dining in the Bay State's capital. Daniel Webster liked to toss back oysters at the **Union**

Oyster House, 41 Union Street, (617) 227-2750, and John F. Kennedy's favorite booth in the upstairs dining room is marked with a plaque. This historic restaurant, located right on the Freedom Trail near Faneuil Hall, lays claim to the title of America's oldest continuously operating restaurant—it's been serving seafood since 1826. The building actually dates to the 1600s, and its hand-hewn wood beams and floor boards and warm atmosphere will transport you back to old New England. And yes, they serve Boston Cream Pie for dessert. Another reliable choice for seafood is the regional chain of **Legal Sea Foods** restaurants, (800) 477-LEGAL. You'll find them in Boston at Park Square, (617) 426-4444; Copley Place, (617) 266-7775; Long Wharf, (617) 227-3115; the Prudential Center, (617) 266-6800; Logan Airport Terminal B, (617) 568-2811; and Logan Airport Terminal C, (617) 568-2800; and in Cambridge at Kendall Square, (617) 864-3400. For fish au naturel, try the Massachusetts chain of **Naked Fish** restaurants—there's one right near Faneuil Hall on The Freedom Trail at 16-18 North Street, (617) 742-3333. Naked Fish features Cubanismo style and fresh fish and meats cooked on a wood-fired grill, but the real highlight here is the restaurant's cocktail concoctions. In fact, the Latin Love, an icy drink containing coconut and banana Cruzan Rum, cream of coconut, pineapple juice, and raspberry puree, was named the world's most sensual cocktail in 2000 by a panel of *Penthouse* magazine judges! For something very casual, try **Barking Crab,** 88 Sleeper Street, (617) 426-2722, where you can sit out on the deck peeling your own shrimp and cracking your own crabs to your heart's and tummy's content.

Where's the best clam chowder? You'll have a tough time choosing among the Chowderfest Hall of Fame members that have won the annual Boston Chowderfest three times and been retired from competition: **Mass Bay Company** at the Sheraton Boston Hotel, 39 Dalton Street; (617) 236-6023; **Turner Fisheries** at the Westin Copley Place, 10 Huntington Avenue, (617) 424-7425; and **Chart House,** 60 Long Wharf, (617) 227-1576.

If meat is a must, Boston won't disappoint the steak lover in you. The hunt club atmosphere of **Grill 23,** 161 Berkeley Street, (617) 542-2255, goes perfectly with red meat and red wine, and the upstairs fireplace lounge and cigar nook are great hideaways for a little after-dinner relaxation. The **Palm,** 200 Dartmouth Street, (617) 867-9292, is known for big cuts of meat—and big prices. Other great places to be seen eating steak include the **Capital Grille,** 359 Newbury Street, (617) 262-8900, and the **Oak Room at the Fairmont Copley Plaza Hotel,** 138 St. James Avenue, (617) 267-5300.

You can take a culinary trip around the world without ever leaving the Boston area. In Chinatown, **Grand Chau Chow,** 45 Beach Street, (617) 292-5166, and **Chau Chow,** 52 Beach Street, (617) 426-6266, are across the street from one another. Owned by the same company, both serve Cantonese cuisine and specialize in seafood and fish dishes. The crème de la French restaurants is **Radius,** 8 High Street, (617) 426-1234, where the preparation of modern French delicacies is overseen by James Beard Award winner for best chef in the Northeast, Michael Schlow. Cajun food is on the menu and jazz is on stage at **Bob the Chef's Jazz Café,** 604 Columbus Avenue, (617) 536-6204. **Fajitas & 'Ritas,** 25 West Street, (617) 426-1222, is a fun Mexican restaurant near Boston Common where you can build your own fajitas by buying only the ingredients that you crave—lettuce for twenty-four cents, tomatoes for forty-eight cents, etc. Just outside the city in Brookline, you'll find a Japanese restaurant that claims to be New England's largest, and if you can get over the amusement of saying its name, **Fugakyu,** 1280 Beacon Street, (617) 734-1268, will dazzle you with its artful sushi preparations. The North End is the place to head for Italian delights. **Maurizio's,** 364 Hanover Street, (617) 367-1123, is named for its talented chef, Maurizio Loddo, who will surprise you with generous portions of sumptuous Italian and Mediterranean specialties. At **Bricco,** 241 Hanover Street, (617) 248-6800, you can enjoy cicchetti, the word used in Venice to describe small plates of hot or cold taste bud tantalizers that are meant to be shared around your table. Make the trip to Cambridge for Indian food at **Tanjore** in Harvard Square, 18 Eliot Street, (617) 868-1900, featuring fresh preparations from a variety of India's regions. For a taste of medieval Europe, reserve a spot at the banquet tables at **Medieval Manor,** 246 East Berkeley Street, (617) 423-4900, where you'll be entertained by jesters and minstrels while eating with your hands.

Irish pubs are, of course, another Boston tradition—there are about 100 of them in Boston and Cambridge. The **Black Rose** at Faneuil Hall Marketplace, 160 State Street, (617) 742-2286, features Guinness on tap and live Irish music nightly. **Kitty O'Shea's** first restaurant was in Dublin, and the Boston incarnation of this Irish-themed pub, 131 State Street, (671) 725-0100, is located in a Victorian building in the heart of the Financial District. The **Purple Shamrock** across from Boston City Hall, One Union Street, (617) 227-2060, has bangers and mash and bands playing every night.

HOT SPOT

Boston has a long and proud Irish tradition. More than 600,000 visitors celebrate St. Patrick's Day in Boston each year. In 1999, the Boston Irish Tourism Association, (888) 749-9494, was founded to promote and preserve Irish history and culture. One of the organization's first major accomplishments is the three-mile, fifteen site Irish Heritage Trail, first described in the 1985 book, *Guide to the New England Irish,* by Michael P. Quinlin, Colette Minogue Quinlin, and Colene M. Minogue. Trail map and description available at *www.irishheritagetrail.com.*

Boston is also known for its brewpubs. **Cambridge Brewing Co.,** One Kendall Square, Cambridge, (617) 494-1994, was one of the first brewery restaurants in the United States. **North East Brewing Company,** 1314 Commonwealth Avenue, (617) 566-6699, serves its handcrafted ales and lagers in an upstairs, open-air restaurant, on couches by a fireplace, and downstairs in the **Caske Room,** where you'll also find live entertainment, billiards, foosball, and darts. **Boston Beer Works,** 61 Brookline Avenue, (617) 536-2337, is the place to go before or after a Red Sox game. And there's the **Samuel Adams Brewhouse,** 710 Boylston Street, (617) 536-2739, which might not really count because the beer is made at the nearby brewery, not on the premises.

For casual fare, Quincy Market serves up dozens of food stalls where you can sample everything from bread bowls overflowing with chowder to sushi to pizza to bagels to raw oysters to delectable cookies at the **Boston Chipyard,** (617) 742-9537. Prices are a bit on the touristy side, and a place to sit down may be hard to come by during peak mealtimes. Night owls gravitate to **Buzzy's Fabulous Roast Beef,** 327 Cambridge Street, (617) 242-7722, which stays open twenty-four hours. And there's a Dunkin' Donuts nearly everywhere you turn—with more than 200 of the donut shops in Greater Boston. The chain's headquarters is in nearby Randolph, Massachusetts.

HOT SPOT

The **Bull & Finch Pub,** 84 Beacon Street, Boston, (617) 227-9605, was the inspiration for the long-running television show, *Cheers*, and is one of the city's top tourist attractions. Visit the Bull & Finch for a great lunch or dinner, and be sure to take home *Cheers* souvenirs. While you're on Beacon Hill, also explore the antique shops and bookstores along Charles Street. Boston Public Garden is just across the street, too.

Shopping Discoveries

Faneuil Hall Marketplace, a.k.a. Quincy Market, is probably Boston's best-known shopping area, and its location right on the Freedom Trail makes it a natural stop for visitors to the city. Upscale fashion purveyors dominate the more than fifty shops, and you'll also find dozens of carts where you can buy eclectic souvenirs.

When you're ready to get off the trail and do some serious shopping, head for the Back Bay neighborhood's Newbury Street, and, to a lesser extent, Boylston Street, which is a block away. You can drift in and out of fancy boutiques, clever gift shops, high-end jewelers, and galleries as you cover the expanse of Newbury Street that stretches from the Public Garden to Massachusetts Avenue. Don't miss **Loulou's Lost & Found,** 121 Newbury Street, (617) 859-8593, which specializes in authentic and reproduction dinnerware from old ships and resorts. And, if you're feeling adventurous, there's **Condom World,** 332 Newbury Street, (617) 267-7233.

If indoor shopping venues, a.k.a. malls, are more your thing, **Copley Place** in the Back Bay at Huntington Avenue and Dartmouth Street, (617) 369-5000, has more than 100 stores including glamour leaders such as Neiman Marcus, Gucci, and Tiffany. Over in Cambridge, the **CambridgeSide Galleria,** 100 Cambridgeside Place, (617) 621-8666, is a bit more down to earth. While you're in Cambridge, Harvard Square is another popular shopping district.

Charles Street on Beacon Hill is the city's premier hunting ground for antiques. Among the more than forty antique shops here is the **Boston Antique Co-op,** 119 Charles Street, (617) 227-9811, which sells estate antiques of all sorts.

Watch tabaqueros at work rolling cigars at the **Boston Cigar Factory,** 186 Lincoln Street, (617) 695-2822, where you can also purchase the city's only hand-rolled cigars.

If you're a bargain stalker, you won't want to miss the original **Filene's Basement** at the Downtown Crossing, 426 Washington Street, (617) 348-7900. Nearly a century ago, Edward A. Filene devised a clever scheme to deal with unsold merchandise from his father's department store—he'd move it to the basement and automatically discount it every few weeks until it sold. Today, the Basement is often mobbed with shoppers, and yes, the store admits that especially good deals have ignited tug-of-wars.

North of Boston: Salem, the North Shore, and the Merrimack Valley

THE REGION NORTH OF BOSTON gives the city a run for its money when it comes to historic allure. This land of witches, pirates, minutemen, and mill girls will enthrall history buffs as they relive the infamous witch trials of 1692 in Salem, head out on a whale watch or deep-sea fishing excursion from America's oldest seaport—Gloucester, walk the battlefields at Lexington and Concord where the American colonists first stood their ground against the Redcoats, and experience the world of nineteenth-century textile workers in Lowell.

In the summer months, visitors flock to Rockport, a charming fishing village turned artists' haven; to the picturesque harbor of Marblehead with its historic homes, oceanside inns, and sailing adventures; to Ipswich, famous for its tender, fried, whole-belly clams; and to Walden Pond in Concord, the tranquil retreat of writer Henry David Thoreau, which is now a 333-acre state reservation. Gloucester's popularity has been heightened by the Sebastian Junger book, *The Perfect Storm,* and the movie it inspired. You can even stay overnight at the Crow's Nest, the local bar that was a central setting in the tale based on the true events of 1991, when six Gloucester fishermen were lost with the *Andrea Gail.*

Sure, the landmarks and locales north of Boston can make for an interesting side trip from the capital city, but keep in mind, too, that this region steeped in history and blessed with inviting beaches and rugged, scenic coastline makes for a worthwhile vacation destination in its own right. The Cape Ann towns of Gloucester (pronounced Glaw-ster), Rockport, Essex, and Manchester-by-the-Sea make a particularly good home base from which to explore the majesty and history of northern Massachusetts.

Lodging Options

In Salem, the **Hawthorne Hotel,** 18 Washington Square West, (978) 744-4080 or (800) 729-7829, has eighty-nine rooms featuring reproduction eighteenth-century furnishings. Ask about special Salem Magic Packages. **Amelia Payson House,** 16 Winter Street, (978) 744-8304, is a restored 1845 Greek Revival B&B with elegant trappings. The **Salem Inn,** 7 Summer Street, (978) 741-0680 or (800) 446-2995, is comprised of three historic nineteenth-century houses on the National Register of Historic Places and features some rooms with working fireplaces. The **Coach House Inn,** 284 Lafayette Street, (978) 744-4092 or (800) 688-8689, is an 1879 Victorian sea captain's mansion with antique décor. The **Stepping Stone Inn,** 19 Washington Square North, (978) 741-8900 or (800) 338-3022, is the former 1846 home of a naval officer that provides Salem visitors with a central location from which to explore the town.

Along the North Shore you'll find accommodations of every style and for every budget. In Swampscott, **Cap'n Jack's Waterfront Inn,** 253 Humphrey Street, (781) 595-7910 or (800) 958-9930, is a classic New England inn built in 1835 with twenty-four rooms/suites/apartments, sweeping views of Nahant Bay and its own private tidal cove. In Marblehead, the luxurious **Harbor Light Inn,** 58 Washington Street, (781) 631-2186, built in 1729, is a favorite with couples seeking sensuous lodgings with canopied beds and fireplaces—inquire about special romance packages. **Spray Cliff on the Ocean,** 25 Spray Avenue, (781) 631-6789 or (800) 626-1530, is the place to stay if you want to be lulled to sleep by crashing surf. The **Marblehead Inn,** 264 Pleasant Street, (781) 639-9999 or (800) 399-5843, is an 1872 Victorian that has been an inn since 1923. Choose from ten suites, all with kitchenettes. The **Seagull Inn B&B,** 106 Harbor Avenue, (781) 631-1893, is a Shaker-furnished, century-old, smoke-free B&B with ocean views from every guestroom. In Danvers, you'll find some affordable chain hotel options including the **Comfort Inn,** 50 Dayton Street, (978) 777-1700, which has indoor and outdoor pools and free continental breakfast. The **Days Inn,** 152 Endicott Street, (978) 777-1030 or (800) 329-7466, also offers free continental breakfast. For something with a few more amenities, try the **King's Grant Inn,** Route 128 North, (978) 774-6800 or (800) 782-7841, a 125-room hotel with a lush, tropical, 1,600-square-foot indoor pool and Jacuzzi® complex. In Gloucester, you're walking distance from Good Harbor Beach when you stay at **Vista Motel & Efficiencies,** 22 Thatcher Road, (978) 281-3410 or (866) VISTAMA. **Cape Ann's Marina Resort,** 75 Essex Avenue, (978) 283-2116, is a boater's dream with fifty-two water-view rooms and whale watch and other water excursions departing from right outside your door. The **Manor Inn,** 141 Essex Avenue, (978) 283-3154, is a Victorian B&B with two adjacent motel buildings that offers a variety of room choices and a wraparound porch where all guests can watch boats gliding along the Annisquam River. If camping is your thing, you'll find 200 tent and RV sites at **Cape Ann Camp Site,** 80 Atlantic Street, (978) 283-8683. Or, for something truly unique, stay upstairs at the **Crow's Nest,** 334 Main Street, (978) 281-2965, the fisherman's hangout featured in the movie, *The Perfect Storm.* In Rockport, **Captain's Bounty Motor Inn,** 1 Beach Street, (978) 546-9557, offers affordable accommodations right on the beach. The historic **Emerson Inn by the Sea,** One Cathedral Avenue, (978) 546-6321 or (800) 964-5550, has welcomed guests since 1846 and has its own spa and saltwater swimming pool. The **Seaward Inn,** 44 Marmion Way, (978) 546-3471, is an oceanfront estate turned lodging complex with a Main Inn, Carriage House, and several cozy cottages—

thirty-eight rooms in all. Travel back in time when you stay at the **Tuck Inn B&B,** 17 High Street, (978) 546-7260 or (800) 789-7260, a renovated 1790 colonial home that has been a B&B since the 1940s. The **Yankee Clipper Inn,** 96 Granite Street, (978) 546-3407 or (800) 545-3699, is the quintessential oceanside retreat—a 1929 Art Deco mansion with only gorgeous gardens standing between it and the churning sea. In Ipswich, the **Inn at Castle Hill,** 280 Argilla Road, (978) 412-2555, is nestled within the 2,100-acre Crane Estate, which features the Castle Hill mansion, a National Historic Landmark open for tours, and the Crane Wildlife Refuge, a sanctuary for birds and animals. In Salisbury, you'll find family-friendly motels including **Ocean Gate Motel,** 233 Beach Road, (978) 462-2712, with fifty-two air-conditioned rooms and a heated outdoor pool, and **Salisbury Beach Casino Resort Motel,** 406 North End Boulevard, (978) 462-2228 or (888) 825-2228, where guest rooms have decks overlooking the beach.

In the Merrimack Valley, the 119-room **Sheraton Lexington,** 727 Marrett Road, Lexington, (781) 862-8700, is central to area attractions. The **Courtyard by Marriott** in Lowell, 30 Industrial Avenue, (978) 458-7575, has 120 guest rooms, a restaurant, and lounge. Concord's **Colonial Inn,** 48 Monument Square, Concord, (978) 369-9200 or (800) 370-9200, dates to 1716—long before the shot heard 'round the world—and it's been an inn since 1889. You'll be in good company—Franklin D. Roosevelt, J.P. Morgan, John Wayne, Kurt Russell, Goldie Hawn, Shirley Temple, Steve Martin, Faye Dunaway, Dan Quayle, Glenn Close, Bruce Springsteen, and Queen Noor of Jordan are on the long list of notable folks who have stayed here! The **Hawthorne Inn,** 462 Lexington Road, Concord, (978) 369-5610, wasn't built until 1870, but it's located right on the famed Battle Road of 1775 on land that was once owned by Ralph Waldo Emerson, the Alcotts, and Nathaniel Hawthorne. If that's not old enough for you, **Longfellow's Wayside Inn,** Boston Post Road/Route 20, Sudbury, (978) 443-1776, was first licensed in 1716 and purports to be America's oldest operating inn.

Bewitching Salem

There's more to Salem than witch stuff, but don't worry—there's plenty of witch stuff. Start your Salem adventure at the **National Park Service's Salem Visitor Center,** 2 New Liberty Street, (978) 740-1650. From this convenient starting point, you can follow Salem's Heritage Trail. Much like Boston's Freedom Trail, the Heritage Trail is marked by a red line winding through town, and if you follow it, it will lead you to many of Salem's most popular attractions.

One of the trail's first stops is the **Peabody Essex Museum,** East India Square, (978) 745-9500 or (800) 745-4054, founded in 1799 and home to intriguing art and history collections including the Real Witchcraft Papers, the 500-plus documents from the witchcraft trials, which are on view to the public during limited, weekday hours.

You'll want to stop at the **Salem Witch Museum,** Washington Square, (978) 744-1692, where the story of the 1692 witch hysteria and ensuing trials is vividly told through a series of life-size dioramas that are illuminated in sequence as you sit on the floor in a darkened room. This presentation might be a bit too scary for younger children, but it serves as the perfect introduction to Salem's tarnished history. At the **Witch Dungeon Museum,** 16 Lynde Street, (978) 741-3570, actors recreate the witch trials based on the 1692 transcripts. A discounted Hysteria Pass admits you to both the **Salem Wax Museum of Witches & Seafarers,** 288 Derby Street, (978) 740-2WAX or (800) 298-2WAX, and the **Salem Witch Village,** 282 Rear Derby Street, (978) 740-9229, where costumed tour guides tell tales of witchcraft. If there's time for one last witch spot, visit the **Witch House,** 310 Essex Street, (978) 744-0180, the former home of witch trials judge Jonathan Corwin.

Ready to see the seafaring side of Salem? The **New England Pirate Museum,** 274 Derby Street, (978) 741-2800, exhibits memorabilia from the days when notorious seamen—Blackbeard, Captain Kidd, and others—terrorized the waters off Boston's North

Shore. Also visit the **Salem Maritime National Historic Site,** 174 Derby Street, (978) 740-1680, a waterfront complex where you can see a free movie about Salem's maritime history and tour three wharves, the **U.S. Custom House,** the **Derby House,** the **Narbonne House,** and the West India Goods Store.

At the **House of the Seven Gables,** 54 Turner Street, (978) 744-0991, you can not only tour one of the oldest surviving seventeenth-century wooden mansions in New England—immortalized in the book of the same name by Nathaniel Hawthorne—but also see the house in which Hawthorne was born. Two other historic homes that might capture your fancy are the **Stephen Phillips Memorial Trust House,** 34 Chestnut Street, (978) 744-0440, a Federal mansion filled with artifacts, and **Pickering House,** 18 Broad Street, (978) 744-1647, the oldest house continuously occupied by the same family.

HOT SPOT

Each October, Salem kicks the spooky stuff up a notch with a jam-packed schedule of Halloween events including ghost tours, haunted houses, parades, and psychic fairs. For information on **Haunted Happenings,** call the Salem Office of Tourism and Cultural Affairs, (877) SALEM-MA, or visit *www.salemhauntedhappenings.com*.

North Shore Sights

In between sunbathing stints, you may want to pull yourself away from the North Shore's tantalizing beaches to explore some of the region's diverse attractions.

Historic homes are plentiful. **Beauport,** 75 Eastern Point Boulevard, Gloucester, (978) 283-0800, was the summer home masterminded by interior designer Henry Davis Sleeper, who filled its rooms with amusing objects and recycled architectural finds. The home is open for tours Monday through Friday from May 15 through

September 15 and weekends September 15 through October 15. **Castle Hill at the Crane Estate,** 290 Argilla Road, (978) 356-4351, was the fifty-nine-room Great House built by Chicago industrialist Richard T. Crane. Tours are offered Wednesdays and Thursdays during the summer season. The **Jeremiah Lee Mansion,** 161 Washington Street, Marblehead, (781) 631-1768, was built in 1768 for a wealthy ship owner and merchant. Tours of the home are available daily from mid-May through October. The **Spencer-Pierce-Little Farm,** 5 Little's Lane, Newbury, (978) 462-2634, dates to about 1690. Here, you can tour the imposing manor house and participate in nature walks Wednesday through Sunday from June 1 through October 15. And be sure to tour the **Hammond Castle Museum,** 80 Hesperus Avenue, Gloucester, (978) 283-7673, the Medieval-style castle built in the 1920s by prolific inventor John Hays Hammond, Jr. to house his extensive collection of Roman, Medieval, and Renaissance artifacts.

Lovers of folk art will want to find their way to Essex, where they can visit **Cogswell's Grant,** 60 Spring Street, (978) 768-3632, the former farmhouse summer home of art collectors Bertram K. and Nina Fletcher Little, who assembled one of the nation's pre-eminent collections of American folk art. While you're in Essex, relive the town's shipbuilding history at the **Essex Shipbuilding Museum,** 66 Main Street, (978) 768-7541. More two-masted ships have been built in Essex than anywhere else in the world, and visiting a working waterfront shipyard is part of your adventure here.

One of the most recognized landmarks in the region is the Fisherman's Memorial Statue, more commonly called the "Man at the Wheel," located on Western Avenue in Gloucester. Dedicated in 1925, the bronze statue stands as a tribute to Gloucester fishermen who have perished at sea.

Looking for something free to do? **Saugus Iron Works National Historic Site,** 244 Central Street, Saugus, (781) 233-0050, is open free daily to visitors who'd like to see a reconstruction of North America's first integrated ironworks, founded in 1646, including a blast furnace, forge, rolling mill, and restored seventeenth century house.

For a completely unique experience, visit **Wolf Hollow,** 114 Essex Road, Ipswich, (978) 356-0216, home of the North American Wolf Foundation. On weekends, weather permitting, visitors are invited to see the resident pack of British Colombian timber wolves in their natural habitat.

TRAVEL TIP

Ocean beaches north of Boston:

- Crane Beach, Argilla Road, Ipswich
- Good Harbor Beach, Thatcher Road, Gloucester
- Half Moon Beach, Stage Fort Park, Gloucester
- Long Beach, Route 127A, Gloucester/Rockport
- Lynch Park Beach, Ober Street/Route 127, Beverly
- Plum Island, Newburyport
- Salisbury Beach State Reservation, Route 1A, Salisbury
- Singing Beach, off Route 127, Manchester-by-the-Sea
- Wingaersheek Beach, Atlantic Avenue, Gloucester

Merrimack Valley—Museums and More

The Merrimack Valley is loaded with juxtapositions–you can listen to the thunderous clacking of power looms at a restored 1920s textile mill in the morning, then spend the afternoon soaking up the quietude of Thoreau's Walden Pond retreat; you can whitewater raft on the rapids of the Concord River one day, then drift peacefully along Lowell's 5 miles of canals aboard a canal boat the next.

The most compelling attractions in this pocket of Massachusetts are concentrated in Concord, Lexington, and Lowell.

Since 1959, visitors to **Minute Man National Historical Park,** (781) 862-7753, have been able to roam the battlefields that served as the opening arena for the American Revolution. The park consists of more than 900 acres of land in Lexington, Concord, and Lincoln that wind along original segments of the April 19, 1775

Battle Road. The park also preserves and interprets the nineteenth-century literary revolution through the Wayside, former home of three New England writers—Nathaniel Hawthorne, Louisa May Alcott, and Margaret Sidney. The best place to begin your exploration of the site is the Minute Man Visitor Center located off Route 2A in Lexington near the eastern entrance of the park. Here, a multimedia presentation, "The Road To Revolution," tells the story of the "shot heard 'round the world" and the opening battles of the American Revolution at Lexington Green, North Bridge, and along the Battle Road. Pick up a map that will identify highlights as you hike or drive along the five-mile Battle Road Trail. Ask about ranger-led programs that may be available as well.

While you're in Concord you can also visit the **Concord Museum,** 200 Lexington Road, (978) 369-9763, where collection highlights include the lantern hung in the Old North Church steeple on the night of Paul Revere's famous ride, American Revolution artifacts, and the world's largest collection of Thoreau possessions including furnishings from his cabin at **Walden Pond.** There are also two literary-linked sites to visit: **Orchard House,** 399 Lexington Road, (978) 369-4118, where Louisa May Alcott wrote the classic novel, *Little Women*, and **Sleepy Hollow Cemetery,** Route 62, final resting place for Alcott and fellow literary greats Thoreau, Emerson, and Hawthorne.

Lexington's additional highlights include the **Museum of Our National Heritage,** 33 Marrett Road, (781) 861-6559, open free daily for a look at changing exhibits that thematically tackle time periods in American life, and the **Lexington Battle Green,** 1875 Massachusetts Avenue, (781) 862-1450, site of the first skirmish in the American Revolution.

If you do only one thing in Lowell, visit the **Lowell National Historical Park,** 246 Market Street, (978) 970-5000. At the Visitor Center, you'll begin to glimpse the life of nineteenth-century textile workers through hands-on activities and an orientation film. From there, board a turn-of-the-century trolley to the Boott Cotton Mills Museum, where you'll see enormous power looms in action.

The human story behind the Industrial Revolution comes to life at the Boott Mills Boardinghouse, where you'll learn about a typical day in the life of a mill girl. Two museums in Lowell also highlight the city's history as a major textile producer. The **American Textile History Museum,** 491 Dutton Street, (978) 441-0400, looks at textile production from colonial days to the present. The **New England Quilt Museum,** 18 Shattuck Street, (978) 452-4207, features permanent and changing exhibits of both traditional and contemporary quilts. Lowell is also home to the **Whistler House Museum of Art,** 243 Worthen Street, (978) 452-7641, birthplace of painter James McNeill Whistler, and to the **New England Sports Museum,** 25 Shattuck Street, (978) 452-6775, where the region's sports heritage is celebrated.

The Merrimack Valley is also home to a few off-the-beaten-path attractions. **Butterfly Place,** 120 Tyngsboro Road, Westford, (978) 392-0955, is a 3,000-square-foot atrium filled with 500 colorful specimens from around the world. **Fruitlands,** 102 Prospect Hill Road, Harvard, (978) 456-3924, bills itself as the museum of the New England landscape. Here, you'll find archeological excavations, galleries, nature trails, and a tea room with a view. The **Nashoba Valley Winery,** 100 Wattaquadoc Hill Road, Bolton, (978) 779-5521, is so much more than a winery—it's a 55-acre orchard where you can pick your own fruit, picnic, and partake of special festivals, tours, and tastings.

TRAVEL TIP

Freshwater beaches north of Boston:

- Breakheart Reservation, 177 Forest Street, Saugus
- Walden Pond, 915 Walden Street, Concord
- Wyman's Beach, 48 Wyman's Beach Road, Westford

Dining Highlights

In Salem, feast on slow-roasted prime rib accompanied by an all-you-can-eat salad bar at **Victoria Station,** Pickering Wharf, (978) 745-3400. For light but delicious fare and locally made beer, pop into **Salem Beer Works,** 278 Derby Street, (978) 745-2337. If you're in town on a Sunday, don't miss the Jazz Brunch at **Nathaniel's,** the restaurant at the Hawthorne Hotel, 18 Washington Square West, (978) 825-4311. Feed your sweet tooth at **Ye Olde Pepper Candy Companie,** 122 Derby Street, (978) 745-2744, America's oldest candy company, which has been a fixture in Salem since 1806.

Dining overlooking the water is definitely the thing to do when you're vacationing along the North Shore. At the **Landing,** 81 Front Street, Marblehead, (781) 639-1266, you may find the views of Marblehead Harbor so distracting you forget to eat! The **Gloucester House Restaurant,** Seven Seas Wharf on Route 127, Gloucester, (978) 283-1812 or (888) 283-1812, features traditional New England lobster bakes and harbor views, too. Want gourmet take-out to prepare or eat in your own little seaside bungalow? The **Ipswich Shellfish Fish Market,** 8 Hayward Street, Ipswich, (978) 356-6941 or (888) 711-3060, is the place to go for lobster pie, clam fritters, fish cakes, and even sushi to go.

The biggest dining dilemma you may face is deciding where to eat clams. It's been more than eighty years since Lawrence "Chubby" Woodman invented the fried clam at the restaurant he opened in 1914. Now, his family still operates **Woodman's of Essex,** 121 Main Street/Route 133, Essex, (800) 649-1773, and the fried clams are every bit as delectable as the day they were discovered. Then again, Ipswich is renowned for its clams, and the town boasts its own venerable clam institution, the **Clam Box of Ipswich,** 246 High Street, (978) 356-9707, which has been serving the bivalves since 1938.

Legendary dining is in store in the Merrimack Valley. The **Bull Run Restaurant,** Route 2A, Shirley, (978) 425-4311 or (877)

536-7190, is a pre-Revolutionary tavern, which may have been visited by Paul Revere if you believe the legend. The **Four Sisters Owl Diner,** 244 Appleton Street, Lowell, (978) 453-8321, was there to serve the mill girls, and now you can stop in for a meal or a cup of coffee. Lowell's oldest tavern, **Old Worthen House,** 141 Worthen Street, (978) 459-0300, dates to the 1830s and is known for affordable meals.

Foods and wines are matched harmoniously at J's, the restaurant at **Nashoba Valley Winery,** 100 Wattaquadoc Hill Road, Bolton, (978) 779-9816, where you can polish your meal off with Pumpkin Crème Brûlé and the winery's own Peach Wine.

Shopping Discoveries

In Salem, **Pickering Wharf,** Derby Street, (978) 740-6990, is a quaint waterfront commercial area dominated by shops selling antiques and handcrafted items. Salem is also home to a proliferation of shops selling New Age wares. The **Broom Closet,** 3 Central Street, (978) 741-3669, bills itself as "Salem's largest shop for witches and others." You'll find wands and cauldrons, herbs and incense, ritual robes and velvet capes, and spell books and supplies for sale. If you're traveling with children, be sure to stop into the **Magic Parlor,** 230 Essex Street, (978) 740-3866. It's chock full of tricks and gags and even has its own resident witch, Sharon Graham, who is available for in-store tarot card readings.

Antique aficionados will want to head for Main Street in Essex, the North Shore's best hunting grounds for treasures from bygone days. If it's art and fine crafts you're after, the charming fishing village of Rockport is a thriving art colony, and there are dozens of galleries to tickle your fancy. Don't miss the **Rockport Art Association,** Main Street, (978) 546-6604, an artists' cooperative founded in 1921 that welcomes the public to browse in its galleries. In the downtown and Bearskin Neck areas of Rockport, you'll also find nearly 100 exceedingly diverse shops touting everything from

Christmas collectibles to antiques, to clothing, to fine jewelry. The peninsula across the harbor from Gloucester, Rocky Neck, is home to another enclave of artists. In fact Rocky Neck is one of America's oldest art colonies. John Singer Sargent and Winslow Homer painted here, and you'll still find dozens of galleries and studios of artists who find inspiration in the ever-shifting seascape.

For an authentic "Perfect Storm" souvenir, visit **Cape Pond Ice Company,** 104 Commercial Street, Gloucester, (978) 283-0174, where you can purchase a "Cape Pond Ice–The Coolest Guys Around" T-shirt identical to the one worn by actor John Hawkes, who played "Bugsy" Moran in the movie.

In the Merrimack Valley, shop or simply observe at the **Brush Art Gallery and Studios,** 256 Market Street, Lowell, (978) 459-7819, a restored mill that is home to thirteen working artists and craftspersons. A 260-year-old New England home in North Andover is the unique setting for **Margot's Gallery,** 1070 Salem Street, (978) 683-6333, specializing in an international array of folk art and sculpture.

FAST FACT

Rockport has been "dry," meaning no alcoholic beverages are served in restaurants, since 1856, when seamstress Hannah Jumper led a crusade to drive the "demon rum" out of town. Most restaurants will allow you to bring your own spirits to enjoy with your meal, but it's a good idea to inquire ahead.

South of Boston

THE LAND OF PILGRIMS, CRANBERRIES, AND WHALES makes for an appealing family vacation pick not only for its selection of historic attractions but also for its proximity to Boston—without the city's family-unfriendly prices. As an added bonus, your youngsters will never dismiss history as dull again once they've chatted with Myles Standish in person at the re-created Pilgrim village at Plimoth Plantation.

The region south of Boston is comprised of three counties—Norfolk, Plymouth, and Bristol. It's a compact area with sights that can be savored in the space of a short getaway. Or, you may decide to stay longer, just as the *Mayflower*'s occupants did back in 1620. Regardless of the duration of your visit, you're bound to depart with a new appreciation for the enduring American traditions that originated on this stretch of New England shore.

Lodging Options

Plymouth is a popular family destination, and reasonably priced accommodations abound. The kids will adore the Pilgrim Theme Pool at the **John Carver Inn,** 25 Summer Street, (508) 746-7100 or (800) 274-1620, which is on the site of the original Pilgrim settlement. **Cold Spring**

Motel, 188 Court Street, (508) 746-2222 or (800) 678-8667, offers comfortable accommodations within walking distance of waterfront attractions. The **Governor Bradford Motor Inn,** Water Street, (508) 746-6200 or (800) 332-1620, also boasts ninety-four guest rooms and an enviable location overlooking Plymouth Harbor. Want to rent a single-family home or cottage for your stay in the area? Call **Absent Innkeeper,** 15 Clearwater Drive, (508) 224-6728, for several rental options—they'll even book in-home spa services for you.

Bristol County claims one of New England's most bizarre lodging establishments—the **Lizzie Borden Bed & Breakfast,** 92 Second Street, Fall River, (508) 675-7333. For all of you craving a stay at the scene of a notorious crime, this inn was once the very house where, allegedly, "Lizzie Borden took an axe, and gave her mother forty whacks. And when she saw what she had done, She gave her father forty-one."

For something a bit less macabre, try the eighty-four-room **Comfort Inn of North Dartmouth/New Bedford,** 171 Faunce Corner Road, North Dartmouth, (508) 996-0800 or (800) 228-5150, or the **Best Western,** 360 Airport Road, Fall River, (508) 672-0011 or (800) 528-1234, which has an indoor pool.

Pilgrim Points and Other Pleasures

Time is frozen in 1627 at **Plimoth Plantation,** 137 Warren Avenue, (508) 746-1622. Half a million people descend upon this living history attraction in Plymouth each year to interact with costumed interpreters and to glimpse the life of New England's first settlers and their Native American neighbors. While you're in Plymouth, other Pilgrim sites that you'll want to visit include the ***Mayflower II,*** Water Street at the State Pier, (508) 746-1662, a replica of the Pilgrims' ship; **Pilgrim Hall Museum,** 75 Court Street, (508) 746-1620, which exhibits Pilgrim possessions and Native American artifacts; and **Plymouth National Wax Museum,** 16 Carver Street, (508) 746-6468, where the story of the Pilgrims' journey to America and their first Thanksgiving is told via realistic, life-size wax figures.

Here are two interesting ways to see Plymouth. **Splashdown Amphibious Duck Boat Tours,** (508) 747-7658 or (800) 225-4000, depart from Harbor Place for one-hour land and sea tours aboard a World War II-era amphibious craft. Or, **Colonial Lantern Tours,** 5 North Street, (508) 747-4161 or (800) 698-5636, will provide you with your own tin lantern and lead you on an evening exploration of Plymouth's past or of local ghosts and legends. Nightly tours are offered April through Thanksgiving.

Plymouth is also home to **Ocean Spray Cranberry World,** 225 Water Street, (508) 747-2350, where, from May through November, you can learn about the history and process of cranberry cultivation and sample cranberry products. Admission is free. In nearby South Carver, the **Edaville Railroad's Cranberry Belt Line,** Route 58, (508) 866-8190 or (877) EDAVILLE, will take you on a five and one-half-mile trip through cranberry country on weekends in September and October.

Further south in Bristol County, major attractions are devoted to Massachusetts' whaling and seafaring history. At the **New Bedford Whaling Museum,** 18 Johnny Cake Hill, New Bedford, (508) 997-0046, the largest American museum devoted to the history of the whaling industry, you'll be awed by a complete skeleton of a rare blue whale, the world's largest ship model, and the world's most extensive collection of whaling artifacts. The museum is open daily. The **Marine Museum,** 70 Water Street, Fall River, (508) 674-3533, has among its exhibits one of the largest collections of *Titanic* artifacts and memorabilia in the United States. And while you're in Fall River, don't miss **Battleship Cove,** 1 Central Street, (508) 678-1100, where you'll see historic World War II ships including the battleship *Massachusetts,* the submarine *Lionfish,* and the destroyer *Joseph P. Kennedy Jr.*

Tucked away in Westport, you'll find one of the country's leading producers of sparkling wines and New England's largest vineyard. **Westport Rivers Vineyard and Winery,** 417 Hixbridge

Road, (508) 636-3423, welcomes the public for tastings daily and for tours on weekends.

Dining Highlights

Each November, the public can sample seventeenth-century dishes as **Plimoth Plantation,** 137 Warren Avenue, Plymouth, recreates the Pilgrims' First Thanksgiving. Advance reservations are required, and these historical dining experiences book up fast. Call (508) 746-1622, ext. 8366 for a schedule, prices, and reservations.

For outdoor dining overlooking Plymouth Harbor, head to **Wood's Seafood** at the Town Pier, (508) 746-0261, which has been serving seafood for more than seventy years. Wood's made headlines in 1992 when it found a blue lobster among the catch purchased from a local lobsterman. Blue lobsters are one in 20 million, and no, this one did not suffer the fate of being dunked in butter. The lobster was donated to the New England Aquarium for study.

In Fall River, you can watch tomorrow's chefs prepare your meal in the kitchen laboratory of the **Abbey Grill,** the dining room at the International Institute of Culinary Arts, 100 Rock Street, (508) 675-9305 or (888) 383-2665, where lunch is served daily and dinner is served on weekends. In New Bedford, grab a bite at **Freestone's City Grill,** 41 William Street, (508) 993-7477, a two-time first place winner in the Newport Chowder Cook-Off. It's housed in a historic 1877 bank building and is also a showcase for funky art.

Shopping Discoveries

Did you know that factory outlet shopping was "invented" in New Bedford in the 1950s? Today, outlet centers abound in this area. **Quality Factory Outlets,** 638 Quequechan Street, Fall River, (508) 677-4949, features Levi's, Corning/Revere, and even a Karaoke outlet. Save on sweaters and knitwear at the **Northeast Knitting Mills Factory Outlet Store,**

(508) 678-1383, located at the Tower Mill Outlet Center, 657 Quarry Street, Fall River, (508) 674-4646, where you'll also discover more than a dozen other outlet stores. **Wampanoag Mill Factory Outlet Center,** 420 Quequechan Street, Fall River, (508) 678-5242, features outlets from Bay State Trading Co., Fall River Shoe and Luggage Too, and more.

You can visit one of the oldest general stores in America in Dartmouth. **Davoll's General Store,** 1228 Russell's Mills Road, (508) 636-4530, has been in business since 1793 and today sells an assortment of clothing, antiques, and collectibles. Antiquers will also want to stop at Plymouth Antique Trading Co., Eight Court Street, Plymouth, which represents treasures from 125 dealers.

FAST FACT

The **Fall River Historical Society,** 451 Rock Street, Fall River, (508) 679-1071, is the keeper of all of the clues in the 1892 mystery of whether Lizzie Borden really whacked her folks, including Lizzie's hatchet, pillow shams dotted with blood, locks of the victims' hair, and crime scene photos. Lizzie was acquitted in 1893, and the murder case remains one of Massachusetts's great unsolved mysteries. Call ahead, as the museum's days and hours of operation vary seasonally.

Worcester and Central Massachusetts

WORCESTER IS NEW ENGLAND'S SECOND LARGEST city, out-populated only by Boston, and while it is a destination for quite a few business travelers, the city and its surrounding central Massachusetts environs are often overlooked by the tourists. What are vacationers missing? A host of cultural and historic attractions, prime recreational facilities, one of New England's finest living history museums, and a trail of discoveries that winds through the countryside.

Central Massachusetts also offers that hard to quantify but nevertheless all-important benefit—location, location, location. If you're looking for a central spot from which to explore New England, Worcester puts you within a few hours' drive of most of Massachusetts and parts of Connecticut, Rhode Island, and New Hampshire, too.

FAST FACT

Unlike other legendary figures, Johnny Appleseed was a real person. His name was John Chapman, and he was born in Leominster, Massachusetts. What possessed him to travel an area of about 100,000 square miles sowing the seeds of apple trees? No one is completely certain, but legend has it that Chapman had a dream in which he saw a vision of a land filled with blossoming apple trees where no one went hungry.

Worcester Regional Airport

For New England travelers whose destination is in central or western Massachusetts, **Worcester Regional Airport** (ORH), Airport Drive, (508) 799-1741 or (888) FLY-WORC, is a viable, growing alternative to the much more congested Logan International Airport in Boston. Four major carriers offer flights in and out of Worcester: American Eagle, (800) 433-7300; Delta, (800) 282-3424; Pan American Airways, (800) 359-7262; and US Airways (800) 428-4322.

Worcester Regional Airport is located north of the Mass Pike (I-90) off I-290. Worcester Airport Limousine Service, (800) 660-0992, provides door-to-door transportation between the airport and surrounding areas.

Lodging Options

The list of lodging possibilities in Worcester reads like a laundry list of who's who in hotels—Courtyard by Marriott, Crowne Plaza, Days Inn, Hampton Inn, Holiday Inn, Ramada Inn, Regency Suites. That said, there are some more distinctive choices, too. The **Beechwood Hotel,** 363 Plantation Street, (508) 754-5789 or (800) 344-2589, has antique and elegant touches and both standard rooms and executive suites. About ten miles from Worcester in Spencer, you'll find the **Red Maple Inn,** 217 Main Street, (508) 885-9205, a circa-1780 Federal-style colonial home turned B&B that is on the National Register of Historical Places.

Staying in Sturbridge? You'll find charming choices such as the **Publick House Historic Inn,** Route 131, (508) 347-3313 or (800) PUBLICK, built in 1881, it features seventeen rooms and suites, many with canopied beds and other period touches. **Sturbridge Country Inn,** 530 Main Street, (508) 347-5503, is a white-columned, 1840s Greek Revival farmhouse that has a fireplace and whirlpool tub in every guest room. The **Thomas Henry**

Hearthstone Inn, 453 Main Street, (508) 347-2224 or (888) 781-7775, invites you to sip complimentary tea, cognac, or brandy by the two-story fireplace before retiring to your whirlpool-equipped suite. For extensive amenities, try the **Sturbridge Host Hotel,** 366 Main Street, (508) 347-7393, which offers business services, room service, a gift shop/newsstand, fitness center, indoor pool, tennis, private lake with beach, racquetball, tennis, child care, a lounge, a tavern, and a restaurant. You can also stay right at Old Sturbridge Village in the **Old Sturbridge Village Lodges** and the **Oliver Wight House**. Call (508) 347-3327 for rates and reservations.

The **Worcester County Convention & Visitors Bureau,** 30 Worcester Center Boulevard, Worcester, (508) 753-2920, offers a central online reservation service via its Web site, *www.worcester.org*. Check availability at area properties with just a few clicks.

Exploring the Core of Massachusetts

Where to begin will be the burning question on your mind once you've arrived in the heart of Massachusetts. Why not start in Worcester, where you can catch a glimpse of a past that predates New England's at the **Higgins Armory Museum,** 100 Barber Avenue, (508) 853-6015, the only museum in the Americas dedicated to arms and armor. The amazing collections of John Woodman Higgins are grandly displayed in a Great Hall that resembles those found in European castles. Children will enjoy making their own brass rubbings and modeling medieval garb. The museum is open Tuesday through Sunday. While in Worcester, don't overlook the **Ecotarium,** 222 Harrington Way, (508) 929-2700, an environmental center with indoor and outdoor wildlife habitats, a planetarium, nature trails, a railroad, and interactive exhibits that is open daily. The **Worcester Art Museum,** 55 Salisbury Street, (508) 799-4406, showcases fifty centuries of art and even has a thirteenth-century French chapel rebuilt stone by stone tucked away inside. Worcester is also home, believe it or not, to the **American Sanitary Plumbing Museum,** 39 Piedmont Street, (508) 754-9453. Call ahead, as hours are limited, and you wouldn't want to have your hopes of seeing fabulous fixtures flushed down the toilet.

Old Sturbridge Village, Route 20, Sturbridge, (508) 347-3362, attracts thousands of tourists each year. The living history site re-creates New England life in the 1830s, and visitors can get in on the act by talking with costumed interpreters, riding the river, tasting foods prepared hearthside, learning nineteenth-century crafts, and attending special annual events such as an 1830s wedding and Militia Day.

If the notion of a scenic country drive past farm stands, orchards, vineyards, and other points of interest calls to you, visit *www.appleseed.org* or call (978) 534-2302 for your free guide to the **Johnny Appleseed Trail,** the nickname given to the stretch of Route 2 that runs from I-495 west until it connects with the Mohawk Trail around Westminster. This stretch of Route 2 traverses twenty-five classic New England towns and offers dozens of reasons to pull over and explore.

Central Massachusetts can claim Johnny Appleseed as its famous native son, and it can claim a famous native daughter, too. Clara Barton, known for her efforts to provide medical care to Civil War soldiers and for founding the American Red Cross, was born in North Oxford, Massachusetts. Today, you can visit the **Clara Barton Birthplace Museum,** 68 Clara Barton Road, North Oxford, (508) 987-5375, Wednesday through Sunday in the summer months and on Saturdays or by appointment in the fall through Thanksgiving.

Love to explore the outdoors? At **Purgatory Chasm State Reservation,** Purgatory Road, Sutton, (508) 234-3733, you can climb or simply picnic beside the 70-foot granite walls left behind by the last Ice Age. The **Quabbin Reservoir,** Ware Road, Belchertown, (413) 323-7221, is a popular free spot for hiking, fishing, and boating. Built in the 1930s, it is one of the largest man-made reservoirs in America. Beneath its tranquil surface lie the "lost towns" of Dana, North Dana, Greenwich, Enfield, and Prescott,

Massachusetts, all flooded and destroyed so that metropolitan Boston could have an additional water supply. Though the towns no longer exist, their history and fate is preserved by the **Swift River Valley Historical Society** at the Whitaker-Clary House, Elm Street, New Salem, (978) 544-6882, which is open on Wednesdays and Sundays in July and August.

TRAVEL TIP

The first covered bridge in the United States was built in 1806 by Massachusetts native Timothy Palmer—in Philadelphia. During the balance of the nineteenth century, New England carpenters made the covered bridge an art form all their own. The red-stained **Gilbertville Bridge,** Bridge Street, Hardwick, was built in 1886 to span the Ware River and remains open to vehicular traffic. **Bissell Bridge,** Route 8A, Charlemont, (413) 339-4045, was built in 1951 to span the Mill River. **Sheffield Bridge,** Covered Bridge Lane, Sheffield, was rebuilt in 1999 to replace the state's oldest covered bridge, which was destroyed by vandals. The **Pumping Station Bridge,** Eunice Williams Drive, Greenville, was built in 1972 to replace its fire-damaged 1870 predecessor. **C. Waterous Bridge,** Groton Street, Pepperell, was originally built in 1848 and rebuilt in 1962.

Dining Highlights

From hearty chowder to broiled Boston scrod to lobster pie to baked Indian pudding, if it's traditional Yankee cooking you're seeking, the dining room at the **Publick House,** Route 131, Sturbridge, (508) 347-3313 or (800) PUB-LICK, delivers. The historic **Salem Cross Inn,** Route 9, West Brookfield, (508) 867-2345, is open daily for lunch and dinner, but call ahead to try to time your visit with one of their special Fireplace Feasts, when you can sample early American fare including prime rib roasted on the only known roasting jack still operating in America and apple pie baked in a 1699 beehive oven.

Another historic dining choice is the **Cocke 'n Kettle Restaurant,** South Main Street/Route 122, Uxbridge, (508) 278-5517, a Georgian-style mansion that was built in the early 1800s by Revolutionary War veteran Hon Bazalee Taft. It's been a restaurant since 1971, and the dinner menu features hearty steak and seafood preparations.

The **Restaurant at Tatnuck Bookseller,** 335 Chandler Street, Worcester, (508) 756-7644 or (800) 64-BOOKS, features curious, glass-topped tables, each with its own theme—the Star Trek table, the historic Worcester table, the dessert table, the money table, and more.

Shopping Discoveries

Sturbridge has tantalizing shops for travelers to explore. At **Sturbridge Pottery,** 99 New Boston Road, (508) 347-9763, Gary and Ann Malone have been selling their one-of-a-kind creations for twenty-five years. **Wrights Factory Outlet,** 559 Main Street, (508) 347-2839, sells ribbons, lace, and other creative supplies at a discount. **Sadie Green's Curiosity Shop,** Route 131, (508) 347-1449, specializes in antique glass.

For bargains, head to **Worcester Common Outlets,** 100 Front Street, Worcester, (508) 798-2581, where you'll find more than fifty outlet stores including Saks Fifth Avenue, Dress Barn, Bass, Reebok, and more.

Springfield and the Pioneer Valley

MOM WANTS TO SHOP AND TOUR OLD HOUSES. Dad's a sports nut. And the kids won't be satisfied unless they get themselves on a roller coaster pronto. No need for anyone in this family to pout. That is, if they've selected Massachusetts' Pioneer Valley for their holiday away.

There's a monumental mix of sightseeing and amusement opportunities along the Connecticut River in the Pioneer Valley. You'll find two historic villages, the Basketball Hall of Fame, New England's largest theme park, and Yankee Candle's headquarters. Familial harmony is practically guaranteed.

HOT SPOT

The Six Flags theme park company made its mark on New England in 2000 when it took over the former Riverside amusement park. **Six Flags New England,** Route 159, Agawam, (413) 786-9300 or (877) 4-SIXFLAGS, features thrill rides including the Superman Ride of Steel—one of the fastest and tallest roller coasters in the world, children's rides and amusements, shows, Looney Tunes Movietown, and the Island Kingdom Water Park. The park is open daily from late May through Labor Day and on weekends and select holidays in early May, September, and October. Admission includes all rides and is discounted after 4 P.M.

Lodging Options

In the Pioneer Valley, you'll find both business-class hotels and classic inns beset with nostalgic allure. In Springfield: the **Sheraton Springfield,** One Monarch Place, (413) 781-1010 or (800) 426-9004, overlooks the Connecticut River from its convenient location off I-91. In Holyoke: the **Yankee Pedlar Inn,** 1866 Northampton Street, (413) 532-9494, offers lavishly decorated rooms and its own Oyster Bar and Grill Room. In Northampton: The grandeur of an old New England hotel awaits at the **Hotel Northampton,** 36 King Street, (413) 584-3100 or (800) 547-3529, a 1927 Colonial Revival gem that is a member of Historic Hotels of America. In Amherst: the **Lord Jeffery Inn,** 30 Boltwood Avenue, (413) 253-2576 or (800) 742-0358, dates to 1926 and offers both authentic New England fare in the **Windowed Hearth** restaurant and a lighter menu at **Elijah Boltwood's Tavern,** in addition to forty-eight guest rooms. For reasonable rates, book a room at the **Campus Center Hotel at the University of Massachusetts,** 918 Campus Center, (413) 549-6000. In Deerfield: If you're looking for the quintessential New England inn, look no further than the **Deerfield Inn,** 81 Old Main Street, (413) 774-5587 or (800) 926-3865. Located in the heart of Old Deerfield, this 1884 National Historic Landmark has twenty-three individually furnished guest rooms with four-poster beds and other pleasing touches.

HOT SPOT

Historic, 750-acre **Forest Park,** Sumner Avenue, Springfield, (413) 733-3800, is transformed each holiday season into Bright Nights, a two and one-half-mile, drive-through display featuring more than 350,000 lights. One of New England's largest holiday light displays, it features Seuss Land, Noah's Ark, North Pole Village, Winter Woods, and a Victorian Village.

Pioneer Places

Did you know that basketball was invented in Springfield by Dr. James Naismith? The **Basketball Hall of Fame,** 1150 West Columbus Avenue, Springfield, (413) 781-6500 or (877) 4HOOPLA, celebrates this truly American sporting invention and the great players, coaches, and teams that have captured fans' imaginations. The Hall is open daily, and you'll even have a chance to get in the game yourself, although without the typical NBA player's salary. Watch the Basketball Hall of Fame Web site, *www.hoophall.com,* for news of the new Hall that is under construction and scheduled to open in Springfield during the summer of 2002. While you're in the area, sports fans may also want to visit the **Volleyball Hall of Fame,** 444 Dwight Street, Holyoke, (413) 536-0926. Volleyball was invented in Holyoke.

Where can you see art masterpieces, dinosaurs, an aquarium, a planetarium, early aviation artifacts, and arms and armor, all in one place? The **Springfield Museums at the Quadrangle,** 220 State Street, Springfield, (413) 263-6800, is a unique collection of four museums clustered around a central green. The Museum of Fine Arts and the George Walter Vincent Smith Art Museum are here, as are the Springfield Science Museum and the Connecticut Valley Historical Museum. One admission fee admits you to all four museums, which are open daily except Monday year-round. A national memorial dedicated to beloved children's book author and Springfield native Theodor Geisel, better known as Dr. Seuss, is scheduled to be unveiled at the Quadrangle on June 1, 2002.

The 300-year-old **Historic Deerfield,** located off Routes 5 and 10 in Deerfield, (413) 774-5581, is one of the Pioneer Valley's most popular day trip destinations. Admission includes guided tours of the village's fourteen eighteenth- and nineteenth-century houses, a self-guided tour of the Flynt Center of Early New England Life, a walking tour of the village (weather permitting), and all special events on the day of your visit. Historic Deerfield is open daily. You can also visit the **Storrowton Village Museum,** 1305 Memorial

Avenue, West Springfield, (413) 787-0136, a restored nineteenth-century New England village including a meetinghouse, schoolhouse, blacksmith shop, and homes on the grounds of the Eastern States Exposition.

Tours of the **Emily Dickinson Homestead,** 280 Main Street, Amherst, (413) 542-8161, are available from March through mid-December and provide fascinating insight into the life of the reclusive poet, who lived here for most of her life.

If you're traveling with children, consider a stop at the **Zoo at Forest Park,** Sumner Avenue, Springfield, (413) 733-2251, which is home to a variety of domestic and exotic animals.

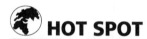

HOT SPOT

The **Eastern States Exposition,** more commonly known as "The Big E," is a New England extravaganza! This celebration of the history and agriculture of the six New England states is North America's ninth largest fair. It's held each September in West Springfield. Call (413) 737-2443 for dates and the schedule of top entertainment.

Dining Highlights

Bountiful buffet breakfasts featuring pancakes, French toast, scrambled eggs, home fries, bacon, sausage, ham, milk, juice, coffee, and pure maple syrup (hungry yet?) are served during sugaring season (late February through early April) and in the fall at **High Hopes Sugar House,** Route 112, South Worthington, (413) 238-5919 or (800) 627-5374. **Bluebonnet Diner,** 324 King Street, Northampton, (413) 584-3333, caters to late risers and the enormous local college student population by serving breakfast all day.

For a taste of New England at lunchtime, grab a sandwich and some hot cheddar soup at the **Vermont Country Deli & Café,** 48 Main Street, Northampton, (413) 586-7114.

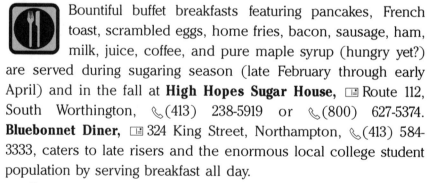

The **Northampton Brewery,** 11 Brewster Court, Northampton, (413) 584-9903, is a good choice for lighter fare and locally crafted beers. Don't miss the crostini appetizer, a toasted baguette topped with fresh basil, diced tomato, cucumber, and red onion relish in a balsamic and olive oil dressing. You'll also find pub food and beers microbrewed in the Pioneer Valley at **Amherst Brewing Company,** 36 North Pleasant Street, Amherst, (413) 253-4400.

For one blowout eating experience, make reservations at one of the dining rooms at the **Deerfield Inn,** 81 Old Main Street, (413) 774-5587 or (800) 926-3865, in the heart of Historic Deerfield.

Shopping Discoveries

The **Yankee Candle** flagship store, Routes 5 and 10 North, South Deerfield, (413) 665-2929 or (877) 636-7707, draws 2.5 million visitors each year and is one of New England's most popular tourist attractions. You can spend hours lost inside its cavernous showrooms. The 90,000-square-foot complex includes a candle-making museum, a dip-your-own candle area, a Winter Wonderland where it snows indoors, a car museum, a restaurant, and more.

Shoppers may just believe they've reached nirvana when they discover Main Street in Northampton. This funky little college town is the perfect destination for travelers looking to spend an afternoon drifting in and out of clever shops discovering the work and wares of New England artists and entrepreneurs. Don't miss the enormous selection of designer jewelry at **Silverscape Designs,** 11 King Street, (413) 584-3324, and the endless greeting card department at **Faces,** 175 Main Street, (413) 584-4081, one of the quirkiest gift shops on the planet.

Brimfield is the site of the largest outdoor antique show in New England—more than 5,000 dealers from across the nation converge to display their wares along a 1-mile stretch of Route 20. Shows are held each year in May, July, and September. Contact the **Quaboag Valley Chamber of Commerce,** (413) 283-2418, for dates and details.

The Berkshires

WHAT WOULD YOU GET IF YOU TOOK the sophisticated cultural enticements of Boston or Manhattan and transplanted them to a place of wide-open spaces, lush vegetation, statuesque mountains, sleepy towns, vigorous rivers, and tranquil country roads? You'd get the Berkshire Hills of western Massachusetts, of course. And the good news is, you can be there in just over a two-hour drive from either Boston or New York City. You'll be joined by the Boston Symphony Orchestra, which takes up residence at Tanglewood each summer; by the nation's leading actors, who escape Manhattan and Los Angeles. for summer stock stages; by world-renowned ballet troupes, and by dozens of other artists, writers, and performers. Don't be intimidated—tourists are welcome here, too!

Lest you think that the Berkshires are percolating with activity in the summertime only, this accessible destination in the mountains offers four-season recreational possibilities, from white-water rafting when rivers are raging with spring runoff to scenic autumn explorations along one of New England's oldest and most picturesque routes to downhill schussing at numerous ski areas. You just may find, as generations of vacationers have, that transplanting yourself regularly to an inn, B&B, or even a weekend or summer home here allows you to leave the hassles of city life behind without sacrificing the richness.

HOT SPOT

Imagine lazing back on your picnic blanket, feasting on gourmet goodies, sipping something bubbly, and listening to the rich strains of a symphony or the cool sounds of jazz. A musical evening at Tanglewood, the Boston Symphony Orchestra's summer home in the Berkshires since 1936, may just be the most memorable event of your stay in the region. Located in Lenox, **Tanglewood** is open from late June through early September each year and hosts a variety of performances. Call SymphonyCharge at (617) 266-1200 or (888) 266-1200 for tickets, or purchase them online at *www.bso.org*. Even if you haven't planned ahead, you may still be able to get lawn tickets at the gate.

Lodging Options

If you're looking for a truly romantic, historic, and extraordinary inn, western Massachusetts won't disappoint. Try **Blantyre,** 16 Blantyre Road, Lenox, (413) 637-3556, a Tudor-style mansion modeled after a Scottish ancestral home of the builder's wife, which features hand-carved four-poster beds, leaded glass windows, tennis, and fine dining. The historic **Red Lion Inn,** 30 Main Street, Stockbridge, (413) 298-5545, was originally a 1773 stagecoach stop rebuilt in 1897 after a devastating fire. The inn was immortalized in Norman Rockwell's painting, *Main Street, Stockbridge*. **Cranwell Resort & Golf Club,** 55 Lee Road, Lenox, (413) 637-1364 or (800) 272-6935, is a 380-acre estate with an 1894 Tudor mansion as its focal point where you can enjoy a host of outdoor activities including golf, tennis, bicycling, and cross-country skiing. The elegant **Cliffwood Inn,** 25 Cliffwood Street, Lenox, (413) 637-3330 or (800) 789-3331, was once home to America's ambassador to France–it has ten fireplaces including six in guest rooms. **Wheatleigh,** Hawthorne Road, Lenox, (413) 637-0610, was a wedding gift from Henry H. Cook to his daughter in 1893, and now the magnificent estate, with landscaping designed by Frederick Law Olmstead, the same fellow responsible for New York's Central Park, welcomes guests seeking exquisite accommodations year-round.

Lenox is home to one of the world's most highly regarded health spas, the **Canyon Ranch Health Resort,** 165 Kemble Street, (413) 637-4100 or (800) 326-7080, where you can relax, be pampered, and learn healthy-living secrets that will extend your spa vacation long past your stay in the Berkshires. In Lenox, you'll also find the **Kripalu Center for Yoga and Health,** West Street, (413) 448-3152 or (800) 741-7353, a vacation sanctuary featuring workshops on yoga and meditation, plus health services including massage, acupuncture, facial therapy, and more.

Bed and breakfast accommodations are plentiful as well. **Applegate Bed & Breakfast,** 279 West Park Street, Lee, (413) 243-4451 or (800) 691-9012, is a 1920s Georgian Colonial with six individually detailed guest rooms and a baby grand piano in the living room. **Baldwin Hill Farm B&B,** 121 Baldwin Hill Road, Egremont, (413) 528-4092 or (888) 528-4092, is situated on a 450-acre hilltop farm. Those with a penchant for music and poetry will feel right at home at **Brook Farm Inn,** 15 Hawthorne Street, Lenox, (413) 637-3013 or (800) 285-7638, where a poem of the day is highlighted each morning, Saturday tea is accompanied by poetry readings, and Sunday breakfasts in the summer feature performances by student musicians from Boston University Tanglewood Institute. The **Weathervane Inn,** Route 23, South Egremont, (413) 528-9580 or (800) 528-9580, is a 1785 farmhouse with an 1835 Greek Revival addition that is listed on the National Register of Historic Places. A full country breakfast featuring locally grown ingredients is served each morning in the Garden Dining Room. Looking for something a bit more rustic? **Race Brook Lodge Bed & Breakfast,** 864 Under Mountain Road, Sheffield, (413) 229-2916, is a transformed New England timber peg barn with exposed wood beams, wide plank floors, and warm, inviting nooks. **Bear Haven Bed & Breakfast,** 22 Mechanic

Street, Shelburne Falls, (413) 625-9281, is a rest home for teddy bears where you can hibernate, too.

If you're seeking something a bit more standard, you'll find hotels and motor inns throughout the region as well. Among the larger options are the 179-room **Crowne Plaza** in Pittsfield, One West Street, (413) 499-2000; the 120-room **Quality Inn,** 130 Pittsfield Road, Lenox, (413) 637-4244 or (800) 442-4201; the fifty-two-room **Best Western Black Swan Inn,** Route 20, Lee, (413) 243-2700 or (800) 876-7926; and the **Orchards,** 222 Adams Road, Williamstown, (800) 225-1517, a forty-seven-room Preferred Hotels & Resorts member inn.

For additional help in locating accommodations, contact the **Berkshire Visitors Bureau's Lodging Reservation Service,** (800) 237-5747, ext. 140.

Berkshires Diversions

M Tie on your running shoes—there are so many unique things to see and do that you may have to scurry to fit them all into your time in the Berkshires. Of course, you don't have to do them all on your first visit.

Put the **Norman Rockwell Museum,** Route 183, Stockbridge, (413) 298-4100, high on your "to visit" list. Rockwell was one of America's best-loved artists, and his gift for capturing a slice of American life is even more evident when you see his original works up close. The museum is open daily year-round.

At the **Berkshire Museum,** 39 South Street, Pittsfield, (413) 443-7171, see a diverse collection of art, history, and science exhibits year-round and a breathtaking display of Christmas trees during the annual Festival of Trees from mid-November through December.

Climb aboard the Sensory Integrator at the **Dark Ride Project, Historic Beaver Mill,** Route 8, North Ada (413) 663-6662, where futuristic art and a theme park ride combine. It's open Wednesday through Sunday, June through October.

If you're a dance fan, catch a summertime ballet, modern, or ethnic dance performance at **Jacob's Pillow Dance Festival,** George Carter Road, Becket, (413) 243-0745. Many free talks and demonstrations are open to the public, too.

Stroll through 15 acres of pretty plantings at the **Berkshire Botanical Garden,** Routes 102 and 183, Stockbridge, (413) 298-3926, open daily May through October.

The Berkshires have sung their siren song to artists and writers for centuries, and today you can visit the historic homes where prominent figures lived and worked. **Herman Melville's Arrowhead,** 780 Holmes Road, Pittsfield, (413) 442-1793, was the author's home while he was hard at work penning *Moby Dick*. **Chesterwood,** 4 Williamsville Road, Stockbridge, (413) 298-3579, was the home of sculptor Daniel Chester French, best known for the statue of the sitting president at the Lincoln Memorial. Visit his studio and gardens May through October. Edith Wharton, a prolific writer and the first woman to win the Pulitzer Prize for fiction, is remembered at her home, the **Mount,** 2 Plunkett Street, Lenox, (413) 637-1899 or (888) 637-1902, which is open for tours Memorial Day through October as it undergoes extensive renovations. The **William Cullen Bryant Homestead,** off Route 112, Cummington, (413) 634-2244, was the poet's summer home, and it is open now to visitors from the end of June through Columbus Day.

For a study in contrasts, visit **Hancock Shaker Village,** Route 20, Pittsfield, (413) 443-0188 or (800) 817-1137, for a firsthand look at the simplicity advocated by the Shaker religious sect. Then head to the **Museum of the Gilded Age,** 104 Walker Street, Lenox, (413) 298-3952, for a look at living at its opposite, extravagant extreme.

Individual and group pilgrimages to the **National Shrine of the Divine Mercy,** Eden Hill, Stockbridge, (413) 298-3931, are always welcome. Built in the 1950s, the shrine is dedicated to Saint Faustina Kowalska, a Polish nun who recorded 600 pages of revelations she received about God's mercy.

Traveling with children? Hike with the llamas at **Hawkmeadow Farm,** 322 Lander Road, Lee, (413) 243-2224; learn how

Japanese shiitake mushrooms are grown at **Delftree Mushroom Farm,** 234 Union Street, North Adams, (413) 664-4907 or (800) 243-3742; board a historic train at the **Berkshire Scenic Railway Museum,** Housatonic Street and Willow Creek Road, Lenox, (413) 637-2210; and experience a working farm at **Holiday Farm,** Holiday Cottage Road, Dalton, (413) 684-0444.

Dining Highlights

Dining at the **Red Lion Inn,** 30 Main Street, Stockbridge, (413) 298-5545, is not just an experience—it's three! That's because you can select from the formal main dining room, the more casual Widow Bingham's Tavern, or the dark and intimate pub atmosphere of the Lion's Den. Whichever you choose, make a reservation.

A culinary blast from the past awaits at **Old Mill,** Route 23, South Egremont, (413) 528-1421, a 1797 grist mill and blacksmith shop turned restaurant. Or chug on over to **Sullivan Station,** Railroad Street, Lee, (413) 243-2082, and dine inside an old train depot.

Spencer's Restaurant at the Thornewood Inn, 453 Stockbridge Road, Great Barrington, (413) 528-3828 or (800) 854-1008, provides lovely mountain views and live jazz or swing music most weekends. Or, for a cozy, candlelit dinner in front of a glowing fireplace, try the **Williamsville Inn,** Route 41, West Stockbridge, (413) 274-6118 or (800) 457-3971. Another romantic choice is the **Old Inn on the Green and Gedney Farm,** Route 57, New Marlborough, (413) 229-3131 or (800) 286-3139, where dining rooms are lit exclusively by candles.

Dine alfresco on barbecued chicken and corn on the cob in the courtyard at the **Candlelight Inn,** 35 Walker Street, Lenox, (413) 637-1555 or (800) 428-0580. For beer brewed in the Berkshires and hearty burgers and sandwiches, head for **Barrington Brewery & Restaurant,** 420 Stockbridge Road, Great Barrington, (413) 528-8282.

In the mood for afternoon tea? The **Village Inn,** 16 Church Street, Lenox, (413) 637-0020 or (800) 253-0917, serves a traditional English tea with homemade scones daily in the summer and fall and on Fridays and Saturdays in the winter and spring.

Shopping Discoveries

As you ramble through the Berkshires, you'll find shopping surprises around every bend—antique shops, flea markets, church tag sales, galleries, boutiques.

Even if you're not in the market for ski gear and warm sweaters, it's worth the trip to **Kenver,** 39 Main Street, South Egremont, (413) 528-2330 or (800) 342-7547, where winter wear is displayed in a former eighteenth-century stagecoach stop and free apples, cider, and coffee are served by a roaring fire. Kenver is open September through March.

Find a unique piece for your home or a one-of-a-kind gift at **Holsten Galleries,** Elm Street, Stockbridge, (413) 298-3044, which represents the creations of dozens of contemporary glass sculptors. And while you're in Stockbridge and thinking about sprucing up your décor, stop into the headquarters of mail order success story **Country Curtains,** Main Street, (413) 298-5565, founded in 1956.

At **Great Barrington Pottery,** 391 North Plain Road, Housatonic, (413) 274-6259, you purchase Japanese-inspired pottery by artist Richard Bennett and visit the Tea House, where the ancient tea ceremony is performed each day between 1 and 4 P.M.

Save some serious shopping time to search for deals at **Prime Outlets,** 50 Water Street, Lee, (413) 243-8186, home to more than sixty name brand outlet stores including Gap, J. Crew, Jones New York, Liz Claiborne, and Polo Ralph Lauren.

Cape Cod and the Islands (Martha's Vineyard and Nantucket)

IN THE 1950s, PATTI PAGE SANG, "You're sure to fall in love with Old Cape Cod," and in the 1970s, Rupert Holmes sang about "piña coladas" and the "dunes of the Cape." You'll be singing the Cape's praises, too, once you've discovered its sea-scented breezes, sandy beaches, adorable B&Bs, enticing shops, and uncanny ability to recharge your life force.

Cape Cod and the nearby islands of Martha's Vineyard and Nantucket are surrounded not only by glittering water but also by a mystique and nostalgia that is unmatched in New England. There is a pervasive sense of a simpler time preserved in the rituals and rhythms of day-to-day living. And at night, the stars shine brighter than you remembered they could, the crickets croon, and the churning surf lulls you to sleep. Whatever the length of your stay, you'll long for just another day in this much-loved corner of New England.

TRAVEL TIP

Want to find ways to get around Cape Cod and the Islands without a car? Call toll free, (888) 33-CAPECOD, to request your free Smart Guide to car-free travel choices, or visit *www.smartguide.org*.

HOT SPOT

Did you know that 43,604 acres of land including forty miles of shoreline from Wellfleet to Provincetown are actually a national park? **Cape Cod National Seashore** is New England's most visited national park, drawing nearly 5 million visitors annually. The park features lighthouses and historic structures, numerous Cape Cod–style houses, six beaches for swimming, eleven self-guided nature trails for walking and hiking, and a variety of picnic and scenic overlook areas. The Salt Pond Visitor Center off Route 6 in Eastham is a good place to get oriented. Entrance fees are charged at beaches, and a vehicle season pass may be your best buy if you plan to visit for several days. For visitor information, call (508) 255-3421.

Getting to Cape Cod

To reach Cape Cod, you must cross the Cape Cod Canal via the Bourne or Sagamore bridges. From the bridges, Provincetown at the Cape's tip is about seventy miles. Beware—traffic crossing the bridges can back up significantly in the summer, particularly on Fridays if you're trying to get to the Cape and on Sundays if you are departing.

You can fly to the **Cape's Barnstable Municipal Airport** in Hyannis from Boston, Providence, and LaGuardia in New York. Hyannis is a hub for Cape Air, (508) 771-6944 or (800) 352-0714; and Nantucket Airlines, (508) 790-0300 or (800) 635-8787.

Getting to Martha's Vineyard

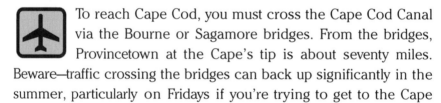

Martha's Vineyard is situated 7 miles off the coast of Cape Cod. The **Steamship Authority,** (508) 477-8600 or (508) 693-9130, provides the only year-round ferry service to the island and also the only car transport. Vehicle reservations are absolutely required in the summer and highly recommended at other times of the year. Ferries depart on a regular schedule from Woods Hole. If your stay on Martha's Vineyard will be three days or less, you may find that leaving your car behind is your best bet. Take advantage of other transportation options on the island including public shuttle buses, taxis, rental cars, mopeds, and bicycles.

Other passenger ferry service is provided seasonally (usually mid-May through early October): **Cape-Island Express Lines,** ✆(508) 997-1688, connects New Bedford and Vineyard Haven; **Falmouth Ferry Service,** ✆(508) 548-9400, transports passengers from Falmouth to Edgartown; the **Island Queen,** ✆(508) 548-4800, will whisk you from Falmouth to Oak Bluffs in thirty-five minutes; **Hy-Line Cruises,** ✆(508) 778-2600, connects Hyannis and Oak Bluffs; **Viking Ferry Lines,** ✆(516) 668-5700, departs from Montauk, New York; and **Fox Navigation,** ✆(888) SAILFOX, sails from New London, Connecticut.

Hy-Line Cruises, ✆(508) 693-0112, connects Martha's Vineyard and Nantucket in the summer months.

Martha's Vineyard can also be reached by air. **Cape Air,** ✆(508) 771-6944 or ✆(800) 352-0714, offers flights to the island from Boston, New Bedford, Hyannis, Nantucket, and Providence, Rhode Island.

If you wish to reach the island via your own boat, contact the harbormaster in Edgartown, ✆(508) 627-4746; Menemsha, ✆(508) 645-2846; Oak Bluffs, ✆(508) 693-9644; or Vineyard Haven, ✆(508) 696-4249.

Getting to Nantucket

The **Steamship Authority,** ✆(508) 477-8600 or ✆(508) 693-9130, provides regular, year-round ferry service to Nantucket from Woods Hole, and, as with Martha's Vineyard, this is your only option if you're planning to take a car to the island. Reserve your vehicle's spot early if you're traveling during the summer months. Passenger ferry service is provided seasonally by **Hy-Line Cruises,** (508) 778-2600, between Hyannis and Nantucket, and by **Freedom Cruise Line,** (508) 432-8999, between Harwich Port and Nantucket.

Hy-Line Cruises, (508) 693-0112, connects Martha's Vineyard and Nantucket in the summer months.

Nantucket Memorial Airport is served by **Cape Air,** (508) 771-6944 or (800) 352-0714; **Colgan Air/US Airways Express,** (800) 428-4322; **Continental Express,** (800) 525-0280; **Island Airlines,** (508) 228-7575 or (800) 248-7779; and **Nantucket Airlines,** (508) 790-0300 or (800) 635-8787.

Lodging Options

Cape Cod has lodging establishments of every conceivable size and type, from family motor inns to chain hotels to rental homes to distinctive B&Bs to elegant inns to exclusive resorts. Keep in mind that higher rates apply during the peak summer season. The Cape is lovely year-round, so take advantage of off-season discounts and a quieter Cape when you can.

Can't agree on a hotel versus a B&B? The perfect compromise is the centrally located **Lamb and Lion Inn,** 2504 Main Street/Route 6A, Barnstable, (508) 362-6823 or (800) 909-6923, which blends the warmth and personality associated with bed and breakfast inns with amenities, including a swimming pool and hot tub, typically only found at larger, more impersonal hotels. For a touch of history, stay at the **Daniel Webster Inn,** 149 Main Street, Sandwich, (508) 888-3622 or (800) 444-3566. After a 1971 fire, the inn was rebuilt in the style of the original 1692 tavern on the site where Daniel Webster and his patriot pals gathered to plot the course of the American Revolution. Or stay at an 1830 estate that belonged to whaling captain Henry Harding—the **Whalewalk Inn,** 220 Bridge Road, Eastham, (508) 255-0617, offers sixteen different accommodations choices in five buildings.

For elegance on the Cape, try the oceanfront **Chatham Bars**

Inn, Shore Road, Chatham, (508) 945-0096 or (800) 527-4884. This 1914 landmark is known as "The Grande Old Dame of New England." Getaways include access to the private, exclusive Cape Cod National Golf Club when you stay at **Wequassett Inn,** Pleasant Bay, Chatham, (508) 432-5400 or (800) 225-7125. Another good choice for golfers is **Ocean Edge Resort,** Route 6A, Brewster, (508) 896-9000 or (800) 343-6074, which has its own acclaimed championship course. Intimacy and romance await at **Heaven on High,** 70 High Street, West Barnstable, (508) 362-4441 or (800) 362-4044, which serves a heavenly breakfast to the small number of guests accommodated in its three individually furnished rooms. Or for Jacuzzis built for two in every room and suite, book your stay at **International Inn,** 662 Main Street, Hyannis, (508) 775-5600. You'll have access to a private beach at **By the Sea Guests Bed & Breakfast,** 8 Inman Road Extension, Dennis Port, (508) 398-8685. Five of the rooms have wood-burning fireplaces at **Snug Cottage,** 178 Bradford Street, Provincetown, (508) 487-1616 or (800) 432-2334, making it a great off-season choice.

For an extended family stay, **Cape Cod Harbor House Inn,** 119 Ocean Street, Hyannis, (800) 211-5551, offers eighteen mini-suites with kitchenettes. The first two children under twelve stay free at **Americana Holiday Motel,** 99 Main Street/Route 28, West Yarmouth, (508) 775-5511 or (800) 445-4497.

Want to find a rental property for your stay on the Cape? The **All Seasons Vacation Rental Network,** online at *www.weneedavacation.com,* connects you to hundreds of houses, cottages, and condos that can be rented directly from homeowners. Getting away at the last minute? The Cape and the Islands Visitor Information Network Services has a Web page, updated daily, which lists available accommodations at *www.capecodchambers.com.*

Because this is far from an exhaustive look at the lodgings possibilities on the Cape, be sure to call the **Cape Cod Chamber of Commerce,** (508) 862-0700, to request your free guide to the area including extensive accommodations listings.

Nantucket Lodging

On Nantucket, you'll find close to 1,200 guest rooms available, even though the tiny island is only fourteen and one-half by three and one-half miles in size. B&B accommodations in historic homes are predominant, and a variety of architectural time periods is represented. **Stumble Inne,** 109 Orange Street, (508) 228-4482 or (800) 649-4482, has been around since 1704, when it was built by one of Nantucket's founding families—ask about packages that include round-trip airfare or ferry fare. The **Carlisle House Inn,** 26 North Water Street, (508) 228-0720, dates to 1765 and offers fourteen rooms including some with canopied beds and working fireplaces. The **Cliff Lodge,** 9 Cliff Road, (508) 228-9480, was built in 1771 as a whaling master's home and now offers twelve rooms for guests. The **Pineapple Inn,** 10 Hussey Street, (508) 228-9992, was built for a prominent island whaling captain in 1838 and the Greek Revival home offers luxurious touches in its twelve guest rooms. When you stay at the **1849 Hawthorn House,** 2 Chestnut Street, (508) 228-1468, your stay includes a voucher for breakfast at your choice of several local restaurants. The **Westmoor Inn,** Cliff Road, (508) 228-0877 or (888) 236-7310, was built in 1917 as a wedding gift for Alice Vanderbilt, and now it offers fourteen gracious guest rooms and ocean views. If you're looking for a larger hotel with more amenities, the 100-room **Nantucket Inn and Conference Center,** 27 Macy's Lane, (508) 228-6900 or (800) 321-8484, has indoor and outdoor pools, a fitness center, tennis courts, a billiards room, a restaurant, and complimentary island shuttle service. The **Beachside,** 30 North Beach Street, (508) 228-2241 or (800) 322-4433, has ninety rooms, an outdoor pool, and complimentary continental breakfast.

Martha's Vineyard Lodging

On Martha's Vineyard, charming inns, rental cottages, and seaside homes turned B&Bs abound. For grand style, choose the landmark **Harbor View Hotel,** 131 North Water Street, Edgartown, (800) 225-6005, with 124 guest rooms, suites, and cottages and harbor views from rows of rocking chairs on the fabulous porch. The **Daggett House,** 59 North Water Street, Edgartown, (508) 627-4600 or (800) 946-3400, is comprised of four historic buildings including a 1660 structure that was the island's first licensed tavern. The **Victorian Inn,** 24 South Water Street, Edgartown, (508) 627-4784, is the former home of a whaling captain and has an English courtyard garden where breakfast is served when the weather is cooperative.

HOT SPOT

The only museum in Onset, Massachusetts, is dedicated to thermometers . . . 2,600 of them, from antiques to the latest, high-tech models! The **Porter Thermometer Museum,** 49 Zarahemia Road, (508) 295-5504, is open free every day, but you must make an appointment in advance.

Edgartown Commons, Pease Point Way, Edgartown, (508) 627-4671, is the place to stay if you want to live like an islander—thirty-five studio, one- and two-bedroom housekeeping units are available. Traveling with kids? **Winnetu Resort,** South Beach, Edgartown, (978) 443-1733, was just built in 2000 and caters to families with its organized programs for children and teens. **Beach Plum Inn,** Beach Plum Lane, Menemsha, (508) 645-9454 or (877) 645-7398, is an upscale, adults-only retreat with a distinguished restaurant. The **Wesley Hotel,** 1 Lake Avenue, Oak Bluffs, (508) 693-6611, is the last of the grand Victorian hotels that once dotted Oak Bluffs at the turn of the twentieth century. You can fulfill your childhood dream of climbing to the top of a cupola and gazing out at everything that surrounds you at the **Oak Bluffs Inn,** Circuit Avenue, Oak Bluffs, (508) 693-7171 or (800) 955-6235. The **Oak House,** Beach Road, Oak Bluffs, (508) 693-4187 or (800) 245-5979, was once the summer home of former Massachusetts Governor William Claflin. Want to play where you stay? **Martha's Vineyard Resort and Racquet Club,** 111 New York

Avenue, Oak Bluffs, ✆(617) 524-7300 or ✆(800) 874 4403, offers sports lovers two championship clay tennis courts, an eighteen-hole golf putting green, and a Pro Shop offering professional tennis and golf lessons.

The **Martha's Vineyard Chamber of Commerce,** ✆(508) 693-0085, *www.mvy.com,* is a wonderful source for additional accommodations ideas.

TRAVEL TIP

Already on Nantucket and find that you want to stay for the night but don't have a reservation? Don't panic. Head to the **Visitor Services and Information Bureau,** 25 Federal Street, ✆(508) 228-0925, which maintains a list of rooms available each day and posts available options outside after business hours.

Cape Cod Excursions and Diversions

Cape Cod has more than 550 miles of coastline, and you're never far from a public beach where you can swim, sunbathe, and breathe deeply of the salty air. Most beaches have a parking or admission fee. In general, waters are warmer on the southern Nantucket Sound coast than on the northern Cape Cod Bay side. The most vigorous surf can be found along the Outer Cape at the beaches that are within the National Seashore. Warm ocean breezes help keep the climate of Cape Cod more moderate than other New England spots—another great reason to visit in the off-season.

Many of the Cape's best excursions are on the omnipresent waters. The Ocean Street docks in Hyannis are a great place to catch an outgoing voyage. See Kennedy family homes and other landmarks from the **Catboat,** ✆(508) 775-0222, a thirty-four-foot sailing vessel that will whisk you out to sea on an exhilarating ninety-minute trip. **Hy-Line,** ✆(508) 778-2600, operates both fishing cruises and leisurely lobster luncheon and harbor sightseeing outings. Provincetown is a popular departure point for whale watches. **Portuguese Princess Whale Watch,** departing from MacMillan Wharf, Provincetown, (508) 487-2651 or (800) 442-3188, boasts a 99 percent whale-spotting success rate, and in the unlikely event that you don't see a whale, you'll receive a free pass for another excursion.

You may be reluctant to interrupt your relaxation for a visit to an historic site or museum, but you'd be remiss if you didn't consider visits to the **John F. Kennedy Hyannis Museum,** 397 Main Street, Hyannis, (508) 790-3077 or (877) HYANNIS; and the **Pilgrim Monument,** High Pole Hill Road, Provincetown, (508) 487-1310, the 252-foot tower that commemorates the site of the Pilgrims' first landing in America. Also popular is **Heritage Plantation,** Grove and Pine Streets, Sandwich, (508) 888-3300, home to diverse collections of Americana including an automobile museum and a military museum, plus gardens and an antique carousel. The facility is open mid-May through late October.

On a summer's eve, nothing quite beats a concert at the **Cape Cod Melody Tent,** 21 West Main Street, Hyannis, (508) 775-9100, which hosts popular performers and features a round, revolving stage. The Cape is also home to the country's oldest professional summer theater, the **Cape Playhouse,** 820 Route 6A, Dennis, (508) 385-3911 or (877) 385-3911. Stars who have appeared here include Gregory Peck, Lana Turner, Ginger Rogers, Humphrey Bogart, Tallulah Bankhead, Helen Hayes, and Bette Davis, who worked there as an usher before she made her stage debut. The whole family will enjoy the old-fashioned fun of watching a movie from the car at the **Wellfleet Drive-In,** Route 6 at the Eastham/Wellfleet town line, (508) 349-7176.

Children will enjoy seeing where potato chips are born on a free tour of **Cape Cod Potato Chip Company,** Breed's Hill Road, Hyannis, (508) 775-3358—there are free chips at the end of the self-guided tour. If they've been good, take them to **Water Wizz,** Routes 6 and 28, East Wareham, (508) 295-3255, too.

Nantucket Nuances

Nantucket—the name is derived from a Native American word meaning "far away island." Truly only thirty miles separate Nantucket from Hyannis on Cape Cod, but you're likely to feel, just as the island's earliest inhabitants did, that you are worlds apart. Nantucket was the world's whaling capital from 1800 to 1840, and during those days, its population of 10,000 made it Massachusetts's third largest city. Today, about 9,000 people occupy the island year round, but that number swells to 50,000 during the summer months. Nantucket is a popular day-trip destination from Cape Cod, but it also makes a wonderful vacation destination in its own right.

Travelers choose Nantucket for its aura of affluence, its old homes, its idyllic beaches, and its preserved natural expanses. You'll likely want to spend your days biking, basking, or building sandcastles on one of the island's ten public beaches, ducking in and out of cute shops and galleries along cobblestone streets, or embarking on an ocean adventure for a day of whale watching or fishing.

A few special sights you'll want to see during your stay include the **Brant Point Light,** Eaton Street, (508) 228-1894, America's second oldest lighthouse and one of three on the island. The **Nantucket Life-Saving Museum,** 158 Polpis Road, (508) 228-1885, is open daily from mid-June through Columbus Day and tells the story of the heroic rescuers who have saved hundreds from the perils of the seas. The **Jethro Coffin House,** Sunset Hill, (508) 228-3451, is the island's oldest, and it's open for tours from Memorial Day to Columbus Day. From late May to mid-October, you can also visit the **Old Gaol,** Vestal Street, (508) 228-1894, which began housing prisoners in 1806 and is distinguished as the first jail in America that allowed prisoners to go home at night. The **Whaling Museum,** Broad Street, (508) 228-1736, portrays Nantucket's whaling history—it is open year-round but operates on a very limited schedule in the winter.

Exploring the Vineyard

In 1602, explorer Bartholomew Gosnold came upon an island populated with wild grapes, which explains the inspiration for part of Martha's Vineyard's name, though the definitive identity of Martha remains a mystery. New England's largest island is just 7 miles off of Cape Cod and just 20 miles across, but it has a personality and magnetism all its own and a deserved reputation for seclusion.

Because getting a car to the island is tricky, you'll find that tourists take advantage of the availability of bike paths and rentals to explore the Vineyard. Ferries arrive at Vineyard Haven, which is the island's busiest town. Oak Bluffs and Edgartown, the other two "down-island" towns, are also popular with visitors. Much like the Cape and Nantucket, the island is teeming with activity in the summer months and much quieter the remainder of the year. Stop into the office of the **Martha's Vineyard Chamber of Commerce,** Beach Road, Vineyard Haven, when you arrive on the island to pick up a free guide and map, or call ahead at (508) 693-0085.

Martha's Vineyard is known for its beaches, nineteen in all. In general, beaches with public access are concentrated in the down-island area. The two-mile Joseph Sylvia State Beach located between Oak Bluffs and Edgartown along Beach Road is one of the island's most popular.

Avid golfers can choose from two public golf courses on the island: **Farm Neck Golf Club,** County Road, Oak Bluffs, (508) 693-3057, or **Mink Meadows Golf Club,** 320 Golf Club Road, Vineyard Haven, (508) 693-0600. Both require tee time reservations two days in advance for nonmembers.

While you're ensconced on Martha's Vineyard, you'll also want to see the **Flying Horses Carousel,** 33 Circuit Avenue, Oak Bluffs, (508) 693-9481, the oldest operating platform carousel in the United States and a National Historic Landmark. You can tour the island's oldest residence, **Vincent House,** off Main Street, Edgartown, Monday through Saturday from May 1 until Columbus

Day. Lighthouse buffs will also be charmed by the small island's large collection of lighthouses—there are five to see in a compact area along the island's north shore. **West Chop Lighthouse,** West Chop Road, Vineyard Haven, was the island's last manned light. The present brick structure dates to 1838. The red-brick Gay Head Lighthouse, also known as **Aquinnah Light,** Lighthouse Road, Aquinnah, (508) 627-4441, was built in 1844, but its perilous cliff-side location made it necessary to move its two-story Fresnel lens to the Vineyard Museum in Edgartown, where it is still lit every evening after dark. The **East Chop Lighthouse,** Beach Road, Oak Bluffs, (508) 627-4441, was built in 1877. The **Edgartown Lighthouse,** Edgartown Harbor, (508) 627-4441, you'll see today is the 1938 structure that replaced its 1828 predecessor. The wooden **Cape Pogue Lighthouse,** Chappaquiddick Island, Edgartown, (508) 693-7662, was built in 1922 and is accessible by four-wheel drive or a two and one-half-mile hike. Limited interior access to lighthouses is available primarily on weekends, so call ahead.

Dining Highlights

Seafood, seafood, seafood! That should be your dining mantra when you're vacationing on the Cape and Islands. Something about the salty air and the laid-back surroundings makes lobster, clams, scallops, fish, and other fruits of the sea taste even more succulent.

On Cape Cod

You'll be overwhelmed by the feasting possibilities. One option is to stop at one of the box lunch restaurants in Brewster, Eastham, Falmouth, Hyannis, Orleans, Provincetown, Wellfleet, or Yarmouth for a picnic pack that you can take with you wherever your Cape Cod meanderings lead. Combine eating and sightseeing on a dinner train excursion with **Cape Cod Central Railroad,** 252 Main Street, Hyannis, (508) 771-3800 or (888) 797-RAIL.

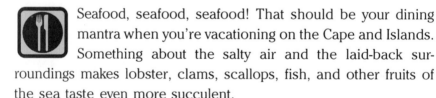

Slurp lobster stew and enjoy native scallops and other seafood specialties with a view of Hyannis Harbor at the **Black Cat,** 165 Ocean Street, Hyannis, (508) 778-1233. For fried clams you'll be talking about long after you leave the Cape, head to **Baxter's,** Pleasant Street, Hyannis, (508) 775-4490. The **Impudent Oyster,** 15 Chatham Bars Avenue, Chatham, (508) 945-3545, boasts some of the Cape's most clever culinary combinations.

At the **Dolphin Restaurant,** 3250 Main Street/Route 6A, Barnstable Village, (508) 362-6610, you can sit beside the fireplace and enjoy sophisticated dishes including some of the freshest and tastiest seafood offerings you'll find anywhere. Dine inside an old sea captain's home at the **Barley Neck Inn,** 5 Beach Road, East Orleans, (508) 255-0212. Or have dinner inside a 200-year-old barn at the **Red Pheasant,** 905 Route 6A, Dennis, (508) 385-2133, which specializes in local ingredients and traditional New England cooking. Be sure to ask your innkeepers and folks you meet for additional restaurant recommendations.

On Nantucket

You're in for not only a culinary treat but also a trip back in time when you dine at the restaurant at the **Woodbox Inn,** 29 Fair Street, (508) 228-0587, which is housed inside one of the island's oldest homes. If you're looking to savor one "money is no object" dinner, try the French seafood preparations at **Chanticleer,** 9 New Street, (508) 257-6231. **Topper's at the Wauwinet Inn,** 120 Wauwinet Road, (508) 228-0145, has two elegant indoor dining rooms and an outdoor deck with views of Nantucket Bay, or take advantage of one of the restaurant's dining adventures: enjoy a tasting menu of all of the day's best dishes at lunchtime, or, with four hours' notice, the kitchen will prepare a gourmet basket lunch and the inn's 21-foot open cruiser will deliver you to a secluded, beach for a memorable picnic. **Club Car,** 1 Main Street off Straight Wharf, (508) 228-1101, is an authentic, historic railroad car turned restaurant that is open mid-May to mid-December. Or for another unique dinner experience, make reservations for one of the two nightly sittings mid-May to mid-December at the

Company of the Cauldron, 5 India Street, Nantucket, (508) 228-4016, where romantic, candlelit dinners are all-inclusive and frequently accompanied by a harpist.

On Martha's Vineyard

The **Beach Plum Inn Restaurant,** North Road, Menemsha, (508) 645-9454, receives consistent accolades for its romantic ambience, panoramic views, and regional cuisine. **David Ryan's Restaurant Café,** North Water Street, Edgartown, offers creative, casual dining for lunch and dinner and some of the island's best entertainment at night. **O'Brien's Serious Seafood & Grill,** 137 Upper Main Street, Edgartown, (508) 627-5850, is a great spot for fresh island seafood and more in an intimate setting. Choose from the candlelit dining room, outdoor rose garden seating, or a more casual pub downstairs for lighter dining. For views that will wow you spring through fall, the dining room at the **Outermost Inn,** Lighthouse Road, Gay Head, (508) 645-3511, is hard to top. Definitely call for reservations. Don't climb back on the ferry without enjoying one last sumptuous meal and a bowl of fish chowder at the **Black Dog Tavern,** Beach Street Extension, Vineyard Haven, (508) 693-9223, which serves breakfast, lunch, and dinner daily. Keep in mind that alcoholic beverages can be served in restaurants or purchased in liquor stores only in Oak Bluffs and Edgartown. The rest of the island is "dry," but you may be able to bring your own beer or wine to restaurants; inquire ahead. **Chicama Vineyards,** Stoney Hill Road, West Tisbury, (508) 693-0309 or (888) CHICAMA, is a great place to pick up a bottle of wine produced right on the island.

Shopping Discoveries

It would be easier to list the places where you can't find cool shops on the Cape and islands than it is to point you to all of the retail riches of this region. Shopaholics should definitely plan to spend some concentrated time in Hyannis,

Chatham, Wellfleet, Provincetown, Vineyard Haven, Oak Bluffs, Edgartown, in the heart of Nantucket Town, and cruising along the Cape's Route 6A. Keep in mind that Provincetown is a very open-minded community and a popular gay and lesbian resort, and some shop window displays may evoke questions from younger children.

If you want to take home a souvenir made in this region, popular choices include scrimshaw, cranberry food products, chichi and very expensive Nantucket lightship baskets, pottery, nautical wood carvings, braided rugs, shell gifts, and designer clothing. Antique shops and flea markets are very popular in this region, too.

For bargains, head to the **Cape Cod Factory Outlet Mall** at the Sagamore Bridge, ✆(508) 888-8417. There's a **Christmas Tree Shop**—one of seven on the Cape—across the street. Call ✆(800) 876-9677 for location information for these wildly popular discount centers.

Even if you're not a shopper per se, you'll be enthralled by the eclectic array of curiosities for sale at **Yankee Ingenuity,** 525 Main Street, Chatham, ✆(508) 945-1288. The **Yankee Craftsmen,** 220 Route 6A, Brewster, ✆(508) 385-4758 or ✆(800) 385-4758, specializes in Cape collectibles and work by local crafters. At **Scargo Stoneware Pottery,** 30 Dr. Lord's Road, Dennis, ✆(508) 385-3894, one-of-a-kind works are displayed in a mesmerizing indoor/outdoor gallery setting. Gain an appreciation for the art of hand carving ivory at **Edgartown Scrimshaw Gallery,** Main Street, Edgartown, ✆(508) 627-9439. Dress yourself in traditional Nantucket Reds at **Murray's Toggery Shop,** 62 Main Street, Nantucket, ✆(508) 228-0437 or ✆(800) 368-2134, an island institution since 1945.

Itineraries

PERSONAL ITINERARY NOTES

A LONG FALL WEEKEND IN WESTERN MASSACHUSETTS

Day One Begin your long weekend in the Berkshires with a leisurely drive along the 63-mile **Mohawk Trail** beginning in Westminster at the eastern end. Stop often to visit such engaging sights as the **Bridge of Flowers** in Shelburne Falls and the **Natural Bridge** in North Adams—they're even more spectacular against a backdrop of fall colors.

Day Two Stay overnight in one of the Berkshires' charming country inns, and set out the next day to tour the **Norman Rockwell Museum,** Route 183, Stockbridge, (413) 298-4100, in the morning. Have lunch at the **Red Lion Inn,** 30 Main Street, Stockbridge, (413) 298-5545, which is straight out of a Rockwell painting. Visit the home of famous sculptor Daniel Chester French, **Chesterwood,** 4 Williamsville Road, Stockbridge, (413) 298-3579, in the afternoon. A fireside dinner makes a perfect end to the day, or, if your inn has a fireplace, leave an hour in the evening to enjoy its warm flicker.

Day Three Head back east a bit on your last day away to the central part of the state and spend the morning exploring the eclectic shops in Northampton. You'll find plenty of great choices in this offbeat town for lunchtime dining. In the afternoon, sports fans may want to squeeze in a visit to the **Basketball Hall of Fame,** 1150 West Columbus Avenue, Springfield, (413) 781-6500. Or, spend the afternoon at scent-sational **Yankee Candle Co.,** Route 5 and 10 North, South Deerfield, (413) 665-2929 or (877) 636-7707, where you can pick up autumn-scented souvenirs—cinnamon, spiced pumpkin, harvest, fireside, and warm apple crisp are just some of the Yankee scents that will remind you of your brief stay in Massachusetts.

A CAPE COD LIGHTHOUSE TOUR

Early A.M. Start in Chatham at the **Stage Harbor Light,** which dates to 1880 and can only be viewed from outside. It's also about a mile's walk from the nearest parking area on Harding Beach Road. Just north, you'll find the **Chatham Light** just off Main Street on Shore Road. The 1877 metal tower replaced a brick beacon built on this site in 1808.

Late A.M. Follow Route 6 North to Eastham, where you can visit the **Nauset Light,** relocated to this spot from Chatham in 1923, and the **Three Sisters Lighthouses,** wooden lighthouses built at Nauset in 1892 and now housed safely within the National Seashore area. All can be viewed from within an easy walk of the Nauset Light Beach parking lot on Ocean View Drive.

Early P.M. Continue north to North Truro, then follow Highland Road for three miles to Lighthouse Road, where the **Highland Light** proudly stands. Built originally in 1798, the first light was replaced by the present brick structure in 1857. It was moved inland in 1996 due to cliff erosion.

Late P.M. The final stop on your lighthouse itinerary is Provincetown. In the summer, you can take a boat from MacMillan Wharf to **Long Point Light** at the entrance to Provincetown Harbor. First lit in 1827, the current replacement structure was built in 1875. This lighthouse can also be reached by walking the 1½ miles to the end of Long Point. You'll need to walk or take a boat from the wharf, too, to see the **Wood End Light,** originally erected in 1873 and now solar powered. Finally, save **Race Point Light,** about a 2-mile walk from the parking lot at the Race Point Coast Guard Station on Race Point Road, for last. Why? You just might decide to spend the night here as a lighthouse keeper's guest! Call ☏(508) 888-9784, as reservations are definitely a necessity.

A WHIRLWIND WEEK IN MASSACHUSETTS

Day One If you're one of those folks who likes to cram as much as possible into a week's vacation, Massachusetts is a great destination for you. Start your trip with a day at **Old Sturbridge Village,** Route 20, Sturbridge, (508) 347-3362, where you can immerse yourself in the happenings of an early New England village. Dine in the evening on traditional Yankee fare at the **Publick House,** Route 131, (508) 347-3313 or (800) PUBLICK.

Day Two Head east to Boston, "The Hub of the Universe." Get acquainted with the city by first taking in the view from atop one of New England's tallest buildings, the **Prudential Building,** 800 Boylston Street, 50th Floor, (617) 236-3318. In the afternoon, explore the shops at Quincy Market and Downtown Crossing. Dine at the **Union Oyster House,** 41 Union Street, (617) 227-2750, America's oldest continuously operating restaurant, which dates to 1826.

Day Three Wake up a bit early and walk Boston's Freedom Trail. You may want to make a full, leisurely day of exploring Boston's landmarks along the trail. If you can pick it up a notch (usually around four hours can get you through without missing anything), leave time in the afternoon to visit the **Museum of Science,** Science Park, (617) 723-2500, or one of Boston's other fine museums. At the Museum of Science you might want to start off with an IMAX film to get off your feet for a while.

Day Four Can you believe your week is nearly half over already? Head north from Boston for a day trip to Salem. Visit the **Salem Witch Museum,** Washington Square, (978) 744-1692; the **Witch Dungeon Museum,** 16 Lynde Street, (508) 741-3570; the **House of Seven Gables,** 54 Turner Street, (978) 744-0991; and other sights along the Heritage Trail. Dine overlooking Salem Harbor on slow-roasted prime rib at **Victoria Station,** Pickering Wharf, (978) 745-3400.

Day Five On day five, drive south from Boston to New Bedford and Fall River, where you can board a whaling ship at the **New Bedford Whaling Museum,** 18 Johnny Cake Hill, New Bedford, (508) 997-0046, and stroll the decks of a destroyer at **Battleship Cove,** One Central Street, (508) 678-1100. If you weren't completely spooked by Salem, you may even want to spend a night at the **Lizzie Borden Bed & Breakfast,** 92 Second Street, Fall River, (508) 675-7333.

Day Six Head for Cape Cod and a relaxing day of biking or basking on the beach on day six. You may want to choose the central town of Hyannis as your base from which to explore the Cape.

Day Seven Day seven has arrived. If you don't need to head for home just yet, drive further east to the very tip of the Cape and visit Provincetown, the Pilgrims' first landing spot and home now to an appealing array of shops and galleries. Wellfleet is also an adorable town you might explore on your way to Provincetown.

PART V

Maine

Maine

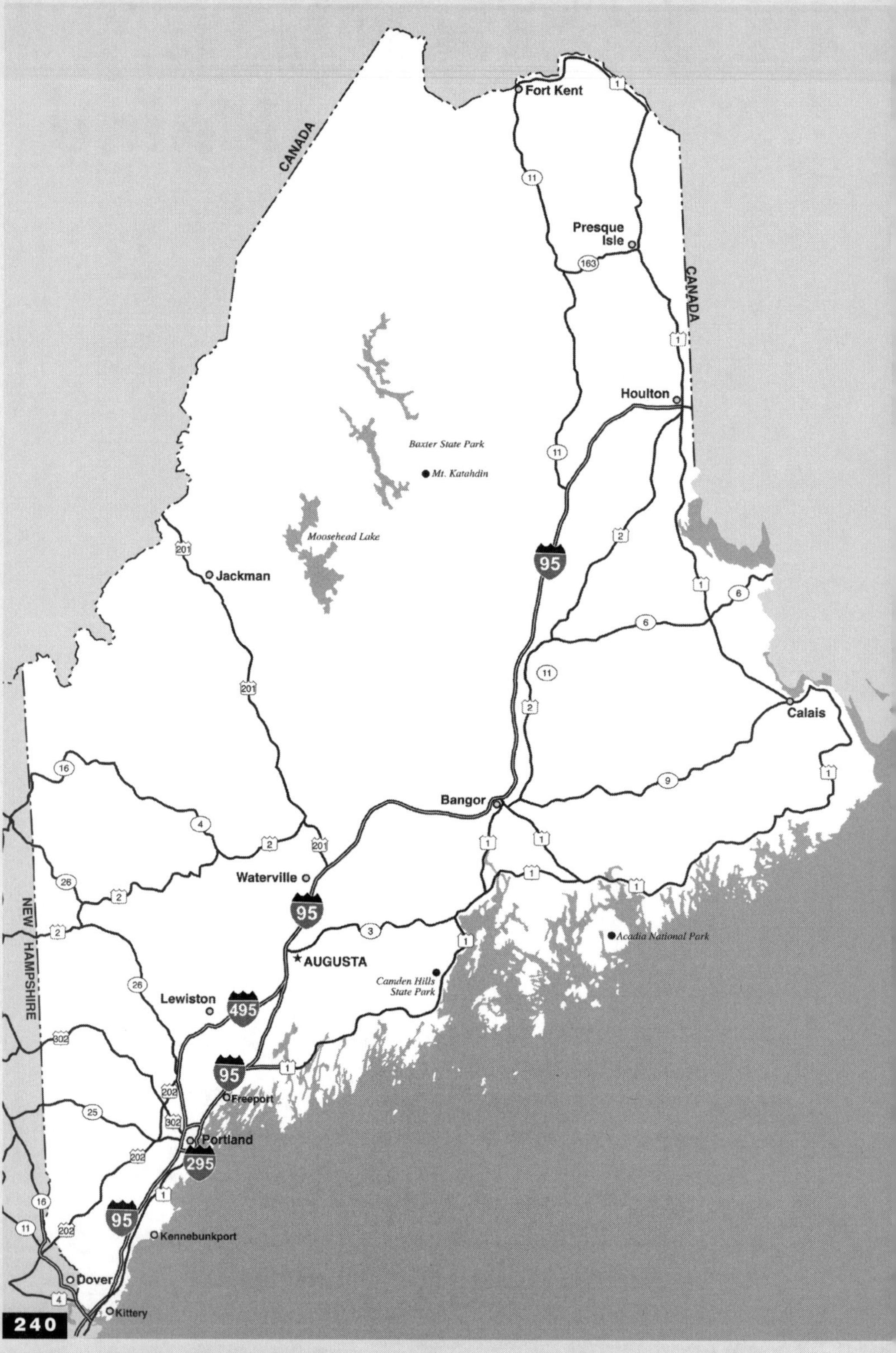
CANADA
Fort Kent
Presque Isle
Houlton
CANADA
Baxter State Park
Mt. Katahdin
Moosehead Lake
Jackman
Calais
Bangor
Waterville
AUGUSTA
Acadia National Park
Camden Hills State Park
Lewiston
NEW HAMPSHIRE
Freeport
Portland
Kennebunkport
Dover
Kittery
1
11
163
95
201
2
6
9
16
4
26
3
495
302
202
25
295

Acadia National Park, Maine

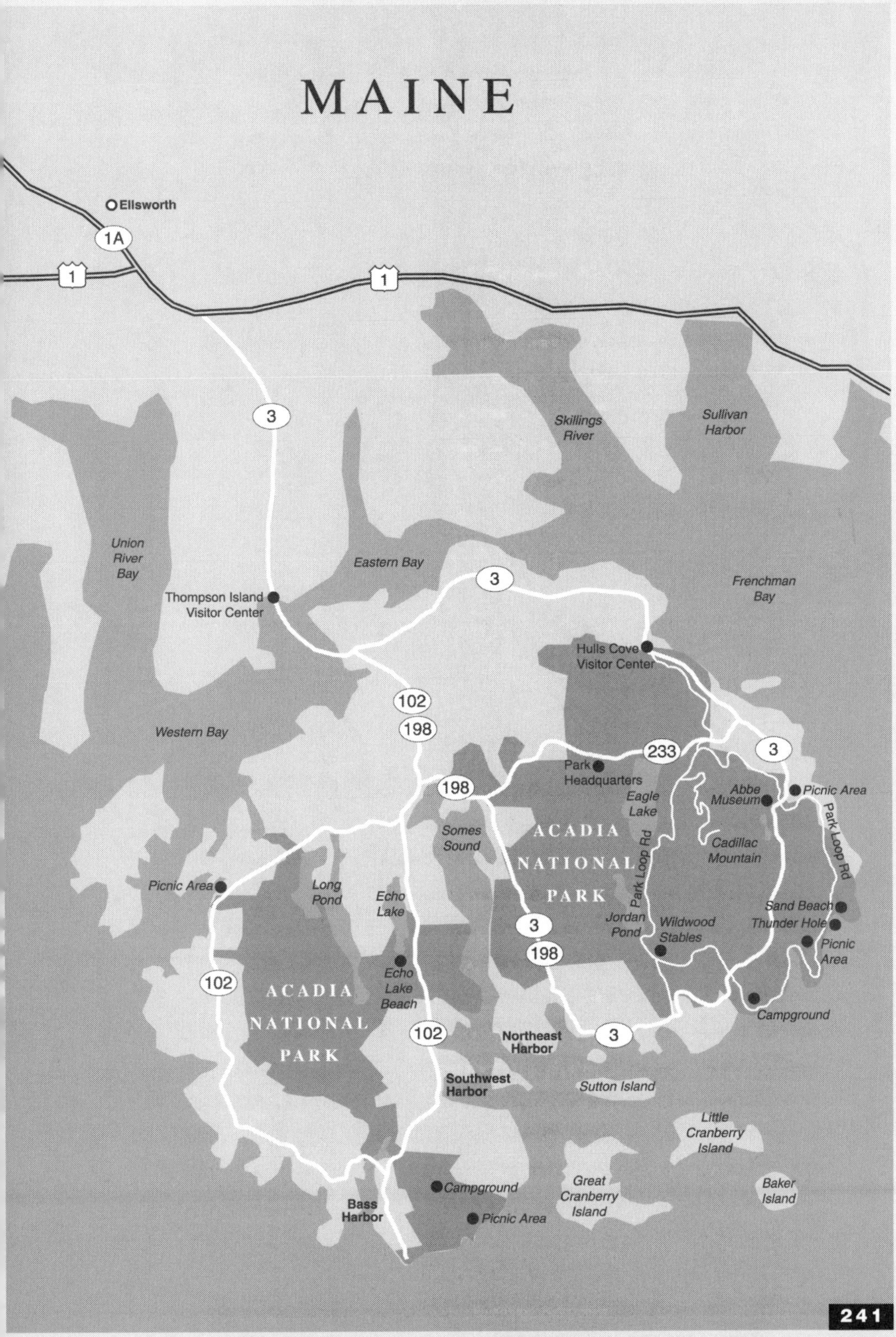
MAINE
Ellsworth
1A
1
1
3
Skillings River
Sullivan Harbor
Union River Bay
Eastern Bay
3
Frenchman Bay
Thompson Island Visitor Center
Hulls Cove Visitor Center
102
198
Western Bay
233
3
Park Headquarters
198
Eagle Lake
Abbe Museum
Picnic Area
Park Loop Rd
Somes Sound
ACADIA NATIONAL PARK
Park Loop Rd
Cadillac Mountain
Picnic Area
Long Pond
Echo Lake
Jordan Pond
Wildwood Stables
Sand Beach
Thunder Hole
3
198
Picnic Area
Echo Lake Beach
102
ACADIA NATIONAL PARK
Campground
102
3
Northeast Harbor
Southwest Harbor
Sutton Island
Little Cranberry Island
Campground
Great Cranberry Island
Baker Island
Bass Harbor
Picnic Area

Portland, Maine

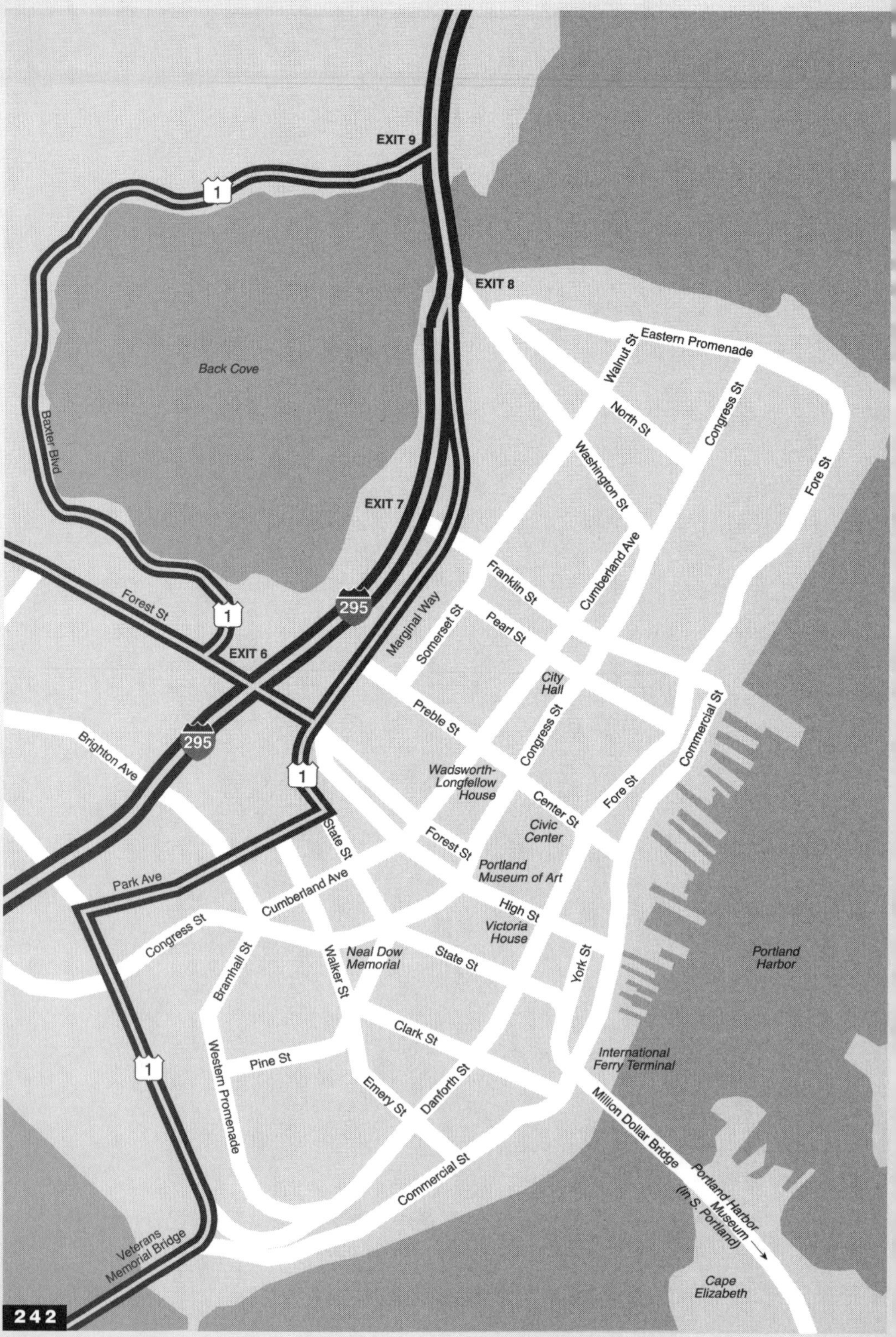

An Introduction to Vacationland

ONCE YOU'VE GOT MAINE ON YOUR MIND, you'll find that the addiction runs deep—to the cellular level, even. But it still won't compare to the true blue affection harbored by Mainers whose families have called the state home for generations. In fact, even if you fall in love with Maine, move there and have children, your youn-guns will still be considered to be "from away." As the locals just might tell you, "Hatchin' chickens in the stove doesn't make 'em muffins, does it?" The rule of thumb is that if at least three generations of your ancestors aren't from Maine—or even if your ancestors are from Maine, but you've moved away and then returned—you're "from away." But don't for a moment think that you won't feel welcome among the natives. Mainers are renowned for their hospitality, and tourism is one of the state's most important industries.

The vast territory that is Maine was actually governed by Massachusetts until 1820, when it was admitted to the Union as the twenty-third state. Early, pre-Pilgrims, European settlement attempts at St. Croix Island in 1604 and at Popham Beach in 1607 were unsuccessful, but in 1641, York became the first city in America with a charter from the English crown. Choose Maine for a family beach vacation or for a hunting, fishing, or snowmobiling retreat with a few pals, for a frenetic weekend of outlet shopping or for quiet time alone or with one special someone in a woodsy lake-front cabin, for a wet and woolly white-water adventure, or for a more leisurely but nevertheless stimulating moose safari. Whatever type of escape you choose, don't let being "from away" cause you to stay away.

TRAVEL TIP

If you have a computer and a charge card, the Maine Innkeepers Association makes it easy to research and book your accommodations at *www.maineinns.com*. Choose a region, enter your arrival date, and you'll see all available properties. Select one, and you'll be able to make secure online reservations and receive instant confirmation.

Ten Maine Highlights

While much of Maine's 230-mile Atlantic coastline is quite well developed, the northern, inland regions are largely uninhabited. As you travel, keep in mind that Maine's large size means distances between cities and towns can be much more significant than in other New England states.

Acadia National Park

Hulls Cove Visitor Center, Route 3, Bar Harbor
(207) 288-3338
www.nps.gov/acad

Acadia was the first National Park established east of the Mississippi River. Each year, millions flock to this 47,633-acre preserved paradise. Popular activities include driving the 27-mile Park Loop Road to view spectacular mountain and coastal scenery; walking, hiking, and biking on 45 miles of carriage roads; hiking 115 miles of trails rated from easy to strenuous; fishing; boating; carriage rides; cross-country skiing; snowshoeing; and ranger-led bird walks and other nature programs.

TRAVEL TIP

Registered Maine Guides are a phenomenon unique to the state. Maine began licensing Guides in 1897—1,700 Guides were registered that first year, and the first one was a woman. Today, there are 3,000 Registered Maine Guides in nine categories: hunting, fishing, recreation, hunting and fishing, hunting and recreation, fishing and recreation, sea kayaking, tidewater, and master. If you're planning to spend time in the Maine outdoors, a Registered Guide, who has passed oral and written licensing exams, can help to ensure an enjoyable, successful outing. To find a Maine Guide, visit the Web site of the Maine Professional Guides Association, *www.maineguides.org,* or call them at (207) 785-2061. Maine Guides Online, *www.maineguides.com,* is another helpful resource.

Baxter State Park

64 Balsam Drive, Millinocket

(207) 723-5140

This 202,064-acre wilderness was a gift to Maine from former governor Percival P. Baxter. It's an ideal place for camping, fishing, hiking, and moose watching. The state's tallest peak, mile-high Mt. Katahdin, offers spectacular views to those who hike the sometimes treacherous Knife Edge trail.

TRAVEL TIP

Camping and Maine are a natural fit, and the sheer number of campsites in the state is proof positive of camping's popularity. The Maine Campground Owners Association counts 235 RV parks and campgrounds with more than 17,000 campsites among its ranks, and you can search the database online at *www.campmaine.com* or call (207)782-5874 to request your free camping guide.

Kennebunkport

President George Bush helped put Kennebunkport on the map, and with his son now occupying the Oval Office, attention will once again be focused on the family's summer home compound in this very cute if overcrowded town. While you can't do much more than drive by the Bush's home, you can enjoy all of Kennebunkport's other enticements–the shops, galleries, and restaurants of Dock Square, whale-watching cruises, sea kayaking, just-plucked-from-the-ocean seafood, and Kennebunk Beach.

Kittery Outlets

www.thekitteryoutlets.com

The densely packed factory outlet stores of Kittery can get even reluctant shoppers' blood pumping. You'll find savings on men's, women's, and children's wear, footwear, housewares, giftware–even underwear–at the more than 120 outlet stores that line Route 1.

L.L. Bean Flagship Store

95 Main Street, Freeport

(800) 341-4341

www.llbean.com

What's open 365 days a year, twenty-four hours a day, and draws more than 3.5 million visitors each year? It's the flagship store of legendary Maine retailer L.L. Bean, which has been a Main Street fixture in Freeport since 1917. The locks on the doors were removed in 1951 when the twenty-four-hour schedule was initiated.

Maine Lobster

Lobstering is one of Maine's oldest industries, and it remains a major contributor to the economy today. Believe it or not, the ultimate "other white meat" has less cholesterol than an equivalent serving of skinless chicken. Of course, you don't usually dunk skinless chicken in drawn butter before you devour it! Feasting on lobster is a must in Maine. Lobster boat excursions are offered along the shore if you'd like to see firsthand the life of a Maine lobsterman.

Old Orchard Beach

Route 1 at exits 5 and 6 off I-95

When summer shines, so does Old Orchard Beach, a seaside family playground that hearkens back to an earlier era with its arcades, rides, amusement pier, and boardwalk lined with pizza and fried dough vendors. Fall brings opportunities to ride horseback along the beach, and winter turns this oceanside nook into a cozy hideaway for a romantic interlude.

Portland Head Light

Fort Williams Park, 1000 Shore Road, Cape Elizabeth

(207) 799-2661

www.portlandheadlight.com

You've probably seen photographs of Portland Head Light in lighthouse books and calendars. When you travel to Maine, you can join the 350,000 to 400,000 people who visit the first lighthouse erected on Maine's seacoast each year. Portland Head Light was first lit in 1791, and George Washington appointed its first keeper.

White-Water Rafting

There are more than a dozen white-water adventure outfitters in Maine, where river rafting is serious business. From late April until mid-October, controlled daily dam releases from hydropower dams on the Penobscot and Kennebec Rivers guarantee excellent rafting conditions. You can check out *www.visit-maine.com* for extensive listings of white-water rafting areas.

The Wyeth Center at the Farnsworth Museum

Union Street, Rockland

(207) 596-6457

www.wyethcenter.com

www.farnsworthmuseum.org

The Wyeth Center opened in 1998 in an historic church building on the property of the Farnsworth Art Museum. The Center is home to the world's most extensive collection of works by the

Wyeth family's three generations of celebrated Maine painters. N.C. Wyeth relocated his family to the small fishing harbor of Port Clyde in 1920. His son, Andrew, and his grandson, Jamie, continued the family legacy of capturing some of the most striking and enduring images of the state.

TRAVEL TIP

Maine is New England's northernmost state, and you'll find overall that temperatures are a bit cooler than in the rest of the region. While this can be an impediment to winter travelers, it means that summers are more comfortable, particularly when it comes to outdoor activities such as biking and hiking. Maine's four seasons also begin and end on a slightly different timetable than elsewhere in New England. Summers get off to a slower start, and peak fall colors can arrive two weeks or more ahead of the rest of New England. Summer and fall are definitely the tourism "high season," so look for bargain accommodations at other times. Keep in mind, though, that tourist businesses may be closed during the slow months.

The Gateway to Maine: York County and the South Coast

MAINE'S 60-MILE SOUTHERN COAST CLAIMS many titles—it is here that you'll find the state's best beaches, oldest towns, choicest outlet shopping . . . and largest crowds. After all, this part of Maine, unlike the far northern reaches, is close to the rest of New England, and it's also an area that most Maine visitors must traverse on their way to more remote regions. Southern Maine is just over an hour's drive from Boston and is a popular day-trip destination and weekend escape for city dwellers. On a Friday night in season, you can definitely spend a bit longer than you'd hoped snarled in traffic heading into Maine on I-95.

Of course, even southern Maine isn't exactly the most tropical of places—ocean temperatures may make you say, "Brr!" even in July and August, so the peak season in this waterside destination is a bit abbreviated. On the flip side, if you plan your vacation for the off-season, you're likely to find some bargains and to feel as if you have the place largely to yourself. That is, until you make your obligatory stop at the legendary outlets in Kittery, where bargain hunting is always in season.

Lodging Options

Family motels, beachside cottages, antique inns, spacious resorts, sea captains' homes turned B&Bs . . . the only option conspicuously absent for the most part from the list of available accommodations in southern Maine is large, "name brand" hotel chains. But that's okay. After all, staying in a place with local character is all a part of getting to know Maine. This does mean that you should take some extra care in asking questions before you book your reservations, and keep in mind that competition for rooms along the shore can be fierce during the peak summer season.

In Kittery, York Harbor, and Ogunquit

If you want to be right in the thick of the outlet shopping opportunities, the forty-three-room **Coachman Motor Inn,** 380 Route 1, (207) 439-5555, is located adjacent to the Kittery Outlet Mall in the heart of the Route 1 shopping strip. For something quieter, **Enchanted Nights Bed & Breakfast,** 29 Wentworth Street/Route 103, Kittery, (207) 439-1489, is an 1890 Princess Anne Gothic Victorian with lavishly decorated rooms including some with whirlpool tubs for two, which could come in very handy after a long day of hauling outlet purchases.

The **York Harbor Inn,** Route 1A, (207) 363-5119 or (800) 343-3869, and its adjacent **Harbor Cliffs Bed & Breakfast,** offer forty rooms with all of the warmth and individuality of a small B&B, yet the oceanside inn also boasts its own restaurant and pub and other amenities you'd associate with a larger hotel. **Tanglewood Hall,** 611 York Street, York Harbor, (207) 351-1075, is an 1889 Victorian bed and breakfast decorated with a 1940s theme, which is appropriate considering that big band greats Jimmy and Tommy Dorsey made this their summer home.

Ogunquit Resort Motel, 719 Main Street, (207) 646-8336 or (877) 646-8336, is a solid choice for extended family stays. Features include a pool, hot tub, exercise room, game room, and free continental breakfast, plus kids twelve and under stay free, and it's right on the trolley route for convenient beach access. For something upscale in Ogunquit, consider **Hartwell House,** 118 Shore Road, (207) 646-7210, where the sixteen guest rooms are furnished with English and early American antiques, and rates include a full breakfast and afternoon tea.

Village By the Sea, Route 1, Ogunquit, (207) 646-1100 or (800) 444-8862, is an all-suite resort situated on 11 acres abutting the Rachel Carson Wildlife Preserve and tidal salt marsh, where you'll be surrounded by Maine's natural riches without sacrificing easy access to the region's attractions.

In Wells and Kennebunkport

The **Captain Jefferds Inn,** 5 Pearl Street, Kennebunkport, (207) 967-2311 or (800) 839-6844, is a romantic, circa-1804, Federal-style mansion with sixteen guest rooms and a dog-friendly policy. For a full menu of amenities and the historic charm of an inn that has welcomed guests since 1884, the **Nonantum Resort,** Ocean Avenue, Kennebunkport, (207) 967-4050 or (800) 552-5651, provides 115 rooms including some with kitchenettes, a restaurant, a heated pool, and more.

Captain Lord Mansion, 6 Pleasant Street, (207) 967-3141, was built for a shipbuilder in 1912. This B&B is listed on the National Register of Historic Places and features an octagonal cupola, a four-story spiral staircase, sixteen rooms, and fourteen fireplaces.

In Old Orchard Beach

At **White Lamb Cottages,** 3 Odessa Avenue, (207) 934-2221 or (800) 203-2034, you can stay privately nestled within one of ten cottages just 100 feet from the beach and have muffins, coffee, and the newspaper delivered to your door each morning. **Royal Anchor Resort,** 203 East Grand Avenue, (207) 934-4521 or (800) 934-4521, provides beachfront family accommodations about a mile away from the hubbub of Old Orchard Pier. Want to rent a beach home? **Wight Agency,** 125 West Grand Avenue, (207) 934-4576, specializes in waterfront rentals in Old Orchard Beach. The **Old Orchard Beach Chamber of Commerce** provides information on the dozens of additional motels and cottages in the area at its Web site, *www.oldorchardbeachmaine.com*, or call them at (207) 934-2500 or (800) 365-9386 to request a free vacation planner.

A Southern Maine "To Do" List

Walk through three centuries in Old York, the collection of historic buildings along York Street and Lindsay Road operated by the **Old York Historical Society,** (207) 363-4974. Costumed guides lead tours of six museum buildings Tuesdays through Sundays from mid-June through mid-October. Park at Jefferds' Tavern, Lindsay Road and Route 1A, where you can purchase your admission ticket.

While you're in York, don't miss the **Cape Neddick "Nubble" Light,** a picturesque 1879 lighthouse that can be viewed from the free parking area at Sohier Park, Nubble Road. The lighthouse is particularly spectacular when it is illuminated each year during the Christmas holiday season.

Have you ever dreamed of riding in a Model T? At the **Wells Auto Museum,** Route 1, Wells, (207) 646-9064, you can literally travel through automotive history. More than seventy cars of forty-five makes are on display daily from mid-June through Labor Day and weekends thereafter through mid-October. For another dose of transportation nostalgia, visit the **Seashore Trolley Museum,** 195 Log Cabin Road, Kennebunkport, (207) 967-2800, where you can ride the rails in an early 1900s streetcar and learn about the bygone trolley era.

In Kennebunkport, don't miss the chance from Memorial Day through Columbus Day to head out to sea with **First Chance Whale Watch Cruises,** 4 Western Avenue/Route 9, (800) 767-BOAT. They offer not only whale watch expeditions with guaranteed sightings but also lobster harvesting and scenic lighthouse cruises.

A quick way to see the sights of Kennebunkport, including the home of former President George Bush, is to take the forty-five-minute, narrated tour offered by **Intown Trolley,** Ocean Avenue, (207) 967-3686.

The perennial favorite among southern Maine's more than a dozen public beaches is Old Orchard Beach, which is not just a 7-mile sandy strip but a family amusement center with rides, games, arcades, restaurants, and fireworks popping near the Pier every Thursday night from late June through Labor Day. Call **Horseback Riding Plus,** (207) 883-6400, to inquire about the availability of horseback riding excursions on the beach in the spring and fall.

TRAVEL TIP

After summertime, the next best season to visit Kennebunkport is the holiday season, when the town goes all out for its annual, old-fashioned **Christmas Prelude** the first two weekends in December. Events include caroling, sleigh rides, tree lightings, bonfires, candlelight tours, and Santa's arrival by boat. Find details at: *www.christmasprelude.com.*

Dining Highlights

Salty air definitely whets the appetite, but no worries. There are dining delights aplenty in southern Maine, whether you want to grab a fried bite on the Pier in Old Orchard Beach or relax in a romantic restaurant.

Need a break from outlet shopping? **Weathervane Seafood Restaurant,** Route 1, Kittery, (207) 439-0330, is located in the heart of "outlet row" and serves lobster and other sea treats in a boisterous, casual environment.

At the **Goldenrod,** Route 1A, York Beach, (207) 363-2621, you can watch candy makers at work concocting world-famous Goldenrod Kisses, much as they have been since 1896 when this restaurant and saltwater taffy shop opened. Breakfast is served all day, and lunch and dinner are available, too, from late May through Columbus Day.

Clay Hill Farm, 220 Clay Hill Road, Cape Neddick, (207) 361-2272, is the country's only restaurant that has been designated as a wildlife habitat and bird sanctuary by the National Wildlife Association. Enjoy fine dining, plus a piano bar on select evenings.

For sophisticated fare and gorgeous ocean views, head to **Seascapes,** Pier Road, Cape Porpoise, (207) 967-8500–a favorite of George and Barbara Bush. Or catch a glimpse of the president's place from the **Cape Arundel Inn,** Ocean Avenue, Kennebunkport, (207) 967-2125, where you can enjoy a cocktail on the wraparound porch before heading inside to the ocean-view dining room.

For an extraordinary, four-course, prix fixe dinner, the restaurant at the **White Barn Inn,** 37 Beach Street, Kennebunk, (207) 967-2321, is the region's most distinguished dining enclave. Reservations and jackets for men are required.

Near Old Orchard Beach, kids can feed the friendly seagulls at **Clambake Seafood Restaurant,** Route 9, Scarborough, (207) 883-4871, which specializes in lobster dinners and seats 700.

The **Maine Diner,** 2265 Post Road/Route 1, Wells, (207) 646-4441, is known for its New England cooking, generous portions, affordable prices, and daily specials. Be prepared to wait in line.

If your hunger is for contact with the folks back home, **Bartley's Dockside Dining Internet Café,** By the Bridge, Kennebunkport, (207) 967-5050, will serve you free coffee, tea, or soft drinks while you surf and send e-mail.

Shopping Discoveries

Finding **Route 1 in Kittery** is akin to discovering the pot at the end of the rainbow for retail addicts and casual shoppers alike. More than 120 brand name outlets are packed into this stretch of highway. Plan your outlet shopping strategy before you get to Maine by viewing the online map at *www.thekitteryoutlets.com*, or by calling (207) 439-4367 or (888) KITTERY to request a printed copy.

Lest you think that it's all about the outlets when it comes to opportunities to drop some cash in southern Maine, here are a few other interesting spots to shop. Start with **Dock Square** in Kennebunkport, where you can easily lose hours wandering in and out of boutiques, gift shops, and art galleries. Kennebunk is home to natural health and beauty products maker **Tom's of Maine,** 302 Lafayette Center, (800) 985-3974, where you can shop at the Natural Living Store. Free tours of the company's manufacturing facility are available by reservation Monday through Thursday. Call (800) 775-2388 to reserve your spot on a tour. **Lighthouse Depot,** Route 1, Wells, (207) 646-0608, lays claim to the title of "world's largest lighthouse gift store," and it's also home to a Lighthouse Museum displaying artifacts from the United States Lighthouse Service.

Greater Portland

PORTLAND IS MAINE'S BOSTON—a city that is old and new all at once, but unlike Boston, Maine's largest city is both compact and easily navigable. Portland was first settled in 1632, and in spite of two devastating fires that destroyed early landmarks, it retains the character etched upon it over its centuries of existence as a thriving commercial port.

Today, the vestiges of history are well preserved in Portland, but this is also a thoroughly hip city—home to sophisticated hotels, coffee nooks, brewpubs, swank shops, ethnic eateries, a minor league baseball team, and world-class entertainment.

Follow Route 1 north along Casco Bay to Freeport, a town synonymous with shopping. Since venerable Maine retailer L.L. Bean set up shop here in 1917, the town has mushroomed into a retail bonanza of designer outlets and specialty stores selling everything from Civil War collectibles to Maine-made products and mooselania.

It was also in Freeport that Maine citizens contemplated a revolution. This may conjure up images of Boston as well, but this was the 1800s, and Mainers were seeking their independence not from Britain but from governance by Massachusetts. In 1819, Massachusetts gave Maine the go-ahead to petition for statehood, and in 1820, Maine became the last New England state to join the Union.

HOT SPOT

Self-guided walking tours of Portland are available at the **Visitor Information Center,** 305 Commercial Street. Or, from May through October, opt for a narrated bus tour, which also departs from the Visitor Center several times each day. Call (207) 772-5800 for more information.

Lodging Options

Portland is Maine's largest city, and places to stay are plentiful. Most of the major hotel chains are represented here—Best Western, Comfort Inn, Doubletree, Econo Lodge, Embassy Suites, Hampton Inn, Holiday Inn, Howard Johnson, Marriott, Motel 6, Regency, Radisson, Sheraton, Susse Chalet. Of these, the largest are the 239-room **Holiday Inn By the Bay,** 88 Spring Street, Portland, (207) 775-2311 or (800) 345-5050, which offers an indoor pool and sauna, free parking and airport transportation, and proximity to the Old Port's shops and restaurants; and the 227-room **Marriott at Sable Oaks,** 363 Maine Mall Road, South Portland, (207) 775-6161, which allows pets and has an indoor pool and business amenities.

Outside the city, quieter, seaside accommodations await. **Black Point Inn Resort,** 510 Black Point Road, Scarborough, (207) 883-2500 or (800) 258-0003, is a grand seaside inn listed on the National Registry of Historic Hotels of America that has been welcoming guests since 1878. You'll have your choice of eighty-four individually appointed rooms and cottages, plus golf privileges at several local courses. Families will be quite comfortable at **Inn By the Sea,** 40 Bowery Beach Road, Cape Elizabeth, (207) 799-3134 or (800) 888-IBTS, where each of the forty-three one- and two-bedroom suites has a porch or deck with ocean views, a kitchen, living room, two televisions, and a VCR.

The Freeport area offers both value-priced family motels and historic bed and breakfast inns. **Freeport Inn & Café,** 📇 Route 1, Freeport, ☏(207) 865-3106 or ☏(800) 99-VALUE, has eighty rooms, an outdoor pool and play area for children, and two restaurants on-site. **White Cedar Inn,** 📇 178 Main Street, Freeport, ☏(207) 865-9099 or ☏(800) 853-1269, is a seven-room, historic Victorian B&B that is just two blocks from L.L. Bean. Ask about the "Serious Shopper" package at the **Harraseeket Inn,** 📇 162 Main Street, Freeport, ☏(207) 865-9377 or ☏(800) 342-6423, a classic, eighty-four-room, antique-filled New England inn with twenty-three fireplaces and an indoor pool.

For additional help with locating a Freeport inn, call the **Freeport Area Bed & Breakfast Association,** ☏(207) 865-1500 or ☏(800) 853-2727.

HOT SPOT

New England is not exactly known for its deserts, but thanks to a glacier that left behind a large sand deposit some 11,000 years ago, Freeport is home to a genuine desert, which visitors can tour. The **Desert of Maine,** 📇 95 Desert Road, Freeport, ☏(207) 865-6962, is open from early May to mid-October.

Portland-Area Points of Interest

Historic homes in Portland give visitors a look at the city's evolution. The **Wadsworth-Longfellow House,** 📇 489 Congress Street, ☏(207) 774-1822, dates to 1785 and was the city's first brick home. It was also the childhood residence of one of Portland's most famous native sons, the poet Henry Wadsworth Longfellow. The house is open for tours daily June through October and during special holiday hours in December. The **Neal Dow Memorial,** 📇 714 Congress Street, ☏(207) 773-7773, is an 1829 brick mansion that was owned by General Neal Dow, the "father of Prohibition." It is open for free tours on weekdays. **Victoria Mansion,** 📇 109 Danforth Street,

(207) 772-4841, is a National Historic Landmark built between 1858 and 1860 for hotel baron Ruggles Morse. The Italianate brownstone's interior is the only surviving example of the work of famed New York designer Gustave Herter. Guided tours are available May through October every day except Monday.

The **Portland Museum of Art,** 7 Congress Square, (207) 775-6148, is Maine's largest art repository and a must for art lovers visiting the state. The museum has a focus on the artistic heritage of the United States and particularly Maine and features works by Winslow Homer, Andrew Wyeth, John Singer Sargent, and other acclaimed American painters. The museum is open daily Memorial Day through Columbus Day and every day except Monday the rest of the year. Time for another museum? See a working lighthouse, a nineteenth-century fort, and historic exhibits at the **Portland Harbor Museum,** Fort Road, South Portland, (207) 799-6337. Located on the campus of Southern Maine Technical College, it is open to visitors daily July through September, Friday through Sunday in June, and weekends only in April, May, October, and November.

HOT SPOT

When the dog days of summer arrive, it's time to cheer on the **Portland Sea Dogs,** the Eastern League Double-A Affiliate of Major League Baseball's Florida Marlins. Kids will love the antics of the team's mascot, Slugger the Sea Dog, and a day at the ballpark makes for an affordable outing for the whole family. The Sea Dogs play at Hadlock Field, 271 Park Avenue, Portland. Tickets may be purchased online at *www.portlandseadogs.com* or by calling (207) 879-9500 or (800) 936-DOGS.

Ready for something wild? You have two choices. Head inland to the **Maine Wildlife Park,** Route 26, Gray, (207) 657-4977, home to Maine animals that need protection or healing from an injury including moose, lynx, bobcats, mountain lions, coyotes, bald eagles, turkey vultures, and more. Or head out to sea to spy on seals with **Atlantic Seal Cruises,** Freeport Town Wharf, South Freeport, (207) 865-6112.

Casco Bay Lines, Commercial and Franklin Streets, Portland, (207) 774-7871, is the nation's oldest continuously operating ferry company, and you should definitely check their sailing schedule for scenic and music cruises. You can even ride along on the mail boat that delivers letters and parcels to the residents of the islands in Casco Bay.

Treat yourself to a free peek behind the scenes at a candy factory when you take the self-guided tour at **Haven's Candies,** 87 County Road, Westbrook, (207) 772-1557 or (800) 639-6309, which has been making saltwater taffy, fudge, chocolate lobsters, and other sweets since 1915. It's open Monday through Saturday. Or visit **Len Libby Handmade Candies,** 419 Route 1, Scarborough, (207) 883-4897, to see the world's only life-size chocolate moose—Lenny is made of 1,700 pounds of chocolate!

Fort Williams Park, 1000 Shore Road, Cape Elizabeth, (207) 799-2661. Fort Williams Park also offers a beach, tennis courts, and areas for cross-country skiing and ice skating in the winter and kite flying on breezy days. The ruins of the large, old fort are enticing to children and adults alike.

Pay a visit, too, to **Two Lights State Park,** off Route 77, Cape Elizabeth, (207) 799-5871, which is home to remnants of a World War II coastal defense installation, picnic areas, and scenic views of the adjacent Cape Elizabeth Light. Out on Cape Elizabeth, visit Maine's first lighthouse, Portland Head Light.

HOT SPOT

Embark on an overnight cruise from Portland, Maine, to Yarmouth, Nova Scotia, and back aboard the ***M/S Scotia Prince.*** Dinner, breakfast, and a private cabin are included, and the ship boasts its own casino and late-night floor show. Call (800) 845-4073 for a schedule and reservations.

Dining Highlights

While brewpubs are certainly popular with Portland diners, there are other unique eating experiences to contemplate when you're in the city. For starters, you can float while you feast at **DiMillo's Floating Restaurant,** Commercial Street/Route 1A, (207) 772-2216, a former car ferry turned into one of the largest floating restaurants in the country. For something extraordinary, make reservations to dine at the Chef's Table at the **Café Stroudwater at the Embassy Suites,** 1050 Westbrook Street, (207) 775-0032, where one lucky party of two to eight people each evening can observe the workings of the restaurant's kitchen while dining.

It might not look like much from the outside, but dining at **Fore Street,** 288 Fore Street, (207) 775-2717, is a coveted experience, so you'll need reservations. Specialties include turnspit-roasted chicken and pork loin and wood-oven–roasted halibut and sea bass.

The **Great Lost Bear,** 540 Forest Avenue, (207) 772-0300, isn't a brewpub, but it does showcase more than a dozen Maine beers among the fifty on tap—you're bound to find just the right brew to wash down every item on the restaurant's eclectic menu.

The **Portland Public Market,** 25 Preble Street, (207) 228-2000, is the perfect place for picnic purchases. About two dozen vendors sell fresh meat, poultry, produce, seafood, cheese, bread, pies, wine, beer, and other made-in-Maine goodies here. Free parking is available in the Public Market Garage, which is accessible from Preble and Elm streets.

New York restaurateur and Maine native Matthew Kenney has opened a restaurant in the Public Market—**Commissary,** (207) 228-2057, that takes its cue from its surroundings, featuring a menu that incorporates local ingredients.

For home-style Maine cooking, head inland to **Cole Farms,** Route 100, Gray, (207) 657-4714, which has been serving filling food to travelers and locals since 1952.

In Freeport, just like L.L. Bean, which is a mere block away,

The **Lobster Cooker,** 39 Main Street, (207) 865-4349, is open every day of the year, serving lobster, homemade chowders, and other seafood selections. The **Muddy Rudder Restaurant at the Freeport Inn,** Route 1, (207) 865-3106, has been a Freeport institution for more than twenty years—just don't get your tongue so twisted trying to say it that you can't enjoy your meal! The menu features seafood, steaks, pasta, and more. Or step back in time at the **Jameson Tavern,** 115 Main Street, (207) 865-4196, the 1799 pub where Freeport folks first talked about asserting their freedom from Massachusetts.

Shopping Discoveries

Leon Leonwood Bean invented the Maine Hunting Shoe in 1911. In 1912, he initiated mail order sales with a four-page flyer sent to out-of-state sportsmen. In 1917, L.L. Bean set up shop on Main Street in Freeport, and the rest, as they say, is history. Today, visitors to the **L.L. Bean Flagship Store,** 95 Main Street, Freeport, (800) 341-4341, can shop twenty-four hours a day, 365 days each year. Part of L.L. Bean's mystique comes from the company's 100 percent satisfaction guarantee—a promise that was born in 1912 and remains to this day. Any L.L. Bean purchase, whether made at the flagship store, at outlet shops, or via mail order, can be returned at any time for a replacement or refund.

Speaking of outlets, Freeport also boasts an **L.L. Bean Factory Store,** Depot Street, (207) 552-7772. It's just one of the dozens of outlet stores and specialty shops concentrated in this vibrant town. Other name brand retailers with factory stores here include Dexter, Nine West, Dansk, Cuddledown of Maine, Levi's, Calvin Klein, and Polo Ralph Lauren. And, unlike Kittery, Freeport also goes beyond outlets to offer shoppers a nifty array of specialty stores selling made-in-Maine gifts and unique souvenirs. Wander into **Mangy Moose,** 112 Main Street, (207) 865-6414 (800) 606-6517, and just try to get yourself out of there without purchasing one moose-shaped or emblazoned item. At **20th Maine,** 49 West

Street, (207) 865-4340, shop for collectibles and commemoratives at the only shop north of Gettysburg dedicated to the Civil War. And when the kids tire of traipsing in and out of outlets, take them to the **Maine Bear Factory,** 294 Route 1 South, (207) 865-0600, where they can design, stuff, and sew their own cuddly companions. Plan your Freeport shopping trip by calling the **Freeport Merchants Association** at (207) 865-1212 or (800) 865-1994 to request a free map and brochure.

I'm afraid you're not done shopping yet! **Portland's Old Port District** with its cobblestone walkways and Victorian red brick buildings housing dozens of specialty boutiques, galleries, restaurants, antique emporiums, and craft shops selling Maine-made items, is also well worth a visit. This five-block, easily walkable area extends from the bustling, working waterfront to Congress Street between Exchange and Pearl streets.

If uniquely Maine jewelry is your desired souvenir, there are several distinctive jewelers you should visit in this region. **Cross Jewelers,** 570 Congress Street, Portland, (207) 773-3107 or (800) 433-2988, creates one-of-a-kind pieces incorporating Maine granites and other stones. **Lovell Designs,** 26 Exchange Street, Portland, (207) 828-5303 or (800) 533-9685, specializes in Maine-inspired pins, pendants, and earrings in pewter. **Fairbanks, Frost & Lowe,** 21 Main Street, Freeport, (207) 865-0011 or (877) MAINE-GEMS, sets dazzling Maine tourmaline in rings, earrings, pendants, bracelets, and brooches.

HOT SPOT

You'll find L.L. Bean Factory Stores in these New England locations:

Maine: Ellsworth, Freeport, Portland
New Hampshire: Concord, Nashua, North Conway

Western Maine: Lakes, Mountains, Rivers, Valleys

LOBSTER AND MOOSE—the tasty crustacean and the gangly mammal symbolize Maine's duality, and when you leave the rocky coastline behind for inland reaches, you'll experience a different Maine entirely. The western part of the state is freshwater Maine—a land where mountain peaks reflect in shimmering lakes, rivers roar, and snow piles up on pine branches.

Outdoor adventures, particularly water sports, are what draw most travelers to this region. Make this your vacation destination if you are longing to canoe or kayak on limpid lakes, to bond with your loved ones on a camping trip, to brave Maine's most vigorous rivers on a white water rafting run, to snowmobile along miles of powdery trails, or to ski by day and hunker down in front of a tension-melting fire at night. Western Maine is also home to the state's capital, Augusta, a riverside city that began as a frontier trading post and now showcases the state's history and way of life.

You may just come snout-to-snout with a moose as you play in Maine's watery wilderness, and don't worry—lobster is still a menu staple.

TRAVEL TIP

Rustic sporting camps that cater to hunting and fishing enthusiasts are a uniquely Maine phenomenon. In their early 1900s heyday, they numbered in the hundreds, but today, only about fifty remain. The **Maine Sporting Camp Association** was founded in 1987 to preserve these havens for outdoor enthusiasts. Their Web site, *www.mainesportingcamps.com,* provides links to member camps that welcome visitors. You can also request a guide to sporting camps by writing to: The Maine Sporting Camp Association, P.O. Box 119, Millinocket, Maine 04462.

Lodging Options

There are plenty of places where families will feel right at home. **Point Sebago Resort,** 261 Point Sebago Road, Casco, (207) 655-3821 or (800) 530-1555, is a 775-acre family playground with an extensive menu of organized and supervised activities for toddlers to teens, and adults, too. Facilities include an eighteen-hole championship golf course, a driving range, a marina, tennis courts, and a nightclub. Camp in your own tent or RV, or stay in one of the resort's rental cottages or park homes. If your family seeks seclusion, **Attean Lake Lodge,** Attean Road, Jackman, (207) 668-3792, is situated on a wild island within the lake. All meals are included. Family reunions are welcomed.

Dreaming of an elegant country inn where the two of you can steal away? **Lake House,** Routes 35 and 37, Waterford, (207) 583-4182 or (800) 223-4182, was built in the 1790s as the town's first tavern; its eight guest rooms are designed to reflect that time period. **King's Hill Inn,** 56 King Hill Road, South Paris, (207) 744-0204 or (877) 391-KING, was once the home of Horatio King, postmaster general under presidents Buchanan and Lincoln. Six rooms are available inside this restored Victorian farmhouse. The

Pressey House Lakeside Bed & Breakfast, 32 Belgrade Road, Oakland, (207) 465-3500, is an octagonal inn built in the 1850s on Messalonskee Lake that offers five suites complete with kitchens for guests.

Spas are few and far between in Maine, but Augusta has one. The **Best Western Senator Inn & Spa,** Western Avenue, (207) 622-5804 or (877) 772-2224, has 125 rooms and offers a variety of spa services, free breakfast, and a gorgeous indoor pool.

For all of the amenities of a four-season resort, the 200-acre, 140-room **Bethel Inn & Country Club,** Broad Street, Bethel, (207) 824-2175 or (800) 654-0125, offers unlimited golf, cross-country and snowshoeing trails, tennis courts, a heated outdoor pool, and breakfast and a four-course dinner daily.

Keep in mind that many white-water rafting outfitters include lodging with their excursion packages.

FAST FACT

The **Appalachian Trail** is a 2,167-mile hiking path that connects Maine's Mt. Katahdin with Springer Mountain in Georgia. It traverses every New England state except Rhode Island. The trail opened in 1937 thanks to extensive volunteer efforts, and, in 1968, it was designated the first National Scenic Trail. More than 99 percent of the trail is protected by federal or state ownership of the land or by rights-of-way. Trail information may be obtained by calling (304) 535-6331. The Appalachian Mountain Club (AMC), (617) 523-0636, *www.outdoors.org,* was founded in 1876 and is America's oldest conservation and recreation organization. The AMC operates back-country lodges along the Appalachian Trail in New Hampshire and a hostel in Maine's Acadia National Park. They also offer guided trail adventures and trail publications.

A Dozen Things to Do in Western Maine

1. Visit the **Sabbathday Lake Shaker Village,** 707 Shaker Road, New Gloucester, (207) 926-4597, open daily except for Sunday from Memorial Day through Columbus Day. This is the last practicing community of Shakers in America.
2. Cruise Long Lake aboard the 92-foot ***Songo River Queen II,*** Route 302, Naples, (207) 693-6861, a Mississippi riverboat replica that operates from July through Labor Day.
3. Rent a kayak or canoe at **Saco River Canoe & Kayak,** Route 5, Fryeburg, (207) 935-2369 or (888) 772-6573, and explore one of New England's most perfect-for-paddling rivers.
4. Take your camera or sketchpad along to the **Sunday River Covered Bridge,** Sunday River Road, Newry. Also known as Artists' Bridge, it is Maine's most-painted and photographed covered bridge.
5. Visit the **Wilhelm Reich Museum** and the **Orgone Energy Observatory at Orgonon,** Dodge Pond Road, Rangeley, (207) 864-3443, open Wednesday through Sunday in July and August and Sundays only in September. A student of Sigmund Freud, Reich claimed to have discovered a previously unknown form of energy—orgone—and he even developed the Orgone Energy Accumulator, later labeled a fraud by the U.S. Food and Drug Administration, to make it accessible to people who needed a boost.
6. See the collection of Stanley Steamer automobiles at the **Stanley Museum,** 40 School Street, Kingfield, (207) 265-2729, open daily except for Mondays from May through October. The Stanley brothers were born in Kingfield.
7. Head to Western Maine Snowmobile Rentals at **Tommy's Marine,** Route 5, Lovell, (207) 925-1075, and hit the trails.
8. Book a white-water rafting adventure with **Northern Outdoors,** Route 201, the Forks, (207) 663-4466 or (800) 765-RAFT. Northern Outdoors also offers sportyak

(inflatable kayak), rock climbing, fishing, and snowmobiling excursions.

9. Learn about Maine's evolution at the **Maine State Museum,** 83 State House Station, Augusta, (207) 287-2301, where four floors of exhibits showcase the state's land, history, products, and people.
10. Take your mountain bike and ride the 30-mile rail bed trail from Jackman to Rockwood.
11. Embark on a ride aboard the only steam train in Maine at the **Belfast & Moosehead Lake Railroad Company,** 1 Depot Square, Unity, (207) 948-5500 or (800) 392-5500.
12. Drive U.S. Route 201, a National Scenic Byway along the Kennebec River.

Dining Highlights

Groovy! You won't need a time machine to travel back to the 1950s—just directions to **Fast Eddie's Drive-In Restaurant and Movie Theatre,** Route 202, Winthrop, (207) 933-4782, where waiters and waitresses on roller skates or blades whisk your order right to your car window.

For romantic, fireside dining, try the **Victoria,** 32 Main Street, Bethel, (207) 824-8060 or (888) 774-1235, a Victorian inn with three charming dining rooms. Or, for casual fireside dining and views of Big Wood Lake, head to **Moose Point Tavern,** 16 Henderson Road, Jackman, (207) 668-4012.

Gourmet preparations and White Mountains views are dished up at the **Oxford House Inn,** 105 Main Street, Fryeburg, (207) 935-3442 or (800) 261-7206, where you can dine indoors or outside on the screened porch. Reservations are required.

The Lakes Region's first brewpub, **Bray's Brewpub & Eatery,** Routes 302 and 35, Naples, (207) 693-6806, opened in 1995 in a 120-year-old Victorian farmhouse. Lunch, dinner, and tours of the brewing operation are available daily.

HOT SPOT

Maine's largest agricultural fair is held in Fryeburg each fall. The 150-year-old **Fryeburg Fair** features livestock exhibitions, woodworking demonstrations, sheepdog trials, harness racing, a midway with rides and games, musical entertainment, and more. For a schedule and information, visit *www.fryeburgfair.com* or call (207) 935-3268.

Shopping Discoveries

While western Maine can't hold a candle to the shopping splendors of Kittery and Freeport, there are some notable retail outposts here.

- At **Cabin Candlery,** 1246 Roosevelt Trail, Raymond, (207) 655-2520 or (800) 343-3838, candles are still made the old-fashioned way—by hand pouring. Take home scents that will remind you of Maine: Ocean Breeze, Blueberry, White Christmas, and more.
- The **Cry of the Loon Gift Shop,** Route 302, South Casco, (207) 655-5060, can keep shopaholics occupied for hours with its multiple buildings filled to overflowing with Maine-made gifts and goodies in every nook and cranny.
- Buy bison meat and gifts at the **Beech Hill Trading Post at the Beech Hill Bison Ranch,** 630 Valley Road, North Waterford, (207) 583-2515. Call ahead for a schedule of hayrides among the herd.
- **Mount Mica Rarities,** 191 Main Street, Greenwood, (207) 875-3060, specializes in jewelry featuring tourmaline mined at Mt. Mica.
- Winnie the Pooh fans will adore **Pooh Corner Farm,** 436 Bog Road, Mason Township, (207) 836-FARM or (800) 625-4708, a greenhouse and garden shop complex where

the kids can chat with a live pig, donkey, rabbit, and kangaroo named Piglet, Eeyore, Rabbit, and Roo, while you shop for garden gifts and Pooh collectibles.

- If you simply must own earrings made from, uh . . . moose droppings, then head to **Maine Line Products,** 297 Main Street, Greenwood, (207) 875-2522 or (800) 874-0484, where you can also buy "mooseltoe" made of the same . . . er . . . stuff.

FAST FACT

Maine's state mineral wasn't discovered in large quantities until 1972. Now, mines in Maine are known for producing some of the world's finest tourmaline. This unusual gemstone comes in a rainbow of colors. Particularly prized are the green and pink "watermelon" stones that have two distinctive bands of color. Maine jewelers set tourmaline stones in glittering settings, and you can even hunt for your own tourmaline at the abandoned quarries within **Mount Apatite Park,** Stevens Mill Road, Auburn, (207) 784-0191, where amateur geologists and rock collectors are permitted to use hand tools to explore for mineral specimens. Two warnings—this is rugged terrain, and there are no toilets.

Midcoast Maine

YOU CAN GET A SENSE OF THE PSYCHE of Midcoast Maine—the coastal region that runs from Brunswick to Searsport—simply by examining the calendar of annual events held here. Winter brings the Christmas by the Sea celebration and the National Toboggan Championships. Warmer weather sprouts events such as the Fishermen's Festival, where Miss Shrimp Princess is crowned, the annual Lobster Boat Races, and Windjammer Days. At the height of summer, Midcoast Maine is home to the Maine Blueberry Festival and the Maine Lobster Festival. And when the leaves begin to turn, an annual Fall Foliage Festival and a Festival of Scarecrows mark this season's splendor as well.

In essence, Midcoast Maine is all about everything that makes Maine delicious. From the vibrancy of the changing seasons to the majesty of rocky ledges standing starkly against the azure ocean, from the loveliness of tiny island towns to the palpable energy of fishing villages, this is a region that is at once both exhilarating and soothing.

Many New England devotees make a trek to Midcoast Maine an annual event in their lives. If nothing else, the promise of eight tons of lobster steaming in the world's largest lobster cooker just might be enough to convince you to mark the Maine Lobster Festival in Rockland on your August calendar this year.

Lodging Options

While you'll find some modern motor and chain hotels in the Midcoast region, particularly in the Brunswick area, by far the most enchanting options are the historic, seaside inns and the snug bed and breakfasts that dot the lodgings landscape.

The **Captain Daniel Stone Inn,** 10 Water Street, Brunswick, (207) 725-9898, is a palatial 1819 Federal-style home turned thirty-four-room inn with its own restaurant.

In Bath, the **Kennebec Inn Bed & Breakfast,** 1024 Washington Street, (207) 443-5202, is a circa 1860 Italianate mansion with seven guest rooms furnished with four-poster beds—some have Jacuzzis and fireplaces, too. The **Galen C. Moses House,** 1009 Washington Street, (207) 442-8771 or (888) 442-8771, is an 1874 "painted lady" Victorian listed on the National Register of Historic Homes. The four-room B&B is full of surprises including ornamental mantels, stained glass windows, and resident ghosts.

At the **Grey Havens Inn,** Seguinland Road, Georgetown Island, (207) 371-2616, four of the fourteen guest rooms are located in the circular turret, providing 180-degree ocean views. Crisp white rockers on the wraparound porch are another prime vantage point from which to watch the waves. The 1904 inn is believed to be the last classic "shingle-style" hotel still operating on Maine's coast.

The **Samoset Resort,** 220 Warrenton Street, Rockport, (207) 594-2511 or (800) 341-1650, has welcomed guests to Midcoast Maine since 1889. Located on 230 rugged, oceanside acres overlooking the Rockland Breakwater and Rockland Lighthouse, it is known for one of New England's most scenic golf courses, with ocean vistas from fourteen of the eighteen holes.

The **Hartstone Inn,** 41 Elm Street, Camden, (207) 236-4259 or (800) 788-4823, is an 1835 Mansard-style, Victorian B&B that offers gourmet getaways including five-course dinners in its award-winning restaurant. Ask about cooking class weekends.

For families, **Brown's Wharf Motel,** 121 Atlantic Avenue,

Boothbay Harbor, ✆(207) 633-5440 or ✆(800) 334-8110, offers balcony rooms with marina views and a restaurant on-site. At **Ocean Gate Inn,** ✉ Route 27, West Southport, ✆(207) 633-3321, children under twelve stay free, and the whole family will enjoy the amenities of this 85-acre, waterfront resort, including a heated pool, tennis courts, and a playground.

Escape to the **Spruce Point Inn,** ✉ Atlantic Avenue, Boothbay Harbor, ✆(207) 633-4152 or ✆(800) 553-0289, which is situated on its own private, 15-acre peninsula. Enroll the kids in the inn's children's program, then relax in a hammock or enjoy the saltwater and heated freshwater pools, two whirlpools, clay tennis courts, and more.

For an affordable vacation, the off-season rates are great at the **Belfast Harbor Inn,** ✉ Route 1, Belfast, ✆(207) 338-2740 or ✆(800) 545-8576, which overlooks Penobscot Bay.

On select weeks and weekends, particularly in the off-season, you can rent the whole house at **EdgeWater Farm Bed & Breakfast,** ✉ 71 Small Point Road, Phippsburg, ✆(207) 389-1322 or ✆(877) 389-1322, and enjoy six rooms, an indoor pool and spa, nearby beaches, and acres of gardens and fruit trees.

HOT SPOT

The **Keeper's House Inn,** ✉ Isle Au Haut, ✆(207) 367-2261, is a former lighthouse keeper's house turned six-room inn that is situated on the site of the still working Robinson Point Lighthouse within Acadia National Park. Listed on the National Register of Historic Places, the inn provides guests with an opportunity for time travel—there is no electricity, meals are served by candlelight, and rooms are lit by kerosene lanterns. Access the island via the mail boat from Stonington. Meals are included during your stay.

Captivations along the Coast

No matter what the sea-son, the sea plays an integral part in the activities and attractions you'll find in Midcoast Maine.

HOT SPOT

The **Maine Maritime Museum,** 243 Washington Street, Bath, (207) 443-1316, is a good place to become acquainted with the state's seafaring history. Located on the site of a nineteenth-century shipyard, the museum features paintings, models, artifacts, and exhibits related to maritime technology and life at sea. It is open daily year-round.

Explore the thirteen historic fishing village buildings at the **Penobscot Marine Museum,** Route 1 and Church Street, Searsport, (207) 548-2529, which are home to twenty-five galleries of marine art and artifacts. The museum is open daily Memorial Day weekend through mid-October.

If you can't take the time for a full-blown Windjammer cruise, there are day excursions that will allow you to see Midcoast Maine from the water side. Board the ***Balmy Days II,*** Pier 8, Commercial Street, Boothbay Harbor, (207) 633-2284 or (800) 298-2284, for a scenic harbor tour, a mackerel fishing trip, or a journey to Monhegan Island, where you can spend a day hiking, picnicking, and visiting art galleries and a lighthouse. The ***Lively Lady Too,*** Bay View Landing, Camden, (207) 236-6672, will take you on a lighthouse tour, a nature cruise, or to an uninhabited island for an evening lobster bake. For a sampling of windjamming, the 1918 tall ship ***Schooner Surprise,*** Camden Public Landing, Camden, (207) 236-4687, offers two-hour sightseeing sails.

If history fascinates you, you'll want to pay a call to ***Montpelier,*** Routes 1 and 131, Thomaston, (207) 354-8062, the re-created retirement home of Revolutionary War hero General Henry Knox.

The **Farnsworth Art Museum,** 352 Main Street, Rockland, (207) 596-6457, is one of Maine's premier art habitats. Home to six galleries, plus the Jamien Morehouse Wing, the Farnsworth Homestead, a great museum shop, and the Wyeth Center featuring the works of Maine's painting dynasty—N.C., Andrew, and Jamie Wyeth—you could easily spend a day or even a weekend here. The museum is open daily year-round, and admission to the Homestead is included between Memorial Day weekend and Columbus Day.

You'll find three lovely beaches at **Reid State Park,** off Route 127, Georgetown Island, (207) 371-2303, a favorite oceanside destination for birding, hiking, swimming, biking, saltwater fishing, cross-country skiing, and snowshoeing. **Popham Beach State Park,** Route 209, Phippsburg, (207) 389-1335, is also a good "day at the beach" destination. It's open mid-April through October. Day-use fees are charged at Maine State Parks.

Visit the **Shore Village Museum,** 104 Limerock Street, Rockland, (207) 594-0311, open June through mid-October, for a look at the largest collection of lighthouse artifacts in the U.S. You might also plan a scenic drive to the end of Route 130, where you'll find Pemaquid Point Light, originally constructed in 1827 and rebuilt in 1835, and the **Fishermen's Museum,** Pemaquid Point Road, New Harbor, (207) 677-2494.

When the kids get fidgety, take them to visit the endangered animals at the **Kelmscott Rare Breeds Foundation,** Route 52, Lincolnville, (207) 763-4088, a working farm open daily except Mondays and home to twenty rare breeds of livestock. Or chug on over to **Boothbay Railway Village,** Route 27, Boothbay, (207) 633-4727, and ride a vintage train through a re-created, turn-of-the-century New England village. This attraction is open from early June through mid-October.

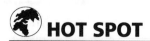

HOT SPOT

Ever dreamed of being part of the crew aboard a tall ship? The thirteen schooners that are members of the **Maine Windjammer Association,** (207) 374-2993 or (800) 807-WIND, make that dream a reality for hundreds of folks during the sailing season each year. Actually, you can do as much or as little as you like on a Maine Windjammer cruise. These tall ships depart from Camden, Rockport, and Rockland in Midcoast Maine from mid-May to mid-October for three- to six-day excursions that include all meals. Because the ships sail in protected inlets for the most part, you're not likely to get seasick. Be forewarned, though, that there are no electrical outlets and only a few hot showers on board.

Dining Highlights

Start your day off with fresh-baked pastries at **Kristina's Restaurant & Bakery,** Centre Street and High Street, Bath, (207) 442-8577, where breakfast is served Tuesday through Friday, brunch on Saturday and Sunday. Lunch and dinner are served every day except Monday, as well.

If you're in Camden at lunchtime, head to **Camden Deli,** 37 Main Street, Camden, (207) 236-8343, for what may arguably be the best views from any deli in America. The restaurant is situated atop a waterfall and offers Camden harbor views, too. Dine inside an 1893 drugstore complete with an original soda fountain at **Boynton-McKay Food Co.,** 30 Main Street, Camden, (207) 236-2465.

By now you know that lobster is the mainstay of Maine coast menus. At **Young's Lobster Pound,** 4 Mitchell Avenue, Belfast, (207) 338-1160, you can select your own from a lobster aquarium that holds 30,000 of the crustaceans! Indoor and outdoor waterfront seating areas are available, and they'll pack seafood to go, too. You'll find ocean views from every table and an affordable children's menu at **Kaler's Crab and Lobster House,** 48 Commercial Street,

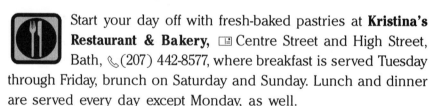

Boothbay Harbor, (207) 633-5839. Lobster, local brews, and ocean views go together at the **Whale's Tooth Pub and Restaurant,** Route 1, Lincolnville, (207) 789-5200. Watch the lobstermen hard at work bringing home your dinner at the **Lobstermen's Co-op,** Atlantic Avenue, Boothbay Harbor, (207) 633-4900, a casual restaurant where you can eat indoors or out.

On Bailey Island, you'll find **Cook's Lobster House,** off Route 24, (207) 833-2818, a highly regarded, casual, seafood spot that's been around since 1955. If the name sounds familiar, you may have heard it in a credit card commercial! From the restaurant, you'll have views of the Bailey Island Bridge, a crib bridge that is a civil engineering marvel listed on the National Register of Historic Places.

Moody's Diner, Route 1, Waldoboro, (207) 832-7785, opened for business in 1934, and travelers and locals have been drawn to its traditional, down-home cooking and reasonable prices ever since.

HOT SPOT

What happens when you turn an auto shop into a waterfront restaurant? Find out at **Le Garage,** Water Street, Wiscasset, (207) 882-5409, where you can select from seafood, meat, and vegetarian entrees.

For an exquisite meal, try out the **Robinhood Free Meetinghouse,** Robinhood Road, Georgetown, (207) 371-2188, a five-star gem housed in a restored 1855 meetinghouse. Save room for a slice of Obsession in Three Chocolates, and inquire ahead about special wine tasting dinners and Thursday Theme Nights.

Keep in mind that January is a month when many Midcoast restaurants take a winter breather.

Shopping Discoveries

Wiscasset is a picturesque shopping village. Main Street (Route 1) and several side streets are clustered with antique purveyors, galleries, and curiosity shops. Don't miss the **Musical Wonder House** and the **Merry Music Box Shop,** 18 High Street, (207) 882-7163, where you can see and shop for all variety of mechanical musical instruments, exhibited in an 1852 Victorian Sea Captain's mansion.

If you'd like to support the work of Maine artisans, you'll find the Midcoast region home to many shops and galleries where you can do just that. **Yankee Artisan,** 56 Front Street, Bath, (207) 443-6215, is an artists' cooperative whose members are selected by a jury to ensure quality. **Sheepscot River Pottery,** Main Street, Damariscotta, (207) 882-9410, sells original, hand-painted pieces featuring uniquely Maine designs. Michael David Brown's mixed media collages put a modernistic slant on Maine and New England scenes. You can see his work at **Red Door Gallery,** 235 Old County Road, Rockport, (207) 596-6202, open daily except for Monday from Memorial Day weekend through mid-October, and you're welcome to stop in to watch the artist at work in his neighboring studio. At **Gallery-By-The-Sea,** Route 131, Port Clyde, (207) 372-8280, the works of a dozen artists who live and work in Maine are represented.

If you cross-stitch, pop into **Stitchery Square,** 11 Elm Street, Camden, (207) 236-9773, where you can purchase needlepoint kits depicting Maine scenes.

Take home maple syrup made in Maine from **Maine Gold Marketplace,** Route 1, Rockport, (800) 752-5271. Or visit Maine's first vineyard, **Cellardoor Winery**, 4150 Youngtown Road, Lincolnville, (207) 763-4478 or (877) 899-0196, where tours, tastings, and wine sales are offered May through October.

Reny's, 33 and 48–54 Main Street, Damariscotta, (207) 563-5757, is a chain of Maine discounters that was founded in Damariscotta in 1949. Visit the original bargain store, with outlets on both sides of Main Street—one for clothing and one for everything else.

Downeast Maine and Acadia

HOW DID A PLACE THAT'S SO FAR UP THERE in Maine ever earn a nickname like "Downeast"? The term originated with sailors en route to this region from Boston, who had to sail downwind and to the east to reach the harbors of Maine. Today, the label is applied to the entire northern coastal region of the state, stretching to the Canadian border.

This is a land chock full of superlatives . . .

- The easternmost point in the United States—Lubec
- The highest tides in the Continental United States—near Calais
- The highest point on the Atlantic coast north of Rio de Janeiro—Cadillac Mountain
- Maine's largest island—Mount Desert Island
- The oldest national park east of the Mississippi River and Maine's top tourist attraction—Acadia National Park. Each year, nearly 3 million visitors descend on the 54-square-mile park, which encompasses 41 miles of coastline, plus mountains, forests, and lakes.

However you choose to encounter the natural wonders of Downeast Maine—on foot, on two wheels, behind the wheel of your automobile, from a boat off the coast, or even aboard a trolley or horse-drawn carriage—you'll gain a renewed appreciation for the formations and creations of nature that could never be replicated by human hands.

TRAVEL TIP

The town of Lubec is the easternmost point in the United States, and thus the spot where the first rays of sunlight touch the nation each morning. Rise early, and head down to the Lubec Municipal Marina on Lubec Harbor to watch the sun rise.

Lodging Options

From campgrounds and rustic log cabins to elegant inns, modern hotels, and spacious resorts, whatever your style, there's likely a perfect lodging complement for you in Downeast Maine.

If you need to stay near Bangor International Airport, you'll have your choice of several business-class and chain hotels. The **Four Points By Sheraton,** 308 Godfrey Boulevard, (207) 947-6721 or (800) 228-4609, provides the greatest convenience, as it is connected to the airport by an enclosed walkway. The **Holiday Inn,** 404 Odlin Road, (207) 947-0101 or (800) 914-0101, has 207 rooms and provides complimentary shuttle transportation to and from the airport. Just fifteen minutes from Bangor in East Holden, you'll find a touch more charm at the **Lucerne Inn,** Bar Harbor Road, (207) 843-5123 or (800) 325-5123, a country inn established in 1814 with views of Phillips Lake and its own golf course.

For your own little log cabin hideaway, **Castine Cottages,** Route 166, Castine, (207) 326-8003, has six waterside units available—all furnished with lobster cooking equipment.

Seclusion is also on the menu at **Goose Cove Lodge,** Goose Cove Road, (207) 348-6615, a Deer Isle resort offering a private beach, nature trails, weekly stargazing evenings, and proximity to the quaint fishing village of Stonington. Choose a private cottage or a room in the main lodge.

Located near Acadia National Park, Bar Harbor is Downeast Maine's most popular destination, and the diversity and number of lodging establishments definitely reflects this distinction. There are more than 9,000 rooms available in the Bar Harbor area. At the top of the lodgings pyramid is the four-star **Bar Harbor Hotel-Bluenose Inn,** 90 Eden Street, (207) 288-3348 or (800) 445-4077, which offers expansive ocean views, heated indoor and outdoor pools, a spa, fitness center, restaurant, and ninety-seven rooms and suites. The main entrance to Acadia National Park is just two minutes from the hotel. **Acadia Inn,** 98 Eden Street, (207) 288-3500 or (800) 638-3636, offers a free continental breakfast plus free shuttle transportation to Acadia and downtown Bar Harbor. For a dramatic ocean setting, it's difficult to top **Bar Harbor Inn,** Newport Drive, (207) 288-3351 or (800) 248-3351, once home to the elite Oasis Club, a social club that counted Vanderbilts, Morgans, and Pulitzers as members.

FAST FACT

Bar Harbor also boasts a bevy of bed and breakfasts. **Thornhedge Inn,** 47 Mount Desert Street, (207) 288-5398, is the Queen Anne-style home built as a summer cottage by the publisher of Louisa May Alcott's *Little Women*. It has thirteen guest rooms. The **Wayside Inn,** 11 Atlantic Avenue, (207) 288-5703 or (800) 722-6671, is a Tudor mansion with a variety of accommodations including rooms with fireplaces and Jacuzzi tubs and even a separate Victorian guest house that sleeps six.

There are two campgrounds in Acadia National Park. Make reservations for **Blackwoods campground** by calling (301) 722-1257 or (800) 365-2267. **Seawall campground** operates on a first-come, first-served basis and fills up early for July through September.

TRAVEL TIP

For more Bar Harbor lodging ideas, request the free guidebook from the Bar Harbor Chamber of Commerce, (207) 288-5103.

There are some intriguing accommodations as you continue east along Maine's coast. **Pleasant Bay Bed & Breakfast and Llama Keep,** West Side Road, Addison, (207) 483-4490, has three guest rooms and is situated within a 110-acre working llama farm.

Doings Downeast

Auto touring, biking, bird watching, boating, camping, climbing, cross-country skiing, fishing, hiking, horseback riding, skiing, snowshoeing, stargazing, swimming, walking, wildlife viewing—that's the laundry list of Acadia activities provided by the National Park Service. Acadia National Park on Mount Desert (pronounced "dessert") Island and Isle au Haut is the gem of Downeast Maine; its 47,633 acres of mountains, forest, lakes, ponds, and shore provide millions of visitors each year the opportunity to reconnect with the natural world.

In Acadia

A one-week entrance permit for Acadia costs $10 per vehicle or $5 per motorcycle, or purchase an annual pass for $20. The park is open year-round, though some roads are closed in the winter. There are many ways to see and experience the park, with a drive along the twenty-seven-mile Park Loop Road serving as a good introduction. Get oriented first at one of the park's two Visitor Centers, the **Thompson Island Information Center,** Route 3, (207) 288-3411, or the **Hulls Cove Visitor Center,** Route 3, (207) 288-3338. There, you can pick up trail and driving maps and other free literature describing the park's history and facilities, plus the schedule of ranger-led activities. In the winter, visitor operations move to the **Park Headquarters,** Route 233 near Eagle Lake, (207) 288-3338.

Within the Park, you'll find the **Abbe Museum,** just off the Park Loop Road and off Route 3, (207) 288-3519, where you can learn about Maine's Native American cultures from mid-May through mid-October.

FAST FACT

The Wabanaki tribe of Native Americans inhabited what is now Acadia National Park 6,000 years ago. European explorer Samuel Champlain landed on and named Mount Desert Island in 1604—sixteen years before the Pilgrims arrived. The English and French battled over the region for a century and a half, with Britain finally winning out in 1759.

Outside of Acadia

While Acadia dwarfs other attractions in the region, there are a few you may want to visit while you're in the Downeast and Acadia region.

West Quoddy Head Light, located in Quoddy Head State Park, off Route 189, Lubec, (207) 733-0911 or (207) 941-4014, is one of Maine's most recognizable lighthouses with its red and white candy cane stripes. This active light was first established in 1808, and the present, photogenic structure was completed in 1858. The park is open mid-May through mid-October.

Fort Knox, Route 174, Bucksport, (207) 469-6553, was built of Maine granite in the mid-nineteenth century for protection against the British, who had twice invaded the Penobscot River. A third attack never came, but the fort served as a garrison during the Civil War and the Spanish-American War. The fort is open daily from May through November with tours available on weekends.

See the cottage and the grounds where President Franklin Delano Roosevelt vacationed at the 2,800-acre Roosevelt

Campobello International Park, 459 Route 774, (506) 752-2922, located at the southern end of Campobello Island in New Brunswick, Canada, and accessible from Lubec, Maine, via the FDR International Bridge.

Head out to sea aboard New England's only four-masted schooner, ***Margaret Todd,*** 27 Main Street, Bar Harbor, (207) 288-4585, on a morning, afternoon, or sunset cruise.

See baby lobsters at the Lobster Hatchery at the **Mount Desert Oceanarium,** Route 3, Bar Harbor, (207) 288-5005. Learn about the history of telephones at the **New England Museum of Telephony,** 166 Winkumpaugh Road off Route 1A, North Ellsworth, (207) 667-9491, open Wednesdays and Sundays July through September and by appointment. Visit the **Wendell Gilley Museum of Bird Carving,** 4 Herrick Road, Southwest Harbor, (207) 244-7555, to watch carvers at work and see examples of this American art form. Tour **Raye's Mustard Mill,** 83 Washington Street, Eastport, (207) 853-4451, where mustard has been made the same way since 1903. Call ahead for a tour schedule.

FAST FACT

Since 1973, the National Audubon Society's Project Puffin has worked to restore the Gulf of Maine habitats of the bird with such colorful nicknames as "clown of the ocean" and "sea parrot." Want to see them up close?

Norton of Jonesport, Sawyer's Square Road, Jonesport, (207) 497-5933 or (888) 889-3222, takes passengers to see the 3,000-plus population of puffins on Machias Seal Island from Memorial Day weekend through August. **Hardy Boat Cruises,** Route 32, New Harbor, (207) 677-2026 or (800) 278-3346, offers Puffin Watch cruises to Eastern Egg Rock with an Audubon naturalist mid-May through early October.

Dining Highlights

You may not think that your taste buds could ever tire of lobster, but just in case, it's good to know that lobster is prepared ten different ways at **Poor Boy's Gourmet Restaurant,** 300 Main Street, Bar Harbor, (207) 288-4148, where you'll also find affordable early bird deals including an all-you-can-eat pasta menu. "Lobster 10 Ways" is a claim of **Jasper's**, High Street, Ellsworth, (207) 667-5318, too, and there's a motel right there in case you want to stay over and try lobster another way tomorrow. If you want to stick to tradition, **Fish House Grill,** 1 West Street, Bar Harbor, (207) 288-3070, serves classic lobster bakes all day every day, indoors and outdoors overlooking the water.

Save some room for lobster ice cream. Believe it or not, **Ben and Bill's Chocolate Emporium,** 66 Main Street, Bar Harbor, (207) 288-3281, dishes up this cold, creamy blend of vanilla and lobster chunks.

The open-air tavern at **Atlantic Brewing Company,** Knox Road, Bar Harbor, (207) 288-BEER, is a great place to enjoy estate-brewed beers with a meal. Free brewery tours are offered at 2, 3, and 4 P.M. daily, and free tastings take place every half hour beginning at noon. Beer and bocce ball go together at the **Lompoc Cafe and Brewpub,** 36 Rodick Street, Bar Harbor, (207) 288-9392, where there's a bocce court in the beer garden.

Meals feature Maine ingredients at **Sisters Restaurant at Eggemoggin Landing,** Route 15, Little Deer Isle, (207) 348-6115, which serves dinner and a breakfast buffet daily.

If you want to take something tasty home as a souvenir, head to **Nervous Nellie's Jams and Jellies,** Sunshine Road, Deer Isle, (207) 348-6182 or (800) 777-6845, where you can watch the action in the jelly kitchen Monday through Thursday mornings or shop daily from May through Christmas and most days the rest of the year.

Shopping Discoveries

Bar Harbor's village center is popular with shoppers. Boutiques, galleries, and specialty stores are clustered in the area of West, Cottage, Mt. Desert, and Main Streets. Stores stay open late into the evening during the summer months to accommodate the tourist population. Don't miss the **Maine Made Outlet,** 110 Main Street, (207) 288-0129 or (888) 270-0129, where you can shop for items made by more than seventy Maine artisans.

There's a small concentration of outlet stores along Route 3 in Ellsworth, so you may want to leave time to pull over on your way to Acadia National Park.

Horror writer Stephen King calls Bangor home, and **Betts Bookstore,** 584 Hammond Street, Bangor, (207) 947-7052, is the place to find signed limited editions and directions to area landmarks that appear in King's books.

How can you resist a place called **Big Chicken Barn**? The 21,600 square foot antique store, Route 1, Ellsworth, (207) 374-2715, holds an ever-changing selection of books and collectibles.

It's Christmas year-round at the **Christmas Shoppe,** Route 1A, East Holden, (207) 989-4887 or (800) 720-XMAS, a fun place for kids and collectors.

For something truly Maine-made, head to **Rackliffe Pottery,** Route 172, Blue Hill, (207) 374-2297 or (888) 631-3321, where hand-crafted pieces are made from native Maine clay. Or stop into **Blue Heron Gallery & Studio,** Church Street, Deer Isle, (207) 348-6051, which sells the works of faculty at the Haystack Mountain School of Crafts, founded to teach fine craftsmanship in 1950.

Moosehead Lake and Maine's North Woods

IF YOU WANT TO SEE WILD, UNTAMED MAINE, point your compass north and inland and drive, drive, drive. It's a long way from Maine's southern border to the vast, unspoiled region that features Moosehead Lake, the largest lake in the Northeast, and Maine's only mile-high mountain, glorious Mt. Katahdin.

It's further still to "The County," as Maine's northernmost county, Aroostook, is called. Just about 76,000 people live in this county, which is the size of Connecticut and Rhode Island combined. Aroostook is home to more than 2,000 rivers, lakes, and streams. Agriculture and forestry play a dominant role in the economy, and the County is renowned for its annual potato crop.

If you're feeling a bit wild and untamed yourself, you'll find some of the state's best white-water rafting here and challenging kayaking and canoeing on the St. John, the Northeast's longest, free-flowing river. Landlubbers can hike the Knife's Edge trail atop Mt. Katahdin, embark on a moose photo safari or, what the heck—you only live once, try mashed potato wrestling at the annual Maine Potato Blossom Festival held each July in Fort Fairfield.

TRAVEL TIP

Are you a snowmobiling enthusiast? Or do you want to try sledding for the first time? Maine's vast network of more than 12,000 miles of mapped and maintained snowmobile trails makes the state a snowmobiler's heaven. The most popular snowmobiling areas are Baxter State Park, the Jackman/Moose River area, the Moosehead Lake and Rangeley Lakes regions, and Aroostook County. **Sled ME,** *www.sledme.com,* (877) 275-3363, is an organization of outfitters that can help you plan your Maine snowmobiling adventure, or visit *www.sledmaine.com,* for a directory of businesses that cater to snowmobilers.

Lodging Options

In many parts of northern Maine, the critters outnumber the people, so it's not surprising that lodging choices can be a bit more limited here than in other regions of the state. Some accommodations are rather primitive, too, designed primarily for those who have come to fish, hunt, raft, snowmobile, and engage in other outdoor activities that aren't necessarily compatible with frilly bed canopies and antique appointments. That said, while you won't find any massive, luxury hotels, you will find lodgings that offer a charm all their own and provide a cozy nest to tuck yourself into at the end of an active day.

Gateway Inn, Route 157, Medway, (207) 746-3193, is a perfect landing spot for snowmobilers, as it's located adjacent to Maine's network of snowmobiling trails. It also welcomes pets and features an indoor pool, spa, sauna, exercise room, and some rooms with Mt. Katahdin views. **Katahdin Inn,** 740 Central Street, Millinocket, (207) 723-4555 or (877) 902-4555, is convenient to the region's prime outdoor sporting activities and features eighty-two rooms including some with Jacuzzis, an indoor pool, fitness room, free continental breakfast, and a massage therapist on-site.

Moosehead Lake is surrounded by diverse accommodations choices. The **Birches Resort,** One Birches Drive, Rockwood, (207) 534-7305 or (800) 825-9453, is situated within an 11,000-acre wilderness preserve on the lake's shores. It is the home base for Wilderness Expeditions, a rafting and paddling outfitter, and also offers a variety of other adventures including ice fishing, cross-country skiing, snowmobiling, moose cruises, biking, and hiking. Choose from cabins, lodge rooms, cabin tents, and even yurts—updated versions of the primitive, circular shelters that originated in Siberia.

The **Lodge at Moosehead Lake,** Lily Bay Road, Greenville, (207) 695-4400, is an award-winning small inn that cleverly blends pampering and elegance with a rustic theme. Eight unique rooms and suites with names like the Bear Room, the Moose Room, and the Katahdin Suite come complete with Jacuzzis for two, fireplaces, and bedposts hand-carved to reflect the room's theme.

Greenville Inn, Norris Street, Greenville, (207) 695-2206 or (888) 695-6000, is the Victorian mansion built by lumber baron William Shaw in 1895. It now offers inn rooms, cottages, and a complimentary breakfast buffet.

For one-stop shopping for a variety of Moosehead region accommodations, call **Moosehead Lodging & Recreation,** (207) 695-0223, which has a B&B, RiverView Lodge, and a private cottage available.

In Aroostook County, **Rum Rapids Inn Bed and Breakfast,** Route 164, Crouseville, (207) 455-8096, offers sophisticated amenities including a hydrotherapy whirlpool, candlelight dining, and full Scottish breakfasts, plus guests are supplied with cross-country skis, mountain and road bikes, tennis racquets, and fishing gear at no charge. **Caribou Inn & Convention Center,** 19 Main Street, Caribou, (207) 498-3733, has seventy-three rooms and three suites and modern hotel amenities including a heated indoor pool and restaurant. **Northern Lights Motel,** 72 Houlton Road, Presque Isle, (207) 764-4441, provides family-friendly accommodations and special touches such as in-room refrigerators and "Internet by the minute" access. **Oxbow Lodge,** Oxbow Road, Oxbow, (207) 435-6140, was built in the late 1800s and serves as a hunting and snowmobiling outpost where meals are served family-style.

Points North

Baxter State Park, 64 Balsam Drive, Millinocket, (207) 723-5140, is the largest state park in Maine. Its 202,064 acres were gifted to the state by one of its governors, Percival P. Baxter. Within its boundaries, you'll discover legendary Mt. Katahdin—its summit is known as Baxter Peak—just one of forty-six peaks and ridges within the park. There are also 175 miles of trails, ten campgrounds, canoe rentals, and plenty of wildlife to entrance and entertain birdwatchers, photographers, and hikers. The Appalachian Trail also begins (or ends) here within the park, so you may just have a chance to greet hikers who have completed the long trek from Georgia to Maine. Stop at the park headquarters in Millinocket or at the Togue Pond Visitor Center for maps and information on all of the park's recreational possibilities.

The Penobscot River, which flows through Baxter State Park, provides some of New England's finest white-water rafting rapids. **New England Outdoor Center,** 240 Katahdin Avenue, Millinocket, (207) 723-5438 or (800) 766-7238, is one of the largest outfitters, offering day and overnight trips. They also offer hunting, fishing, kayaking, and snowmobiling trips.

Moosehead Lake is forty miles long with 400 miles of shoreline, and it beckons to those who want to canoe or kayak on its waters, fish, search for moose from a pontoon boat, or watch seaplanes take off and land. A wonderful way to get to know the lake is to set out on the 1914 steamship S/S *Katahdin* from **Moosehead Marine Museum,** Route 15, Greenville, (207) 695-2716. Cruises are available Memorial Day weekend through early October; call ahead for a schedule and reservations.

A few sites of historic and cultural interest are worth a visit while you're in Maine's Great North. **Katahdin Iron Works State**

Historic Site, off Route 11, Brownville, (207) 941-4014, is the site of a once thriving iron works that dates to 1843. From Memorial Day through Labor Day, visitors can see the restored stone blast furnace and charcoal kiln. At the **Lumberman's Museum,** Shin Pond Road, Patten, (207) 528-2650, you'll find 4,000 artifacts from Maine's lumbering history displayed in nine buildings, open daily except for Mondays in July and August, Friday through Sunday from mid-May through June and September through mid-October. **Acadian Village,** Route 1, Van Buren, (207) 868-2691, is a collection of original and replica buildings that display artifacts related to the life of the French Acadians who populated the St. John Valley in the mid-eighteenth century.

The University of Maine at Orono boasts the state's first planetarium. The **Maynard F. Jordan Planetarium & Observatory,** 5781 Wingate Hall, Orono, (207) 581-1341, offers a regular schedule of public planetarium shows, and the observatory is open on clear Friday and Saturday evenings. Also at the university, don't miss the **Hudson Museum,** 5746 Maine Center for the Arts, (207) 581-1901, which showcases the arts and culture of Maine's native tribes. You can even learn to speak Penobscot with the help of a computer program. The museum is open free year-round.

Dining Highlights

Food always seems to taste better after a day of fresh air and outdoor activity. If you're staying at a remote resort or sporting camp or participating in an organized rafting or other outing, it's likely that your meals will be provided. If not, take your appetite to one of the region's down-home eateries.

If white-water rafting isn't your cup of tea, you can still dine at the **New England Outdoor Center's River Drivers Restaurant,** Medway Road, Millinocket, (207) 723-5438 or (800) 766-7238, where entrees range from fresh seafood preparations to slow-roasted pork loin.

What will you find at the sign of the "Moosetacean?" **Lost Lobster Seafood Café,** North Main Street, Greenville Junction, (207) 695-3000, is an indoor/outdoor family seafood restaurant with a very interesting logo.

You could literally step right into Moosehead Lake from your table on the deck at **Kelly's Landing,** Routes 6 and 15, Greenville Junction, (207) 695-4438, where hungry vacationers will love the all-you-can-eat breakfast bar on Sundays.

In Aroostook County, the **Blue Moose,** Route 1, Monticello, (207) 538-0991, welcomes snowmobilers—the log cabin restaurant with a cozy wood stove is just 400 feet from snowmobile trails. The **Elm Tree Diner,** Bangor Road, Houlton, (207) 532-3181, has been serving home cooked breakfasts, lunches, and dinners for more than fifty years. At the **Lakeview Restaurant,** 9 Lakeview Drive, St. Agatha, (207) 543-6331, taste Maine potatoes as only a former potato farmer can prepare them.

Your palate may not appreciate just any potatoes once you've tasted the Maine-grown variety. The good news is, you can order organic potatoes grown in Aroostook County from **Wood Prairie Farm** online at *www.woodprairie.com* or by calling (800) 829-9765. They even have a Maine Potato Sampler-of-the-Month Club.

Shopping Discoveries

Need fishing supplies, camping supplies, hiking supplies, or a canoe of your own? **Indian Hill Trading Post & Supermarket,** Routes 6 and 15, Greenville, (207) 695-2104, sells everything you need for your northern Maine adventures.

For a sweet souvenir, visit **Bob's Sugar House,** 146 East Main Street, Dover-Foxcroft, (207) 564-2145, which sells its own Maine maple syrup, maple sugar candy, and even maple popcorn.

Search for old, out-of-print titles at **Mountain & Meadow Books,** 59 Bangor Street, Houlton, (207) 532-9285, which specializes in local history.

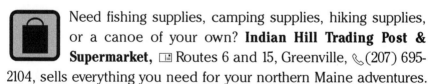

Itineraries

PERSONAL ITINERARY NOTES

A SHORE AND SHOPPING LONG WEE KEND

Day One Start on day one in Kittery, Maine's outlet shopping capital, and spend a half-day searching for bargains. You won't be able to see it all, so plan your outlet strategy ahead of time. In the afternoon, drive along coastal Route 1 to Kennebunkport. The forty-five-minute, narrated tour offered by **Intown Trolley,** Ocean Avenue, (207) 967-3686, is a good way to get acquainted with the town. Have dinner overlooking the water, and if you can, stay overnight in one of Kennebunkport's historic inns.

Day Two In the morning, continue north on Route 1 to Old Orchard Beach, and spend the bulk of the day relaxing beside the ocean, browsing boardwalk stores, and riding the rides at the Pier. Off-season, **Horseback Riding Plus,** (207) 883-6400, offers horseback riding excursions—another memorable way to enjoy the beach. In the evening, continue north to Portland and dine and shop in the Old Port District.

Day Three On your last day, continue north to Freeport. Get there as early as you like—**L.L. Bean,** 95 Main Street, (800) 341-4341, is open twenty-four hours a day. The assortment of other outlets and retail stores in town will keep you busy until it's time to head for home.

FIVE FOLIAGE DRIVES

Day One Start out by looping through Maine ski country and see the mountains ablaze, plus catch views of the fall colors reflecting in Rangeley Lake. Start in Farmington and follow Route 2 West into Wilton, where you will pick up Route 156. Follow Route 156 northwest through Weld, then head north on Route 142. When 142 meets Route 4, take Route 4 northwest into Rangeley. Your next turn will be onto Route 16 East. You'll stay on Route 16 through Kingfield and in North Anson, pick up Route 201A South into Norridgewock. There, you'll rejoin Route 2, which you can follow back to Farmington, completing the 132-mile loop.

Day Two Head west on Route 2 again, this time traveling all the way to Newry, where you will pick up Route 26 north, which crosses just into New Hampshire before meeting up with Route 16, which you will follow back into Maine. In Oquossoc, take Route 4 West to Route 17 and follow 17 South into Mexico. In Mexico, pick up Route 2 West, which will take you back to Farmington once again. Scenic sites along this 138-mile loop include Screw Auger Falls, Grafton Notch State Park, Aziscohos Dam, and Mooselookmeguntic Lake.

Day Three Begin your drive in Skowhegan, which is farther east on Route 2. From Skowhegan, take Route 201 north through Bingham and nearly to Jackman, where you will connect with Route 15. Follow Route 15 south and east through Greenville and then on to Dover-Foxcroft, where you will pick up Route 7 South to Newport. In Newport, take Route 2 West into Palmyra. Then take Route 151 West to Athens. In Athens, pick up Route 150 South, which returns to Skowhegan, completing the 210-mile loop. Along this route, you'll see Moosehead Lake, Moxie Falls, and Mount Kineo dressed up in fall colors.

Day Four Travel to Acadia National Park and drive the 27-mile Park Loop Road to view spectacular mountain and coastal scenery. You can drive to the top of Cadillac Mountain, the highest point north of Rio de Janiero on the Atlantic coast, to watch one of the most spectacular sunsets in all of New England.

Day Five Start out from Ellsworth on Route 1A North. In Ellsworth Falls, pick up Route 179 North into Aurora. In Aurora, take Route 9 East, which winds through Beddington, Wesley, and Alexander. Follow signs in Alexander to Route 191, on which you will travel east to Route 214. Take 214 South into West Pembroke, where you will pick up Route 1 South through Machias and into Cherryfield. In Cherryfield, take Route 182 West through Franklin to Route 1 once again, which you will follow south back into Ellsworth. This 180-mile scenic drive will take you through the heart of Downeast Maine, past lakes, streams, forests, and Cobscook Reversing Falls.

LIGHTHOUSE TOUR OF MAINE

Early A.M. Start at **Camden Hills State Park,** Route 1, Camden, (207) 236-3109 or (207) 236-0849, where you can hike or drive to the summit of Mt. Battie. There's no lighthouse on Mt. Battie, but with a pair of binoculars, you can spot as many as sixteen lighthouses from there on a clear day.

Late A.M. Take Route 1 North to Lincolnville Beach, where you can board the Isleboro Ferry, (207) 734-6935, to **Grindle Point Light** and the **Sailor's Memorial Museum.** The ferry trip is about twenty minutes. You'll want to call ahead for a schedule. This active beacon was first built in 1851, and the present lighthouse dates to 1874.

Early P.M. Nearby in Rockport, **Indian Island Light** is visible from **Rockport Marine Park,** Andre Street, (207) 236-4404. The present light here was built in 1875 and taken out of service in 1934.

Continuing south on Route 1 to Rockland, visit the 1902 **Rockland Breakwater Light,** which is visible from the end of Samoset Road. Tread carefully if you decide to walk out on the breakwater for a closer look.

Late P.M. Also see **Owls Head Light** in nearby Owls Head, which is a short walk from the end of Lighthouse Road. The grounds only are open to the public at this 1825 lighthouse that is still an active navigational aid. To get to the lighthouse, you'll have to walk up a steep ramp and climb dozens of steps, but the views are worth the exertion.

A fitting end to your lighthouse expedition is a stop at the **Shore Village Museum,** 104 Limerock Street, Rockland, (207) 594-0311, which is open June through mid-October. The museum boasts the nation's largest collection of lighthouse artifacts.

PART VI

New Hampshire

New Hampshire

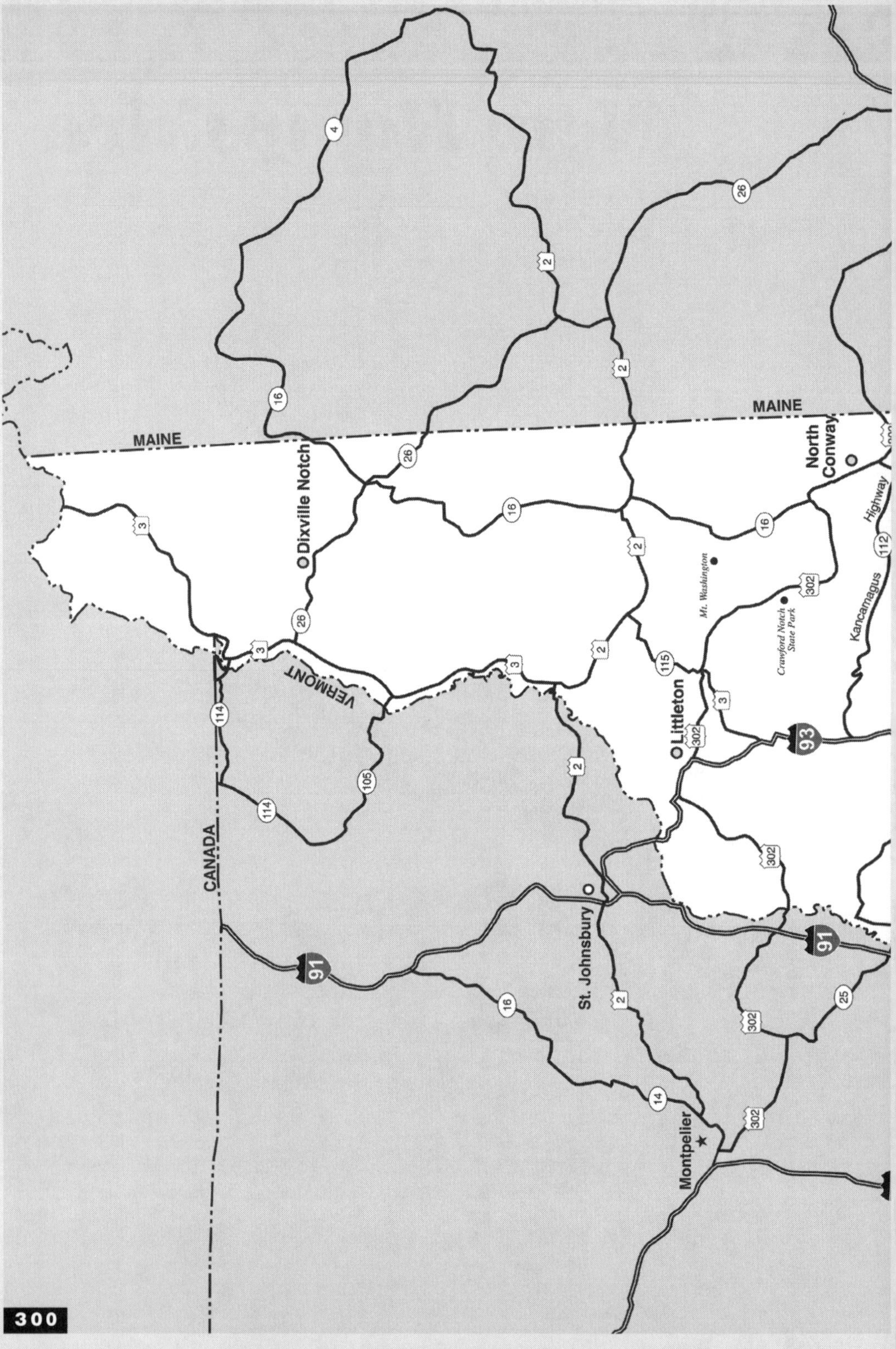

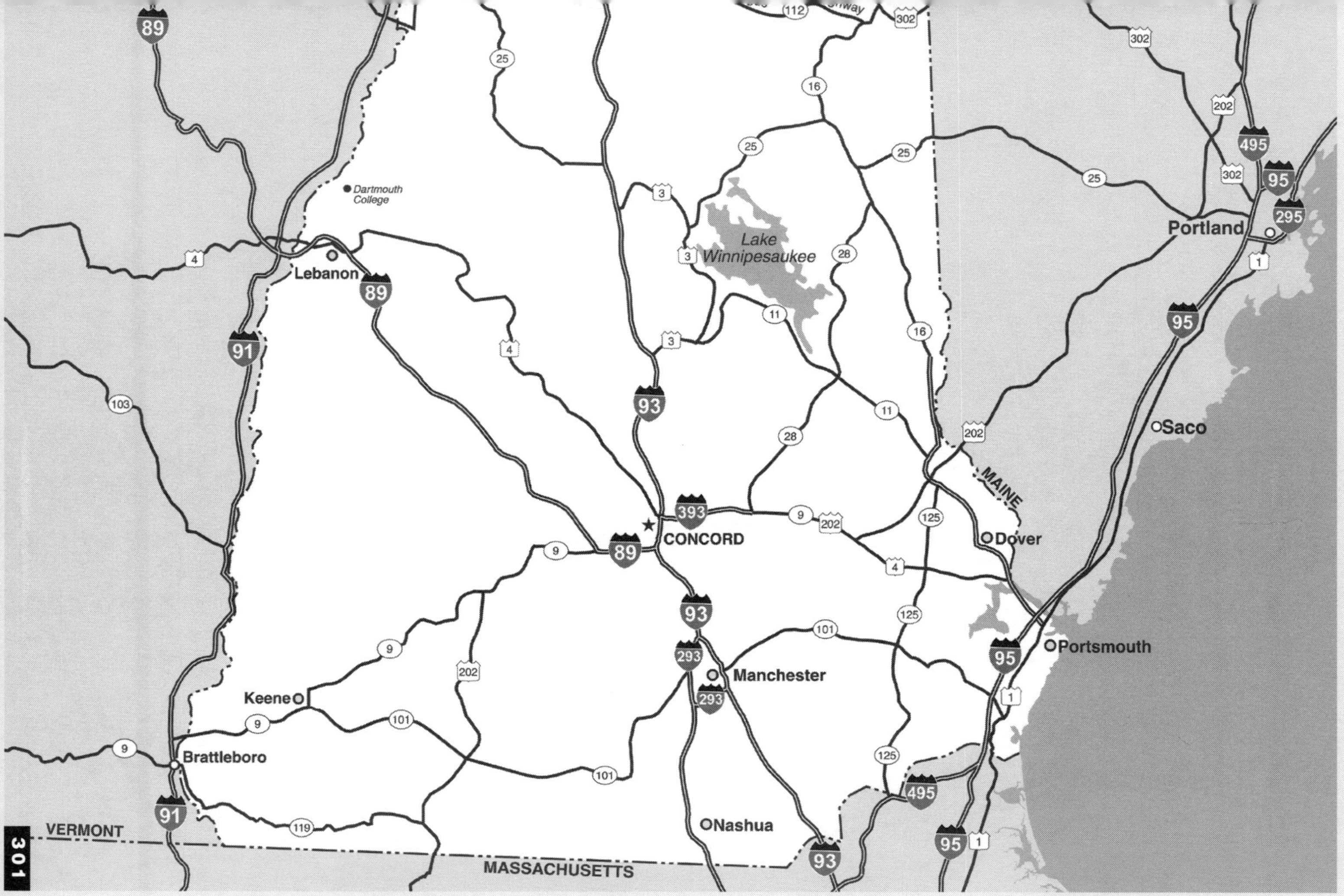
Portland
Saco
Portsmouth
Dover
MAINE
Lake Winnipesaukee
Dartmouth College
Lebanon
CONCORD
Manchester
Nashua
Keene
Brattleboro
VERMONT
MASSACHUSETTS

Portsmouth, New Hampshire

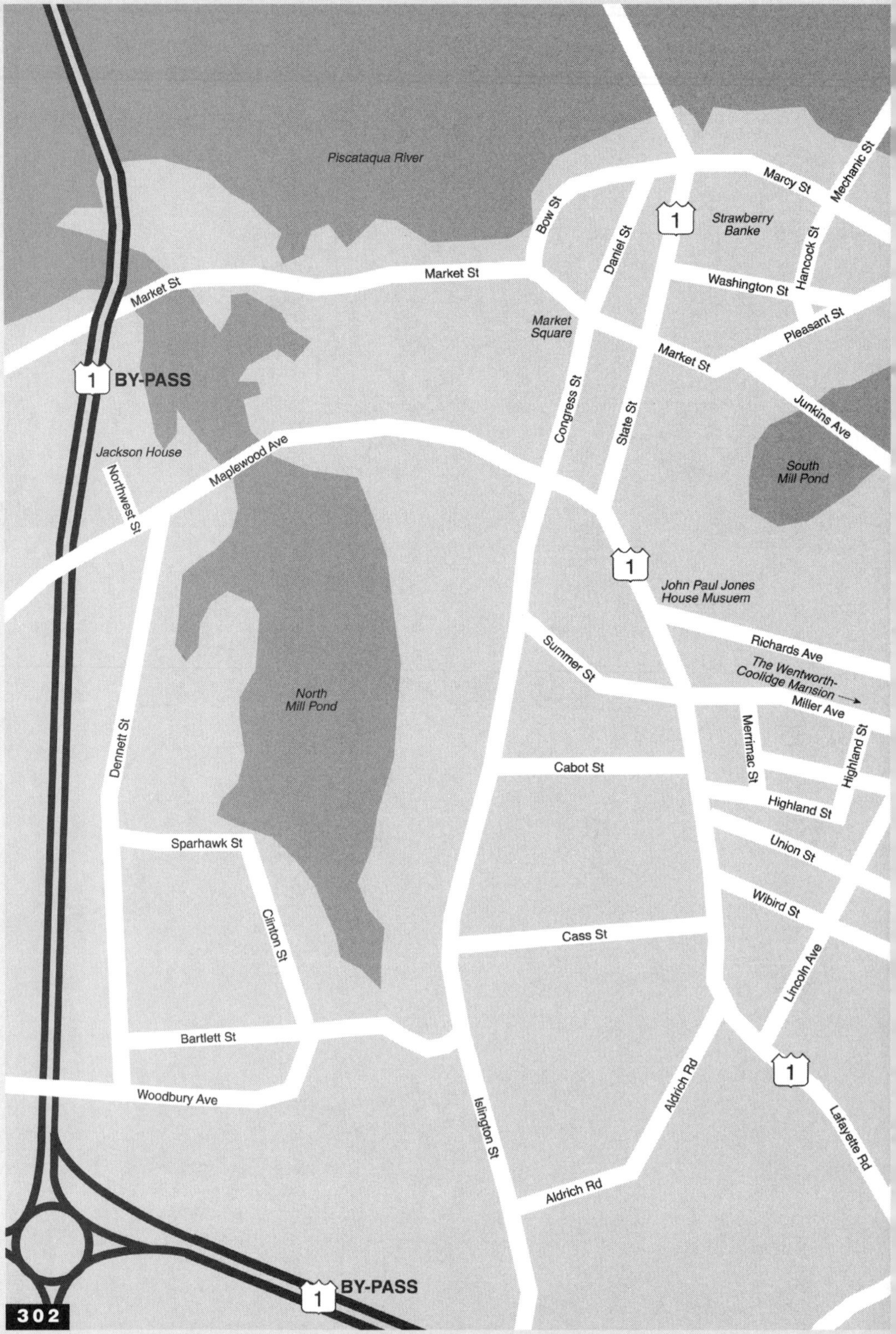

Piscataqua River
Market St
Market St
1 BY-PASS
Jackson House
Northwest St
Maplewood Ave
Bow St
Daniel St
1
Strawberry Banke
Marcy St
Mechanic St
Hancock St
Washington St
Market Square
Pleasant St
Market St
Junkins Ave
Congress St
State St
South Mill Pond
1
John Paul Jones House Musuem
Richards Ave
The Wentworth-Coolidge Mansion
Summer St
Miller Ave
Merrimac St
Highland St
Cabot St
Highland St
Union St
Wibird St
North Mill Pond
Dennett St
Sparhawk St
Clinton St
Cass St
Lincoln Ave
Bartlett St
Woodbury Ave
Aldrich Rd
1
Lafayette Rd
Islington St
Aldrich Rd
1 BY-PASS

An Introduction to the Granite State

WHETHER YOU PICTURE MAJESTIC MOUNTAINS, sparkling lakes, rushing rivers, bustling cities, sleepy villages, or seashore as the backdrop to your New England adventure, you can find the perfect setting within New Hampshire's borders.

The first European settlement in New Hampshire was a fishing colony established in 1623. New Hampshire has 1,300 lakes and ponds and 40,000 miles of rivers and streams—115,000 acres of water in all—that provide opportunities for fishing and recreation. Fittingly, in 1865, New Hampshire was the first New England state to establish a fish and game department and to promote active conservation. New Hampshire also has an ocean coast, and while it is just eighteen miles long, it provides not only fertile saltwater fishing and lobstering grounds, but vacation enticements for those who heed the call of the beach.

Mountains are another prominent feature of New Hampshire's landscape, and the state's peaks hold the promise of skiing in the winter, hiking in the spring and summer, and fabulous fall foliage sightseeing come autumn. Thanks to the dream of one man, Sylvester Marsh, the summit of Mt. Washington is accessible via the world's first mountain-climbing cog railway. Though members of the New Hampshire Legislature scoffed at Marsh and told him he "might as well build a railway to the Moon," this 1869 engineering feat continues to take visitors the 6,288 feet to the mountain's top.

TRAVEL TIP

Outdoor adventurers will want to avoid New Hampshire's infamous three-week "black fly season," which generally occurs in late April in the southern part of the state and may occur as late as mid-June in the far north. An insect repellent containing DEET is your best defense against the painful bite of these pests.

Ten New Hampshire Highlights

Choosing just one New England state to visit is an unenviable task, but if you must, New Hampshire is a solid bet. Not only will you find a smattering of all that is New England here but also you'll discover one-of-a-kind attractions, such as the Mt. Washington Cog Railway, that are unique to this realm. After all—with "Live Free or Die" as a motto, you can almost guarantee that fiercely independent New Hampshire will dish up a few surprises all its own.

America's Stonehenge

105 Haverhill Road, Salem
(603) 893-8300
www.stonehengeusa.com

You don't have to travel to the old England to see a prehistoric archaeological enigma. New England has its own Stonehenge in Salem, New Hampshire. Explore 30 acres of cave-like dwellings, astronomically aligned rock formations, and other mysterious structures left behind on "Mystery Hill" by an unknown people.

Canterbury Shaker Village

288 Shaker Rd, Canterbury
(603) 783-9511 or (800) 982-9511
www.shakers.org

Step back in time to the simple ways espoused by the Shaker religious community formed at Canterbury in 1792. This 694-acre National Historic Landmark has twenty-five original Shaker buildings to explore, plus nature trails, gardens, costumed guides, daily craft demonstrations, a gift shop featuring Shaker reproductions, and an award-winning restaurant, the Creamery, which serves traditional Shaker cuisine.

HOT SPOT

Wine and spirits are common souvenirs of New Hampshire. That's because they're sold at discounted prices and with no sales tax at more than seventy state-operated **Liquor Outlet stores.** For up-to-date information on sales and locations, visit *www.state.nh.us/liquor* or call (603) 271-3755.

Cathedral of the Pines

75 Cathedral Entrance, Rindge

(603) 899-3300

www.cathedralpines.com

This outdoor memorial honors Americans who have died in service to their country. The Altar of the Nation is constructed of rock from every U.S. state and territory. Norman Rockwell designed the bronze tablets you'll see inside the Memorial Bell Tower, which also houses bells from around the world.

Christa McAuliffe Planetarium

3 Institute Drive, Concord

(603) 271-7831

www.starhop.com

Teacher Christa McAuliffe captured the world's imagination when she became the first civilian astronaut. Her untimely death in the 1986 explosion of the space shuttle *Challenger* devastated a nation that had followed her dream. The New Hampshire Technical Institute's planetarium in Concord, named for McAuliffe, features hands-on exhibits, a 40-foot dome telescope, and a changing menu of shows that take visitors on a virtual flight through space.

FAST FACT

In England in the 1760s, Ann Lee became the leader of a religious order that was an offshoot of the Quakers. The name "Shakers" was shorthand for "Shaking Quakers," a label derived from this group's unorthodox worship practices, which featured loud singing, wild dancing, and violent trembling. Lee and her followers believed Jesus would soon return to judge the world and that salvation would come only via a life of celibacy, confession of sin, and hard labor. Persecuted in England, Shaker communities began to arrive in America in 1776—New Hampshire's Canterbury Shaker Village dates to 1792. The Shaker population in America peaked at about 6,000 just before the Civil War. Today, only a handful of practicing Shakers remains at the Sabbathday Lake community in Maine.

Clark's Trading Post

Route 3, Lincoln
(603) 745-8913
www.clarkstradingpost.com

One of the White Mountains' most unusual attractions, Clark's Trading Post is best known for its dancing black bears that perform daily. Clark's has been delighting families for seventy years with its interesting collection of entertainment, which includes a scenic train ride on the White Mt. Central Railroad, water bumper boats, the mysterious Tuttle House, Merlin's Mystical Mansion, and a museum of Americana.

The Isles of Shoals Steamship Co.

315 Market Street, Portsmouth
(603) 431-5500 or (800) 441-4620
www.islesofshoals.com

The Isles of Shoals Steamship Co. is New England's oldest

whale-watch company, and it's based in one of the best whale-spotting departure points in the Northeast—Portsmouth. Daylong whale-watch adventures also include a narrated tour of historic Portsmouth Harbor and a chance to see two lighthouses, five forts, and the Portsmouth Naval Yard. Also check Isles of Shoals' schedule of picnic cruises to Star Island, foliage cruises, lobster clambake dinner cruises, and even excursions to a working buffalo farm.

Saint-Gaudens National Historic Site

Off Route 12A, Cornish
(603) 675-2175
www.sgnhs.org

The former home, studio, and gallery of one of America's foremost sculptors, Irish immigrant Augustus Saint-Gaudens, is now a national historic site. The 150-acre estate that Saint-Gaudens called home from 1885 to 1907 has hiking trails, gardens, a stable with antique carriages, the sculptor's historic eighteenth-century home, and three exhibition galleries.

Scenic Railways

Three railroad sightseeing options provide New Hampshire visitors with a nostalgic, leisurely means of viewing the state's natural beauty. Most famous is the Mt. Washington Cog Railway in Bretton Woods, (800) 922-8825. The coal-fired steam engine trains take passengers up one of the steepest tracks in the world—6,288 feet to the summit of Mt. Washington. Conway Scenic Railroad, (800) 232-5251, offers scenic excursions aboard the vintage Valley Train from Conway to Bartlett or the Notch Train through Crawford Notch, one of the state's most scenic spots. Or, climb aboard the historic Winnipesaukee Railroad, (603) 279-5253, from departure points at Weirs Beach or Meredith for a fabulous tour of the lake's shore.

Tax-free and Outlet Shopping

There is no sales tax on purchases anywhere in New Hampshire. That makes the state's outlet shopping centers an even better bargain for shoppers. Many New Hampshire shops will gladly ship purchases for visitors.

Water Country

Route 1, Portsmouth

(603) 427-1111

www.watercountry.com

Water Country is New England's largest water amusement park, with eighteen different water rides ranging from big thrillers to tamer options appropriate for the tiniest of tots. Water Country also boasts New England's largest wave pool; it's 700,000 gallons! One admission price includes all water rides and attractions.

TRAVEL TIP

New Hampshire has four distinct seasons—five if you count the "mud season," which occurs in late March and early April. Snow in the mountains makes for wonderful skiing vacations beginning in late November and lasting through April. New Hampshire really comes to life in late spring and early summer, and you'll find festivals celebrating the state's floral bounty, including lilac festivals in Rochester and Lisbon and a lupine festival in Sugar Hill. Summer is a great time to explore New Hampshire's seacoast beaches and to take a whale-watch cruise. New Hampshire is at its most breathtaking in autumn, when the White Mountains are ablaze with color. You'll bring home vacation photos of crystal-smooth lakes and covered bridges against a background palette of autumn hues.

Seacoast New Hampshire

YOU'RE THE FIRST PRESIDENT of the United States, and you've just wrapped up the first session of the first Congress–where do you go to get away from it all? Well, in 1789, George Washington chose Portsmouth, the Seacoast region's largest city, as the final destination of his tour through New England. Since then, millions of other vacationers have followed suit, choosing the diminutive shoreline area with 350 years of history for its family attractions, sandy beaches, ocean excursions, old-fashioned clambakes, boutiques and antiques, and regional brews.

Proximity also makes the region a popular choice. Portsmouth is just an hour north of Boston, and a stay in the Seacoast region puts you within a short drive of the outlets and other enticements of southern Maine and the beaches and seafood delights of Massachusetts' North Shore.

The bad news is, you won't be greeted with quite the pomp and ceremony that accompanied George Washington's arrival in Portsmouth. The good news is, you won't have to steal away quietly on your fifth day of vacation in order to have some seaside fun without your military entourage cramping your style.

HOT SPOT

Seabrook Greyhound Park, Route 107 West, Seabrook, (603) 474-3065, hosts live greyhound racing year-round, plus simulcast wagering. Call for a schedule of matinee and evening sessions, and ask about special weekend packages and all-you-can-eat buffet dinners on Thursdays, Fridays, and Saturdays.

Lodging Options

The Seacoast region is quite compact, so wherever you choose to stay, you'll find the area's attractions are just minutes away. The **Sheraton Harborside Hotel Portsmouth,** 250 Market Street, Portsmouth, (603) 431-2300, is one of the larger options with 205 rooms and its own restaurant and nightclub. Another location convenient to the shops and sights of Portsmouth is the **Inn at Strawberry Banke,** 314 Court Street, (603) 436-7242 or (800) 428-3933, an historic early-1800s home turned B&B.

The bustling Hampton Beach area is your best bet for waterfront lodging. **Ashworth by the Sea,** 295 Ocean Boulevard, (603) 926-6762 or (800) 345-6736, has offered lodgings overlooking the Atlantic for more than ninety years. Book a two-room suite with its own ocean-view deck at **Sea Spiral Suites,** 449 Ocean Boulevard, (603) 926-2222 or (800) 303-9933. Couples will find luxury and a quiet haven at **D.W.'s Oceanside Inn,** 365 Ocean Boulevard, (603) 926-3542, with ten individually furnished guest rooms.

The **Hampton Beach Area Chamber of Commerce** will gladly send you a free accommodations guide with dozens of additional choices. Call them at (603) 926-8718, or mail your request to Hampton Beach, P.O. Box 790W, Hampton, NH 03843.

Historic choices are available in the Seacoast region, too. **Inn by the Bandstand,** 4 Front Street, Exeter, (603) 772-6352 or

(877) 239-3837, is a restored 1809 Federal townhouse listed on the National Register of Historic Places. **Three Chimneys Inn,** 17 Newmarket Road, Durham, (603) 868-7800, provides accommodations within a restored 1649 mansion and carriage house and dining beside the 1649 cooking hearth at the ffrost Sawyer Tavern or outdoors on the Conservatory Terrace. **Sise Inn,** 40 Court Street, Portsmouth, (603) 433-1200, is a restored 1881 Queen Anne mansion with thirty-four elegant, Victorian-inspired rooms, some with fireplaces and whirlpool tubs, and a free light buffet breakfast served each morning. **Rock Ledge Manor,** 1413 Ocean Boulevard, Rye, (603) 431-1413, is a classic gingerbread Victorian that was once part of a resort colony and is now a B&B with sea views from all guest rooms.

FAST FACT

When the $1 million **Rockingham Park** thoroughbred horse track opened in Salem in 1906, 10,000 fans came by train from Boston, Rhode Island, and New York City. Then, the track closed down for twenty-five years. You see, gambling on horseracing was illegal in New Hampshire.

Luckily, there's no danger that betting on horses will be declared illegal in the Live-Free-or-Die state these days, and this historic racetrack is a wonderful place to spend a New England afternoon wagering on the ponies. It's located just a half-hour north of Boston at exit 1 off I-93. Rockingham Park is open June through September. Call (603) 898-2311 for a complete schedule of racing action.

What to See by the Sea

Get a glimpse of New Hampshire's origins at the **Strawberry Banke Museum,** Marcy Street, Portsmouth, (603) 433-1100, a 10-acre, waterfront living history complex on the site of one of the city's oldest neighborhoods. It is open daily from May through October. Winter walking tours are also available on a limited basis from November through April. If you're a history and architecture buff, you may also want to visit **Jackson House,** 76 Northwest Street, Portsmouth, (603) 436-3205, New Hampshire's oldest house, built in 1664. Tours are offered on weekends June through mid-October. The **Wentworth-Coolidge Mansion,** Little Harbor Road, Portsmouth, (603) 436-6607, is also an interesting structure, and it was home from 1741 to 1767 to New Hampshire's first royal governor. Learn about the Father of the American Navy at the **John Paul Jones House Museum,** 43 Middle Street, Portsmouth, (603) 436-8420, where the Revolutionary War hero stayed on his two visits to the city. Operated by the Portsmouth Historical Society, the 1758 boarding house is open to visitors from June through mid-October. If the house looks uncannily familiar, that's because it has appeared in Sears house paint commercials!

The Seacoast region dishes up a full menu of family fun, too. Let the kids brave the water slides while you float along lazily on the Adventure River tube ride at New England's largest water amusement park, **Water Country,** Route 1, Portsmouth, (603) 427-1111. At **Albacore Park,** 600 Market Street, Portsmouth, (603) 436-3680, tour the world's fastest submarine year-round. Walk the nature trails at the 350-acre **Odiorne Point State Park,** Route 1A, Rye, (603) 436-8043, which is also home to the Seacoast Science Center, with natural history exhibits including a tide-pool touch tank. And don't miss the chance to head out to sea with northern New England's oldest whale-watch company, **Isles of Shoals Steamship Co.,** 315 Market Street, Portsmouth, (603) 431-5500 or (800) 441-4620. Spend the evening playing games, listening to live music, and eating ice cream on the boardwalk at Hampton Beach.

The **Hampton Beach Casino Ballroom,** 169 Ocean Boulevard, Hampton Beach, (603) 929-4100, brings top musical acts and entertainers to the seashore each summer. Call ahead to see who'll be in town while you're visiting.

HOT SPOT

Fuller Gardens, 10 Willow Avenue, North Hampton, (603) 964-5414, is a Colonial Revival, seaside estate garden planted in the early 1920s at the former summer home of Massachusetts Governor Alvan T. Fuller. Designed by landscape architect Arthur Shurtleff, it features 1,500 rose bushes of all types, brilliantly colored annuals, a Japanese garden, perennial borders, a hosta display garden, and a conservatory filled with tropical and desert plants. The gardens are open for a small charge daily from early May through mid-October.

Dining Highlights

The Seacoast region is known for two things–seafood and beer.

Don't miss the affordable Lobster Clambake dinners piled high on paper plates at the casual and fun **Little Jack's Seafood Restaurant & Lobster Pool,** 539 Ocean Boulevard, Hampton Beach, (603) 926-8053. Go for the Triple Lobster Dinner if you're really hungry, or save room for some of the other sea specialties served here including clam fritters, scallop rolls, fisherman's chowder, seafood stew, crab legs, and fresh fried salmon. Prefer your seafood au naturel? The **Ketch 22 Raw Bar at the Sea Ketch Restaurant & Lounge,** 127 Ocean Boulevard, Hampton Beach, (603) 926-0324, features entertainment nightly.

For upscale seafood dining, the **Oar House,** 55 Ceres Street, Portsmouth, (603) 436-4025, is located in the city's historic Merchant's Row building overlooking the old harbor. You can also choose to dine on the outdoor deck opposite the restaurant. **Lindbergh's Crossing,** 29 Ceres Street, Portsmouth, (603) 431-0887, is a Bistro and Wine Bar in a 200-year-old building featuring exposed brick and beams. Menu selections feature creative seafood preparations.

Portsmouth is home to the East Coast operations of **Redhook Ale Brewery,** 35 Corporate Drive, (603) 430-8600. Explore the beer-making process on a guided tour—they're offered daily and end with a sampling session—then, belly up to the bar in the Cataqua Public House for tasty eats and more crafted-in-New Hampshire beers. **Portsmouth Brewery,** 56 Market Street, Portsmouth, (603) 431-1115, is the region's original brewpub. In addition to beers brewed on the premises, you'll also find selections brewed at the brewpub's sister company, Smuttynose Brewing Company, plus pub-style food and a schedule of beer dinners.

Isles of Shoals Steamship Co., 315 Market Street, Portsmouth, (603) 431-5500 or (800) 441-4620, has both of the region's specialties covered—book passage on either their Downeast Lobster Clambake Cruise or their Smuttynose Brews Cruise. Be sure to call ahead for a schedule and reservations.

For another truly unique experience, eat dinner on a tugboat! The ***John Wanamaker*** is docked at One Harbour Place, Portsmouth, (603) 433-3111, and gourmet dinners are served onboard.

Want ice cream for breakfast? The **University of New Hampshire Dairy Bar** housed in the old Durham train station, Durham, (603) 862-1006, is open year-round, except during school breaks, as a training facility for restaurant management students, and yes, ice cream is served during all hours of operation.

Shopping Discoveries

The Kittery, Maine, outlets are just minutes away, but don't overlook some shopping finds tucked away right in Seacoast New Hampshire, including the **North Hampton Factory Outlet Center,** Route 1, North Hampton, (603) 964-9050.

Market Square in the center of Portsmouth is a popular shopping district with dozens of galleries, gift shops, cafés, and boutiques.

Select from fine jewelry, pottery, glass, and other handworks by more than 250 local artisans at the **League of New Hampshire Craftsmen,** 61 Water Street, Exeter, (603) 778-8282. For traditional New England salt-glaze pottery, visit **Salmon Falls Pottery,** Oak Street Engine House, Dover, (603) 749-1467 or (800) 621-2030. Watch candles being made at the **Candle Mill,** 2454 Lafayette Road, Portsmouth, (603) 430-0277.

The stretch of Route 4 between Portsmouth and Concord is called "Antique Alley," and you'll find more than forty antiques shops to poke around in when you drive this 30-mile route.

Northern New England's only rose grower welcomes visitors. **Elliot & Williams,** 32 Dover Point Road, Dover, (800) NE-GROWN, offers greenhouse tours on weekends, pick-your-own apples beginning in late August at Thornwood Farms, and the Rose Garden Florist Shop, open Monday through Saturday.

The Lakes Region

HOW MANY LAKES AND PONDS DOES IT TAKE to make a Lakes Region? In New Hampshire, the answer is 273. If you love lakes and the quiet, calming influence a day on or beside the water can have, you may actually find yourself emitting a squeal of delight when you catch your first glimpses of these sparkling blue gems as you drive the region's rolling, winding roads.

The crown jewel is Lake Winnipesaukee, the state's largest lake. How large is it? It's 182 miles around, covers 72 square miles, and contains 238 confirmed islands—some estimates put the number over 300. The lake's unusual shape and jagged coastline provide for sheltered coves, bays, and inlets that create a sort of optical illusion, making Winnipesaukee appear much less enormous from many perspectives. Situated around the lake you'll find storybook New England towns, private residential areas, resorts, and even a carnival-esque boardwalk area at Weirs Beach.

And while your natural tendency may be to gravitate toward the big blue diamond that is Winnipesaukee, don't overlook some of the region's smaller, less crowded and hurried lakes, including Squam Lake, Winnisquam Lake, and Newfound Lake.

HOT SPOT

The Lakes Region is home to New Hampshire's oldest summer theater, the **Barnstormers,** Main Street, Tamworth Village, (603) 323-8500, a resident, equity theater company that produces a full schedule of musicals and dramas each season. Founded in 1931, the 282-seat theater was formerly a general store.

Lodging Options

From lakefront cottages, family-oriented motels, and B&Bs to sprawling resorts, you'll have your choice of intimate accommodations or grand lodgings when you visit the Lakes Region.

Christmas Island, 630 Weirs Boulevard, Laconia, (603) 366-4378 or (800) 832-0631, offers a variety of Winnipesaukee lakefront accommodations including motel rooms, efficiency apartments, and housekeeping cottages. Whichever you choose, your family will have access to two beaches, a boat dock, and an indoor pool. The **Anchorage on Lake Winnisquam,** 725 Laconia Road, Tilton, (603) 524-3248, has thirty cottages with screened front porches and 30 private acres for peaceful recreation.

If a B&B appeals to you, here are a few you might consider. The **Glynn House Inn,** 59 Highland Street, Ashland, (603) 968-3775 or (800) 637-9599, is a life-size Victorian dollhouse with nine unique rooms including one in the cupola, many with working fireplaces and relaxing whirlpool tubs. **Ferry Point House Bed & Breakfast on Lake Winnisquam,** 100 Lower Bay Road, Sanbornton, (603) 524-0087, was built by the Pillsbury family in the early 1800s as a lakeside summer retreat. **Manor on Golden Pond,** Route 3, Holderness, (603) 968-3348 or (800) 545-2141, was built in the early 1900s by a wealthy English land developer, and now you can have your own luxurious room with a fireplace, Jacuzzi, or both at this captivating estate.

HOT SPOT

Each year, about 400,000 motor sports fans descend on the **New Hampshire International Speedway,** Route 106, Loudon, (603) 783-4931. New England's largest sports facility hosts not only NASCAR Winston Cup races but also a variety of professional and amateur motor sports competitions, bicycle racing, driving and racing schools, and soap box derby trials from late spring through early fall. Call for a schedule of racing events or to order reserved seats. General admission tickets may also be purchased online at *www.nhis.com*. Free car and RV parking is available to ticket holders.

Looking for a larger hotel or resort? The **Inns at Mill Falls,** 312 Daniel Webster Highway, Meredith, (603) 279-7006 or (800) 622-6455, is a complex that actually includes three country inns, a covered bridge, a waterfall, and a marketplace with fifteen adorable shops, restaurants, and galleries—all overlooking Lake Winnipesaukee. The selection of getaway packages here is unparalleled, so be sure to ask about deals that include meals, skiing, or sightseeing excursions. The **Margate on Winnipesaukee,** 76 Lake Street, Laconia, (603) 524-5210, is a full-service luxury hotel that boasts its own private white sand beach, indoor and outdoor pools, tennis courts, a health club and tanning salon, a bar, and a restaurant. **Wolfeboro Inn,** 90 North Main Street, Wolfeboro, (603) 569-3016, was built in 1812 as a private residence and now has expanded to feature forty-four guest rooms. Overnight guests are treated to a cruise aboard the inn's own *Winnipesaukee Belle,* May through October. **Shalimar Resort,** 660 Laconia Road/Route 3, Winnisquam, (603) 524-1984 or (800) 742-5462, offers guests an indoor pool and a private beach, plus free use of paddleboats, rowboats, and canoes.

Renting a vacation home for a week or more is also a popular option in the Lakes Region. **Preferred Vacation Rentals,** 32

Whittier Highway, Center Harbor, (603) 253-7811, provides an extensive online directory of available rental properties at *www.preferredrentals.com,* or call for a free brochure.

Call the **Lakes Region Association,** (603) 744-8664 or (800) 605-2537, for additional lodgings assistance.

TRAVEL TIP

Seacoast Harley-Davidson, 17 Lafayette Road, North Hampton, (603) 964-9959, rents motorcycles to licensed bikers April through October. You must be at least twenty-five years old, carry a valid motorcycle license, have one year of motorcycle operating experience, wear a helmet, and be able to charge a $1,000 security deposit on a credit card. You will also find an incredible selection of Harley-Davidson fashions, accessories, and gifts for sale.

Places to Explore On- and Offshore

By far the most enthralling tour you can take while in the Lakes Region is of the 5,200-acre **Castle Springs Estate,** Route 171, Moultonborough, (800) 729-2468, home to not only Castle in the Clouds—the architecturally extravagant and eccentric home of industrialist Thomas Plant, but also Castle Springs Premium Natural Spring Water and the Castle Springs microbrewery, where Lucknow ales and lagers are crafted and bottled using natural mountain spring water. After paying your admission at the entrance gate, you'll be in for scenic treats including views of Lake Winnipesaukee as you follow the winding road up the mountain. Take the time to hike the 200 yards from the first parking area to Falls of Song, a 50-foot natural waterfall. Guided tours of the castle, brewery, and spring water bottling operation are available, and you can hike or even rent a horse from the estate stables to explore the magnificent property further.

TRAVEL TIP

Each year in mid-June, an estimated 350,000 motorcycle enthusiasts converge on the Lakes Region for **Laconia Motorcycle Rally & Race Week,** one of the largest rallies of its kind in America and the oldest continuously held event of the sort. While the races are held at the New Hampshire International Speedway, Route 106, Loudon, (603) 783-4931, Weirs Beach is also a central hub of activities during the nine-day event. For bikers, this is an annual opportunity to see custom bikes and the latest motorcycle accessories and to mingle with fellow members of the leather set. Nonbikers in the know usually avoid the overrun area entirely during this annual powwow.

One of the best ways to enjoy Lake Winnipesaukee is to get out on it. So rent a canoe, kayak, or boat, or sit back and relax aboard the 230-foot M/S ***Mount Washington,*** (603) 366-5531 or (888) 843-6686, which departs for scenic lake cruises daily from late May through mid-October from docks in Weirs Beach, Wolfeboro, Center Harbor, Meredith, and Alton Bay. Ask about dinner dance and Sunday brunch cruises, too.

Weirs Beach on Lake Winnipesaukee is a summertime family favorite, and the kids will hardly know in which direction to pull you first. At **Surf Coaster,** Route 11B, (603) 366-4991, you pay one admission price for daylong access to all of the wet and wild slides and rides. Clamber aboard the **Winnipesaukee Scenic Railroad,** (603) 279-5253, which departs hourly from Weirs Beach Station for scenic shoreline rides. The train operates weekends from late May through late June and during fall foliage season, and daily from late June through Labor Day. Along the wooden boardwalk, you'll find arcades, bumper cars, mechanical fortunetellers, shops, restaurants, miniature golf, bowling, and bingo. You can always simply lie on the beach, or, if you're feeling more adventurous, rent a boat or jet-ski. For an afternoon treat, head to **Franken Sundae,** Route 3, Meredith, (603) 279-5531, where you can select the toppings to build your own ice cream monstrosity. At night, a blast from the past awaits at the **Weirs Drive-In Theater,** Route 3, (603) 366-4723, New Hampshire's oldest drive-in movie theater with four screens and room for 800 cars.

At the **Wright Museum,** 77 Center Street, Wolfeboro, (603) 569-1212, exhibits and special events transport you to the era of World War II on the American home front. The museum is open daily from May through October.

HOT SPOT

Remember *On Golden Pond,* the 1981 movie for which Henry Fonda and Katharine Hepburn won Oscars? That was no pond—it was New Hampshire's Squam Lake. Two tour companies offer boat tours of the scenic lake and behind-the-scenes narration about the making of the film. The two-hour **Original Golden Pond Tour,** (603) 279-4405, departs daily from Memorial Day through foliage season from Squam Boat Dock, Route 3 at the bridge in Holderness. **Squam Lake Tours,** (603) 968-7577, takes passengers on a two-hour pontoon tour of movie filming locations with three daily excursions from May through October. Squam Lake Tours is on Route 3 a half-mile south of Holderness.

Dining Highlights

It's Thanksgiving every day at **Hart's Turkey Farm,** Routes 3 and 104, Meredith, (603) 279-6212, where, on a busy day, they serve 1 ton of turkey, 40 gallons of gravy, 1,000 pounds of potatoes, 4,000 rolls, and 100 pies.

All-you-can-eat lobster? Yup—that's the deal at the all-you-can-eat **Surf 'n Turf Buffet at Cherrystone Lobster House,** 40 Weirs

Road, Gilford, (603) 293-7390. What's the catch? Your dining time is capped at two hours.

Dine inside a rustic, homey, nineteenth-century farmhouse and barn at the **Woodshed,** Lees Mill Road, Moultonborough, (603) 476-2311. **Stafford's in the Field,** 88 Philbrick Neighborhood Road, Chocorua, (603) 323-7766 or (800) 833-9509, is an inn set against the backdrop of an old apple orchard that also offers historic New England ambience in its main dining room—a tin ceiling, fireplace, and five-course prix fixe dinners. Reservations are required.

HOT SPOT

Kirkwood Gardens at the Science Center of New Hampshire, Routes 3 and 113, Holderness, (603) 968-7194, is a 3-acre, low-maintenance plant kingdom featuring a fern garden, a butterfly garden, and a bird garden comprised of native New England shrubs and flowers. Admission to the gardens is included with Science Center admission from May through October.

The **Hilltop Restaurant at Steele Hill Resorts,** 516 Steele Hill Road, Sanbornton, (603) 524-0500, has one of the region's most extensive and affordable Sunday brunches. a casual dinner menu, and best of all, the incredible mountain and lake views are included, free. **Walter's Basin,** Route 3, Holderness, (603) 968-4413, is another great choice for lunch, dinner, or Sunday brunch with a view—Squam Lake is so close you can almost dip your toes in.

Stone Coast Brewing Co., 546 Main Street, Laconia, (603) 528-4188, is the Lakes Region's only brewpub, and it's the perfect spot to wash down a lobster salad roll with a brewed-in-New Hampshire beer.

Italian food and music go perfectly together, and at **Giuseppe's Show Time Pizzeria,** Routes 3 and 25, Meredith, (603) 279-3313, there's live entertainment on the menu every night. "Hot Food, Hot Bands, and Cool Decks" is what the **Bay View Pavilion,**

Route 11, Alton Bay, (603) 875-1255, advertises. This Lake Winnipesaukee waterfront dining and dancing spot has been an institution for decades, from the days of the big bands to today's country, bluegrass, blues, and groove-reggae performers. Drive up in your car or boat, dine, dance the night away, and cool off on the outdoor wraparound deck.

FAST FACT

What's that haunting cry you hear in the night? It's the call of the common loon, a water bird common to the lakes of New Hampshire. Loons are fascinating creatures that have legions of fans and much lore associated with them. The Chippewas called the loon "mang," meaning "the most handsome of birds." They believed the loon's cry was an omen of death. Other Native tribes believed loons held magical powers. New Hampshire's Loon Preservation Committee operates the **Loon Center,** Lee's Mills Road, Moultonborough, (603) 476-5666, which is open free daily July through mid-October. Here you can learn more about these birds, known for staying underwater for minutes at a time, and walk two nature trails.

Shopping Discoveries

If you appreciate handcrafted things, you'll be tickled pink by the selection of shops in the Lakes Region. Whether you're a beginning quilter or an expert, you'll lose yourself inside America's largest quilt shop, **Keepsake Quilting,** Route 25B, Center Harbor, (603) 253-4026. If you collect Annalee dolls, you'll definitely want to pop into the **Annalee Doll Museum,** Hemlock Drive, Meredith, (603) 279-6542 or (800) 433-6557, to see where these whimsical creations come to life, and shop for hard-to-find items on your wish list. At **Hampshire Pewter,** 43 Mill Street Wolfeboro, (603) 569-4944 or (800) 639-7704, free tours are offered in the summer and fall, giving you the opportunity to watch craftsmen transform pewter into beautiful objects. Watch crystal cutters at work on a free tour of **Pepi Herrmann Crystal** and the **Pepi Herrmann Glass Museum,** 3 Waterford Place, Gilford, (603) 528-1020. At **Country Braid House,** 462 Main Street, Tilton, (603) 286-4511, you can purchase traditional New England braided wool rugs made on the premises, or buy a kit and teach yourself this old-world craft.

Savvy shoppers won't want to miss the **Lakes Region Factory Stores,** 120 Laconia Road, Tilton, (603) 286-7880 or (888) SHOP-333, where outlets include J. Crew, Eddie Bauer, Mikasa, Reebok, and Black & Decker.

For a yesteryear shopping experience, visit the **Old Burlwood Country Store,** Route 3, Meredith, (603) 279-3021, for penny candy, old-fashioned root beer, New Hampshire gourmet foods, weathervanes, lawn furniture, and other finds. Or stop into the **Old Country Store and Museum,** Moultonborough Corner, Moultonborough, (603) 476-5750, which has been peddling wares since 1781.

HOT SPOT

Lakes Region Greyhound Park, Route 106, Belmont, (603) 267-7778, offers live greyhound racing from June to September and simulcast wagering for forty dog, harness, and thoroughbred tracks year round. For free programs, racing forms, food, and beverages, sign up for the free Players Advantage Club and accumulate credits based on your wagering.

The White Mountains and the Great North Woods

THERE ARE A FEW PLACES ON EARTH that seem to have been tailor-made for vacationers. The White Mountains of New Hampshire certainly make that list. This hospitable region opens its arms to visitors, providing just the right mix of grand, romantic inns and affordable motels; out-of-the-ordinary family attractions and natural wonders; novelty shopping and serious outlet bargains. With thousands of acres of public park land including the 780,000-acre White Mountain National Forest, twenty-six covered bridges, more than 100 waterfalls, thousands of miles of walking and hiking trails, northern New England's only National Scenic Byways—the Kancamagus Highway and the White Mountains Trail, the Northeast's tallest mountain peak, ten downhill ski areas, and a posse of performing bears at Clark's Trading Post, you may just be able to tick off everything on your New England checklist, all in one spot.

The White Mountains didn't always seem so inviting to visitors, though. The rugged terrain served as a deterrent to travelers until about 200 years ago, when tourists first began to discover the region's scenic riches. Businesses catering to the needs of travelers followed quickly on their heels, and today, vacationers will find that everything they need is at hand. However, scenic vistas and back-country treasures have been left mostly undisturbed.

If the White Mountains aren't quite remote enough for you, continue north to New Hampshire's largely undeveloped, pristine Great North Woods, a favorite among hunters, snowmobilers, fishing enthusiasts, and those who truly are looking to get away from it all.

HOT SPOT

It is the "Live Free or Die" state, after all. **Snowvillage Inn,** Stuart Road, Snowville, (603) 447-2818 or (800) 447-4345, offers clothing optional cross-country ski tours on winter full-moon weekends. Call for dates and package pricing.

Lodging Options

Lodgings in the White Mountains quite literally come in every size, shape, and variety. Availability is the only potential problem during the peak fall foliage season and busy summer weekends, when you should definitely make reservations well in advance. In the Great North Woods, lodgings are sparser, and hunting lodges and cabins are predominant.

Relive the days of the Great North Woods and White Mountains grand hotels at one of the two turn-of-the-century landmarks that remain. The **Balsams,** Route 26, Dixville Notch, (603) 255-3400 or (800) 255-0600, is a four-season paradise that is a destination all by itself. The 15,000-acre resort dates to 1866 and has skiing, ice skating, golf, tennis, and a private lake within its confines. All meals are included with your stay. The **Mount Washington Hotel & Resort,** Route 302, Bretton Woods, (603) 278-1000 or (800) 258-0330, still treats guests to the same lavish hospitality afforded visitors who arrived in 1902. Winston Churchill, Thomas Edison, Babe Ruth, and three U.S. presidents have stayed here. You may never want to check out once you discover the resort's indoor and outdoor pools, health spa, cozy Cave Lounge, golf course, clay tennis courts, horseback riding trails, downhill and cross-country ski trails, daily music performances, and supervised children's programs.

HOT SPOT

The **"Old Man of the Mountain"** is one of state's most intriguing natural attractions. The rock formation is depicted on the U.S. Mint's New Hampshire state quarter. Viewed from the right angle, the 40-foot, five-layer, Conway red granite formation looks distinctly like the profile of a weathered old man. It is believed that the carving was created when the ice that covered the Franconia Mountains during the last Ice Age receded some 2,000 to 10,000 years ago. If you'd like to see this natural wonder for yourself, you'll find well-marked viewing spots with parking areas in Franconia Notch State Park, ✆(603) 823-5563.

The **Wentworth,** ✉ Route 16A, Jackson Village, ✆(603) 383-9700 or ✆(800) 637-0013, is a primo country inn with elegant appointments, rooms with fireplaces and/or whirlpools, cross-country ski trails, and an eighteen-hole golf course. No matter what the season, you'll be close to everything or never have to leave at all when you choose to stay at **Golden Eagle Lodge,** ✉ Route 49, Waterville Valley, ✆(603) 236-4600 or ✆(800) 910-4499, which has a soothing indoor pool and Jacuzzi to chase away the winter chills and a complimentary shuttle bus that will whisk you around the valley.

The **Woodstock Inn,** ✉ Route 3, North Woodstock, ✆(603) 745-3951 or ✆(800) 321-3985, isn't just a 100-year-old, twenty-one-room B&B, it's a microbrewery, and you can become an apprentice brewer on select Brewer's Weekends. Arrive single and depart hitched at **Notchland Inn,** ✉ Route 302, Harts Location, ✆(603) 374-6131, where innkeeper Ed Butler is a justice of the peace. Had to leave Fido at home? At **Bungay Jar,** ✉ Easton Valley Road, Franconia, ✆(603) 823-7775 or ✆(800) 421-0701, a B&B housed in an eighteenth-century barn, innkeepers Gordon and Joanne Haym will let you take *their* dogs out for a walk. Ask for the Stargazer Suite, which comes furnished with a telescope.

Sportsmen will feel at home at **Tall Timber Lodge,** Back Lake, Pittsburg, (603) 538-6651 or (800) 835-6343, which offers rustic log cabins and luxury cottages with Jacuzzis and access to fishing, snowmobiling, and other outdoor pursuits in New Hampshire's Great North Woods.

For an array of accommodations options all in one place, call **Luxury Mountain Getaways,** Route 16, Jackson, (603) 383-9101 or (800) 472-5207, which operates a string of resort complexes featuring everything from townhouses and penthouses to four-bedroom homes to inn rooms at the Victorian Nestlenook Farm Inn. The **Mill at Loon Mountain,** Route 112, Lincoln, (603) 745-6261, is another resort village with three hotels, plus restaurants and shops, all on the site of an old lumber mill.

For more lodging ideas, be sure to call the **White Mountains Attractions Association,** (603) 745-8720 or (800) 346-3687, to request a free vacation planning kit. You might also want to visit the Web sites of the **White Mountains Bed & Breakfast Association,** *www.wmbandbs.com,* and **Country Inns in the White Mountains,** *www.white-mountains-inns.com.*

HOT SPOT

New Hampshire is home to New England's only commercial caves, and they're cool places to visit during the hot summer months. Take an hour-long, self-guided tour of **Lost River Gorge,** Route 112 Kinsman Notch, North Woodstock, (603) 745-8031, see caverns, steep-walled gorges, and plummeting waterfalls left behind by the last ice age. Or, head to **Polar Caves Park,** 705 Old Route 25, Plymouth, (603) 536-1888 or (800) 273-1886, for an intriguing look at caves and passageways formed about 50,000 years ago when the third continental glacier began to recede.

Mountain Highpoints

You really should get to the top of Mt. Washington, the Northeast's tallest peak, while you're in the neighborhood. The good news is that even though folks have been climbing the mountain since explorer Darby Field first did it in 1642, you don't have to. The 7.6-mile **Mt. Washington Auto Road,** Route 16, Gorham, (603) 466-3988, was opened to travelers in 1861. Once the snow is cleared away sometime in May, it is open daily to travelers through late October. The private car toll is $16 for the vehicle and driver and includes an audio tour on cassette. There is a charge of $6 for each additional adult, $4 for each child ages 5 through 12. You can also opt for a guided tour aboard an Auto Road van. Prices are $22 for adults, $20 for seniors, and $10 for children ages 5 to 12.

Another route up the mountain is aboard the world's first mountain-climbing cog railway. The **Mt. Washington Cog Railway,** Route 302, Bretton Woods, (603) 278-5404 or (800) 922-8825, makes the steep, 3-mile climb up the mountain in an hour and a half, May through October. It's a good idea to call ahead for schedule information and to purchase your ticket in advance, particularly during leaf-peeping season.

HOT SPOT

At the summit of Mt. Washington sits the **Mount Washington Observatory,** (603) 356-2137, where you can visit the Weather Discovery Center, which is open daily, in season. Mt. Washington is located in the path of three major storm tracks, and its reputation for extremely cold temperatures, high winds, and icing conditions has earned it the nickname, "Home of the World's Worst Weather."

The hazard of quickly changing and severe weather can endanger climbers, who should be sure to heed the U.S. National

Forest trail signs that say, "Turn back at the first sign of bad weather." More than a quarter of hiking- and climbing-related deaths on the mountain have been due to exhaustion and exposure.

HOT SPOT

At 6,288 feet above sea level, Mt. Washington in New Hampshire's White Mountains is not just the tallest peak in New England, it's the highest point east of the Mississippi.

Scenic Touring in the White Mountains

Whether you choose to explore on foot, in the car, on a train, or aboard a skyride, your most indelible vacation memories are likely to be of the dramatic scenery you soaked up during your stay. The scenic touring possibilities are endless. Here are a few highlights.

Arethusa Falls

Crawford Notch State Park, Route 302, Harts Location
(603) 374-2272

Of all of New Hampshire's waterfalls, Arethusa Falls has the longest drop. The access road to the start of the 1 3/10-mile Arethusa Falls Trail, a fairly rocky and moderately steep hike, is off Route 302 just south of Dry River Campground. Return via the same route, or complete the 3-mile loop past Frankenstein Cliff, which also brings you back to the starting point.

Cannon Aerial Tramway

Franconia Notch Parkway Exit 2, Franconia Notch
(603) 823-8800

See the scenery from aloft aboard the eighty-passenger aerial tramway that takes you 4,200 feet up to the summit of Cannon Mountain for views of New Hampshire, Vermont, Maine, and Canada.

HOT SPOT

Each June, the Franconia Area Chamber of Commerce, (800) 237-9007, celebrates spring during the three-week **Fields of Lupine Festival** in the Franconia/Sugar Hill area. Lupines are wildflowers that bloom in an array of shades—blue, purple, pink, white, red, orange, and yellow—creating a spectacular color explosion. The chamber publishes a guide to the best lupine viewing spots; tours, teas, and demonstrations are held throughout the festival.

Conway Scenic Railroad

Route 16, North Conway

(603) 356-5251 or (800) 232-5251

www.conwayscenic.com

Both railroad aficionados and sightseers alike won't want to miss this stop. At the Conway Scenic Railroad, you can embark on your choice of three scenic excursions through the Mount Washington Valley aboard a restored antique train.

Lost River

Route 112, Kinsman Notch, North Woodstock

(603) 745-8031

See waterfalls, caverns, and gorges created by the powerful forces of water, wind, weather, and time as you amble along wooden walkways.

Robert Frost Farm

Ridge Road, Franconia

(603) 823-5510

www.npu2.org/frostfarm

The famous American poet lived here from 1900 to 1909. From late May to mid-October, you can tour the poet's home and wander the grounds that inspired his works, including a nature trail where excerpts from his poems are posted.

FAST FACT

The Connecticut River forms the border between Vermont and New Hampshire. In 1934, a U.S. Supreme Court ruling gave control of the river to New Hampshire. The state's western border is the low water mark on the Vermont side of the river.

White Mountains Trail/Kancamagus Highway

(603) 528-8721

This 100-mile loop is the most scenic drive in New Hampshire and perhaps all of New England. Begin at the White Mountain Visitor Center, Route 3, North Woodstock, and head north to I-93 to the Franconia Notch Parkway. In Conway, pick up "The Kang," Route 112, and continue west to complete the loop. Along this route, you'll see waterfalls, covered bridges, and some of the region's most popular natural and man-made attractions. There are also abundant opportunities to park and hike.

Dining Highlights

- For a divine breakfast, eat at **Polly's Pancake Parlor,** Route 117, Sugar Hill, (603) 823-5575, a local institution since 1938.
- The **Café Lafayette Dinner Train,** Route 112, North Woodstock, (603) 745-3500 or (800) 699-3501, combines a sumptuous, five-course meal with a two-hour scenic ride.
- For romantic atmosphere, mountain views, and award-winning gourmet selections, make reservations at the **1785 Inn,** 3582 White Mountain Highway, North Conway, (603) 356-9025.
- At **Stonehurst Manor,** Route 16, North Conway Village,

(603) 356-3113, you can watch your pizza being made and baked in indoor and outdoor, wood-fired, stone ovens. Dine in one of four elegant but casual indoor dining rooms or outside on the summer porch.

- Fussy kids? They're sure to find something they like on the ninety-item menu at **Dad's Restaurant at the Beacon Resort,** Route 3, Lincoln, (603) 745-8118.

HOT SPOT

Llamas are gentle pack animals that make ideal hiking companions. You may hike with your personal llama on any state or national land in New Hampshire. Not traveling with your own llama? **Llongneck Llamas,** 321 Shaker Road, Northfield, (603) 286-7948, has llamas available for leisurely treks and farm tours. **Fairfield Llama Farm,** Elm Street, Freedom, (603) 539-2865, offers guided White Mountains llama treks by appointment. **Snowvillage Inn,** Route 16N, Snowville, (603) 447-2818 or (800) 447-4345, llama expeditions include a gourmet champagne picnic. Visit the New Hampshire Lama Association at *www.nhlama.org*.

Shopping Discoveries

North Conway is the outlet shopping capital of New Hampshire. In fact, the outlets along Route 16 are some vacationers' primary reason for visiting the region! Remember, the savings are multiplied here because New Hampshire has no state sales tax. The largest outlet center along Route 16 is **Settlers' Green Outlet Village Plus,** (603) 356-7031, with more than fifty stores including Brookstone, Harry & David, Rockport, Levi's, and Banana Republic. For a free guide to outlet shopping, call the **Mt. Washington Valley Chamber of Commerce,** (603) 356-3171.

For one-stop shopping for American-made crafts and New England specialty foods, visit the **Handcrafters Barn,** Route 16,

North Conway, ✆(603) 356-8996, which showcases the works of more than 350 artisans and sells gourmet delights from all six New England states.

Looking for an old-fashioned Main Street shopping district? You'll find craft shops, gift boutiques, antiques stores, gourmet food purveyors, and other retail treasures along Main Streets in Lincoln, North Woodstock, and Littleton.

The **Franconia Marketplace,** ✉ Main Street, Franconia, ✆(603) 823-5368, specializes exclusively in products made right in Franconia.

Dartmouth–Lake Sunapee Region

DO YOU OFTEN RETURN HOME FROM VACATION screaming, "I need another vacation!" because you've tried to pack too much activity into your time away? The perfect New England solution may just be New Hampshire's quiet, compact Dartmouth–Lake Sunapee region, where travelers get a wee respite from the racks of brochures that tempt them to run around seeing and doing everything. Here, you can simply hunker down at a country B&B and reconnect with someone you love, watching the world and the wildlife go by.

Of course, that's not to say that you won't find plenty of diversions once you're fully rested and rejuvenated. This region's identity is shaped in part by Ivy League college Dartmouth, an educational and cultural leader in New England since 1769. And both Lake Sunapee and the Connecticut River provide recreational opportunities such as canoeing, fishing, and birding. There are also mountains to ski in Sunapee, though they can't rival the state's White Mountains farther north.

What are you waiting for? Hurry to New Hampshire's unhurried western frontier, and treat yourself to a true relaxation vacation.

HOT SPOT

The longest-running craft fair in America is the annual **League of New Hampshire Crafts** held each August on the grounds of Mt. Sunapee State Park. The fair, which originated in the 1930s, features vendors, demonstrations, music, and food. For dates and information, call (603) 224-3375.

Lodging Options

Your lodging choices in this region are dominated by traditional New England inns and bed and breakfasts.

The **Inn at Sunapee,** Burkehaven Hill Road, Sunapee, (603) 763-4444 or (800) 327-2466, is an 1875 New England farmhouse that sits up on a hill overlooking the lake. Sixteen guest rooms, including five family suites, feature period décor. The ten-room **Thistle & Shamrock Inn,** 11 West Main Street, Bradford, (603) 938-5553 or (888) 938-5553, is an old hotel that played host to traveling salesmen visiting the region's mills at the turn of the century. The **Hanover Inn at Dartmouth College,** Main Street, Hanover, (603) 643-4300 or (800) 443-7024, is a classic, New England hotel that puts you right in the heart of this college community.

If you're fascinated by the ways and beliefs of the Shaker religious community, two lodging establishments in this area are housed within old Shaker structures. The **Shaker Inn at the Stone Dwelling,** 447 Route 4A, Enfield, (603) 632-7810 or (888) 707-4257, was built from 1837 to 1841 and is the largest main dwelling ever erected by any Shaker community. Today, the inn, located on Lake Mascoma, has twenty-four guest rooms replete with Shaker-style furnishings. **Shaker Farm Bed & Breakfast,** Route 4A, Enfield, (603) 632-7664, is housed within a 1794 Shaker home and also features period décor.

Couples seeking cozy B&B retreats have quite a selection at their disposal. **Highland Lake Inn Bed & Breakfast,** 32 Maple

Street, East Andover, (603) 735-6426, was originally built in 1767 and is nestled on 12 rustic acres featuring stone walls and sugar maples. **Candlelite Inn Bed & Breakfast,** 5 Greenhouse Lane, Bradford, (603) 938-5571 or (888) 812-5571, is a cute 1897 country Victorian with five guest rooms. **Goddard Mansion B&B,** 25 Hillstead Road, Claremont, (603) 543-0603 or (800) 736-0603, is a dramatic 1929 estate that offers spectacular views and a private world all its own.

FAST FACT

Does the name Donald Ross ring a bell? Then you are probably an avid golfer! Ross designed an amazing 413 golf courses during the first half of the twentieth century—notably North Carolina's Pinehurst No. 2 and Florida's Seminole—including seven in New Hampshire: the Panorama Course at the Balsams, Tory Pines Golf Resort, Wentworth by the Sea, and the Carter, Kingswood, Lake Sunapee, and Manchester Country clubs. Ross also redesigned the courses at Mount Washington Golf Club and the Bethlehem Country Club. New Hampshire has so many public golf courses that you could play a different one each day for nearly three months, so pack your clubs.

Places to Go

When you are ready to get out and explore the Dartmouth–Lake Sunapee region, here are some stops you should consider.

The **Saint-Gaudens National Historic Site,** off Route 12A, Cornish, (603) 675-2175, celebrates the life and work of one of the country's most accomplished sculptors, Augustus Saint-Gaudens, who made his home at this 150-acre estate from 1885 to 1907. Saint-Gaudens is famous for public monuments such as the Sherman monument in New York City's Central Park and the "Standing

Lincoln" in Chicago. The site is open daily from late May through late October.

While you're in Cornish, don't miss the chance to see four covered bridges, including the longest one in the United States, which connects the town with Windsor, Vermont.

The **Fort at No. 4,** 267 Springfield Road, Charlestown, (603) 826-5700, is a living history museum open from late May through October on the site of the 1743 fortified village built at the northernmost British settlement, which was subject to frequent Native American attacks. Visitors get a glimpse of eighteenth-century life.

HOT SPOT

The Gardens at the Fells, John Hay National Wildlife Refuge, Route 103A, Newbury, (603) 763-4789, feature a 100-foot perennial border, views of Lake Sunapee from the formal Rose Terrace, and a hillside alpine garden with a Japanese water lily pool. The Fells was the summer home of John M. Hay, writer, diplomat, and private secretary to Abraham Lincoln. The Hay Refuge offers gardening workshops and guided walks. There is an admission charge to visit the grounds, which are open daily.

Bring home mineral souvenirs from **Ruggles Mine,** off Route 4, Grafton, (603) 523-4275, a giant, cavernous mica, beryl, and feldspar mine that first opened in 1803. Rock hunters are welcome to collect specimens when they visit from mid-May to mid-October.

Tours of the historic **Dartmouth campus** are available daily; call (603) 646-2875 for a schedule. While you're on campus, the **Hood Museum of Art,** Wheelock Street, Hanover, (603) 646-2808, is worth a visit. It is one of the largest and oldest college museums in the country and home to a varied collection of masterworks.

Two other museums in the region that you might want to venture out to are the **Enfield Shaker Museum,** 2 Lower

Shaker Village, Enfield, (603) 632-4346, open late May through mid-October, preserves the legacy of this town's Shaker community, and the **Mt. Kearsarge Indian Museum,** Kearsarge Mountain Road, Warner, (603) 456-2600, New Hampshire's only museum dedicated to Native American culture.

Dining Highlights

For a hearty, New England breakfast, **Lou's Restaurant,** 30 South Main Street, Hanover, (603) 643-3321, across the street from the Dartmouth Co-op, has been an institution since 1947. Breakfast is served until closing time.

Dine afloat aboard the MV *Kearsarge*, operated by **Sunapee Cruises,** 39 Lake Avenue, Sunapee, (603) 763-5477. A hot dinner buffet and two-hour narrated lake cruise is offered daily in season.

For eclectic fare served on a deck overlooking Sunapee Harbor, head to the **Anchorage,** Sunapee Harbor, Sunapee, (603) 763-3334, which just may be the only place in New England where you can pull up in a boat and order Yankee pot roast.

Sample Shaker-inspired cuisine at the **Shaker Inn,** 447 Route 4A, Enfield, (603) 632-7810 or (888) 707-4257, where the restaurant is located inside the Shaker community's former dining hall.

Shopping Discoveries

While this region isn't a shopping destination per se, there are a few finds that you shouldn't miss while vacationing here. Premier among them is the opportunity to visit the original **Mesa International store,** Elkins Road, Elkins, (603) 456-2002. This nationally known designer and importer of handcrafted glassware, tableware, home accessories, and garden items offers factory-direct savings to visitors to its New Hampshire outlet.

You'll also find outlet prices on sweaters and other woolen goods from Pendleton and Dorr Woolen Mills at the **Woolen Mill Store,** Routes 11 and 103, Guild, (603) 863-6377.

If you're an avid reader, lose yourself for a while inside the **Dartmouth Bookstore,** 33 South Main Street, Hanover, (603) 643-3616, one of the largest independent bookstores in America. Founded in 1872 by Dartmouth students, it was purchased in 1883 by the Storrs family and is operated by family members to this day—making it the oldest bookstore in the United States continuously owned by the same family.

Before you head for home, visit **Nunsuch Dairy & Cheese,** Route 114, South Sutton, (603) 927-4176, and purchase some of the farm's herbed or plain goat cheese to take back with you.

The Merrimack Valley and Monadnock Region

PEOPLE FLY IN AND DRIVE THROUGH, but few linger long enough to appreciate the wealth of history that is preserved in New Hampshire's capital region. Even more frequently overlooked is the state's southwest corner, the lovely land of little, quintessentially New England towns with Mt. Monadnock at its core. Luckily, convincing you that southern New Hampshire is worthy of a visit is an easy task.

Surely one of these names pulls at your heartstrings–Robert Frost, Christa McAuliffe, Uncle Sam, NASCAR. The beloved New England poet, the heroic *Challenger* astronaut, and Samuel Wilson, inspiration for the American icon, all called southern New Hampshire home. Landmarks that bear their names should definitely be on your "must see" list. And as for NASCAR–if motor sports get your heart pumping, the New Hampshire International Speedway has your ticket to a day of exhilarating racing action. Dublin-based *Yankee* magazine and *The Old Farmer's Almanac,* two publications that carry the pulse of New England to the nation and the world, call this region home, too.

So don't blitz blindly up I-93 en route to the lakes and mountains or land in Manchester only to take off immediately for far-flung parts of the state. Take a day or more and explore this region's historic and recreational riches. Uncle Sam would want you to.

TRAVEL TIP

The New Hampshire Campground Owners' Association has 140 members, so campers have plenty of choices in all of the state's diverse regions. The association's online campground directory, *www.ucampnh.com,* is a great place to start your search, or call toll free, (800) 822-6764, to request a campground guide. New Hampshire also boasts more than a dozen state parks that offer everything from tent sites to full RV hookups. For complete information and state park camping reservations, call (603) 271-3628.

Lodging Options

The Merrimack Valley is New Hampshire's business and urban hub, and available accommodations tend to be of the business-class and chain hotel variety. If you're looking for something a bit more classic New England, the nearby Monadnock region is loaded with inns and B&Bs that are the embodiment of old-fashioned New England charm and hospitality.

If you need to stay near Manchester Airport, there are more than a dozen hotels in the vicinity that offer complimentary airport shuttle service. A few to consider include the 119-room Sheraton **Four Points Hotel,** 55 John Devine Drive, Manchester, (603) 668-6110, which has an indoor pool, room service, and business amenities; **Holiday Inn—The Center,** 700 Elm Street, Manchester, (603) 625-1000, with 250 rooms, two restaurants, and business services; and the 194-room **Wayfarer Inn,** 121 South River Road, Bedford, (603) 622-3766, located on the site of an historic mill and featuring country inn décor, three pools including one indoors, and many other high-end amenities.

In New Hampshire's capital, Concord, you'll find reasonably priced family accommodations at the 100-room **Comfort Inn,** 71 Hall Street, (603) 226-4100, which has an indoor pool and complimentary continental breakfast, and at the sixty-six-room

Best Western Concord Inn & Suites, 97 Hall Street, (603) 228-4300, which offers an indoor pool and fitness center and permits pets.

In Salem, the **Susse Chalet,** 8 Keewaydin Drive (603) 893-4722, offers comfortable, budget lodgings with convenient access to New Hampshire highways. In Nashua, larger hotels include the 337-room **Sheraton,** Tara Boulevard, (603) 888-9970, with indoor and outdoor pools and supervised children's activities, and the 251-room **Marriott,** 2200 Southwood Drive, (603) 880-9100, which offers free airport transportation and business services.

It's hard to single out just a few of the appealing inns in the Monadnock area. You may want to call the **Monadnock Travel Council,** (603) 355-8155 or (800) HEARTNH, to request a free brochure describing additional accommodations. **Chesterfield Inn,** Route 9, West Chesterfield, (603) 256-3211 or (800) 365-5515, is a renovated 1787 farmhouse and barn turned fifteen-room inn with views of Vermont's Green Mountains and both modern amenities and old-fashioned touches, including some rooms with fireplaces, whirlpools, and private decks. For the privacy of a mountain hideaway, **Crestwood Chapel & Pavilion,** 400 Scofield Mountain Road, Ashuelot, (603) 239-6393, a former religious retreat built at the turn of the century, offers three suites and the even more private Pavilion building for guests seeking solitude. The **Grand View Inn and Resort,** 580 Mountain Road, Jaffrey, (603) 532-9880, is a nineteenth-century country mansion tucked away on 330 acres at the foot of Mt. Monadnock. Kids will get a kick out of the **Inn At East Hill Farm,** 460 Monadnock Street, Troy, (603) 242-6495 or (800) 242-6495, where they'll be enlisted to help hunt for eggs, milk cows, and feed goats.

HOT SPOT

Victorian Park, 350 North Broadway, Salem, (603) 898-1803, is the place to head when the kids tire of gardens. They may not even realize that the eighteen-hole miniature golf course is designed as a Victorian garden with a waterfall, bridges, and plantings that require the care of a full-time gardener. Other amusements include an arcade, a climbing wall, Water Wars, and an old-fashioned ice cream parlor. The park is open mid-April through October, and there is an admission charge.

Southern New Hampshire Sights

Before delving into southern New Hampshire's historic sights, why not visit a prehistoric site? **America's Stonehenge,** 105 Haverhill Road, Salem, (603) 893-8300, is a mysterious series of stone structures including astronomically aligned megaliths. It's open to the public year-round—wear sturdy walking shoes and draw your own conclusions about how these structures came to be.

Fast forward to the eighteenth century, and spend a half-day or more immersed in the world of the Shaker religious community founded in New Hampshire in 1792 at the **Canterbury Shaker Village,** 288 Shaker Road, Canterbury, (603) 783-9511. Tour twenty-five original Shaker buildings and see demonstrations of Shaker crafts. The village is open daily May through October and weekends in April, November, and December.

The wooden, five-room home in Mason where Samuel Wilson spent his teens and early twenties is the only surviving structure that can be directly linked to the man commonly believed to be the inspiration for Uncle Sam. An historical marker located on Route 123 about five miles south of Mason village identifies the home, where the Wilson family took up residence in 1780. Sam's fame came during the War of 1812, when he supplied meat to troops in barrels labeled "U.S."—for United States . . . or Uncle Sam.

The 1804 mansion that was the childhood home of the nation's fourteenth president, Franklin Pierce, is also worth a visit. The **Franklin Pierce Homestead,** Routes 9 and 31, Hillsborough, (603) 478-3165, is open daily in July and August and weekends in June and September through Columbus Day.

Continue your time travel with a visit to the **Robert Frost Farm,** Route 28, Derry, (603) 432-3091, where the poet lived from 1900 to 1909. The grounds are open daily year-round, and you can tour the farmhouse and barn daily from late June through Labor Day and weekends in the late spring and early fall.

One of the great tragedies of the late twentieth century was the explosion of the space shuttle *Challenger* and the death of its seven-member crew, which included the first civilian in space, New Hampshire schoolteacher Christa McAuliffe. Her memory and vision are preserved at the **Christa McAuliffe Planetarium,** 3 Institute Drive, Concord, (603) 271-7831, which opened in 1990. The planetarium's exhibit halls and 40-foot theater dome are open to the public daily.

Art devotees will want to include a visit to the **Currier Gallery of Art,** 201 Myrtle Way, Manchester, (603) 669-6144, on their itineraries. Not only will you see works by Picasso, Matisse, Monet, O'Keeffe, Calder, and Homer but also you'll have the opportunity to tour the Zimmerman House, designed in 1950 by renowned architect Frank Lloyd Wright. The museum is open year-round, but closed Tuesdays.

TRAVEL TIP

To see moose in the Great North Woods, the New Hampshire Fish and Game Department recommends:

Route 3 in Pittsburg
Route 26 between Dixville and Errol
Route 16 between Errol and Berlin

For family fun, head to **Canobie Lake Park,** North Policy Street, Salem, (603) 893-3506. Founded in 1902 as an area of gardens, trolley cars, and strolling promenades, the park is now a modern theme park with more than forty-five rides for all ages including four roller coasters. Don't miss "The Old Man o' the Mountain" rock-climbing wall and the wet and wild Boston Tea Party water ride.

Don't miss the chance to see the famous Budweiser Clydesdales at the **Anheuser-Busch Brewery,** 221 Daniel Webster Highway, Merrimack, (603) 595-1202, where you can also take a tour and view the brewing and bottling process.

When you're tired of touring, find peaceful respite at **Cathedral of the Pines,** 75 Cathedral Entrance, Rindge, (603) 899-3300. This meditative place honors Americans who have died during wars and is open to visitors of all faiths May through October. Organ and other musical recitals are often held in the summer months.

Dining Highlights

Plan your visit to **Canterbury Shaker Village,** 288 Shaker Road, Canterbury, (603) 783-9511, around a mealtime so that you can sample the Shaker specialties prepared at the **Village's Creamery Restaurant,** including desserts such as Maple Sugar Cream Pie and Old-Fashioned Butterscotch Pudding.

Pickity Place, Nutting Hill Road, Mason, (603) 878-1151, serves herb-seasoned, five-course, gourmet lunches every day of the year except holidays. The dining room inside this 200-year-old cottage is open for three luncheon seatings each day—call ahead for times and reservations. Leave time to visit the gardens, greenhouse, and gift shop before or after lunch.

For a special evening, make reservations at **Colby Hill Inn,** The Oaks, Henniker, (603) 428-3281 or (800) 531-0330, where the menu features seasonally inspired, hearty New England favorites. New Hampshire's oldest inn, **Hancock Inn,** 33 Main

Street, Hancock, ✆(603) 525-3318, is also known for its upscale, Yankee-inspired dining.

Shopping Discoveries

If you've got shopping on your mind, the one must-stop spot in the Monadnock Region is the **Colony Mill Marketplace,** 222 West Street, Keene, ✆(603) 357-1240, where a restored, historic 1838 woolen mill is now the setting for a brewpub, a steakhouse, and 65,000 square feet of unique specialty stores including a 200-dealer antiques center. Another unique shopping destination is **Frye's Measure Mill,** 12 Frye Mill Road, Wilton, ✆(603) 654-5345, where colonial and Shaker boxes have been handcrafted since 1858. The **Museum Gift Shop,** open every day except Monday from April through late December, features a selection of local crafts. Mill tours are offered on Saturdays, June through October.

In the Merrimack Valley, crafters will delight in two shops—both housed within 200-year-old barns. The **Fiber Studio,** 9 Foster Hill Road, Henniker, ✆(603) 428-7830, sells hand-dyed yarns, looms and spinning wheels, hand-woven items, and beads from around the world. **Country Quilter,** College Hill Road, Hopkinton, ✆(603) 746-5521, is a working quilt shop that sells finished quilts along with supplies for do-it-yourselfers. Also visit **Gibson Pewter,** 18 East Washington Road, Hillsborough Center, ✆(603) 464-3410, where you can watch the father-son team of Raymond and Jonathan Gibson at work casting, hammering, and spinning traditional and modern designs in pewter.

HOT SPOT

Keene State College Arboretum and Gardens, Keene, ✆(603) 358-2544, welcomes visitors for self-guided tours of the ornamental trees and shrubs, including specimens of historic significance, on the campus. A walking tour brochure is available at the student center on Appian Way.

Itineraries

PERSONAL ITINERARY NOTES

A JAM-PACKED, THREE-DAY NEW HAMPSHIRE SUMMER SAMPLER

Day One Arrive in Portsmouth on your first day of vacation and spend the afternoon at sea on a whale-watch cruise or other excursion with the **Isles of Shoals Steamship Co.,** 315 Market Street, Portsmouth, (603) 431-5500 or (800) 441-4620. In the evening, take a scenic drive along Route 1A, which follows New Hampshire's shoreline, and watch the shadows dance on wave crests as the day disappears. Treat yourself to a seafood feast at **Little Jack's Seafood Restaurant & Lobster Pool,** 539 Ocean Boulevard, Hampton Beach, (603) 926-8053, before calling it a night.

Day Two On day two, head north to Lake Winnipesaukee. Get a fabulous view of the sparkling lake aboard the historic **Winnipesaukee Scenic Railroad,** (603) 279-5253, which departs hourly from Weirs Beach Station. Spend the afternoon tinkering around Weirs Beach, where you'll find swimming, arcades, souvenir shops, kids' rides, and outdoor restaurants.

Day Three On your last day in the Granite State, head back south on I-93 and spend the morning at the historic **Canterbury Shaker Village,** 288 Shaker Road, Canterbury, (603) 783-9511 or (800) 982-9511. Be sure to have lunch at the village's award-winning Creamery restaurant, where you can sample authentic Shaker cuisine. In the afternoon, continue south to Concord and take a side trip to outer space at the **Christa McAuliffe Planetarium,** 3 Institute Drive, Concord, (603) 271-7831, before blasting off for home.

FIVE FABULOUS FALL DAYS

Day One Start in North Conway for sales tax–free outlet stores galore. When you've tired of the shopping frenzy, take a peaceful leaf-peeping trip aboard the **Conway Scenic Railroad,** Route 16, North Conway, (603) 356-5251 or (800) 232-5251. In the evening, head north on Route 16 and pass through the covered bridge gateway to the town of Jackson, where you can sup at the **Wildcat Inn & Tavern,** Route 16A, Jackson Village, (603) 383-4245 or (800) 228-4245.

Day Two Take Route 16 North to Dixville Notch in the Great North Woods, where hopefully you've been able to make reservations at the **Balsams Grand Resort Hotel,** Route 26, Dixville Notch, (603) 255-3400 or (800) 255-0600, a relaxing, elegant mountain escape with a gourmet restaurant.

Day Three Take a morning walk around Lake Gloriette. Ask the Balsams restaurant to pack you a picnic lunch before you set out again, heading north to Franconia Notch for an aerial view of the colorful landscape aboard the **Cannon Aerial Tramway,** Franconia Notch Parkway, Franconia Notch, (603) 823-8800.

Day Four Grab your camera and take the **Mt. Washington Cog Railway,** Route 302, Bretton Woods, (603) 278-5404 or (800) 922-8825, 6,288 feet to the summit for breathtaking views. In the afternoon, head south on Route 3 and explore the amusements at **Clark's Trading Post,** Route 3, Lincoln, (603) 745-8913. A quick drive west to North Woodstock may let you squeeze in a visit to **Lost River Gorge,** Route 112 Kinsman Notch, North Woodstock, (603) 745-8031.

Day Five Follow New Hampshire's most scenic road, the 34-mile **Kancamagus Highway,** back to North Conway. You'll be treated to spectacular mountain scenery as the road climbs to nearly 3,000 feet. Time permitting, make the trip an hour south to explore Castle in the Clouds, a wonderful spot to savor your last images of autumn in New Hampshire.

SEVEN DAYS OF SIGHTSEEING AND SHOPPING

Day One Begin your week-long New Hampshire adventure at the Massachusetts border town of Rindge, where you can visit the one-of-a-kind **Cathedral of the Pines,** 75 Cathedral Entrance, (603) 899-3300. After a meditative morning at this glorious, non-denominational spot, head a bit northwest to the city of Keene, where **Colony Mill Marketplace,** 222 West Street, (603) 357-1240, features New England specialty stores and a 240-dealer antique center.

Day Two Wake up early and follow Route 9 northeast to Concord and visit the **Christa McAuliffe Planetarium,** 3 Institute Drive, (603) 271-7831, for a star-studded show. In the afternoon, travel north to **Canterbury Shaker Village,** 288 Shaker Road, Canterbury, (603) 783-9511 or (800) 982-9511, to sample the simple Shaker lifestyle. Have dinner at the award-winning **Creamery** restaurant at the village, and shop for Shaker-inspired crafts in the museum store.

Day Three Continue north to Plymouth and spend the early hours exploring **Polar Caves Park,** 705 Old Route 25, (603) 536-1888 or (800) 273-1886. In the afternoon, see Squam Lake, setting for the movie *On Golden Pond*, on one of the available guided boat tours.

Day Four Travel north to Lincoln on day four, and spend the morning exploring **Clark's Trading Post,** Route 3, (603) 745-8913—there's something for everyone at this amusing outpost. In the afternoon, drive New Hampshire's most picturesque road, the Kancamagus Highway, east to North Conway.

Day Five Peruse the discounted merchandise at dozens of outlet stores in North Conway in the early part of the day. In the afternoon, drive an hour south to visit **Castle in the Clouds** and the **Castle Spring Brewing Co.,** Route 171, Moultonborough, (800) 729-2468. Drive to Portsmouth in time to set out on a lobster clambake dinner cruise offered by **Isles of Shoals Steamship Co.,** 315 Market Street, Portsmouth, (603) 431-5500 or (800) 441-4620.

Day Six You won't regret spending some time exploring Portsmouth, one of New Hampshire's oldest communities, settled in 1623. You'll find pre-Revolutionary War homes; **Strawberry Banke,** 314 Court Street, (603) 436-7242 or (800) 428-3933, an outdoor living history museum; and shops and galleries to browse in Market Square.

Day Seven Before you leave New Hampshire, see the ancient archaeological mystery that is **America's Stonehenge,** 105 Haverhill Road, Salem, (603) 893-8300. Buy a lucky rock amulet in the gift shop to wear on your journey home and to remind you of your stay in New Hampshire.

PART VII

Vermont

Vermont

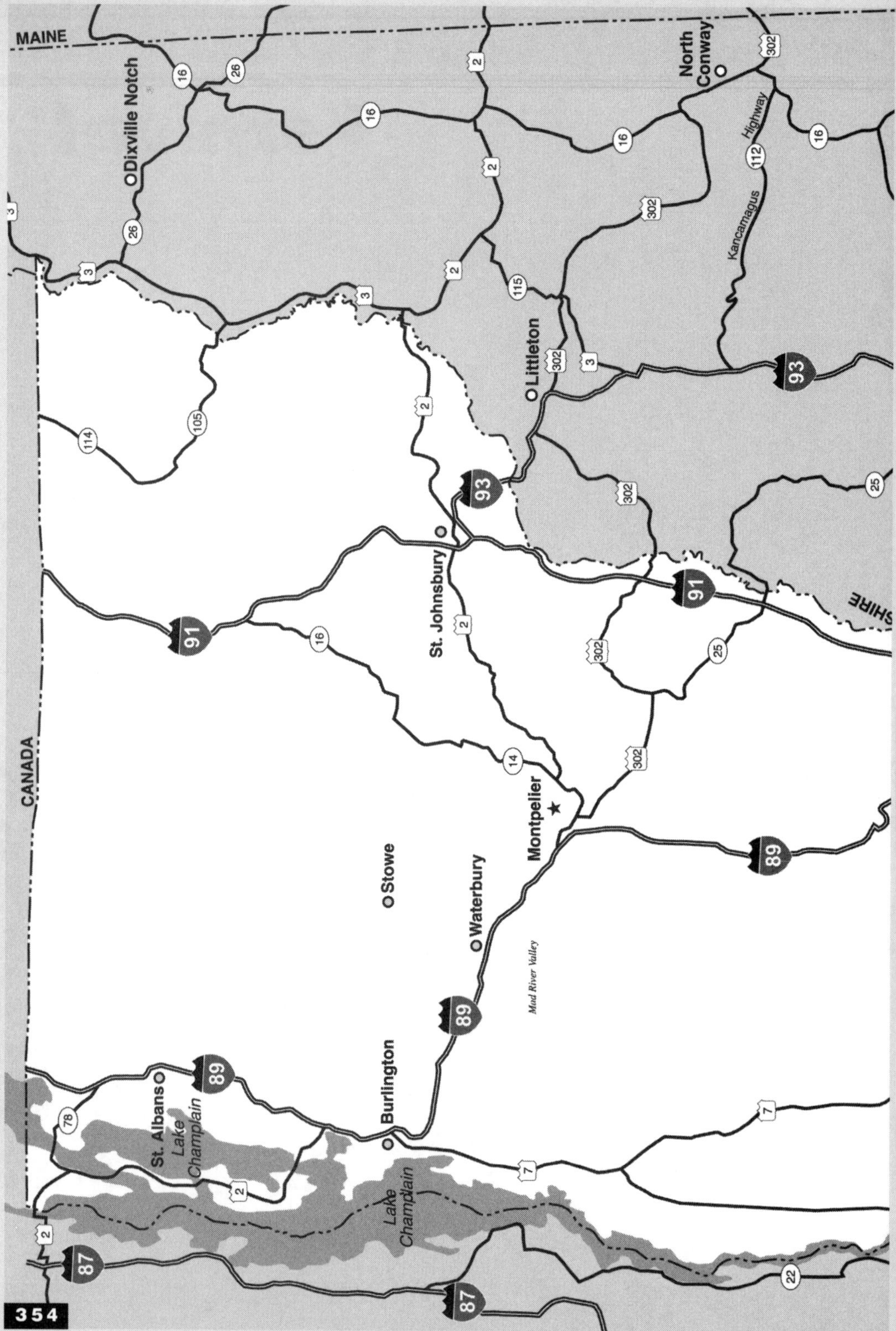

MAINE
CANADA
Dixville Notch
North Conway
Kancamagus Highway
Littleton
St. Johnsbury
Montpelier
Stowe
Waterbury
Mad River Valley
Burlington
St. Albans
Lake Champlain
Lake Champlain
SHIRE

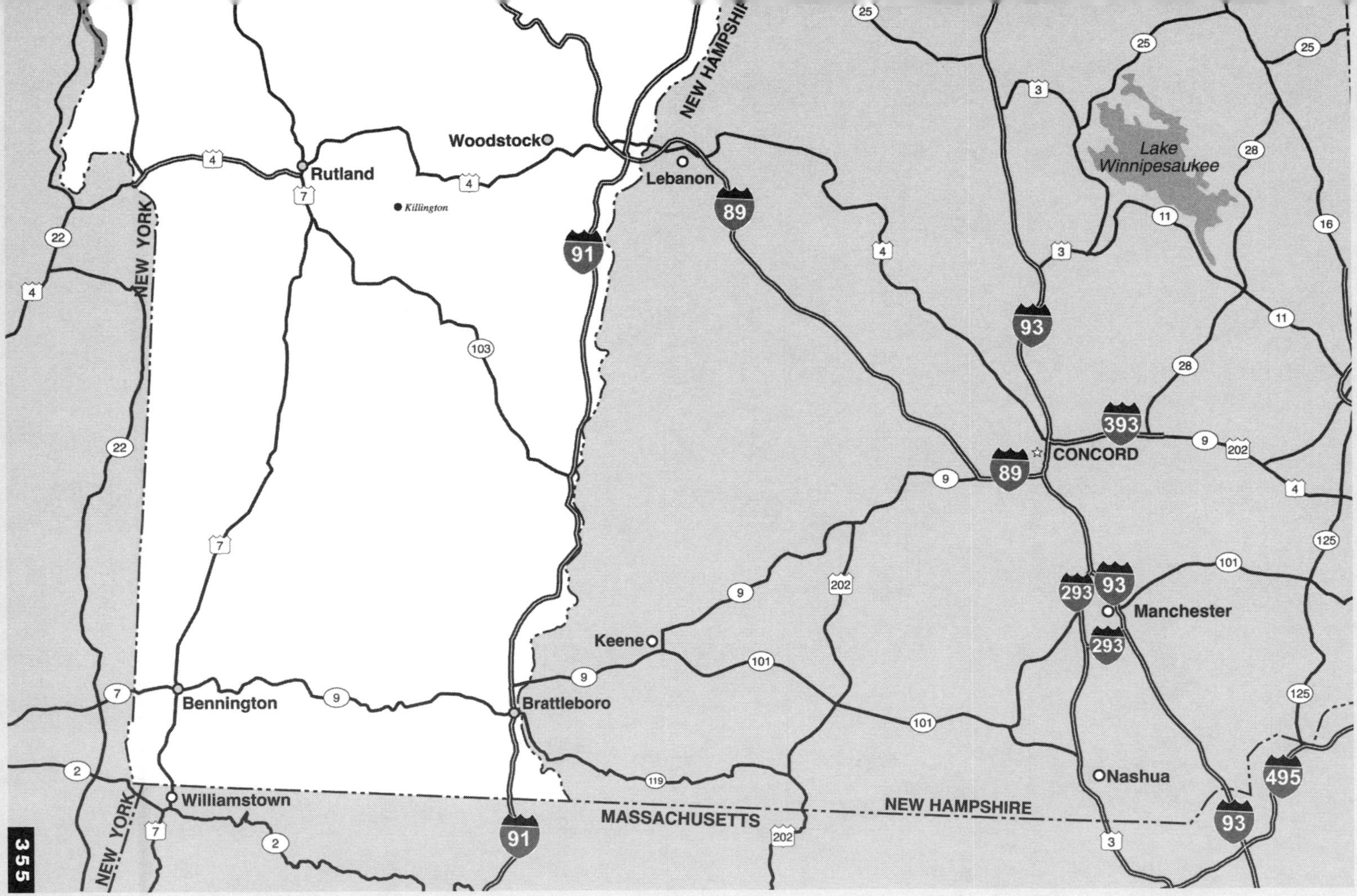
Woodstock
Rutland
Killington
Lebanon
NEW HAMPSHIRE
NEW YORK
Lake Winnipesaukee
CONCORD
Manchester
Nashua
Keene
Brattleboro
Bennington
Williamstown
MASSACHUSETTS
NEW HAMPSHIRE
NEW YORK

Ski and Hiking Trails of Vermont

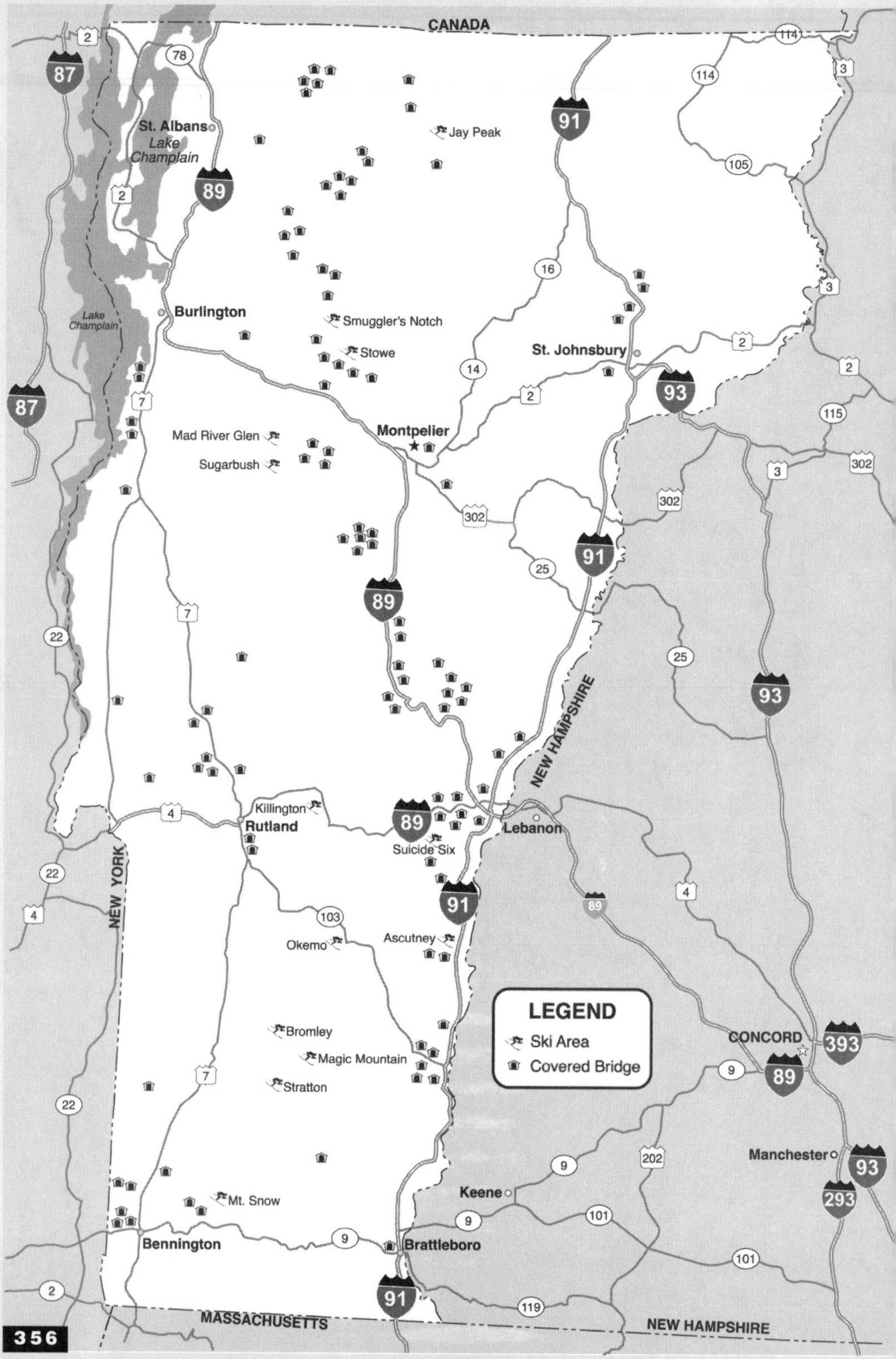

Burlington, Vermont

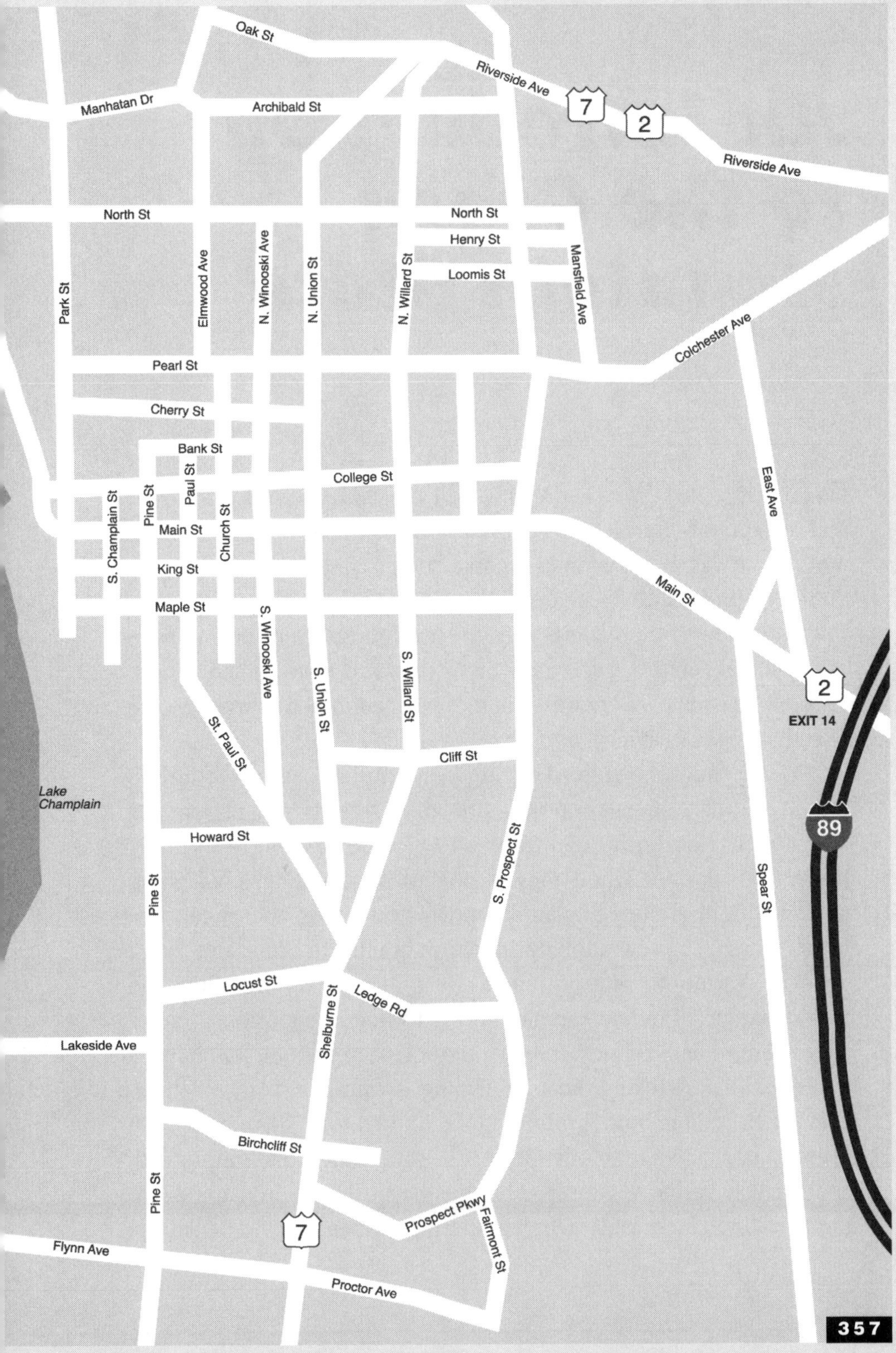

An Introduction to the Green Mountain State

EVEN IF YOU'VE NEVER SET FOOT IN VERMONT, you've probably had a taste of New England's most agrarian state, whether it was Vermont-made maple syrup, cheddar cheese, apple cider, or Ben & Jerry's ice cream. Vermont was the last New England state to be settled, and, for the fourteen-year period from 1777 to 1791, before it became the fourteenth state in the Union, Vermont was its own country—an independent republic with its own postal service, currency, and laws.

Today, there is still a different drummer leading Vermont's march through time. Vermont's unspoiled forests and mountains and countryside beckon to travelers to come and play—and they holler even louder when they're coated in sparkling, cold white stuff. Vermont is New England's undisputed winter sports capital—from skiing to snowmobiling to snowshoeing to sledding. Don't overlook Vermont's other three seasons, though. Spring brings the annual magic of maple sap simmering to become glorious, amber syrup. Summer is chock full of outdoor recreational possibilities including hiking, biking, boating, fishing, swimming, bird watching, horseback riding, and golfing—in fact, Vermont has more golf courses per capita than any other U.S. state. And fall is, in a word, spectacular. Vermont's covered bridges and white church spires are photographed incessantly when autumn provides its vivid backdrop.

TRAVEL TIP

With twenty downhill ski areas and nearly fifty for cross-country skiing, winter is a popular time to be in mountainous, snowy Vermont. And as winter turns to spring, Vermont's ski resorts remain open longer than those in neighboring states, and visitors have the additional treat of being able to observe the annual "sugaring off" as sap is transformed into world-renowned Vermont maple syrup.

Ten Vermont Highlights

In Vermont, the cities are more like small towns, and even though there are no longer more cows than people, the total population barely tops 600,000. You'll feel right at home among the natives and the thousands of transplants who have discovered that a taste of Vermont is simply not enough.

Ben & Jerry's Factory

Route 100, Waterbury

(802) 882-1260 or (866) BJ-TOURS

www.benjerry.com

From its humble 1978 origins in a renovated gas station in Burlington, Ben & Jerry's has grown to become an enormous Vermont success story. The makers of such original ice cream flavors as Cherry Garcia and Chunky Monkey invite you to take a tour and to taste their sweet frozen concoctions daily year-round.

The Bennington Museum

West Main Street, Bennington

(802) 447-1571

www.benningtonmuseum.com

If you've ever for even a second thought you were too old to learn a new trick, you'll be inspired by the large collection of works by Grandma Moses housed at the Bennington Museum. Anna Mary Robertson Moses (1860–1961) didn't start painting until she was in her seventies. Don't miss the selection of children's books illustrated by her great-grandson, Will Moses, in the museum store.

The Cliff House

Stowe Mountain Resort, Stowe

(802) 253-3665

This restaurant sits atop Vermont's tallest mountain, Mt. Mansfield, at the Stowe Mountain Resort, and you'll need to hop a chair lift to enjoy its amazing views. The good news is, the ten-minute aerial ride is free when you have a dinner reservation.

Lake Champlain

Vermont's largest lake is the place to go for scenic cruises, waterfront dining, fishing, and monster watching. You'll find relaxing recreational opportunities here—that is, unless you do spot "Champ," the fabled prehistoric sea serpent that reputedly lives in the lake, in which case, your coronary unit may get more of a workout than you bargained for.

Maple Sugaring

In the late winter and early spring, Vermont turns into a hotbed of boiling sap. Dozens of sugarhouses welcome the public to watch the syrup-making process in action. Even if you don't visit during the annual sugaring season, you'll at least want to be sure to order pancakes with pure Vermont maple syrup for breakfast.

HOT SPOT

Ready to get your hands sticky? Stay at the bed and breakfast at **Mount Pleasant Sugarworks,** 1627 Shackett Road, Leicester, (802) 247-3117 or (800) 439-3117, during maple sugaring season, and you'll have a chance to lend a hand from gathering sap to stoking the wood-fired

Outlet Shopping in Manchester

Manchester rivals Kittery, Maine, when it comes to outlet shopping. If you're looking for designer duds, housewares, shoes, and other retail items at factory store prices, you'll definitely want to include a visit to Manchester on your Vermont itinerary.

The Shelburne Museum

Route 7, Shelburne
(802) 985-3346
www.shelburnemuseum.org

If you want to see a lot of Vermont in a short stretch of time, be sure to visit the Shelburne Museum, where you can explore thirty-seven historic structures including a lighthouse that once stood beside Lake Champlain, a covered bridge, and a one-room schoolhouse. You'll also get a peek at the museum's 80,000-item collection of Americana, including tools, quilts, carriages, circus memorabilia, American paintings, and impressionist works.

Skiing

Vermont is home to twenty alpine (a.k.a. downhill) ski resorts and about fifty cross-country ski areas, making it a winter paradise for skiers and snowboarders. Some of the most popular ski resorts include:

- Ascutney Mountain Resort
- Killington
- Mad River Glen
- Magic Mountain
- Mount Snow
- Stowe
- Sugarbush

TRAVEL TIP

You can check on snow conditions at ski resorts throughout Vermont with one call to (802) 229-0531 or, toll-free, (800) VERMONT.

Vermont Teddy Bear Factory

Route 7, Shelburne

(802) 985-3001

There's a Vermont Teddy Bear for practically every occasion, and you can see where these adorable keepsakes come to life on a tour of the company's factory in Shelburne. While you're there, you can also select, stuff, and stitch up a bear all your own.

Windsor-Cornish Covered Bridge

Route 5, Windsor Village

America's longest wooden covered bridge connects Windsor, Vermont, with Cornish, New Hampshire. It's just one of more than 100 covered bridges scattered across the state.

HOT SPOT

Spirit in Nature, 464 East Main Street, East Middlebury, (802) 388-7244, is a collection of ten, mile-and-a-half-long paths that feature posted sayings that remind walkers of the interconnectedness of faith and nature. The site welcomes visitors from all spiritual traditions, and admission is by donation.

The Gateway to Vermont: Bennington, Manchester, and Southern Vermont

VERMONT'S SOUTHERN GATEWAY ALLOWS YOU to sample a smattering of all of the enticements the state serves up for visitors–pretty little villages, mountains dotted with ski resorts, historic landmarks, quintessential New England inns, made-in-Vermont foods and handicrafts, working farms, and family attractions. The region has characteristics all its own, too, including topnotch outlet shopping and battlefields and monuments that spotlight the state's heroic history.

This is the land, after all, of the Green Mountain Boys—the valiant bunch under Ethan Allen's command that successfully fought attempts by New Yorkers to encroach upon Vermont's independence. They also played a vital role in the American Revolution, capturing Fort Ticonderoga in 1775 and defeating the British in 1777 at the Battle of Bennington.

Your clan just might call you a hero, too, when you choose southern Vermont as the destination for your next family furlough.

HOT SPOT

Vermont Bicycle Tours, ✆(802) 453-4811 or ✆(800) BIKE-TOUR, will lead you on an invigorating inn-to-inn cycling excursion through colorful Vermont towns and exquisite scenery. Call to request their free catalog of bike trips worldwide.

Lodging Options

From cozy motor inns and bed and breakfasts to resort and condominium accommodations at the region's ski areas, lodging choices in southern Vermont are quite diverse.

In Bennington, Manchester, and the Stratton/Mount Snow Area

The **Bennington Motor Inn,** 143 West Main Street, (802) 442-5479 or (800) 359-9900, provides sixteen guest rooms and a central location from which to walk to attractions in town. With fifty-eight rooms, the **Best Western New Englander,** 220 Northside Drive, (802) 442-6311, is the town's largest motor inn. For a touch of history and charm, try the **Molly Stark Inn,** 1067 Main Street, (802) 442-9631 or (800) 356-3076, a Queen Anne Victorian-style home turned B&B.

In Manchester, the **Equinox,** Route 7A, (802) 362-4700 or (800) 362-4747, is a famed old hotel that dates to 1769 and has hosted such distinguished guests as Mary Todd Lincoln, Ulysses S. Grant, and Theodore Roosevelt. The **Inn at Willow Pond,** Route 7A, (802) 362-4733 or (800) 533-3533, features colonial touches in its guest suites and fine dining inside a restored 1770s farmhouse. The **Reluctant Panther Inn,** 17–39 West Road, (802) 362-2568 or (800) 822-2331, is a country hideaway with sixteen guest rooms and was once home to a wealthy blacksmith. **Manchester View,** Route 7A, (802) 362-2739, has thirty-six unique rooms including some with fireplaces and Jacuzzis built for two.

Stratton Mountain provides several of its own lodging options including more than 100 one- to four-bedroom condominiums and the seventy-seven-room, chalet-style **Liftline Lodge.** Call (802) 297-4000 or (800) 787-2886 for reservations. You'll find the 200-room **Grand Summit Resort Hotel,** Route 100, West Dover, (800) 451-4211, right at the base of Mount Snow. The ski resort also has a variety of condominium and other lodging facilities available. Call (800) 845-7690 for information and reservations. Want to stay at a

B&B while you ski? The **Inn at Mount Snow,** Route 100, West Dover, (802) 464-3300 or (800) 577-SNOW, serves a home-cooked country breakfast each morning and offers fifteen inn rooms and thirty-two family-style lodge rooms.

FAST FACT

The **Waybury Inn,** Route 125, East Middlebury, "played" the Stratford Inn on the *Newhart* show, which aired from 1982 to 1990. The inn dates to 1810 and is listed on the National Register of Historic Places. It has fourteen guest rooms and a pub.

Southwestern Vermont

In Bellows Falls stay at **Horsefeathers Inn,** 16 Webb Terrace, (802) 463-9776 or (800) 299-9776, an 1897 Vermont farmhouse turned B&B. Down south a bit in Newfane is the **Four Columns Inn,** 230 West Street, (802) 365-7713 or (800) 787-6633, a Greek Revival mansion turned inn built more than 160 years ago by local craftsmen who used hand-hewn beams and timbers harvested from local forests.

In West Townshend you can spend some quiet time renewing yourself or your relationship at **Windham Hill Inn,** 311 Lawrence Drive, (802) 874-4080 or (800) 944-4080, where tearing yourself away from your gracious guest room may be the most strenuous activity you undertake during your stay.

Brattleboro has the **Latchis Hotel,** 50 Main Street, (802) 254-6300, a thirty-room, 1938 Art Deco landmark that shares a building with a theater, a restaurant, and a brewery. The **Tudor,** 300 Western Avenue, (802) 257-4983 or (800) 232-6392, is an English Tudor-style mansion built between 1929 and 1931 that is now a B&B with three guest rooms.

HOT SPOT

Riding the rails is a wonderful way to see Vermont's scenery, particularly in the fall. **Green Mountain Railroad,** 54 Depot Street, Bellows Falls, (802) 463-3069 or (800) 707-3530, operates two historic sightseeing trains. The Vermont Valley Flyer departs from the North Bennington Depot for excursions along the Battenkill River with stops in Arlington and Manchester. The Green Mountain Flyer provides fabulous views of covered bridges, a waterfall, and farmlands along the ride from Bellows Falls to Chester Depot. Call for summer and fall timetable information, or visit *www.rails-vt.com*.

Things to See in Southern Vermont

Bennington is home to several of southern Vermont's most interesting attractions including the **Bennington Battle Monument,** 15 Monument Circle, (802) 447-0550, which looms over the town. At 306 feet, 4½ inches, it is Vermont's tallest structure, and an elevator trip to the top provides views of three states, which are particularly spectacular in the fall. Don't miss the **Bennington Museum,** West Main Street, (802) 447-1571, one of the oldest and largest decorative and fine arts museums in New England. It dates to 1875 and has been at its present location since 1928. The museum houses the largest public collection of works by Grandma Moses and the Grandma Moses Schoolhouse, the 1834 one-room building where the legendary painter attended school in nearby Eagle Bridge, New York. When you leave the museum, walk next door to the Old First Church, where you'll find the grave of beloved New England poet Robert Frost (1874–1963), which is inscribed, "I had a lover's quarrel with the world."

In Manchester, visit **Hildene,** Route 7A, (802) 362-1788, the former summer home of Robert Todd Lincoln, Abraham Lincoln's son. The twenty-four-room Georgian manor house on the 412-acre estate is open for tours daily mid-May through October. Fishing enthusiasts will want to make a stop at the **American Museum of Fly Fishing,** Route 7A and Seminary Avenue, (802) 362-3300, where you can see tackle that belonged to such notable fishermen as Dwight D. Eisenhower, Ernest Hemingway, Andrew Carnegie, and Bing Crosby. While you're in Manchester, don't miss the chance to drive the 5-mile Equinox Sky Line Drive, which rises from 600 to 3,835 feet in elevation at the top of Mt. Equinox. Many parking and picnic areas are along the drive.

Wonderful family activities abound in southern Vermont. Start with **Santa's Land USA,** Route 5, Putney, (802) 387-5550 or (800) SANTA-99, where it's Christmas every day from Memorial Day through Christmas Eve. From March through mid-April, head to **Harlow's Sugar House,** Route 5, Putney, (802) 387-5852, where you can watch the syrup-making process in action. In Wilmington, you'll find **Adams Farm,** 15 Higley Hill, (802) 464-3762, where kids can enjoy farm fun activities year round from milking goats to gathering eggs to pony or hay or sleigh rides.

Southern Skiing

Ski resorts in southern Vermont are plentiful and very accessible.

- **Mount Snow Resort,** Route 100, West Dover, (802) 464-3333 or (800) 245-SNOW, is the big mountain closest to major cities in the Northeast. It boasts five mountain faces including Haystack Mountain, 130 ski and snowboard trails, twenty-three lifts, and snowmaking on 476 acres.
- **Stratton Mountain Resort,** Stratton Mountain Road, Stratton Mountain, (802) 297-4000 or (800) STRATTON, was the first major ski area to allow snowboarding—back in 1983. Today, you'll find the resort is home to six terrain parks for beginner to expert snowboarders and skiers,

ninety trails, fourteen lifts, and snowmaking on 82 percent of the terrain.

- **Bromley Mountain Resort,** 3984 Route 11, Peru, (802) 824-5522, is known for affordable family skiing. It offers forty trails, nine lifts, and snowmaking on 84 percent of its skiable terrain.
- **Magic Mountain,** Route 183, Londonderry, (802) 824-5645, is home to the Ala Kazaam Tube Park and challenging slopes for skiers and snowboarders. Magic Mountain has thirty-three trails, four lifts, and snowmaking on 87 percent of its terrain.

Dining Highlights

Breakfast is one of the best meals of the day in Vermont. At the **Original Geannelis' Restaurant,** 520 Main Street, Bennington, (802) 442-9833, hearty Vermont breakfasts are served all day. Even if you're not a morning person, you'll want to get to **Up For Breakfast,** 710 Main Street, Manchester Center, (802) 362-4204, for a bistro omelet with Granny Smith apples, brie, and maple-cured bacon or one of this breakfast-only restaurant's other signature selections.

Have lunch at **Zoey's Deli & Bakery,** Route 11/30, Manchester, (802) 362-0005, where the world can see if you've got mustard in the corner of your mouth via the Deli Cam, *www.zoeys.com/zoeycams.shtml.*

Pick up the makings of a picnic at the **Brattleboro Food Co-op,** 2 Main Street, Brattleboro, (802) 257-0236, a natural foods market and deli that has an extensive selection of local wines and cheeses.

For dinner in an out-of-the-ordinary environment, try **Bennington Station,** 150 Depot Street, Bennington, (802) 447-1080, which is housed in a century-old train depot. The **Coach House Inn and Restaurant,** Route 30, Newfane, (802) 365-7952, serves up Northern Italian fare in an 1800s farmhouse. Or take a step back in time at the **Old Tavern at Grafton,**

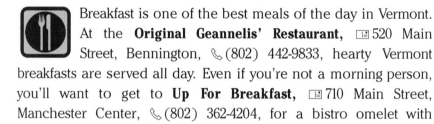

Townshend Road, Grafton, (802) 843-2231 or (800) 843-1801, an 1801 inn where you can sip cocktails in Phelps Barn among the collection of antique quilts—reservations are a must.

For outdoor dining with spectacular views, **Dalem's Chalet,** 78 South Street, West Brattleboro, (802) 254-4323 or (800) 462-5009, offers balcony seating and a menu featuring German, Swiss, and Austrian dishes.

FAST FACT

The **Vermont Fresh Network** is a statewide collaborative of farmers and chefs who share the goal of bringing fresh products grown and made in Vermont to the table. For visitors, this means you'll have bountiful opportunities to feast on tasty, locally inspired cuisine. How can you find a participating restaurant? Links to the dozens of member restaurants are online at the network's Web site, *www.vermontfresh.net/restaurants.htm,* or call (802) 229-4706 or (800) 658-8787.

Shopping Discoveries

Manchester is blossoming as one of New England's premier outlet shopping towns. Routes 7A and 11/30 in Manchester Center are literally littered with outlet centers. Two of the largest are **Manchester Commons,** (800) 955-SHOP, an upscale outlet shopping complex featuring names you know such as Polo Ralph Lauren, Calvin Klein, Timberland and more; and Manchester Designer Outlets, which bills itself as "Fifth Avenue in the Mountains" and features fifty designer outlets including J. Crew, Brooks Brothers, Donna Karan, and Tommy Hilfiger.

Deals can also be found in Brattleboro at the **Outlet Center,** exit 1 off I-91, (802) 254-4594 or (800) 459-4594, which is home to outlet stores such as Dress Barn, Bass, Carters Childrenswear, and more.

For a unique shopping experience, visit the headquarters of **Basketville,** 📇 Main Street, Putney, ☏ (802) 387-5509, where you can learn about traditional basket-making techniques at this family-owned business that was founded in Vermont in 1842, and peruse the myriad of baskets for sale. Nearby, you'll find **Green Mountain Spinnery,** 📇 Depot Road, Putney, ☏ (802) 387-4528 or ☏ (800) 321-9665, another interesting place to shop with its yarn and knit items made from locally harvested wool.

Combine shopping with a history lesson at **Candle Mill Village,** 📇 Old Mill Road, Arlington, ☏ (802) 375-6068 or ☏ (800) 772-3759, a collection of specialty shops housed in an old mill built by one of Ethan Allen's Green Mountain Boys back in 1764.

Central Vermont: Killington, Woodstock, Montpelier, and the Mad River Valley

NEED A REASON TO SET YOUR SIGHTS on central Vermont? If the Northeast's largest ski area, the world's largest granite quarry, or Vermont's oldest golf course don't pique your interest, then perhaps free samples of some of the world's finest cheeses and some of Earth's quirkiest ice cream flavors will do the trick.

The state's central core dishes up more of everything for which folks flock to Vermont–scenic wonders, downhill exhilaration, distinctive inns, fishable lakes and streams, points of historic interest, and unlimited recreational possibilities.

Central Vermont native and thirtieth president Calvin Coolidge was known for being a man of few words. A woman once challenged "Silent Cal"–"I bet I can get you to say more than two words." His response? "You lose."

I'd be willing to bet that if she'd asked Coolidge whether to visit central Vermont, his answer would've been even more succinct: "Go!"

FAST FACT

Dreaming of a white Christmas? According to the National Climactic Data Center, Montepelier, Vermont, is one of your best bets with a 93 percent chance that there will be snow on the ground come December 25. The capital city gets about 9 feet of snow each year.

Lodging Options

You'll find no shortage of places to stay the night in central Vermont. **Killington Lodging and Travel Service,** (800) 621-MTNS, is available to help you book your slope-side accommodations, whether you're seeking a condo, a motor hotel, a country inn, or a ski lodge. Sugarbush skiers will find inn and condominium accommodations available. Call (802) 583-2301 or (800) 53-SUGAR for reservations assistance.

- The **Cortina Inn and Resort,** Route 4, Killington, (802) 773-3333 or (800) 451-6108, is a ninety-six-room complex that offers tennis, an indoor pool, two restaurants, sleigh rides, snowshoeing, a fly-fishing school, and golf packages, and they'll pamper your pet, too.
- The **Vermont Inn,** Route 4, Killington, (802) 775-0708 or (800) 541-7795, is a quaint country inn with historic touches.
- The **Inn at Rutland,** 70 North Mail Street, (802) 773-0575 or (800) 808-0575, is a stately Victorian mansion constructed in 1889 that now offers eleven bed and breakfast rooms.
- **Tulip Tree Inn,** Chittenden Dam Road, Chittenden, (802) 483-6213 or (800) 707-0017, was the former home of Thomas Edison's partner, William Barstow. Now, most of its nine guest rooms have private Jacuzzis, and breakfast and dinner are included with your stay.
- 1,200 acres in the Green Mountains provide the setting for

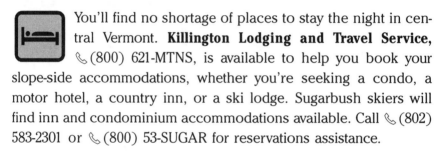

Hawk Inn & Mountain Resort, Route 100, Plymouth, (802) 672-3811 or (800) 685-HAWK, which is comprised of private villas and a fifty-room inn.

- The **Quechee Inn at Marshland Farm,** Clubhouse Road, Quechee, (802) 295-3133 or (800) 235-3133, provides twenty-four rooms inside the 1793 home that once belonged to Vermont's first lieutenant governor.
- **Jackson House Inn,** 37 Old Route 4 West, Woodstock, (802) 457-2065, is an 1890 Victorian mansion on the National Register of Historic Places that has fifteen antique-filled guest rooms.
- For upscale amenities, the 144-room **Woodstock Inn & Resort,** Fourteen the Green, Woodstock, (802) 457-1100 or (800) 448-7900, provides you with access to four restaurants, the Woodstock Ski Touring Center, and the Woodstock Country Club—Vermont's first golf course.
- You'll find the ultimate in seclusion and maybe even a thrill or two at **Blueberry Hill Inn,** Route 32, Goshen, (802) 247-6735 or (800) 448-0707, tucked away at the foot of Romance Mountain.
- The **Swift House Inn,** 25 Stewart Lane, Middlebury, (802) 388-9925, provides accommodations in the 1814 Main House, home of former governor John W. Stewart; the 1906 Victorian Gatehouse; and the 1886 Carriage House—twenty-one rooms in all.
- You can't get any more country than the **Cowbarn Bed & Breakfast,** Route 100 North, Waterbury Center, (802) 244-1844, where the three guest rooms feature quilts handmade by the innkeeper.
- Horse lovers will adore **Birch Meadow Cabins & Riding Stable,** off Stone Road, Brookfield, (802) 276-3156, where you can select B&B lodgings or hide away in your own private log cabin.
- The forty-seven-room **Capitol Plaza Hotel,** 100 State Street, Montpelier, (802) 223-5252 or (800) 274-5252, is

situated directly across the street from the State House.

- The **Inn at Montpelier,** 147 Main Street, Montpelier, (802) 223-2727, is comprised of two Federal-style buildings erected in the early 1800s; a stay here will transport you back to the early days of this capital city.

HOT SPOT

Jimmy LeSage's **New Life Hiking Spa** at the Inn of the Six Mountains, Killington, (800) 228-4676, combines Green Mountains hikes, healthy cuisine, and activities for relaxation and stress reduction. Stay for two days or longer from early May through late October, and leave rejuvenated.

The Sights of Central Vermont

M The region surrounding Killington and Rutland is known as the "Crossroads of Vermont," and features several popular attractions. The **New England Maple Museum,** Route 7, Pittsford, (802) 483-9413, is the world's largest maple museum, where you can watch demonstrations of the syrup-making process, try maple foods at the tasting counter, and shop for Vermont foods and crafts daily from June through mid-October. Vermont is famous for marble, and the world's largest marble display is at the **Vermont Marble Exhibit,** 52 Main Street, Proctor, (802) 459-2300 or (800) 427-1396. You can relive another crucial battle of the American Revolution fought on Vermont soil at the **Hubbardton Battlefield,** Monument Road, East Hubbardton, (802) 759-2412. The **Norman Rockwell Museum,** 654 Route 4 East, Rutland, (802) 773-6095 or (877) 773-6095, commemorates the illustrator's Vermont years with more than 2,500 magazine covers, advertisements, calendars, and other works on exhibit. It is open June through November. From June through mid-October, take a guided tour of **Wilson Castle,** Hollow Road, Proctor, (802) 773-3284, a thirty-two-room, European-inspired architectural fascination.

In the eastern part of the state, the **Old Constitution House,** Main Street, Windsor, (802) 672-3773, was the birthplace of the "Free and Independent State of Vermont" on July 8, 1777. The **President Calvin Coolidge State Historic Site,** Route 100A, Plymouth Neck, (802) 672-3773, celebrates the life of Vermont native and thirtieth president of the United States Calvin Coolidge, the only president born on the fourth of July. Coolidge was actually sworn in here by his father following the death of Warren Harding. The **Billings Farm & Museum,** 12 and River Road, Woodstock, (802) 457-2355, gives you a firsthand look at Vermont dairying past and present. Visit **Quechee State Park,** Route 4, Quechee, (802) 295-2990 or (800) 299-3071, for a picnic and a peek at glacier-carved Quechee Gorge.

Montpelier may be the country's tiniest capital city, but you'll find two of the state's most delicious attractions nearby. **Ben & Jerry's,** Route 100, Waterbury, (802) 882-1260 or (866) BJ-TOURS, offers ice cream factory tours daily. Learn how childhood friends Ben Cohen and Jerry Greenfield turned a $5 correspondence course on ice cream making into one of Vermont's best known businesses and, most importantly, sample a selection of their original frozen flavors after your tour. Head to award-winning cheese maker **Cabot,** Route 215, Cabot Village, (800) 837-4261, for a tour and free tastings of cheeses including their highly acclaimed cheddars. The Cabot Creamery Cooperative was founded by local dairy farmers in 1919. While you're in the capital area, tour the **Vermont State House,** 115 State Street, Montpelier, (802) 828-2231. Free tours are available weekdays year-round. You may also want to set aside time to see the world's largest granite quarry, **Rock of Ages,** 773 Graniteville Road, Barre, (802) 476-3119. The visitors' center is open daily May through October.

HOT SPOT

It's hard to believe that with all of its landmarks and wide open spaces, Vermont couldn't claim a national park within its borders until 1998, when Laurance S. and Mary Rockefeller donated their 26-room Queen Anne mansion and 555 acres including part of Mount Tom to the National Park Service. The **Marsh-Billings-Rockefeller National Historical Park,** Route 12 North, Woodstock, (802) 457-3368, ext. 22, is the only national park to focus on conservation history and the evolving nature of land stewardship in America. The park is open daily for tours late May through late October. The 20 miles of historic carriage roads and trails are open year round. The Billings Farm & Museum is open daily May through October.

Central Peaks

The central region is home to some of Vermont's best skiing.

- **Okemo Mountain Resort,** 77 Okemo Ridge Road, Ludlow, (802) 228-4041 or (800) 78-OKEMO, is a family-owned resort with extensive snowmaking capabilities. Okemo has ninety-eight trails, fourteen lifts, and snowmaking on 95 percent of its terrain.
- **Ascutney Mountain Resort,** off I-91, Brownsville, (802) 484-7711 or (800) 243-0011, has undergone a multimillion dollar expansion and improvement project since the early 1990s, and its popularity is surging. You'll find fifty-six trails, six lifts, and snowmaking coverage of about 95 percent.
- **Killington,** 4763 Killington Road, Killington, (802) 422-6200, has the East's longest ski season, typically running from October to June. Killington consists of a ring of seven mountains with 200 trails, thirty-two lifts, and snowmaking on 61 miles of trails.

- **Suicide Six,** Fourteen the Green, Woodstock, (802) 457-1100 or (800) 448-7900, is the intimate ski area at the Woodstock Inn & Resort. It features twenty-three trails, three lifts, and snowmaking coverage of 50 percent.
- **Middlebury College Snow Bowl,** Middlebury College campus, Middlebury, (802) 388-4356, offers an affordable, uncrowded skiing option. The Snow Bowl has fifteen trails, three lifts, and snowmaking on 20 percent of the skiable terrain.
- **Sugarbush,** off Route 100, Warren, (802) 253-3500 or (800) 53-SUGAR, is an American Skiing Company resort that offers varied terrain on six interconnected mountain peaks and a relaxed, away-from-it-all atmosphere. Sugarbush features 115 trails, eighteen lifts, and 68 percent snowmaking coverage.
- **Mad River Glen,** Route 17, Waitsfield, (802) 496-3551, has a unique story—it is the only cooperatively owned ski area in America. In 1995, loyal skiers were invited to become shareholders when the resort was put up for sale. Today, you'll find Mad River Glen, which gets about 250 inches of natural snowfall annually, home to forty-four trails, five lifts including the last surviving single chair lift in the nation, and snowmaking on 16 percent of its terrain.

TRAVEL TIP

Whether your prefer no-frills camping at a wilderness tent site, renting a woodsy cabin, or parking your RV at a campground with extensive amenities, Vermont has a camping destination for you. The **Vermont Campground Association** has built a helpful Web site at *www.campvermont.com*, where you can research private campgrounds and state parks where camping is allowed. Or request a campground guide from the Vermont Department of Tourism and Marketing, (800) VERMONT.

Dining Highlights

Pubs, taverns, and saloons that appeal to both the after-ski crowd and to families proliferate in central Vermont. Ask the locals for recommendations. The **Long Trail Brewing Company,** Routes 4 and 100A, Bridgewater Corners, (802) 672-5011, serves its craft-brewed beers and light pub fare with Vermont flair daily from 11 A.M. to 5 P.M. You can observe the beer-making process while you enjoy an afternoon snack. At **Black River Brewing Company,** Route 103, Cavendish, (802) 228-3100, you can play darts, sip microbrews, and gobble up English pub fare.

For a unique fine dining experience, **Simon Pearce Restaurant,** The Mill, Quechee, (802) 295-1470, offers gourmet delights served on tablewear by the famed pottery and glass designer. The restaurant overlooks a covered bridge and the falls of the Ottauquechee River. Watch potters and glassblowers at work at the Mill before or after your meal. For a unique casual dining experience, try the **Dugout Restaurant and Lounge,** East Barre Road, Barre, (802) 479-3441, where you just might save 10 percent on your breakfast, lunch, or dinner if you drive up on a snowmobile.

Montpelier is home to the **New England Culinary Institute,** which operates three restaurants in the capital city, plus two in Essex and one in Burlington, where you can sample the culinary creations of up-and-coming chefs in training. Call (802) 223-6324 for complete information and reservations.

Want to dine in an historic environment? **Countryman's Pleasure,** Town Line Road, Mendon, (802) 773-7141, serves German- and Austrian-inspired cuisine by firelight and candlelight within a red-shuttered 1824 farmhouse. **Hemingway's,** Route 4, Killington, (802) 422-3886, is all about ambience—three dining rooms are tucked away inside a nineteenth-century house including the stone-walled wine cellar, which is available for parties of ten to twelve. **Windsor Station Restaurant,** Depot Avenue, Windsor, (802) 674-2052, is a converted 1900 train station. You won't soon forget your visit to the **Common Man,** 3209 German Flats Road,

Warren, (802) 583-2800, where the setting is a 150-year-old barn with hand-hewn beams and an open fireplace, dressed up with crystal chandeliers and art. The chef introduces new dishes each week in addition to the menu of traditional European selections.

If it's steak or seafood you crave, **Nikki's,** Route 103, Ludlow, (802) 228-7797, has been a favorite for more than twenty years. For a taste of Vermont, seek out **Arvad's,** with locations at 3 South Main Street, Waterbury, (802) 244-8973, and Route 100, Waitsfield, (802) 496-9800. Arvad's uses Vermont ingredients and serves products by Green Mountain Coffee Roasters, Miguel's Tortilla Chips, Cabot Dairy, and Ben & Jerry's Ice Cream, plus beers from more than ten Vermont breweries, including their own Arvad's Ale.

FAST FACT

For most New Englanders, zucchini is that omnipresent squash that grows all too well in your garden and can barely be given away come summer's end. Leave it to Vermont to celebrate the green squash with the annual **Vermont State Zucchini Festival** held in Ludlow each August. Call (802) 228-5830 for more details.

Shopping Discoveries

Central Vermont is home to legendary shopping possibilities. The **Vermont Country Store,** Route 100, Weston, (802) 824-3184, is known nationwide for its mail order catalog crammed with items you probably thought no longer existed. The original Vermont Country Store was founded in 1946, and travelers are welcome to explore its unique product array including Vermont foodstuffs and hard-to-find goods Monday through Saturday. The **Bowl Mill,** Route 100, Granville, (800) 828-1005, has been producing wooden bowls in Vermont since 1857. The store is open daily, and you can tour the factory when you visit on a weekday. The **Cold Hollow Cider Mill,** Route 100,

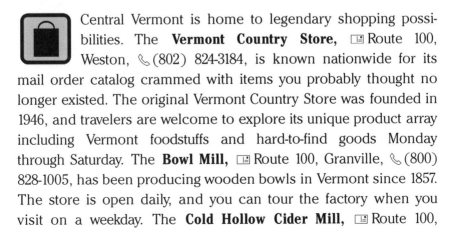

Waterbury Center, ✆(802) 244-8771 or ✆(800) 3-APPLES, is open daily year-round, and you can watch cider being pressed the old-fashioned way and shop for Vermont specialties.

You'll find sweet deals at **Green Mountain Sugarhouse,** ✉ Route 100, Ludlow, ✆(800) 643-9338, an authentic sugarhouse and Vermont country gift shop, and at **Morse Farm Sugar Works,** ✉ 1168 County Road, Montpelier, ✆(802) 223-2740 or ✆(800) 242-2740, open daily year-round for tours, tastings, and shopping for gifts from the farm.

Northern Vermont: Burlington, Stowe, and the Northeast Kingdom

THE TOP OF VERMONT IS A LAND of juxtapositions. You'll find Vermont's largest city here—Burlington. It's tallest peak is here, too—Mount Mansfield, home to the Stowe ski resort. And while we're talking about superlatives, not just Vermont's but New England's largest lake is here—Lake Champlain. However, this is also the location of the Northeast Kingdom, a wild, insular, three-county area where winters are long and hard, forests are dense, and those who have lived here for generations cling fast to traditions. With the national border close at hand, you'll also find bilingual signs and other welcoming touches for tourists visiting from Canada.

With all of this diversity, a getaway in northern Vermont is one that can satisfy all of your dualities. You can join the crowds on the slopes one day, and the next find yourself surging through an uninhabited forest aboard a snowmobile with just one special person. Visit a family-run farm market one summer morning, then tour a multimillion-dollar teddy bear factory later that same day. Delve into history at the Ethan Allen Homestead, or kick back on a scenic cruise aboard the *Spirit of Ethan Allen II*. You may just depart from northern Vermont with the uncanny feeling you've gotten two vacations for the price of one.

FAST FACT

For more than twenty years, northern **Vermont's Jay Peak,** Route 242, Jay, (802) 988-2611 or (800) 451-4449, has accepted Canadian currency at par with U.S. dollars for lift ticket purchases, a great deal considering the gap between the two currencies.

Lodging Options

Accommodations of all varieties are readily available in the Burlington and Stowe areas, but you'll find lodging and other tourist amenities fewer and farther between in the Northeast Kingdom.

In the Burlington Area

You'll find a number of business-class hotels and motor inn chains that appeal to families including a 255-room **Radisson,** 60 Battery Street, (802) 658-6500; the 309-room **Sheraton Hotel & Conference Center,** 870 Williston Road, South Burlington, (802) 865-6600; and a 105-room **Comfort Inn,** 1285 Williston Road, South Burlington, (802) 865-3400 or (800) 228-5150. For something a bit more out of the ordinary, the **Inn at Essex,** 70 Essex Way, Essex, (802) -878-1100, offers 120 individually decorated rooms including some with fireplaces, gas stoves, rocking chairs, kitchenettes, and whirlpool tubs. B&B lovers will jump at the opportunity to stay in a home built by Vermont's first governor—**Catamount Bed & Breakfast,** 592 Governor Chittenden Road, (802) 879-6001, has three guest rooms.

In Shelburne and Jeffersonville

The **Inn at Shelburne Farms,** 102 Harbor Road, Shelburne, (802) 985-8498, is the restored nineteenth-century home of Dr. William Seward and Lila Vanderbilt Webb on the shores of Lake Champlain. When you stay here, you help to support the preservation efforts of the nonprofit environmental education center at Shelburne Farms.

Smugglers' Notch Resort, Route 108, Jeffersonville, (802) 644-8851 or (800) 451-8752, has 375 condos available year-round—they're not just for skiers.

In Stowe

The **Von Trapp Family Lodge,** 42 Trapp Hill Road, (802) 253-8511 or (800) 826-7000, is perhaps the most storied inn in all of New England. It was built by the Von Trapp family, the inspiration for the musical and movie, *The Sound of Music.* Stowe reminded them of their home in the Austrian Alps, from which they fled during World War II. Maria and her husband are buried in the cemetery near the lodge, and Johannes von Trapp, the youngest of the singing Von Trapp children, is president of the inn today.

If it's pampering you're after, **Topnotch at Stowe,** Mountain Road, (802) 253-8585 or (800) 451-8686, is a 120-acre resort and spa where you'll have the freedom to design your own spa program—if you can tear yourself away from the hydromassage waterfall.

For a touch of history, **Edson Hill Manor,** 1500 Edson Hill Road, (802) 253-7371 or (800) 621-0284, is a 1940 Georgian Colonial mansion with living room beams taken from Ethan Allen's barn. The Manor has nine guest rooms, and there are carriage house rooms with fireplaces available, too. The **Stowe Mountain Resort** offers a variety of slope-side accommodations including condominium rentals and the thirty-room Inn at the Mountain. Call (800) 253-4754 for reservations assistance.

In the Northeast Kingdom

Craftsbury Outdoor Center, 535 Lost Nation Rd, Craftsbury Common, (802) 586-7767 or (800) 729-7751, offers sporting packages year round. **Highland Lodge,** Caspian Lake Road, Greensboro, (802) 533-2647, is a peaceful lakeside hideaway with rooms, cottages, and room to roam. The **Fairbanks Inn,** 401

Western Avenue, St. Johnsbury, (802) 748-5666, has forty-five rooms, a heated outdoor pool, and its own putting green.

FAST FACT

Vermont has a remarkable network of more than 5,000 miles of snowmobile trails. The snowmobiling season runs from mid-December through early April. For maps and other trail information, contact the **Vermont Association of Snow Travelers** at (802) 229-0005, or visit their Web site, *www.vtvast.org*.

Explore the North

The Lake Champlain Valley is a perfect family destination. After all, if the kids whine about visiting historic sites, where else can you dangle the prospect of creating their own teddy bears to take home? Start with the **Shelburne Museum,** Route 7, Shelburne, (802) 985-3346, which is home to a compendium of folk art, Americana, and traditional New England structures including a lighthouse.

At the **Ethan Allen Homestead,** off Route 128, Burlington, (802) 865-4556, you can get to know Vermont's founder and flamboyant Revolutionary War hero. Venture back down south to the **Lake Champlain Maritime Museum,** 4472 Basin Harbor Road, Vergennes, (802) 475-2022, for a historic look at the lake and a chance to board a replica of the gunboat *Philadelphia II*. The museum is open mid-May through mid-October.

Finally, tour the factory at **Vermont Teddy Bear Co.,** Route 7, Shelburne, (802) 985-3001, which is open daily. After you see where bears are born, head to the Make a Friend for Life area, where you can actually create your very own bear—don't overstuff him!

While you're enjoying the Northeast Kingdom's scenic and recreational resources, don't miss the chance to also visit two St. Johnsbury landmarks. The **Fairbanks Museum,** 1302 Main Street, (802) 748-2372, features extensive natural history exhibits and

Vermont's only public planetarium. The **St. Johnsbury Athenaeum and Art Gallery,** 1171 Main Street, (802) 748-8291, is a National Historic Landmark and longtime cultural outpost where you'll see an impressive collection of nineteenth-century paintings.

HOT SPOT

Did you know that you can hike Vermont end-to-end by following Long Trail, a 270-mile, backcountry route that runs from the Canadian border to the Massachusetts state line? Long Trail was America's first extensive hiking path, and it remains a unique, scenic, and challenging way to see the Green Mountains and Vermont's rugged landscape. About seventy primitive shelters are located along the route at intervals of about a day's hiking distance. For more information, visit *www.greenmountainclub.org* or *www.hikevermont.com,* or call the Green Mountain Club at (802) 244-7037.

Skiing in Northern Vermont

You'll find Vermont's highest peaks and resorts specializing in family fun when you head up north.

- **Bolton Valley,** Bolton Valley Access Road, Bolton Valley, (802) 434-3444 or (877) 9-BOLTON, is a winter wonderland where you can not only ski downhill, but snowshoe, cross-country ski, snowboard, and even go on a horse-drawn sleigh ride. Bolton Valley visitors will find fifty-one trails, six lifts, and 60 percent snowmaking coverage.
- **Stowe,** 5781 Mountain Road, Stowe, (802) 253-3000 or (800) 253-4754, can brag of Vermont's highest peak and longest average trail length. It also provides spectacular amenities including a mountaintop restaurant and a Web

café. Stowe offers forty-seven trails, ten lifts, and 73 percent snowmaking coverage.

- **Smugglers' Notch,** 4323 Route 108 South, Smugglers' Notch, (802) 644-8851 or (800) 523-2754, is a three-mountain family ski area with a renowned Snow Sport University. You'll find plenty of alpine action with seventy trails, nine lifts, and snowmaking on 62 percent of the terrain.
- **Burke Mountain,** I-91 exit 23, East Burke, (802) 626-3322, is located in Vermont's Northeast Kingdom and provides an alternative to some of the more crowded and commercial ski centers. Burke has thirty-four trails, four lifts, and snowmaking coverage of 75 percent.
- **Jay Peak,** Route 242, Jay, (802) 988-2611, has the highest average annual snowfall of any ski area in the East, so if you're looking for natural snow, this is the place. Jay provides seventy-four trails, seven lifts, and 80 percent snowmaking coverage.

HOT SPOT

Herrmann's Royal Lipizzan Stallions summer on North Hero Island in Vermont's Lake Champlain; see them for free at **Lipizzan Park,** Route 2, North Hero, Performances are held on Thursday and Friday evenings and Saturday and Sunday afternoons from early July until late August. Ticket prices range from $8 to $15; Friday evenings are free for children. For more information, call the Champlain Islands Chamber of Commerce, (802) 372-8400.

Dining Highlights

Burlington is the place to eat if you're craving variety. **Ice House,** 171 Battery Street, (802) 864-1800, is an old icehouse turned steak and seafood restaurant with views of Lake Champlain. **Rí~Rá,** 123 Church Street, (802) 860-9401, is an authentic pub built in Ireland and moved to Vermont. **Isabel's on the Waterfront,** 112 Lake Street, (802) 865-2522, is housed inside a restored mill building with brick walls and large windows that provide panoramic views of Lake Champlain. **Perry's Fish House,** 1080 Shelburne Road, South Burlington, (802) 862-1300, specializes in unusual seafood from across America. **Sweetwaters Bistro,** 120 Church Street, (802) 864-9800, is a European-inspired, outdoor café that's your best bet if you want to watch Burlington go by as you dine.

In Stowe, **Ye Olde England Inn,** 433 Mountain Road, (802) 253-7558 or (800) 643-1553, serves venison, wild boar, and partridge—plus more than 150 different ales—at the casual **Pickwick's Pub.** For Vermont's most sweeping views, make reservations to dine at the **Cliff House Restaurant** at the Stowe Mountain Resort, (802) 253-3665, which is accessible only via gondola. Where can you find more than eighty varieties of Dutch Pancakes? At the **Dutch Pancake Café at Grey Fox Inn,** 990 Mountain Road, (802) 253-8921.

In the Northeast Kingdom, dinner is served in a restored creamery at the **Inn at Mountain View Farm Restaurant,** Darling Hill Road, East Burke, (802) 626-9924 or (800) 572-4509. If you're really hungry, head to **Anthony's Diner,** Railroad Street, St. Johnsbury, (802) 748-3613, for a Woodsman Burger. Got the late night munchies? The **P&H Diner,** Route 302, Wells River, (802) 429-2141, is the Kingdom's only twenty-four-hour restaurant.

Shopping Discoveries

If shopping is in your genes, you will adore the **Church Street Marketplace,** which runs along four blocks in downtown Burlington and features close to 100 retail stores. To encourage visitors, two hours of free parking is provided at the following city lots and downtown garages: Marketplace Garage, South Winooski between Bank and Cherry; College Street Garage at the Radisson Hotel, 60 Battery Street; South Winooski

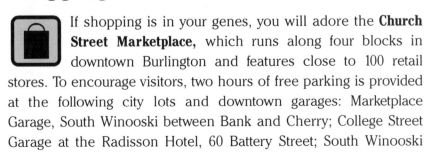

Lot, South Winooski between College and Bank; and Pease West Lot, Burlington waterfront. Blue and white signs with smiling cars indicate free parking.

You'll find discounts on woolen wear and blankets at the **Johnson Woolen Mills,** Main Street, Johnson, (802) 635-2271, an authentic factory store.

You know you're dying to buy a pair of moose antlers. OK, well, even if you're not, you're bound to find something of interest at **Moose River Lake & Lodge Store,** 69 Railroad Street, St. Johnsbury, (802) 748-2423, featuring taxidermy and antlery, hickory furniture, Vermont-made products, and a wine vault. Speaking of wine, Vermont's first winery, **Snow Farm Vineyard,** 190 West Shore Road, South Hero, (802) 372-9463, is open for tours, tastings, and wine purchases May through December, and the vineyard's **Tasting Area,** (802) 244-7118, located on Route 100 between Stowe and Waterbury, is open year-round.

Did you leave northern Vermont souvenir-less? Never fear. You can call **Vermont Teddy Bear** toll free at (800) 829-BEAR twenty-four hours a day and have a furry critter to call your own as quickly as the next day.

FAST FACT

"Champ," Lake Champlain's mysterious monster, was first reported back in 1609 by Samuel de Champlain, who described seeing a "twenty-foot serpent thick as a barrel with a head like a horse." Iroquois stories of a horned serpent in the lake predate European exploration. Champ was sighted more than a dozen times in 2000. The village of Port Henry has a Champ Sightings Board on Route 9N and hosts Champ Day annually on the first Saturday in August. Doubters think "Champ" is an oversized sturgeon. You be the judge!

Itineraries

PERSONAL ITINERARY NOTES

A FIVE-DAY WINTER SPORTS SAMPLER KEEPING NEAR ROUTE 100

Day One Start at **Stratton Mountain Resort,** Stratton Mountain Road, Stratton Mountain, (802) 297-4000 or (800) STRATTON, where the recent addition of two high-speed chair lifts means you'll get in more runs before the day is done. Stratton prides itself on its professional ski instructors who can help beginners master the sport and guide experienced skiers seeking to become experts.

Day Two Drive north to the **Viking Nordic Centre,** Little Pond Road, Londonderry, (802) 824-3933. You may want to consider spending the night at the Viking Guest House, as that entitles you to free access to the center's 40 kilometers of cross-country trails.

Day Three Make day three your day of rest. Continue north along Route 100 at a leisurely pace, exploring the many shops in Weston, particularly the **Vermont Country Store,** (802) 824-3184. Later in the afternoon, visit the **Green Mountain Sugarhouse,** Route 100, Ludlow, (800) 643-9338, for a taste of Vermont-made maple syrup and other goodies. Get to your inn, B&B or condo near Killington early and rest up—tomorrow is another big day on the slopes!

Day Four On day four, conquer **Killington,** 4763 Killington Road, Killington, (802) 422-6200, where good snow is guaranteed. That's right—if you're unhappy with the conditions after at least one run within your first hour of arrival, you can exchange your lift ticket for a voucher to return on another day.

Day Five On your last day, venture off Route 100 just a bit and check in early at the **Woodstock Inn & Resort,** Fourteen the Green, Woodstock, (802) 457-1100 or (800) 448-7900. Spend the afternoon nestled inside the inn's old-world ambience, or venture out on snowshoes at the Woodstock Ski Touring Center. Whatever you do, save some energy for a run or two down the 1,000-foot, torch-lit toboggan run before retiring for the night.

A THREE-DAY SUMMER GETAWAY

Day One Have time for just a brief summer retreat? Head to Burlington on the shores of Lake Champlain, and use that as your central hub of exploration. Spend your first vacation day getting to know Vermont's largest city including the shops and restaurants concentrated in the Church Street Marketplace area. Dine in the evening at one of the area's many waterfront restaurants.

Day Two On day two, head north to **Snow Farm Vineyard,** 190 West Shore Road, South Hero, (802) 372-9463, where you can tour the state's oldest winery and sample a variety of wines. Continue north to **North Hero Island,** where you can visit with **Herrmann's Royal Lipizzan Stallions,** (802) 372-8400, and even see a horse show if it is Saturday or Sunday afternoon. Return to Burlington later in the afternoon, and get a different view of Lake Champlain from aboard the ***Spirit of Ethan Allen II,*** (802) 862-8300, which departs from the Burlington Boathouse, College Street, Burlington.

Day Three On the final day of your getaway, it's time for the ultimate summer activity—eating ice cream. Drive southwest to Waterbury for a tour of **Ben & Jerry's,** Route 100, (802) 882-1260 or (866) BJ-TOURS, which concludes sweetly with the opportunity to sample several of the company's one-of-a-kind flavors. If you haven't ruined your appetite, you may want to have lunch at one of the three **New England Culinary Institute restaurants,** (802) 223-6324, in the nearby Montpelier area before heading for home.

A WEEK OF AUTUMN HUES AND VIEWS

Day One Fall is a glorious time to visit Vermont, but keep in mind that it's also the season when lodging rates are highest and reservations are nearly impossible to come by unless you've planned well in advance. Start your fall foliage journey in Bennington, where you can ascend to the top of the **Bennington Battle Monument,** 15 Monument Circle, (802) 447-0550, for views of three states.

Day Two Follow Route 7A toward Manchester and visit **Hildene,** Route 7A, (802) 362-1788, the summer home of Robert Todd Lincoln, where you can stroll through lush formal gardens and take in spectacular views of the autumn-painted Green Mountains. Spend the afternoon shopping for bargains at the **Manchester outlets,** which are concentrated in the area of Routes 7A and 11/30 in Manchester Center.

Day Three For your third day, pack a picnic and make the drive along the 5-mile Equinox Sky Line Drive to the summit of Mt. Equinox. When you're ready to tear yourself away from the amazing views, leave southern Vermont behind and drive along scenic Route 7. Rutland is a good stopping place for the night.

Day Four Wake up early and venture off Route 7, following Route 4 East to **Killington,** 4763 Killington Road, (802) 422-6200, which boasts the highest Vermont peak serviced by a chair lift. The chair lift ride provides leaf peepers with views of five states and Canada. Return to Route 7 and continue north, stopping whenever the colors warrant reaching for the camera. Spend the night in Middlebury.

Day Five Continue north on Route 7 to Shelburne, where you'll want to photograph the covered bridge at the **Shelburne Museum,** Route 7, Shelburne, (802) 985-3346, against the backdrop of autumn leaves. In the afternoon, tour the **Vermont Teddy Bear factory,** Route 7, Shelburne, (802) 985-3001, and make your own bear dressed for Halloween.

Day Six Again, continue north on Route 7 to Burlington. **Lake Champlain Ferries,** (802) 864-9804, will take you from the King Street Dock in Burlington on a scenic lake cruise, or, if you're dying to know how the fall colors look over in New York State, you can even take the ferry all the way across the lake and back.

Day Seven Make sure you still have plenty of film for your final day of scenic Vermont driving. From Burlington, follow Route 15 East through quaint towns along the way to Jeffersonville, where you'll pick up Route 108 South, which will take you through the mountainous Smugglers' Notch area and eventually to Stowe, home to Vermont's tallest mountain peak. You may want to spend the rest of your day exploring Stowe, or, you can continue south from Stowe on Route 100 for a visit to the **Ben & Jerry's Factory,** Route 100, Waterbury, (802) 882-1260 or (866) BJ-TOURS, before heading for home.

Appendix I: Resources for Visitor Information

CONNECTICUT

Office of Tourism—Connecticut Department of Economic and Community Development

505 Hudson Street
Hartford, CT 06106-7106

(800) CT BOUND

www.ctbound.org

Coastal Fairfield County Convention and Visitors Bureau

297 West Avenue
Norwalk, CT 06850

(800) 866-7925

www.visitfairfieldco.org

The Greater Hartford Tourism District

One Civic Center Plaza
Hartford, CT 06103

(800) 793-4480

(860) 244-8181

www.enjoyhartford.com

Greater New Haven Convention & Visitors Bureau

59 Elm Street
New Haven, CT 06510
(800) 332-STAY
(203) 777-8550
www.newhavencvb.org
mail@newhavencvb.org

Litchfield Hills Travel Council

Box 968
Litchfield, CT 06759
(860) 567-4506
www.litchfieldhills.com

Mystic Convention & Visitors Bureau

P.O. Box 89, 470 Bank Street
New London, CT 06320
(800) TO-ENJOY
(860) 444-2206
www.mysticmore.com
mystic@ctol.net

MAINE

Maine Office of Tourism

59 State House Station
Augusta, ME 04330
(207) 287-5711; (888) MAINE45
www.visitmaine.com

Bangor Convention & Visitors Bureau

P.O. Box 1938
Bangor, ME 04402
(207) 947-5205
www.bangorcvb.org
info@bangorcvb.org

Convention and Visitors Bureau of Greater Portland

305 Commercial Street
Portland, ME 04101-4641

(207) 772-5800

www.visitportland.com

East Penobscot Bay Association

One Schoolhouse Road East
Blue Hill, ME 04629

(207) 374-5174

www.penobscotbay.com

info@penobscotbay.com

Freeport Merchants Association

P.O. Box 452
Freeport, Maine 04032-0452

(207) 865-1212; S(800) 865-1994

www.freeportusa.com

info@freeportusa.com

Kennebec Valley Tourism Council

79 Main Street
Waterville, ME 04901

(800) 393-8629

www.kennebecvalley.org

Southern Maine Coast Tourism Association

(800) 639-2442

www.southernmainecoast.com

MASSACHUSETTS

Massachusetts Office of Travel and Tourism

10 Park Plaza, Suite 4510
Boston, MA 02116

(800) 447-MASS; (617) 727-3201

www.mass-vacation.com
vacationinfo@state.ma.us

Berkshire Hills Visitors Bureau

Berkshire Common Plaza Level
Pittsfield, MA 01201
(800) 237-5747; (413) 443-9186
www.berkshires.org
bvb@berkshires.org

Bristol County Convention and Visitors Bureau

70 North Second Street
P.O. Box 976
New Bedford, MA 02741
(800) 288-6263; (508) 997-1250
www.bristol-county.org
info@southofboston.org

Cape Cod Chamber of Commerce

307 Main Street, Suite 2
P.O. Box 790
Hyannis, Massachusetts 02601
(888) 33-CAPECOD
(508) 862-0700
www.capecodchamber.org
info@capecodchamber.org

Central Massachusetts Tourist Council

33 Waldo Street
Worcester, MA 01608
(508) 755-7400
www.worcester.org

Greater Boston Convention and Visitors Bureau

2 Copley Place, Suite 105
Boston, MA 02116

(888) SEE BOSTON; (617) 536-4100
www.bostonusa.com

Greater Merrimack Valley Convention and Visitors Bureau

22 Shattuck Street
Lowell, MA 01852
(800) 443-3332; (978) 459-6150
www.lowell.org

Greater Springfield Convention and Visitors Bureau

1500 Main Street, Box 15589
Springfield, MA 01115
(800) 723-1548; (413) 787-1548
www.valleyvisitor.com
info@valleyvisitor.com

Martha's Vineyard Chamber of Commerce

P.O. Box 1698
Vineyard Haven, MA 02568
(508) 693-0085
www.mvy.com
mvcc@mvy.com

Mohawk Trail Association

P.O. Box 722
Charlemont, MA 01339
(413) 664-6256
www.mohawktrail.com
info@mohawktrail.com

Nantucket Island Chamber of Commerce

48 Main Street
Nantucket, MA 02554
(508) 228-1700
www.nantucketchamber.org

North of Boston Convention and Visitors Bureau

17 Peabody Square
Peabody, MA 01960
(800) 742-5306; (978) 977-7760
www.northofboston.org

Plymouth County Convention and Visitors Bureau

345 Washington Street
P.O. Box 1620
Pembroke, MA 02359
(800) 231-1620; (781) 826-3136
www.plymouth-1620.com
info@plymouth-1620.com

NEW HAMPSHIRE

New Hampshire Office of Travel and Tourism

P.O. Box 1856
Concord, NH 03302-1856
(603) 271-2665
www.visitnh.gov

Greater Portsmouth Chamber of Commerce

500 Market Street; P.O. Box 239
Portsmouth, NH 03802-0239
(603) 436-3988
www.portcity.org
portsmouthnhchamber@rscs.net

Lakes Region Association

Harbor Business Center
P.O. Box 589
Center Harbor, NH 03226
(800) 60-LAKES; (603) 744-8664
www.lakesregion.org
lra@lakesregion.org

Monadnock Travel Council

P.O. Box 358
Keene, NH 03431

(603) 355-8155 or (800) HEARTNH

www.monadnocktravel.com

Mt. Washington Valley Chamber of Commerce

P.O. Box 2300, Main Street
North Conway, NH 03860

(800) 367-3364 ; (603) 356-5701

www.4seasonresort.com

mwvcc@4seasonresort.com

Northern White Mountain Chamber of Commerce

P.O. Box 298, 164 Main Street
Berlin, NH 03570

(603) 752-6060

www.northernwhitemountains.com

nwmcc@northernwhitemountains.com

Ski New Hampshire

P.O. Box 10
North Woodstock, NH 03262

(603) 745-9396

www.skinh.com

info@skinh.com

Waterville Valley Region Chamber of Commerce

RFD 1, Box 1067
Campton, NH 03223

(800) 237-2307; (603) 726-3804

www.watervillevalleyregion.com

info@watervillevalleyregion.com

White Mountain Attractions

P.O. Box 10
North Woodstock, NH 03262
(800) FIND MTS; (603) 745-8720
www.visitwhitemountains.com
info@visitwhitemountains.com

RHODE ISLAND

Rhode Island Economic Development Corporation—Tourism

One West Exchange Street
Providence, RI 02903
(800) 556-2484; (401) 222-2601
www.visitrhodeisland.com
visitrhodeisland@riedc.com

Blackstone Valley Tourism Council

171 Main Street
Pawtucket, RI 02860
(800) 454-2882; (401) 724-2200
www.tourblackstone.com
bvtourism@aol.com

Block Island Tourism Council

P.O. Box 356
Block Island, RI 02807
(800) 383-BIRI; (401) 466-5200
www.blockislandinfo.com

Newport County Convention & Visitor's Bureau

23 America's Cup Avenue
Newport, RI 02840
(800) 326-6030; (401) 849-8048
www.gonewport.com

Providence/Warwick Convention & Visitors Bureau

One West Exchange Street
Providence, RI 02903
(800) 233-1636; (401) 274-1636
www.providencecvb.com
information@providencecvb.com

South County Tourism Council

4808 Tower Hill Road
Wakefield, RI 02879
(800) 548-4662; (401) 789-4422
www.southcountyri.com
sctc@netsense.net

Warwick Tourism Office

Warwick City Hall, 3275 Post Road
Warwick, RI 02886
(800) 4-WARWICK; (401) 738-2000
www.warwickri.com
info@warwickri.com

VERMONT

Vermont Department of Tourism and Marketing

6 Baldwin Street, Drawer 33
Montpelier, VT 05633-1301
(800) VERMONT
www.1-800-vermont.com
vttravel@dca.state.vt.us

Vermont Chamber of Commerce

P.O. Box 37
Montpelier, VT 05601
(802) 223-3443
www.vtchamber.com

Lake Champlain Regional Chamber

60 Main Street, Suite 100
Burlington, VT 05401
(802) 863-3489 x203
www.vermont.org
vermont@vermont.org

Northeast Kingdom Travel & Tourism Association

P.O. Box 465
Barton, VT 05822
(802) 525-4386
www.travelthekingdom.com
info@travelthekingdom.com

Southern Vermont Regional Marketing Organization

P.O. Box 2413
Manchester Center, VT 05255
(802) 362-5155
www.sovermont.com
info@sovermont.com

Stowe Area Association

Main Street, P.O. Box 1320
Stowe, VT 05672
(802) 253-7321
www.gostowe.com
askus@gostowe.com

Windham Regional Marketing Organization

1484 Middle Road
Dummerston Center, VT 05301
(802) 258-3992
www.southernvermont.com
prime@sover.net

Appendix II: The Best New England Web Sites

For General Info

- *www.newengland.com*
- *www.visitnewengland.com*
- *http://gonewengland.about.com*
- *www.boston.com*
- *www.boston.citysearch.com*
- *www.timeout.com/boston/index.html*

For Places to Stay

- *www.newenglandinns.com*
- *www.bedandbreakfast.com*
- *www.bbonline.com*
- *www.10kvacationrentals.com*
- *www.cyberrentals.com.*
- *www.bnbfinder.com*
- *www.restaurants-inns.com*

For Places to Eat

- *www.zagat.com*
- *www.opentable.com*
- *www.dininginnewengland.com*
- *www.dininginri.com*
- *www.dininginnh.com*
- *www.dininginmass.com*
- *www.capecoddine.com*
- *www.dineonme.com*
- *www.eatri.com*

Major New England Newspapers

Connecticut	
Connecticut Post	www.connpost.com
Hartford Courant	www.hartfordcourant.com
New Haven Advocate	www.newhavenadvocate.com
New London Day	www.theday.com
Stamford Advocate	www.stamfordadvocate.com
Maine	
Bangor Daily News	www.bangornews.com
Kennebec Journal	www.kjonline.com
Portland Press Herald	www.portland.com
Massachusetts	
The Boston Globe	www.boston.com/globe
The Boston Herald	www.bostonherald.com
The Boston Phoenix	www.bostonphoenix.com
Cape Cod Times	www.capecodtimes.com
The Patriot Ledger	www.southofboston.com
The Springfield Union News	www.masslive.com
Worcester Telegram & Gazette	www.telegram.com
New Hampshire	
Concord Monitor	www.cmonitor.com
Nashua Telegraph	www.nashuatelegraph.com
Portsmouth Herald	www.seacoastonline.com
The Union Leader	www.theunionleader.com
Rhode Island	
Bristol Phoenix	www.bristolri.com
The Pawtucket Times	www.pawtuckettimes.com
The Providence Journal	www.projo.com
Vermont	
The Burlington Free Press	www.burlingtonfreepress.com
The Rutland Herald	www.rutlandherald.com

Index

G

H

I

Q, R

T

U, V

W

Y

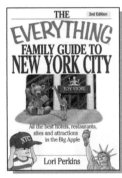

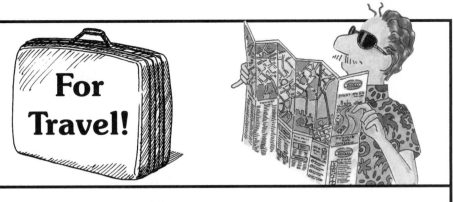

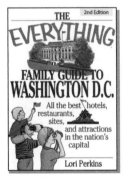

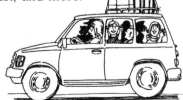

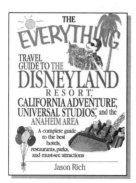

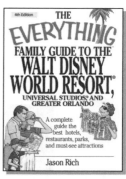

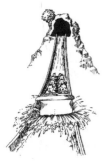